The New York Times

BREAD
AND
SOUP
COOKBOOK

The New York Times

BREAD
AND
SOUP
COOKBOOK

YVONNE YOUNG TARR

Quadrangle

A New York Times Company

ACKNOWLEDGEMENTS

Permission was graciously given by the following who contributed the recipes found in the great restaurants section of this book.

Andre Surmain, Proprietaire of Lutèce Restaurant, N.Y., N.Y. for Potage Aux Grenouilles (Alsace).

Linda Heras, Executive Secretary of The Spanish Pavilion Restaurant, N.Y., N.Y. for Sopa Castilla La Vieja.

Louis Verdi, Executive Chef of The Dallas Cowboy Restaurant, N.Y., N.Y. for Dallas Cowboy Bean Soup.

Mona Martelli, Proprietor of Mona's Trattoria, Croton Falls, New York for Beef and Chicken Broth, Soup Royale, Il Minestrone Di Mona, Tortellini, Passatelli, and Zuppa Regina.

Carlos Jacott, Proprietor of El Parador Cafe, N.Y., N.Y. for Chile Bean Soup.

Doubleday & Company, Inc. for Graupensuppe Mit Huhnerklein, Venison Soup, Fresh Eel Soup, and Liver Biscuits, from LUCHOW'S GERMAN COOKBOOK, by Jan Mitchell. Copyright 1952 by Leonard Jan Mitchell.

Dieter Sauer, Executive Director of Luchow's Restaurant, N.Y., N.Y for recipes in LUCHOW'S GERMAN COOKBOOK by Jan Mitchell.

Barbara Norat of Restaurant Associates Industries, Inc., N.Y., N.Y. for Onion Soup Brasserie from the Brasserie, Cold Senegalese Soup and Cold Milligatawny Soup from the Four Seasons Restaurant, Chilled Minted Pea Soup from The Tower Suite, Charley O's Bean Soup from Charley O's and Ground Floor Cafe Cheese Soup with Bourbon from the Ground Floor Cafe.

Library of Congress Card Number: 72-83084

BOOK DESIGN BY BETTY BINNS

This book is dedicated

to my good friends

ELLA MAZEL,

ESSIE FRIEDBERG,

LILLIAN BARR

and

MARGARET YOUNG

With special thanks to
Ruth, Ruth, Jodie and Ethel

Contents

Introduction

BREAD AND SOUP. These primeval foods became the earliest culinary comforts of primitive peoples. Soups brewed in caves and grains ground on stones and baked between glowing coals became the sustenance from which early civilization flowed. As long ago as yesterday and as near as tomorrow, bread and soup still sustain and comfort us. Here are our primary nutrients contained in golden loaves. Little wonder bread is called the staff of life ... the representation of the body of Christ. For bread is good ... as Life is good ... as health is good. And soup is a simmering secret of vitamins and minerals ready to nourish us and send us forth. It is probably safe to say that as soon as man (or was it woman?) invented the kettle, he or she promptly invented soup. For what easier, more delectable meal could the primitive gourmet concoct than a simmering caldron of bones and bits of meats, berries and roots, fern shoots and fruits, served with an elemental bread of ground wild grain mixed with water and baked on a hot, flat stone? Today, perhaps for the first time in history, we are a nation and a world blessed with a need to strengthen our ties to our origins instead of pursuing some abstract and mechanical goal of imagined bliss in a future time and in some interplanetary place. We are turning away from the plastic meal in the aluminum plate ... synthetically created, artificially preserved ... to a concept of a more natural way of living, a more basic way of cooking, of eating to nourish our bodies as well as please our palates. In light of this trend I submit the following solution ... the Gourmet Bread and Soup Meal. While all of the breads and soups here contained may be considered a welcome addition to any meal, most are hearty and satisfying enough to become a meal on their own when served with cheese, a simple salad and dessert. This basic menu benefits the cook as well as the guest for many breads and soups may be prepared wholly or in part one or two days prior to serving and require minimum cooking time on party day. Use your imagination to combine soups and breads indigenous to one area or from countries half a world apart. The breads and soups marked with three stars *** in this book are recipes I've been asked to prepare most often by my family and friends. Bread and soup with a gourmet touch may bring a refreshing change to your way of eating, of entertaining and of nourishing your body, mind and soul.

BACK
TO
BREAD
AND
SOUP

The
how-to
of
bread
baking

BAKING IS NOT AN ART, it is an act of creation. This is not to say that
the baker is an artist, for, again, baking is not an art. But in the act
of creating a bread, an honest loaf, an object with a presence, a
fragrance, a substance, a taste, some would say even a soul, the
baker has changed grain and flour and liquid into an entity. She or
he has taken yeast, a dormant colony of living plants, and released
and nurtured them in embryonic warmth, has sprinkled in sugar on
which yeast thrives, has sifted in flour that builds the cellular elastic
structure that holds the tiny carbon dioxide bubbles that raise the
framework of the house called BREAD. And in that house is love,
and warmth, and nourishment, and comfort, and care, and caring,
and *taking* care, and time gone by, and time well spent, and things

natural, and things good, and honest toil, and work without thought of reward, and all of those things once had, now lost in a country and a world that has rushed by itself and passed itself, running, and never noticed its loss.

What Do You Need to Know Before you Begin to Bake?

Nothing. That is to say . . . everything. That is to say . . . oneself. If you want to bake, bake, and you will bake well. But if you go beyond desire and on to love, if you become aware of the bread growing under your hands like a child . . . if you knead the dough, if you pat it and care for it and nurture it, if you become the father and mother of the bread, you will bake magnificently.

I have baked over 400 different varieties of bread in the past year and have had only one failure. I dropped a partially baked Easter Bread on its head and so traumatized it that it couldn't rise, although I'm sure it tried. The bread does what bread can do. You must do the rest. Bake with sense and sensitivity and you need remember only four rules:

1. Never shock the living yeast with excess warmth.
2. Scald milk to destroy the enzymes that cause soggy loaves.
3. Allow the bread to rise sufficiently.
4. Bake with love and an accurate oven.

Beyond this there are certain bits and pieces of knowledge gained by experience that might be of some help to you until you gain sufficient experience of your own.

Bread-Making Tools

Bread is elemental, basic, earthy, and simple; as such, it requires no more than the most basic tools to bring it to life . . . a bowl to mix the dough in, a flat surface for kneading, a pan in which to bake it, and an oven to bring it to fruition.

Ideally you should have a neat, clean place, light and airy, in which to work. For kneading, a large board kept clean and dry and used only for bread-making is recommended, although a clean, smooth, sturdy tabletop of sufficient size and comfortable height will also do well. A rough, wet towel between your board and table will keep it from slipping about while you work.

Wooden mixing spoons are a decided asset, and a set of measuring spoons and cups are handy, although old-time bread-makers generally disdain such conveniences, preferring to use their hands for measuring and mixing too.

For baking, aluminum pans do nicely. Rectangular shapes are generally recommended, and the standard sides are 4½x8½ inches and 5¼x9¼ inches. Smaller pans for smaller loaves are also available. Having the right size on hand when you need it is a luxury easily achieved, although in an emergency almost anything will work —from oven-proof glassware to an ordinary cookie sheet. Incidentally, bread pans should only be washed infrequently. After using, simply scrape out the crusts and crumbs, wipe clean with a dry towel, and your pans will soon develop that dark, tempered, professional-baker look . . . a definite asset because breads won't stick and they'll bake a trifle faster too.

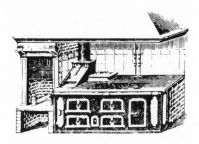

Why Knead?

The most enjoyable part of bread-making is the kneading. The fact that it is also the hardest work may seem to be a paradox, but there is something about kneading bread that is so elemental and satisfying, the work becomes pleasurable. Kneading is the process of "working" the dough with a pushing and pulling manipulation that serves to smooth, blend, and elasticize all at the same time, As you fold and push and refold, the gluten in the dough becomes flexible so that it may stretch and encapsulate each tiny bubble of carbon dioxide produced when the yeast rises. It is through this process that bread attains its fine texture.

An interesting experiment for the novice baker is to prepare enough dough for two loaves. Follow the recipe exactly when mixing the dough, but do not knead half of it. The unkneaded loaf will be uneven and leaden, full of strange bumps and bubbles—an unkind fate for something so honest as "an honest loaf."

The compensations of kneading go beyond quiet satisfaction and the feeling of a job well done. Kneading is also excellent exercise. I can think of no better activity to firm and tone the upper arms and the pectoral and back muscles than to knead bread once or twice a week. Bake two batches of bread, one after the other, and the following day you will be aware of muscles you never knew you had. These side benefits are of little importance, however; the real reason for kneading is to produce as fine a loaf of bread as is possible. Follow these directions, work vigorously, do not stint on kneading time, and you will soon be a bread-baker par excellence.

How to Knead

Sprinkle a bread board, pastry cloth, table, or counter top lightly with flour. The kneading surface should preferably be of wood and comfortably low (about mid-thigh). Dust your hands with flour and turn the dough out onto the board. It will have a rough texture and ragged ends. Press the dough firmly into a ball and flatten it slightly. Begin to knead by folding the upper side of the dough toward you with the fingers of both hands. Now push the dough vigorously away, using the heels of your hands. Rotate the ball of dough a quarter-turn in a clockwise direction, and repeat the folding and pushing process, rotating the dough a quarter-turn after each pulling and pushing motion. About midway into your kneading time, turn the dough over and continue as before. The typical bread requires from 8 to 10 minutes of vigorous kneading. Cover the loaves with a clean cloth and allow to rise.

Tips

1. Withhold 1½ cups of the flour called for in the recipe. Small eggs or a slight measuring miscalculation might make your dough stiffen with less than the entire amount of flour called for. You can always knead in more flour, but once it has been added it can't be removed.

2. Always set your kitchen timer for the amount of kneading time called for in the recipe. It's very easy to daydream while you're working and imagine you've been kneading for hours instead of minutes.

KNEADING

Turn the rough dough out onto the floured board.

Use your fingertips to pull the dough up and over toward you.

Now push the dough away firmly with the heels of your hands.

Rotate the dough ¼ turn. Continue to flour the board when necessary. Repeat this process until the dough is smooth and satiny.

3. The dough should never be too sticky to handle comfortably. If it is, sprinkle the kneading surface with ¼ cup flour, roll the dough in it, and begin kneading. If the recipe calls for a stiff dough and yours *isn't*, sprinkle a *little* extra flour onto the board as you knead. When the dough no longer sticks to your hands or the board, you've added enough flour. Set your timer and begin kneading.

4. Don't be surprised or worried if the dough cracks or crumbles a bit when you first begin to knead it. As mentioned earlier, kneading gives dough its elasticity. By the time you've finished kneading, the dough will be elastic. If it isn't, knead until it is.

5. If your dough does not feel springy after you've kneaded for the allotted time, don't feel discouraged. You may merely be handling it too gently. A really good baker (or cook for that matter) is one who kneads, chops, or beats with vigor. A ladylike touch is no asset in the kitchen. Treat your dough as you would your child—firmly and honestly, but with love.

6. There are some doughs that require more than vigorous kneading—they need a really heavy hand. Some of these are beaten biscuits, brioche, and croissants. These recipes call for the dough to be beaten or slapped against the bread board, and by all means do this with enthusiasm! The aforementioned masochistic doughs thrive on rough treatment, and thwarted bakers may rid themselves of many aggressions in the process of producing a fine loaf or biscuit.

How to Mix

Each recipe in this book delineates the precise procedures for successfully baking each particular bread. Here, for your general information, are the typical steps required in mixing and kneading a yeast bread.

Mixing yeast dough is a relatively quick, easy procedure which requires no special skills or experience. If you follow the steps outlined below, you should achieve perfect results every time. One word of caution, however. As you are aware, yeast is a living plant and therefore requires some special attention. Temperature is important. Too much heat and it becomes overactive, soon exhausts itself, and dies. Too little and it remains insufficiently active, and the rising process is slowed down considerably. To achieve that happy medium —just the right amount of warmth—pay close attention to the following.

MIXING

Dissolve the yeast in warm water. Stir in scalded milk which has cooled to room temperature. Add melted butter, sugar, salt and beaten eggs. Mix well.

Set aside ½ cup of the flour to dust over the kneading board. Stir the remaining flour into the yeast mixture a cup at a time, beating after each addition. The dough is the proper consistency when it stiffens and comes away from the sides of the bowl.

If dry active yeast is to be dissolved in water make sure the temperature is about 105 degrees F. (A few drops on the side of your wrist will feel comfortably warm.) Compressed yeast should be dissolved in lukewarm (95° F.) water. (A few drops on the side of your wrist will not feel especially warm or cool, but rather neutral.) Never mix dissolved yeast into scalded milk or any mixture that has not been cooled to lukewarm.

Step 1
If milk is being used, pour it into a pan and scald (heat to approximately 180° F., or to the point at which it is just about to boil). Remove from the heat and add salt, sugar, and shortening, and allow to stand until mixture is lukewarm.

Step 2
Pour the required amount of warm or lukewarm water (depending on whether you are using dry active or compressed yeast) into a large mixing bowl and stir in the yeast until it dissolves. When the milk mixture is lukewarm, add it to the yeast mixture and then stir in eggs (if called for).

Step 3
Add one-half of the required amount of flour and mix until smooth. Then add the remaining portion of flour. (It may be necessary to add a bit more flour to achieve a rough, sticky, easily handled dough.)

Step 4
Stir the mixture until the dough becomes a ball-shaped mass that pulls away from bowl, leaving no more than small bits adhering to the sides. The dough is now ready to turn out and knead.

Doubled in Bulk

When your dough appears to be twice its original size, it has risen sufficiently or, in bread-making parlance, "doubled in bulk." The time required for this depends upon a number of factors—temperature, type of flour being used, amount and type of yeast, and so on. Also, at high altitudes your loaf will double in bulk much more rapidly than at sea level; so, if you happen to live in the mountains, be prepared for faster rising than your recipe indicates.

DOUBLED IN BULK

Place the kneaded dough smooth-side down in a well-oiled bowl, turning once to oil the top. Cover the bowl lightly and set in a warm, draft-free place. Allow the dough to rise until it is almost doubled in bulk.

Test for "doubled in bulk" by pressing two fingers into the center of the risen dough to a depth of about one inch.

If the indentations remain in the dough it is ready to be "punched down." (Loaves may be shaped at this stage if your recipe calls for only one rising.)

Punch down the dough by pushing your fist forcefully into the center of the bowl. Fold the edges of the dough inward and press out as many bubbles as possible. Turn the dough over, cover it lightly and let it rise once more in a warm, draft-free place until it is nearly doubled in bulk. Punch the dough down once again and form the loaves.

FORMING LOAVES

If your recipe makes two loaves, divide the dough in half.

Roll out the dough to press out any bubbles.

Pull up each flattened oval of dough.

Turn the ends under to form loaves.

A simple, reliable test that will tell you whether your dough has risen sufficiently can be made by poking two fingers deeply into the center of it. If the holes remain after you remove your fingers, the chances are that the dough has in fact doubled in bulk and is ready to be shaped and baked.

How to Shape your Loaf

If the recipe you are following makes two loaves, divide the dough in half by squeezing through the center of the ball of dough with your hand. Using a lightly floured rolling pin, roll each half, gently but firmly, into a rectangle. This helps to rid the dough of gas or air bubbles. Start with the narrow end of the dough farthest away from you, and roll toward you. Carefully pinch all seams together and place the loaf, seam side down, into an appropriately sized, greased pan.

Judging your Bread

In the final analysis, the taste is most important. If the bread tastes good—it is good. There are, however, certain characteristics that the expert looks for to determine whether or not the loaf is a well-baked one.

First of all, how does your bread look? Is the crust smooth and golden brown? Is the top well-rounded and free of bulges, bumps, and cracks? Is the "break" (the division between the top and the sides) even and uniform? In other words, is it a handsome, tempting loaf that invites tasting?

How does your loaf feel when you hold it? Is it too heavy for its size? If so, the chances are that your bread is too dense because you put it in the oven before it had risen adequately. On the other hand, if the bread feels too light and airy, the reverse is probably the case —you allowed the bread to rise too long before putting it in the oven. A good rule of thumb to remember is this: when the middle of the loaf stands just about even or a trifle higher than the side of the pan, the dough has risen enough and the loaf is ready to bake.

The interior of the bread must be attractive and tempting, too. It should be uniform in color; have a fine, soft texture that doesn't crumble under the touch; and the grain (that is, the shape of the air spaces) should be even and devoid of large air bubbles. When you

THE FINISHED LOAVES

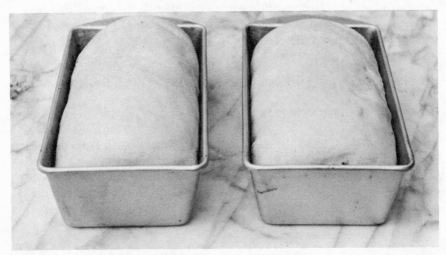

Place the loaves in loaf or bread pans, cover and set in a warm, draft-free place until the dough has risen ¾ of an inch above the top of the pans.

Bake as directed in your recipe until the loaves are golden brown and the pans sound hollow when the sides are tapped with the fingernail.

Remove the loaves from the pans and place them on wire racks to cool. The perfect loaf should be well-formed and have a fine, uniform texture.

roll a small piece of the bread between your fingertips, it should feel moist and soft, give a little, and spring back into shape when released. Finally, it should be tender, easy to chew, and have a tempting, mouth-watering aroma—a yeasty fragrance that is typical of fresh, home-baked yeast bread and nothing else.

Freezing Unbaked Breads and Rolls

Although I don't heartily recommend it, it is possible to freeze unbaked bread dough for periods of up to two weeks. Freezing, to me, seems an unnatural interruption of a beautifully natural process. The best bread is the result of normal baking, which begins with mixing and is followed by kneading, rising, punching down, rising again, and baking. Since no life is, or should be, perfectly planned, there are bound to be unexpected interruptions or emergencies right in the middle of baking. A child's broken tooth must be cared for immediately. A surprise invitation by someone you love should not be missed. The natural life sequence of the bread must not take precedence over your own. These are the times when freezing the dough becomes part of the "perfect order of things."

Freezing

To freeze unbaked bread dough, proceed as directed in your recipe up to the point where you form the loaves. Line the pans with aluminum foil. Shape the loaves to fit loosely in the pans (they expand a bit before they are solidly frozen). Cover the pans with plastic wrap and freeze. When the breads are solidly frozen, lift them from the pans (together with the aluminum foil) and wrap them tightly either in aluminum foil or plastic wrap. Return the frozen loaves to the freezer *immediately*.

If you are preparing round or braided breads or rolls, follow your recipe up to the point where they have been shaped. Then place them on a baking tray or in muffin tins (according to your recipe), cover with plastic wrap, and freeze. When solidly frozen, remove from the pan, and wrap individually in aluminum foil or plastic wrap. Return the frozen braids or rolls to your freezer *immediately*.

Baking

To bake, remove the breads from the freezer 6 or 7 hours before baking time and place them in (or on) greased pans. Cover and allow to double in bulk (about 6½ hours), then bake as directed in your bread recipe. If the breads are to be prepared for breakfast (a lovely idea), thaw them—still wrapped—in your refrigerator overnight. Set your alarm several hours early, unwrap the breads and place them in the pans. You can then go back to bed while you allow them to rise, lightly covered, for 2 hours prior to baking.

For rolls, remove them from the freezer about 2½ hours before baking time, place them in (or on) greased tins, cover lightly, and allow to double in bulk (usually just less than 2 hours). Bake as directed in your recipe.

An ambitious baker with more than one bread in the freezer at a time should date the frozen loaves or rolls and indicate which recipe was used.

Freezing Baked Breads or Rolls

Bread tastes the most delicious when it is eaten immediately after baking. The crust is crispier, the bread more moist, the fragrance more intense and satisfying. However, when you bake you will have extra loaves from time to time, and these *must* be frozen in order to keep them fresh. If freeze you must, here is the correct way to proceed:

Freezing

The secret to successful bread freezing is in the wrapping! After your baked bread has cooled to room temperature, wrap it tightly in aluminum foil, plastic wrap, or air-tight plastic bags. Be sure to do a neat, tight, wrapping job! The objective is to eliminate as much air as possible from the package in order to keep it air-tight during its stay in your freezer. If your bread recipe calls for decoration or icing, do this after the bread has been defrosted and is ready to be served. Date and label your bread for future reference, and bear in mind that after approximately 3 months even the best-wrapped loaf will begin to dry out and lose its flavor.

Thawing

Remove the bread from the freezer, keeping the original wrap intact, and place it on a rack so that air can circulate freely around the loaf. The thawing time is generally around 2 or 3 hours for average-sized loaves at normal room temperature. If the bread is wrapped in foil, it may be defrosted by placing it in an oven preheated to 375° F. for approximately 20 minutes. The foil should be removed during the last 5 minutes to allow the crust to become somewhat crisp. Slices of frozen bread may be popped directly into the toaster.

Bread Ingredients

The type and quality of flour used in preparing bread for baking determines the final product. All yeast-raised breads are made with some portion of wheat flour, which contains a protein called gluten. Gluten acts upon the bread while it is being kneaded by stretching to form the elastic framework holding the gas bubbles produced by the yeast. The amount and quality of gluten is determined by the type of wheat used, where it is grown, and its milling process. Flours with the highest gluten content produce the highest, most handsome loaves.

All-purpose flour used for bread-making is made from a mixture of hard wheat, which is especially gluten-rich, and soft wheat, which has a low gluten and high starch content.

Bread flour is made from gluten-rich hard wheat. Its availability, however, is usually limited to commercial baking firms.

Whole wheat flour is the basic ingredient of whole wheat bread and is complete and unadulterated by man or machine. It contains all of the wheat kernel—the germ, the bran, and the flour, including all of the nutrients put in by Mother Nature herself—and has the highest gluten content of any flour.

Unbleached white flour is wheat flour from which the bran and the germ (as well as their nutrients) have been mechanically removed, but it is not altered otherwise by preservatives or chemicals. High in gluten and far tastier than the commercial bleached flours, unbleached white flour in small quantities makes sticky bread doughs lighter and more workable.

Rye flour contains less gluten than wheat flour, and it tends to produce a denser bread with a finer texture. In small quantities it makes rough-textured doughs smoother and easier to work.

Cornmeal is rich, golden, and of rougher texture than flour—as are all meals. It makes breads crunchier and sweeter, too. Whole cornmeal is richer in nutrients and better tasting than its degermed counterpart, but it is very difficult to obtain.

Rolled oats are, of all the grains, richest in proteins and minerals. When oats are pressed flat between steel rollers, they become rolled oats; they impart a chewy-sweet moistness to breads.

Brown rice flour, although not readily obtainable, increases the nutrients of bread and produces dense, moist, and smooth-textured loaves.

Barley flour enhances the taste of the bread to which it has been added, imparting a moist-sweet, nutty flavor.

Buckwheat flour is a delicious, heavy, and distinctive addition to bread.

Milk is the liquid most frequently used in bread-baking. It imparts a lighter, whiter, smoother, and more velvety grain; helps the bread to remain moist longer; and adds to its nutritional value. Dry, evaporated, or whole milk may be used, although the latter must be scalded (heated close to the boiling point) and then cooled to lukewarm before using in yeast dough. Scalding destroys the enzymes that would otherwise react with the yeast and ultimately produce a rubbery or gummy loaf. Pasteurized milk, heated during the pasteurization process, does not need to be scalded. However, since scalding takes only a few extra moments, I suggest that you include this step even when using pasteurized milk. I generally do so as a precautionary measure.

Water enhances the wheaty flavor of breads and rolls and produces a crustier loaf. Yeast dissolves best and grows fastest in water. Even if a recipe calls for milk, it is best to dissolve the yeast first in luke-warm water (1/4 cup water to 1 package or cake of yeast). If 1/4 cup of water is used with the yeast, reduce the amount of the milk called for in the recipe by 1/4 cup unless your recipe calls for both.

Fruit juice is sometimes used as part or all of the liquid in a bread recipe. It contributes to the flavor and sweetness of the loaf.

Yeast is a wondrous substance, a living microscopic plant which, in the process of fermenting, liberates carbon dioxide; this, in turn, causes batters and doughs to stretch and rise. The texture of bread is actually millions of these tiny gas bubbles, each held in its own small house of dough. These bubbles are responsible for the lightness of the loaf. Yeast comes in two forms. The compressed cakes must be kept refrigerated and only last for a week or two. The newer and more practical dry form remains fresh for several months if stored in a cool place and even longer when refrigerated. Treat your yeast gently; it is living and wants to grow.

Shortening makes for a richer, more tender, and flavorful loaf, and it produces a somewhat softer crust. Liquid vegetable oils are more easily digested than solid fats such as lard, margarine, or butter; therefore, they are better for you. There is no substitute, however, for the richer taste that butter imparts.

Eggs provide extra flavor and nutrition, impart a golden color, and contribute a finer, more delicate texture to the finished loaf. When

beaten and brushed on the surface, they give bread an attractive golden glaze.

Sugar, honey, and molasses are frequently used in yeast bread. Yeast feeds upon sugar (as well as starch) to produce the carbon dioxide bubbles that cause breads to rise. White granulated sugar is the most common sweetener used in baking, but brown and natural sugars may also be used. Liquid sweeteners, such as honey and molasses, have their devotees, particularly in health-food circles. However, if you do substitute a liquid sweetener for sugar, you must reduce the amount of other liquid ingredients accordingly.

Salt promotes flavor in bread just as in other foods, but here it also regulates the yeast and consequently slows the rising of the bread.

Herbs and spices serve to add flavor.

Nuts and seeds contribute crunchiness, nutritional value, and additional taste.

Fruits add sweetness and nutritional value but should be used rather sparingly (as should nuts) since they slow the rising of the bread.

Basic breads

White Bread

3 cups milk	1⅓ cakes compressed yeast
1½ tablespoons butter	¾ cup lukewarm water
3 tablespoons sugar	8–9 cups sifted all-purpose or
3¾ teaspoons salt	unbleached flour

MAKES TWO LOAVES

Scald the milk in a saucepan. Add the butter, sugar, and salt. Set aside and cool to lukewarm. Dissolve the yeast cake in the warm water in a large bowl. Add the milk mixture and flour and beat until smooth. Knead 8 to 10 minutes, or until the dough is smooth and elastic. Shape the dough into a ball and place it in a greased bowl. Roll the dough over to grease the other side. Cover the bowl with a towel. Allow the dough to rise until double in volume (about 1–1½ hours). Punch the dough down, and allow to rise again until double in volume. Punch the dough down again.

Divide the dough in half, shaping each half into a ball. Place on a board and cover, allowing the dough to set 10 to 15 minutes. To shape the dough, flatten it and fold lengthwise. Stretch to a size three times as long as the bread pan. Fold one end to the center, bring the other end up to overlap, and seal the edges. Fold again lengthwise and roll up. Place the dough in two greased bread pans and brush the tops with melted fat. Cover and let rise until double in volume. Bake 50 minutes at 400° F.

Rye Bread

*The whole rye flour gives this unique
bread a texture similar to cracked wheat loaves.*

3 cups milk

1½ tablespoons butter

3 tablespoons sugar

3¾ teaspoons salt

1⅓ cakes compressed yeast

¾ cup lukewarm water

6 cups unsifted 100% rye flour

2–3 cups all-purpose flour

MAKES TWO LOAVES

Scald the milk in a saucepan. Add the shortening, sugar, and salt. Set aside and cool to lukewarm. Meanwhile, dissolve the yeast in the lukewarm water in a large mixing bowl. Stir in the cooled milk mixture. Add the flour and beat until smooth. Knead the dough 8 to 10 minutes. When the dough is smooth and elastic, shape into a ball. Place the dough in a greased bowl, rolling it over to grease the other side. Cover the bowl with a towel and allow the dough to rise until double in volume (about 1½ to 2 hours). Punch the dough down, and allow to rise until doubled in volume again. Punch down once more.

Divide the dough in half, shaping each half into a ball. Place on a board and cover, and allow to set 10 to 15 minutes. To shape the dough, flatten it and fold lengthwise. Stretch each half about three times the length of the bread pan. Fold one end to the center, bring the other end up to overlap, and seal the edges. Fold again lengthwise and roll up. Place dough in two greased loaf pans. Brush the tops with melted fat, cover the pans, and allow to rise once more until doubled in volume. Bake 50 minutes at 400° F.

Bran Bread

Remember—when you bake, all ingredients should
be at room temperature unless otherwise specified.

1¼ cups milk

1 cup water

9 tablespoons butter

4 tablespoons honey

7–8 cups all-purpose or
unbleached white flour

3 cups whole bran cereal

3 tablespoons sugar

¼ teaspoon nutmeg

1 tablespoon salt

3 packages dry active yeast

3 eggs

MAKES TWO LOAVES

Place milk, water, butter, and honey in a small saucepan. Heat for a few minutes until very warm (125° F.); it is not necessary to melt the butter. Meanwhile, combine 1½ cups of flour, the whole bran, sugar, nutmeg, salt, and the yeast in the large bowl of your electric mixer. Stir in the warm milk mixture a little at a time, blending well after each addition. Turn the mixer to medium speed and beat for 2 minutes, stopping the beaters now and then to scrape the bowl. Break the eggs into the mixture. Blend in ½ cup of flour. Beat at high speed, stopping to scrape the bowl occasionally, for 2 more minutes. Stiffen the dough by adding as much of the remaining flour as necessary. Dust a pastry board with flour. Knead the dough for 8 to 10 minutes, or until it has a smooth, elastic consistency.

Grease a large bowl. Set the dough in it and turn it over to grease the top. Allow it to stand, covered, in a warm, draft-free place until its volume has doubled (approximately 1 hour). Punch the dough down. Remove from bowl and cut into two equal pieces. Roll each piece with a rolling pin into a rectangle, about 9x14 inches.

Roll each rectangle up into a loaf by bringing the narrow end farthest away toward you. Use your thumbs to press the edges down. Tuck both ends under and seal with the fingers. Grease two loaf pans. Set the loaves into them with the seams down.

Cover and allow to rise in a warm, draft-free place for about an hour, or until the loaves double in volume. Set the loaf pans on the lowest rack of a preheated 375° F. oven. Bake for 45 minutes or until loaves sound hollow when tapped on the bottom. Remove from pans. Cool on wire racks. Also delicious when served warm.

Cracked Wheat Bread

4½–5½ cups all-purpose or
    unbleached white flour.
    unsifted
2 packages dry active yeast
3 tablespoons sugar
4 teaspoons salt

¾ cup milk
1¼ cups water
3 tablespoons butter
1 cup cracked wheat flour

MAKES TWO LOAVES

Combine 2 cups flour with the yeast, sugar, and salt in a large mixing bowl. Heat the milk, water, and butter together in a small saucepan over a low flame to 125° F. It is not necessary for the butter to melt. Add the milk mixture to the dry ingredients a little at a time, mixing after each addition. Beat with an electric mixer for 2 minutes at medium speed. Scrape the bowl occasionally. Stir in the cracked wheat. Beat 2 minutes more at high speed. Stop to scrape the bowl occasionally. Mix in as much additional flour as needed to make a soft dough. Lightly flour a board and knead the dough about 10 minutes, or until smooth and elastic.

Grease a large bowl and add the dough, turning once to grease the top. Cover the bowl with a towel and allow the dough to rise in a warm, draft-free place until double in bulk (approximately 1 hour).

Punch the dough down and place on a lightly floured board. Cover with a towel and allow to rest for 15 minutes. Divide the dough into two equal parts. Roll each part into a 12x8-inch rectangle. Starting at the short upper end, roll the dough down and seal the seam with your thumbs or the heel of your hand. Seal the ends and fold under. Grease two bread pans and place one loaf in each with the seam down. Cover the loaves and allow them to rise again in a warm, draft-free place until doubled in volume, approximately 1 hour. Preheat the oven to 400° F., and bake the loaves for 30 minutes. Remove from pans and allow to cool on wire racks.

Sourdough Starter

1 cup milk

1 cup all-purpose or unbleached flour

The traditional sourdough starter of pioneer lore, which gold prospectors and lumberjacks utilized for making bread rise, is merely fermented dough made by combining equal amounts of flour and milk. When placed in a glass jar or ceramic bowl for several days and kept warm, the milk's natural organisms launch a bacterial fermentation action in the mixture. The starter will begin to bubble and sour, which you can see and smell, if all goes well. At this point, the starter is ready for use. Store leftover starter in the refrigerator, covered. Be sure to restore the starter to its original volume each time you use some for baking. Add equal amounts of milk and flour to your depleted supply. Allow the starter and its added ingredients to remain overnight at room temperature to bubble and sour again.

Commercially prepared sourdough starter is available at specialty shops or in your grocer's freezer. Follow the instructions on the package for using and storing. The safest bet is to buy sourdough starter, but if you want to work up a first-hand acquaintance with this old standby of the pioneers, here are the directions.

Pour the milk in a glass jar or tightly covered ceramic bowl. Leave uncovered at room temperature for 24 hours. Blend in the flour. Set the uncovered mixture to rest in a warm spot, but not *too* warm, or no fermentation will take place. About 80° F. is the correct temperature. Allow to stand for several days, or until it begins to bubble and sour. Cover and store in the refrigerator until ready for use. Sourdough starter improves with age, but use it at least once a week, and restore it to its original volume each time you use it by adding equal amounts of milk and flour.

Sourdough French Bread

Sourdough starter, whether prepared at home or bought in a store, gives this French-style bread its tantalizing aroma and enticing flavor.

1 package dry active yeast

1¼ cups warm water

1 cup sourdough starter (see page 24)

5½ cups all-purpose or unbleached white flour

2 teaspoons sugar

2 teaspoons salt

½ teaspoon baking soda

MAKES ONE LARGE LOAF

[25]

Place the yeast in a large bowl. Add the warm water and stir briefly. Mix in the starter, 4 cups of the flour, the sugar, and the salt. Stir with a wooden spoon for several minutes. Grease another bowl. Set the dough into it, turning it over once to grease the top. Allow the dough to rise, covered, in a warm, draft-free place (approximately 1½ to 2 hours). When the dough has doubled in volume, add 1 cup of the remaining flour mixed with the baking soda. Dust a pastry board lightly with flour and set the dough on it. Knead slightly and then begin to work in as much of the last cup of flour as necessary. When the dough no longer sticks to the board or your hands, it has enough flour. Knead for 8 to 10 minutes, or until the dough is smooth and elastic. Form into a large ball.

Grease a baking sheet lightly and set the loaf on it. Allow it to rise, covered, in a warm, draft-free place until it nearly doubles in bulk, about 1½ to 2 hours. To ensure a crispier crust, brush the top of the loaf with a little water. Use a very sharp knife to make ¼-inch deep diagonal slashes on the top surface. Preheat the oven to 400° F. and bake this bread for 50 minutes, or until its crust is a deep golden brown.

Dinner Roll Bread***

*This bread both tastes and behaves like
Parkerhouse rolls. It pulls apart, forming individual
rectangular "rolls" of fine-textured bread. Irresistible!*

6–7 cups all-purpose or
    unbleached white flour
3½ tablespoons sugar
  2 teaspoons salt
  1 package dry active yeast

½ cup milk
1½ cups water
5½ tablespoons butter

MAKES TWO LOAVES

Place 2 cups of the flour, the sugar, the salt, and the yeast in a large bowl. Use your fingers to mix these dry ingredients thoroughly. Heat the milk, water, and 3 tablespoons of the butter to 130° F. in a small saucepan. The butter does not need to melt. Stir the warm milk and water mixture gradually into the flour-yeast mixture. Beat 2 minutes at medium speed using a table model or hand electric mixer. Add

¾ cup flour and beat at high speed for 2 minutes more. Scrape the bowl occasionally. Stir in enough of the reserved flour to make a stiff dough. Turn onto a floured board and knead for 8 to 10 minutes, or until the dough is smooth and elastic.

Grease a large bowl and turn the dough into it, turning once to grease the top. Cover and let rise in a warm, draft-free place until double in bulk (approximately 1–1¼ hours).

Punch the dough down, divide it into two equal parts, and place on a lightly floured board. Cover and let rest for 15 minutes. Roll each part into a 12x8-inch rectangle. Brush one rectangle with melted butter and cut into four 8-inch long strips. Stack the strips and cut them into four 2-inch pieces. Stand these slices on end down the center of a 1-pound loaf pan. Repeat the process with the second piece of dough. Cover the loaves and let rise in a warm, draft-free place until double in bulk (about 1 hour). Bake for 30 minutes in an oven preheated to 400° F. Remove the loaves from the pans and cool on wire racks.

Basic Parkerhouse Dough[1]

1 cup milk
½ cup butter
½ cup sugar
1 teaspoon salt
2 packages dry active yeast

¼ cup lukewarm water
5 cups all-purpose or unbleached white flour
2 eggs

MAKES THREE DOZEN ROLLS

Scald the milk in a saucepan, remove from heat, and add the butter, sugar, and salt. Set aside to cool. Stir the yeast into the lukewarm water and allow it to dissolve. Measure the flour. Put 3 cups of it into a large bowl, reserving the rest. When the milk mixture has cooled to lukewarm, blend it into the 3 cups of flour. Add the dissolved yeast and the eggs, which have been beaten until frothy. Mix thoroughly. The result will be a thick batter. Blend in enough of

---

[1] The dough may be kept in the refrigerator two or three days until needed.

the 2 remaining cups of flour, a little at a time, to make a soft dough that will come clean from your hands.

Place the dough on a lightly floured pastry board. Knead until smooth and elastic, about 5 to 8 minutes. Grease a bowl lightly and put the dough into it, turning once to grease the top. Cover with a dishtowel and set the bowl in a warm, draft-free place. Allow it to double in volume. This should take approximately 1½ hours. Punch the dough down; allow it to rest for 10 or 15 minutes before shaping into rolls, or store it in the refrigerator for 2 hours until ready to use.

Parkerhouse Rolls

Basic Parkerhouse dough (page 27)   *Melted butter*

MAKES THIRTY-SIX ROLLS

Divide the dough into two equal parts. Roll each part into a 9-inch circle. Using a 2½-inch wide cookie cutter or drinking glass, cut circles from the dough. Lightly score each circle to one side of the center with a knife, making sure not to cut through. Brush the whole surface of each circle with melted butter, then take the narrower side of the scored line and fold it over so that the edges meet. Pinch lightly to seal. Grease a baking sheet lightly with butter, and arrange the rolls 1 inch apart. Cover lightly and allow to rise in a warm, draft-free place for 1 hour, or until the rolls double in size. Brush lightly with melted butter and bake in a preheated 400° F. oven for 15 minutes, or until golden brown. Serve warm.

Snails

Basic Parkerhouse dough (page 27)   *Melted butter*

MAKES ABOUT TWENTY-FOUR ROLLS

Prepare the Parkerhouse dough as directed. Place dough on pastry board and roll with the hands into long ropes ½-inch thick. Cut the ropes into 8-inch sections. Coil each section by forming a wide circle at the bottom and diminishing circles on top to form snail-shaped rolls. Tuck the loose end under the edge of the roll to hold it in place. Brush rolls lightly with melted butter, place on greased baking sheets, and cover with a dishtowel. Set the baking sheets in a warm, draft-free place and allow the rolls to double in size (approximately 1 hour). Preheat the oven to 400° F. and bake for 15 minutes. When rolls are golden brown, remove from oven and cool slightly on wire racks. Serve warm with plenty of butter.

Cloverleaf Rolls

Basic Parkerhouse dough (page 27)   *Melted butter*

MAKES THIRTY-SIX ROLLS

Prepare the Parkerhouse dough as directed. Divide dough into four equal parts. Shape each part into a 9-inch roll. Cut each roll into nine equal pieces. Divide each piece into thirds and roll the thirds into small balls between your hands. Cover the sides of these balls with melted butter. Grease muffin tins and arrange three balls close together in each cup. Cover the muffin tins loosely with a towel. Allow the small balls of dough to rise in a warm, draft-free place for 1 hour, or until they double in size. Bake for 15 minutes in an oven preheated to 400° F. Remove when they are golden brown and serve hot with butter.

Rosettes

Basic Parkerhouse dough (page 27)   *Melted butter*

MAKES ABOUT TWENTY-FOUR ROLLS

Prepare the Parkerhouse dough as directed. Roll the dough between the hands and form ropes ½-inch thick. Cut each rope into 6-inch pieces. Tie each piece into a loose knot by bringing one end under and up over the circle formed by the knot and placing the other end down into the circle. Brush all surfaces lightly with melted butter. Place on greased baking sheets, cover with a towel, and allow to rise in a warm, draft-free place until doubled in size (approximately 1 hour). Preheat the oven to 400° F. and bake for 15 minutes until golden brown. Serve hot with butter.

Burger Buns

1/3 cup instant nonfat milk powder	1 tablespoon salt
1/4 cup sugar	1/3 cup butter, softened
2 packages dry active yeast	1 1/2 cups warm water (120°–130°F.)
5 1/2–6 1/2 cups all-purpose or unbleached white flour, unsifted	

MAKES TWENTY BUNS

Combine the dry milk powder, sugar, yeast, salt, and 2 cups of flour in a large mixing bowl. Cut in the softened butter. Stir the warm water slowly into the mixture, blending well. Beat for 2 minutes at medium speed of the electric mixer, scraping the bowl from time to time. Blend in ¾ cup of flour and beat for 2 minutes at high speed, stopping occasionally to scrape the bowl.

Make a stiff dough by blending in as much of the remaining flour as necessary. Knead the dough on a lightly floured board 8 to 10 minutes, or until it becomes elastic and smooth. Grease a large bowl and set the dough in it, turning the dough over to grease the top. Allow the dough to rise, covered, in a warm, draft-free place until it doubles in volume (approximately 45 minutes).

Using your fist, punch the dough down. Cover it and allow it to rise again for only 20 minutes. Before it doubles in size, cut the dough into two equal parts and divide each part into ten pieces of equal size. Shape each piece into a ball. Flatten them into bun shapes and place about 2 inches apart on greased baking sheets. Allow them to rise once more, covered, in a warm, draft-free place until doubled in volume. This should take approximately 1 hour. Preheat the oven to 375° F. and bake for 15 or 20 minutes. Slide the buns off the baking sheets and cool on wire racks.

Variations

Any of the following ingredients will yield interesting taste and texture when added to the basic Burger bun dough.

Bacon: Use melted bacon fat instead of butter. Crumble 10 strips of cooked bacon into the dough before adding the remaining flour for kneading.

Cardamom: Mix 1 teaspoon crushed cardamom seeds with the dry ingredients. Glaze the bun tops with melted butter as they come from the oven.

Chives: Mix ¼ cup fresh chopped chives into the dry ingredients. Glaze the bun tops with melted butter as they come from the oven.

Dill: Stir 2 tablespoons of dill seeds into the dry ingredients. Glaze the bun tops with melted butter as they come from the oven.

Sesame Seed: Lightly brown ¼ cup sesame seeds in the oven and add to the dry ingredients. Mix 2 tablespoons of water with 1 lightly beaten egg white and glaze the bun tops *before* baking. Extra sesame seeds may be sprinkled over the glazed tops before the buns go into the oven.

Salt Rising Bread

The rising action in this moist, crumbly bread
is due to the action of salt, milk, sugar,
and cornmeal. A higher temperature (a constant
120°F.) is required for it to rise.

½ cup milk

½ cup cream

⅓ cup white cornmeal

2 tablespoons sugar

1½ teaspoons salt

1 cup lukewarm water

4¼ cups all-purpose or
  unbleached white flour, sifted

2 tablespoons shortening or
  lard, softened

MAKES TWO LOAVES

Scald the milk and cream together in a saucepan. Add the cornmeal, 1 tablespoon of the sugar, and the salt, mixing well. Pour into a wide-mouthed glass jar or large glass bowl. Allow the jar to stand, covered, in a pan filled with water heated to 120° F. while fermentation takes place (about 6–7 hours); the gas in the mixture should escape freely.

Then mix the remaining sugar with the lukewarm water and add to the jar. Sift 2 cups of the flour and blend thoroughly into the fermented mixture. Reheat the water in the pan to 120° F. and set the jar into it. Keep the water temperature as constant as possible while the mixture rises. Add hot water as needed. When light bubbles appear on the surface of the mixture, turn it into a large bowl that has been warmed briefly. Make a stiff dough by adding as much of the remaining flour as necessary; blend it in a little at a time, stirring well after each addition.

Divide dough into two equal parts and form each into a loaf. Grease a baking sheet, place the loaves on the sheet, and spread shortening or lard over the surface of the loaves. Set in a warm, draft-free place and cover with a towel. Allow the loaves to rise until they are 2½ times their original size. Preheat the oven to 375° F. and bake for 10 minutes. Reduce heat to 350° F. and continue baking for an additional 25 minutes. Slide from baking sheet and cool on a wire rack.

Sweet Dough

2 cups milk	½ cup butter, softened
¾ cup sugar	7½–8 cups all-purpose or
2 teaspoons salt	unbleached white flour, sifted
2 packages dry yeast	
2 eggs	

Heat the milk until lukewarm. Place the sugar and salt into a large bowl and add the warm milk. Sprinkle yeast into the mixture, and stir until dissolved. Mix in the eggs and shortening. Add the flour and beat until smooth. Knead 8 to 10 minutes, or until the dough is smooth and elastic. Shape it into a ball and place in a greased bowl. Turn once to grease the top of the dough. Cover with a damp cloth and allow to rise in a warm, draft-free place until double in bulk (about 1½–2 hours). Punch down. Thrust a fist into the dough, pull the edges into the center, and turn upside down in the bowl. Allow the dough to rise again until almost double in bulk. Shape as directed in any sweet dough recipe.

Here's How to Make Perfect Baking Powder Biscuits

Perfect biscuits should be tender and light, with crisp, golden tops. Here's how to make and bake them that way.

Always preheat the oven to the specified temperature.

Assemble all ingredients and utensils. Measure the exact amounts specified in a recipe. Sift the dry ingredients together.

To cut the shortening into the dry ingredients, use two knives held at right angles.

When the dry ingredients and the cut-in shortening have the consistency of very coarse meal, add the milk gradually.

Use only as much milk as is necessary to produce a dough that is smooth to the touch and easy to work with.

If a recipe calls for sour milk or buttermilk and none is available, add a few drops of lemon juice or vinegar to your regular milk.

Dust your hands with flour while you knead the dough lightly and briefly on a flour-dusted pastry board. Turn the dough only two or three times. Firm but gentle is the rule.

Biscuits tend to get tough if your touch is too rough.

After rolling out the dough, dip your biscuit cutter (or the edge of a drinking glass) in flour, shake off the excess, and cut the biscuits out, one next to the other. Gently gather up the pieces of dough left on the board after cutting, shape into a ball, flatten it to the desired thickness without rolling again, and cut out more biscuits.

For soft biscuits, place close together on the baking sheet; for crusty biscuits, space farther apart.

Basic Biscuit Dough

2 cups all-purpose or unbleached
  white flour, sifted

3 teaspoons baking powder

1 teaspoon salt

4 tablespoons shortening

⅔ cup milk

1 egg, beaten

MAKES EIGHTEEN BISCUITS

[33]

Combine the sifted flour, baking powder, and salt, and sift together into a large bowl. Add the shortening and work it into the dry ingredients using two knives or the fingers. When the mixture resembles coarse meal, add the milk and the egg. Stir until the dough leaves the sides of the bowl. Sprinkle flour on a pastry board. Knead the dough lightly for about a minute. Roll out to ½-inch thickness. Dip the edges of a 2½-inch drinking glass or biscuit cutter in flour and cut the dough into rounds. Preheat the oven to 450° F. Arrange the rounds on ungreased baking sheets and bake until lightly browned, approximately 12 minutes. Serve hot.

Basic Biscuit Variation I

JAM SANDWICHES

Basic biscuit dough (see page 33)　　*Assorted jams, preserves, or marmalade*

MAKES NINE SANDWICHES

Prepare the basic biscuit dough. Spread half of the biscuits with a spoonful of jam, preserves, or marmalade, or even an assortment of each. Cover with the remaining biscuits and seal the edges with your fingers. Brush the tops with milk. Preheat the oven to 450° F. Arrange the sandwiches on ungreased baking sheets and bake until lightly browned, approximately 15 minutes.

Basic Biscuit Variation II

MEAT SANDWICHES

Basic biscuit dough (see page 33)　　*Cooked ham or chicken, chopped*

MAKES NINE SANDWICHES

Prepare the basic biscuit dough. Spread a little chopped ham or chicken on half the biscuits. Sprinkle the chicken with curry powder for an added taste treat. Cover with the remaining biscuits and seal the edges with your fingers. Brush the tops with milk. Bake for 15 minutes in an oven preheated to 450° F.

Basic Biscuit Variation III

ORANGE BISCUITS

Basic biscuit dough (see page 33)

2 teaspoons orange zest, (the grated thin outer peel of an orange)

MAKES EIGHTEEN BISCUITS

In preparing the basic biscuit dough, just before adding the milk, stir the orange zest into the flour-shortening mixture. Bake as directed.

Basic Biscuit Variation IV

FRUIT BISCUITS

Basic biscuit dough (page 33)

⅔ cup raisins, dates, figs, or prunes, finely chopped

MAKES ABOUT TWENTY-ONE BISCUITS

While preparing the basic biscuit dough, stir the dried fruit into the ingredients before adding the milk. Bake as directed.

Basic Biscuit Variation V

NUT BISCUITS

Basic biscuit dough (page 33)

⅔ cup walnuts, pecans, or raw cashews, finely chopped

MAKES ABOUT TWENTY-ONE BISCUITS

Stir the nuts into the basic biscuit dough mixture before adding the milk. Bake as directed.

Basic Biscuit Variation VI

CHEESE BISCUITS

Basic biscuit dough (see page   ¼ cup cheese, grated
33)

MAKES ABOUT TWENTY BISCUITS

While preparing the basic biscuit dough, grate any variety of hard
cheese and blend it in with the dry ingredients. Bake as directed.

Basic Biscuit Variation VII

CHEESE BUTTONS

Basic biscuit dough (see page   Sharp cheddar cheese, cubed
33)
⅓ cup butter, at room
    temperature

MAKES ABOUT TWENTY-FOUR BISCUITS

Prepare the basic biscuit dough as directed. Roll out to ¼-inch
thickness. Dust the edges of a 2-inch diameter glass with flour. Cut
the biscuits into circles with the glass and butter the tops, reserving
a little of the butter. Place ½-inch cube of sharp cheddar cheese on
each biscuit. Pull up the edges of each biscuit and seal over the
cheese. Brush with reserved melted butter. Bake as directed.

Basic Biscuit Variation VIII

CHEESE PULL-APARTS

Basic biscuit dough (see page   1 cup sharp cheddar cheese,
33)   grated
Butter, at room temperature

MAKES SIX BISCUITS

Prepare the basic biscuit dough as directed. Knead briefly on a
lightly floured pastry board. With your hands, form the dough into

[36]

a ball. Flatten the ball and roll out into an 8x8-inch square, about ⅓-inch thick. Dust a knife with flour and cut the square into four equal strips. Spread all the strips with softened butter, and cover one strip with a layer of grated cheddar cheese (about ⅓ cup). Place another strip of dough on top of the cheese. Cover it with cheese. Repeat with another strip of buttered dough and the remaining cheese. Top with the final strip of dough. Cut the layers of dough and cheese into six pieces. Arrange each piece, cut side up, in a buttered muffin pan. Bake as directed for basic biscuit dough. Serve immediately.

Basic Biscuit Variation IX

DILL BISCUITS

Basic biscuit dough (page 33)

½ teaspoon baking soda

1 tablespoon fresh dill, chopped (or 1 teaspoon dried dill)

⅔ cup buttermilk

MAKES EIGHTEEN BISCUITS

While preparing the basic biscuit dough, sift baking soda together with the dry ingredients. Add the dill to the flour-shortening mixture. Substitute buttermilk for regular milk. Proceed as directed.

Basic Biscuit Variation X

DROP BISCUITS

Basic biscuit dough (see page 33)   ⅓ cup milk

MAKES EIGHTEEN BISCUITS

In preparing the basic biscuit dough, use an additional ⅓ cup of milk (a total of 1 cup). Grease a baking sheet and drop the dough onto it by rounded teaspoonfuls. Bake as directed.

Basic Biscuit Variation XI

CREAM BISCUITS

Basic biscuit dough (page 33)   1 cup medium cream, minus 1
                                            tablespoon

MAKES EIGHTEEN BISCUITS

While preparing the basic biscuit dough, substitute cream for the shortening and milk. Bake as directed.

Basic Biscuit Variation XII

SHORTCAKE BISCUITS

Basic biscuit dough (page 33)   2 tablespoons shortening
2 tablespoons sugar   1 egg

MAKES EIGHTEEN BISCUITS

Prepare the dry ingredients for the basic biscuit dough as directed. Add the sugar, 2 extra tablespoons of shortening, and the egg. Proceed and bake as directed.

Basic Biscuit Variation XIII

BRAN BISCUITS

Basic biscuit dough (page 33)   ¾ cup whole bran cereal

MAKES EIGHTEEN BISCUITS

While preparing dry ingredients for the basic biscuit dough, use ¾ cup of whole bran and only 1 cup of enriched flour. Proceed as directed.

Basic Biscuit Variation XIV

WHEAT BISCUITS

Basic biscuit dough (page 33)   ⅔ cup 100% whole wheat flour

MAKES EIGHTEEN BISCUITS

[38]

While preparing dry ingredients for the basic biscuit dough, use ⅔ cup of whole wheat flour and only 1 cup of enriched flour. Reduce the amount of salt from 1 teaspoon to ¾ teaspoon. Proceed as directed.

Basic Biscuit Variation XV

RYE BISCUITS

Basic biscuit dough (page 33)   *1 cup 100% rye flour*

MAKES EIGHTEEN BISCUITS

Use 1 cup of rye flour and only 1 cup of enriched flour while preparing the dry ingredients for the basic biscuit dough. Reduce the amount of salt from 1 teaspoon to ¾ teaspoon. Proceed as directed.

Basic Biscuit Variation XVI

WHEAT GERM BISCUITS

Basic biscuit dough (page 33)   *½ cup sweetened wheat germ*

MAKES EIGHTEEN BISCUITS

In preparing the basic biscuit dough, use ½ cup of sweetened wheat germ and only 1½ cups of enriched flour. Reduce the amount of salt from 1 teaspoon to ¾ teaspoon. Proceed as directed.

Basic Buttermilk Biscuits

2 cups all-purpose or unbleached white flour, sifted
¾ teaspoon baking soda
2 teaspoons baking powder

½ teaspoon salt
¼ cup shortening
1¼ cups buttermilk

MAKES TWELVE BISCUITS

Combine the sifted flour, baking soda, baking powder, and salt. Sift these ingredients together three times. Using two knives, cut the shortening into the dry ingredients until the mixture resembles coarse meal. Stir in the buttermilk with a fork, just enough to blend the ingredients. Knead the dough for 30 seconds on a pastry board, lightly dusted with flour. Roll the dough out to ½-inch thickness. Dip the edges of a drinking glass in flour and cut out twelve circles. Arrange on ungreased baking sheets. Bake in a preheated 450° F. oven. Serve the biscuits hot as they come from the oven.

Parmesan Biscuit Sandwiches

Here's a crunchy, cheese-filled biscuit sandwich that goes very well with any vegetable soup.

2 cups all-purpose flour
1¼ teaspoons salt
2 teaspoons double-action baking powder
5 tablespoons butter or shortening

¾ cup milk
Dijon mustard
¾ cup Parmesan cheese, grated

MAKES TWELVE SANDWICHES

Sift together the flour, salt, and baking powder. Work in the butter or shortening quickly with the fingertips. Stir in the milk to make a soft dough. Turn out on a lightly floured board and knead until smooth, from 30 to 60 seconds. Roll the dough until it is ¼-inch thick and cut out 2-inch rounds. Spread the top of each round liberally with mustard. Sprinkle grated Parmesan cheese on half of the rounds. Place the remaining rounds, mustard side down, on top of the cheese-sprinkled rounds. Grease a baking sheet and bake in a preheated 425° F. oven for 12 to 15 minutes, or until the sandwiches are golden brown. Serve hot.

Beaten Biscuits

6 cups all-purpose or unbleached white flour, sifted
1½ tablespoons sugar
½ teaspoon salt

1 cup shortening
1¾ cups ice water

MAKES ABOUT THIRTY-SIX BISCUITS

Combine the sifted flour, sugar, and salt, and sift them together into a large bowl. Work the shortening into the dry ingredients with the fingers. Using the fist, make a well in the center of the mixture, pour in the ice water, and work all ingredients together rapidly. Place the dough on a pastry board and beat it vigorously for 20 minutes with the side of a rolling pin. Add as much flour from time to time as the dough will absorb. If beaten properly, the dough should be blistered and shiny at the end of this time.

Dust the pastry board lightly with flour. Roll the dough out until it is paper-thin. Give the dough a light sprinkling of flour, bring one end up to the other and roll out once more until it is about ⅓-inch thick.

Use a drinking glass or a 3-inch round cookie cutter to cut out the biscuits. Place on ungreased baking sheets and prick each biscuit with a fork several times. Bake at 400° F. for about 20 minutes. Remove biscuits from the oven before they become brown and hard. Cool on wire racks.

Salt Biscuits

2 cups all-purpose or unbleached white flour, sifted

2 tablespoons sugar

2 teaspoons baking powder

⅓ teaspoon baking soda

¾ teaspoon cream of tartar

⅓ pound cream cheese, softened

2 tablespoons butter, softened

⅓ cup buttermilk

1 large egg

Coarse salt

MAKES EIGHT TO TEN BISCUITS

Combine the sifted flour, sugar, baking powder, baking soda, and cream of tartar, and sift together into a large bowl. Work the cream cheese and butter into the dry ingredients until well blended. Stir in the buttermilk. Beat the egg until light and frothy and add to the mixture. Blend thoroughly to form a stiff dough. Lightly flour a pastry board. Turn the dough out and knead for 5 minutes until it is smooth. Roll the dough out until it is ¼-inch thick and cut it into 2-inch squares. Arrange the biscuits on an ungreased baking sheet. Sprinkle each biscuit with a few grains of coarse salt and bake for 15 minutes in an oven preheated to 450° F. Remove biscuits from the oven when they are golden brown and serve with sweet butter.

Here's How to Make Perfect Muffins

Perfect muffins should be tender and light. Here are some hints:

Always preheat the oven to the temperature specified in each recipe.

Melt the shortening at the beginning and allow it to cool slightly while you assemble the utensils and measure the dry ingredients.

The purpose of sifting the dry ingredients together is to mix them thoroughly, thereby ensuring a good texture for your muffins.

Stir the specified liquids into the dry ingredients only enough to moisten the batter. Too much mixing will cause the muffins to be tough.

Grease the muffin cups with any salt-free shortening, butter, or vegetable oil.

Fill your muffin cups, no matter what their size, only ⅔ full. When baked, muffins should be golden brown on top and have a uniform texture.

Basic Muffin Batter

4 tablespoons butter, melted	½ teaspoon salt
2 cups all-purpose or unbleached white flour, sifted	1 egg
	1 cup milk
2 tablespoons sugar	
2¾ teaspoons baking powder	

MAKES TWELVE MUFFINS

Melt butter over hot water and allow to cool. Combine the sifted flour, sugar, baking powder, and salt, and sift together into a large bowl. Beat the egg until light and frothy. Mix the butter and egg with the milk and add all at once to the dry ingredients. Stir 10 or 15 times with a wooden spoon, so that the flour is just moistened. The batter will be lumpy, but that is all right; too much mixing will only produce tough muffins. Pour batter into well-greased muffin cups (or pyrex cups), filling them about ⅔ full. Bake in an oven preheated to 425° F. for 20 to 25 minutes, or until the muffins are golden brown. Serve warm with butter.

Apple Muffins

Basic muffin batter (see page 42)

1 small apple, peeled and thinly sliced

¼ teaspoon cinnamon

Cinnamon sugar

½ cup apples, peeled and finely chopped

MAKES ABOUT SIXTEEN MUFFINS

Prepare Basic muffin batter as directed, sifting the cinnamon with the dry ingredients. Proceed as directed. Stir the chopped apples into the batter, and pour the batter into greased muffin cups. Arrange two slices of apple on top of the batter in each muffin cup. Sprinkle with cinnamon sugar. Bake as directed.

Date and Nut Muffins

Basic muffin batter (see page 42)

¼ cup walnuts, finely chopped

½ cup dates, finely chopped

MAKES ABOUT SIXTEEN MUFFINS

Prepare the dry ingredients for the Basic muffin batter. Mix the chopped dates and walnuts with the dry ingredients. Continue with the recipe for basic muffin batter.

Bacon Muffins

Basic muffin batter (see page 42)

4 tablespoons bacon fat

½ cup lean bacon, chopped

MAKES ABOUT SIXTEEN MUFFINS

Sauté bacon in a skillet until it is brown and drain well on paper towels. Reserve bacon fat. Prepare Basic muffin batter as directed, adding the chopped sautéed bacon to the dry ingredients. Substitute melted bacon fat for the butter. Continue with the recipe for basic muffin batter.

Bran Muffins

Basic muffin batter (page 42)   *1 cup whole bran cereal*

MAKES ABOUT SIXTEEN MUFFINS

Use 1 cup whole bran and only 1 cup of flour. Soften the bran in milk to cover for 5 minutes. After the dry ingredients have been sifted, mix in the softened bran. Proceed as directed.

Cranberry Muffins

Basic muffin batter (page 42)   *¼ cup sugar*
¾ cup cranberries, finely chopped

MAKES ABOUT SIXTEEN MUFFINS

Rinse and dry the cranberries thoroughly. Chop them very fine, add the sugar, and mix with the dry ingredients in the Basic muffin batter recipe. Proceed as directed.

Oatmeal Muffins

Basic muffin batter (page 42)   *1 cup raw quick-cooking oats*

MAKES ABOUT SIXTEEN MUFFINS

In preparing the Basic muffin batter, use 1 cup raw quick-cooking oats and only 1 cup of flour. Add the oats to the sifted dry ingredients. Proceed as directed.

Yeasty Pancakes

2 packages dry active yeast   *4 cups all-purpose flour*
½ cup warm water   *1 teaspoon salt*
3½ cups milk   *2 eggs, beaten*

SERVES EIGHT

Dissolve the yeast in the warm water for 5 minutes. Warm the milk briefly and stir into the yeast mixture. Combine the flour with the salt and sift together. Add the dry ingredients to the yeast mixture, a little at a time, stirring well after each addition. Beat in eggs for a smooth batter. Melt some butter in a 10-inch skillet and allow it to heat. Pour in enough batter to cover the bottom of the skillet completely. Shake the skillet occasionally as the pancake browns to loosen the edges. Turn once to brown the other side. Repeat the procedure until all the batter has been used. Serve the pancakes hot with butter and syrup.

Yeasty Pancakes with Apples

Yeasty pancakes recipe　　　　　3 *tablespoons butter*
(page 44)
4 medium-sized apples

MAKES EIGHT

Prepare Yeasty pancake batter as directed. Peel and core the apples. Heat the butter in a 10-inch skillet. Slice half an apple thinly and arrange the slices in the butter. Pour enough batter over the apple slices to cover the bottom of the skillet. Brown the pancake on one side, shaking the skillet occasionally, then turn and brown the other side. Repeat until all the apples and batter have been used. Serve hot, sprinkled with cinnamon and sugar.

Yeasty Pancakes with Bacon

1 pound lean bacon　　　　　　3 *tablespoons butter*
Yeasty pancakes recipe
(page 44)

MAKES EIGHT

Sauté the bacon strips until brown. Drain on paper towels. Prepare Yeasty pancake batter as directed. Heat the butter in a 10-inch skillet. Arrange two or three strips of bacon in the butter, pour in enough batter to cover the bottom of the skillet, and brown the pancake on both sides. Shake the skillet occasionally and turn the pan-cakes once. Repeat until all the bacon and batter have been used. Serve hot with syrup.

How to Reheat Bread and Rolls

Here are two ways to use leftover or partially stale bread or rolls:

METHOD I: Place bread or rolls in a dampened paper bag. Close the top of the bag and heat for 5 minutes in a 425° F. oven.

METHOD II: Put the bread or rolls in the top of a double boiler over boiling water for 5 minutes. If the bread or rolls are hard, sprinkle with water.

Using Stale or Leftover Breads

Once in a while a home-baked bread may linger around long enough to dry out, or on occasion you may wish to use a freshly baked loaf for some special dish. Here are a few suggestions:

Breadcrumbs

SOFT: Use your fingers to pull small pieces from a slice of fairly fresh bread.

DRY: Break *very* dry bread into small pieces. Pulverize with a rolling pin or whirl in a blender until the crumbs are fine. For uniform size, sift the crumbs and roll or whirl the larger pieces a second time.

DRY-BUTTERED: Heat ½ cup of butter in a fairly heavy skillet. Add 1 cup fine, dry breadcrumbs. Sauté over medium-low heat, stirring constantly until the crumbs are slightly browned. If some of the crumbs seem too dry, add more butter.

Bread Cubes

SOFT: Cut several slices of fresh bread into strips approximately ½-inch wide. Slice again across the strips to form ½-inch cubes.

TOASTED (BROILER METHOD): Preheat the broiler to 400° F. Place soft bread cubes on a cookie sheet and slide it under the broiler flame. Stir the cubes frequently until they are lightly browned on all sides.

TOASTED (OVEN METHOD): Preheat the oven to 325° F. Place soft bread cubes on a cookie sheet and bake, turning occasionally, until cubes are lightly browned on all sides.

French Toast with Sugar and Lime***

French toast brushed with melted butter and
sprinkled with sugar and lime juice is
incredibly good and a favorite
for Sunday brunch.

3 eggs	8 slices fine-textured bread, ½-inch thick
1 cup milk	
3 tablespoons sugar	5 tablespoons butter
1 teaspoon cinnamon	¼ cup coarse sugar
¼ teaspoon nutmeg	2 limes
¼ teaspoon vanilla	

MAKES EIGHT SLICES

Beat the eggs to a froth in a shallow bowl. Beat in the milk, sugar, spices, and vanilla. Dip the bread slices into the egg mixture and fry in melted butter until golden brown on both sides. Spread the French toast liberally with butter while it is still warm. Serve immediately with sugar and lime wedges.

Toast Points

Fresh bread slices, ½-inch thick

Remove crusts from each slice. Toast and cut each slice into four triangles while still hot. Use as garnish for creamed food or soups.

Toast Cups

¼-inch slices of fresh bread   *Melted butter*

Trim the crusts from the bread slices. Brush melted butter on one side of each slice. Form toast cups by pressing each slice into a custard cup or cupcake pan, buttered side up. Bake at 350° F. for 15 to 20 minutes until crisp and brown.

Melba Toast

1 loaf slightly stale bread,
* unsliced*

MAKES TWENTY-FOUR SLICES

Slice bread as thinly as possible, not more than ¼-inch thick. Lay the slices on baking sheets and bake at 300° F. for 15 to 20 minutes, or until brown and dry.

Pain Perdu

Leftover bread put to sweet use!

3 eggs
½ cup milk
⅓ cup sour cream
4½ tablespoons honey
⅓ cup brandy or rum

1 teaspoon cinnamon
¼ teaspoon nutmeg
8 slices fine-textured white
* bread, ½-inch thick*
4 tablespoons sweet butter

MAKES EIGHT SLICES

Beat the eggs to a froth in a shallow bowl. Stir in the milk, sour cream, honey, liquor, and cinnamon. Cut the crusts from the bread and discard. Dip each slice of bread briefly into the mixture, turning to coat both sides. Allow each slice to remain for a minute or two in the bowl to absorb the mixture. Heat some of the butter in a skillet. Brown each slice of bread evenly on both sides. Serve immediately, with syrup, honey, powdered sugar, or cinnamon sugar, as desired.

Cornbread Pudding

2 cups cornbread crumbs

2 cups bread cubes (sweet bread is best)

2 cups milk

4 eggs

1 cup dark brown sugar

¼ cup molasses

¼ cup chopped nuts

½ teaspoon cinnamon

¼ teaspoon allspice

2 tablespoons butter

SERVES EIGHT

Place cornbread crumbs and bread cubes in a buttered, ovenproof bowl. Beat together milk, eggs, brown sugar, molasses, chopped nuts, and spices. Pour this mixture over the bread and stir gently until all of the bread is well soaked. Dot with butter and bake for 1 hour in an oven preheated to 350° F.

Cornbread Stuffing

*Crumbled into small chunks, leftover cornbread, combined
with chopped onion and celery, can make a tasty
Southern-style stuffing for chicken, turkey, or game birds.*

3 tablespoons butter

¾ cup celery, chopped

¾ cup onion, chopped

2 sprigs parsley, minced

2 cups leftover cornbread, crumbled

2 cups bread cubes

¼ teaspoon thyme

½ teaspoon sage

1 teaspoon salt

¼ cup water

1 egg

¼ cup golden raisins (optional)

MAKES ABOUT FIVE CUPS

[49]

Melt the butter in a large skillet or Dutch oven. Add the chopped vegetables and sauté until the onion is golden and transparent. Add the crumbled cornbread, bread cubes, and seasonings. Sprinkle with water, stirring occasionally. Beat the egg lightly and stir into the stuffing. Golden raisins may be added if desired. Allow the filling to cool before stuffing the bird.

Bread Baskets

CROUSTADES

½ loaf of stale white bread, unsliced

Melted butter

MAKES ABOUT SIX BASKETS

Trim the crusts from all sides of the bread. Cut through the loaf at 2-inch intervals. With a sharp knife, carve a 1-inch cube from the center of each slice to form a basket. Brush the baskets with melted butter. Toast to a light golden brown 3 inches from the flame in a preheated broiler. Pour creamed foods over the baskets and serve.

Italian Cheese Sticks

Meltingly good!

½ pound mozzarella cheese

2 eggs

⅓ cup all-purpose or unbleached white flour

1½ cups breadcrumbs, finely ground

1 tablespoon butter

1 tablespoon olive oil

MAKES ABOUT SIXTEEN STICKS

Cut the cheese into sticks ¼ inch thick, 1 inch wide, and 3 inches long. Beat the eggs slightly. Dip the cheese sticks first in the flour, next in the eggs, and then in the breadcrumbs. Heat the butter and oil together in a frying pan, adding more oil or butter if necessary. Brown the cheese sticks until crisp, turning once. Drain on paper towels. Serve immediately with Italian bread, salad, or soup.

Garlic Bread Sticks

3½ tablespoons butter
Garlic salt

8 party rye bread slices

MAKES ABOUT THIRTY-SIX STICKS

Melt the butter and sprinkle with garlic salt. Brush the garlic butter over both sides of the bread slices and cut in thin strips. Toast until lightly browned in an oven preheated to 400° F.

Basic Nut Loaf

*I love the country taste of hickory nuts in this
particular bread. Or use the nuts of your choice, or those on hand.*

2 cups all-purpose or unbleached
white flour, sifted

7 tablespoons sugar

3 teaspoons baking powder

¾ teaspoon salt

1 cup hickory nuts, finely chopped

1 egg

1 cup milk

½ teaspoon nutmeg

MAKES ONE LOAF

Combine the sifted flour, sugar, baking powder, and salt, and sift again into a large bowl. Add the finely chopped nuts to the dry ingredients. Beat the egg lightly. Mix the milk with the egg and add to flour mixture. Stir rapidly, just until all the ingredients are well blended. Pour the batter into a well-greased loaf pan. Bake for 45 minutes in a preheated 350° F. oven. Remove from baking pan and cool the loaf on a wire rack.

Basic Nut Loaf Variation I

DATE AND NUT FRUIT LOAF

Basic nut loaf batter
½ cup dates, finely chopped

½ cup dried apricots, finely chopped
½ cup walnuts, finely chopped

MAKES ONE LOAF

[51]

Prepare the dry ingredients for basic nut loaf batter. Add the chopped dates and apricots to the flour mixture. Use ½ cup chopped walnuts instead of 1 cup of hickory nuts. Proceed as directed.

Basic Nut Loaf Variation II

CITRUS NUT LOAF

Basic nut loaf batter (page 51)
½ cup candied orange peel, finely chopped

½ cup candied lemon peel, finely chopped
¼ cup candied lime peel, finely chopped (optional)

MAKES ONE LOAF

Prepare the dry ingredients. Add the chopped candied citrus peel together with the chopped nuts. Proceed as directed.

Basic Nut Loaf Variation III

HEALTH LOAF

Basic nut loaf batter (page 51)
¾ cup whole wheat flour
¼ cup wheat germ

4 tablespoons brown sugar, firmly packed
1 cup sunflower seeds, hulled

MAKES ONE LOAF

Use ¾ cup of whole wheat flour and ¼ cup of wheat germ and only 1 cup of all-purpose flour. Use brown sugar instead of the granulated sugar. Substitute hulled sunflower seeds for the nuts. Sift only the white flour with the sugar, baking powder, and salt. Stir the whole wheat flour, wheat germ, and hulled sunflower seeds into the flour mixture. Proceed as directed in basic recipe.

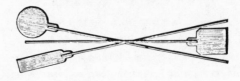

Basic Gingerbread

2 cups all-purpose flour, sifted

1¾ teaspoons ground ginger

1¼ teaspoons ground cinnamon

¼ teaspoon ground cloves

2 teaspoons baking powder

¼ teaspoon baking soda

½ teaspoon salt

⅓ cup shortening

⅓ cup sugar

1 egg

¾ cup milk

¾ cup molasses

SERVES EIGHT

Combine the sifted flour with ginger, cinnamon, cloves, baking powder, baking soda, and salt, and sift again. Place the shortening in a large bowl and beat it lightly. Add the sugar and blend with the shortening. Add the egg and beat the creamed mixture until light and fluffy. Combine the milk and molasses. Add the dry ingredients, a little at a time, alternately with the milk and molasses to the creamed mixture. Stir well after each addition, but only until blended. Pour the batter into a well-greased 8-inch square baking pan. Bake for 45 minutes in a preheated 350° F. oven. Cool in the pan after removing it from the oven. Cut into squares and serve warm or cold.

Basic Gingerbread Variation I

ORANGE MARMALADE GINGERBREAD

Basic gingerbread batter

¾ cup orange juice

2 tablespoons butter

¾ cup orange marmalade

SERVES EIGHT

Preheat the oven to 350° F. Prepare the basic gingerbread batter as directed, substituting orange juice for the milk. Place the butter in the bottom of an 8-inch square pan, melt it in the oven, and remove the pan from the oven. Spread the orange marmalade over the bottom, carefully pour the batter on top, and bake as directed. Remove from oven, loosen the edges, and immediately invert the gingerbread onto a serving plate. Cut into squares after cooling slightly. Serve warm or cold.

[53]

Basic Gingerbread Variation II

UPSIDE-DOWN APPLE GINGERBREAD

Basic gingerbread batter (see page 53)
1 cup apples, sliced and peeled

2 tablespoons butter, melted
¼ cup molasses

SERVES EIGHT

Prepare the basic gingerbread batter as directed. Before putting the batter into the baking pan, peel and slice the apples. Swirl the melted butter over the bottom and sides of the pan. Spread the molasses over the butter. Arrange the sliced apples in rows in the molasses, and pour the batter carefully over them. Bake as directed. Loosen the edges and turn the gingerbread upside down as soon as it is removed from the oven. Cut into squares after cooling slightly. Serve warm or cold.

Basic Spoon Bread I

2 cups water
1 cup white cornmeal
1 teaspoon salt
4 tablespoons butter

5 eggs
1 cup milk
¾ cup medium cream

SERVES EIGHT

Preheat the oven to 350° F. Heat the water to boiling in a large saucepan. Add the cornmeal and salt. Stir briskly and cook for 1 minute or until very thick. Remove from the heat and stir in 2 tablespoons of the butter. Set aside.

Place the remaining butter in a 9-inch square baking pan or pyrex dish, and put it in the oven until sizzling but not brown.

Beat 4 of the eggs and mix in the milk. Stir egg mixture into cornmeal. Beat with electric beater until free from lumps. Take the baking pan from the oven and pour the batter into it. Return to the oven and bake for 15 minutes.

Beat the remaining egg with the cream. Pour the egg mixture

over the top of the bread and continue baking for 25 minutes, or until the top is lightly browned and puffy. Serve immediately. Spoon onto plates and butter generously.

Basic Spoon Bread Variation I

BACON SPOON BREAD

¾ cup lean bacon, diced   4 tablespoons bacon fat
Basic spoon bread I batter
(see page 54)

SERVES EIGHT

Sauté the diced bacon until crisp. Drain on paper towels and reserve the bacon fat. Substitute 2 tablespoons of bacon fat for 2 tablespoons of butter and stir into the hot cornmeal mixture together with the diced bacon. Place the remaining bacon fat in a baking pan to sizzle in the oven. Proceed as directed.

Basic Spoon Bread Variation II

CHEESE SPOON BREAD

Basic spoon bread I batter   ¾ cup sharp cheddar cheese,
(see page 54)   grated

SERVES EIGHT

Stir grated cheddar cheese into the hot cornmeal after the butter has been added. Proceed as directed.

Basic Spoon Bread Variation III

CRACKLING SPOON BREAD

¾ cup salt pork, chopped   2 tablespoons salt pork fat,
Basic spoon bread I batter   rendered
(see page 54)

SERVES EIGHT

Sauté the chopped salt pork over low heat until golden brown, stirring frequently. Drain the cracklings on paper towels and reserve both the fat and the cracklings. Add cornmeal and only ¾ teaspoon of salt to the boiling water. Substitute salt pork fat for 2 tablespoons of the butter and stir into the hot cornmeal mixture together with the cracklings. Proceed as directed.

Spoon Bread II

Moist and delicious—a special touch for any meal.

1 cup white cornmeal	2 eggs
1 cup boiling water	1⅔ cups milk
1 tablespoon butter	1 teaspoon baking powder
¾ teaspoon salt	

SERVES EIGHT

Place the cornmeal in a large saucepan. Pour in the boiling water, stirring vigorously to eliminate all lumps. When the mixture is smooth, add the butter and salt, and stir until the butter is blended in. Separate the eggs. Add the yolks (reserving the whites) to the cornmeal mixture together with the milk. When the mixture has cooled to lukewarm, blend in the baking powder. Beat the egg whites until they form peaks and gently fold into the batter. Spread butter over the sides and bottom of a 9-inch square baking dish and place it in an oven preheated to 375° F. until the butter is hot. Remove the baking dish from the oven, pour in the batter, and then bake for 45 minutes. When the spoon bread turns fluffy and golden and a toothpick inserted in the center comes out clean, remove from the oven and serve immediately.

Spoon Bread with Ham

Spoon bread II batter	
½ cup cooked ham, finely chopped	2 tablespoons butter

SERVES EIGHT

Sauté the finely chopped cooked ham in butter and then drain. Add to spoon bread II batter at the same time that the egg yolks and milk are stirred into the cornmeal mixture. Proceed as directed.

Basic Cornbread

This moist, golden cornbread rises high and handsome.

3 cups all-purpose or
    unbleached white flour, sifted
1½ *cups yellow cornmeal*
2 *tablespoons baking powder*

1 *teaspoon salt*
½ *cup butter*
2½ *cups milk*

SERVES EIGHT GENEROUSLY

Combine the sifted flour, cornmeal, baking powder, and salt. Melt the butter and add it to the milk. Blend the milk mixture into the dry ingredients and stir for a minute or two until lightly mixed. Grease an 8-inch square baking pan and bake for 30 minutes in an oven preheated to 425° F.

Basic Cornbread Variation I

BACON-Y CORNBREAD

1 *cup bacon, diced*   *Basic cornbread batter*

SERVES EIGHT GENEROUSLY

Sauté diced bacon until crisp and nicely browned. Drain on paper towels. Mix with the dry ingredients after they have been sifted. Proceed as directed.

Basic Cornbread Variation II

CORNBREAD WITH CRACKLINGS

3 *ounces salt pork, diced*   *Basic cornbread batter*

SERVES EIGHT GENEROUSLY

Sauté the diced salt pork in a skillet over a low flame, until lightly browned. Drain thoroughly on paper towels. Stir the cracklings into the dry ingredients after they have been sifted. Proceed as directed.

Custard Cornbread***

2 tablespoons butter	1 teaspoon baking powder
½ cup all-purpose or unbleached white flour, sifted	½ teaspoon salt
¾ cup yellow cornmeal	1 egg
2⅓ tablespoons light brown sugar	1½ cups milk

SERVES EIGHT

Melt butter over hot water. Combine the sifted flour, cornmeal, brown sugar, baking powder, and salt, and sift again. Beat the egg lightly. Add 1 cup of the milk and the melted butter to the egg and stir well. Blend the liquids into the flour and cornmeal mixture thoroughly. The result will be a very thin batter. Grease an 8-inch square baking dish and pour in the batter. Spoon the remaining ½ cup of milk over the batter so that it floats on top. Bake in a preheated 400° F. oven for 20 minutes. Remove from oven, cut into squares while hot, and serve immediately.

Corn Sticks

1 tablespoon shortening	½ teaspoon salt
1 cup all-purpose or unbleached white flour, sifted	½ cup yellow cornmeal
½ cup sugar	1 egg
3 teaspoons baking powder	1 cup milk

MAKES TWELVE STICKS

Melt the shortening and set aside to cool a little. Meanwhile, combine the sifted flour, sugar, baking powder, and salt, and sift again. Blend in the cornmeal. Beat the egg lightly, stir in the milk, and add this mixture to the dry ingredients. Mix the shortening into the batter and blend thoroughly. Grease cornstick pans and heat briefly in an oven preheated to 400° F. Remove from oven, pour batter into the pans, and bake for 15 to 20 minutes. Serve golden brown corn sticks with lots of butter on the side.

Batter Bread

Don't be dismayed by the proportions of milk and egg to cornmeal in this tasty bread. Its velvety custard-like texture will surprise and delight you.

2 cups white cornmeal, sifted	6 eggs
2 teaspoons sugar (optional)	4 cups milk
2 teaspoons baking powder	6 tablespoons melted butter
2 teaspoons salt	

SERVES EIGHT

Combine the sifted cornmeal, sugar, baking powder, and salt, and sift again. Break the eggs into a large bowl. Beat until light and frothy. Add the milk to the eggs and stir in the dry ingredients. Blend well. Pour the melted butter into a deep baking dish or casserole, no larger than 8 inches square. Tip the baking dish to make sure that the butter coats the sides thoroughly. Pour the batter into the dish. Bake for 30 minutes in an oven preheated to 350° F. Use a knife blade to test for doneness. If it comes out clean, the bread is ready and should be served immediately.

Spreads for Breads

Old-fashioned Whole Strawberry Preserves

Just like Grandmother used to make . . .

3 quarts of firm, ripe strawberries	Sugar

MAKES ABOUT EIGHT GLASSES

Pick over the berries, discarding only those that are badly bruised, green, or poorly formed. Wash the whole, perfect berries and drain.

Weigh the drained berries and place them in a large preserving kettle. Weigh an equal amount of sugar and add to the berries. Bring slowly to a boil and boil for 8 minutes. Remove from the heat, cover, and cool to room temperature. Pour into sterilized jars and seal with paraffin.

Pear Honey

This unusually tasty "something" to spread on toast, crumpets, or muffins is from an old Southern recipe.

7 large pears

3 medium-sized apples

1 orange

3¾ cups sugar

1 stick cinnamon, broken into pieces

MAKES ABOUT EIGHT GLASSES

Peel, quarter, and remove cores from pears and apples. Grate the zest (or outer skin) from the orange, taking care not to include the bitter white underskin. Squeeze the juice from the orange and reserve.

Finely chop the pears and apples and add them, together with the orange zest and juice, the sugar, and the cinnamon, to a large preserving kettle. Mix well. Place over high heat and cook for 25 minutes, stirring frequently. Pour into sterilized jars and seal immediately with paraffin.

Plum Jam with Peaches

Nice and spicy!

2¾ pounds large blue plums

2 pounds peaches

1¾ ounces fruit pectin

7 cups sugar

1 cinnamon stick, broken into pieces

10 cloves

MAKES ABOUT TEN GLASSES

Peel the fruit and remove the pits. Put the plums through a food grinder and chop the peaches into small pieces. Place the fruit, pectin, 3 cups sugar, and spices in a large preserving kettle. Bring to a hard boil over high heat. Stir in the remaining sugar immediately and bring once again to a high boil; then stir constantly for 1 full minute. Remove from the heat and skim off the foam.

Stir for 1 minute to cool the jam. Skim once again. Repeat the stirring and skimming for 5 minutes. Spoon immediately into sterilized jars leaving ½ inch at the top. Seal with paraffin.

Passion Fruit Jam

This Australian jam is a bit exotic.

4 cups passion fruit pulp

3 cups sugar

3 tablespoons lemon juice

4 slices fresh ginger, or ⅛ teaspoon dry powdered ginger

MAKES ABOUT EIGHT GLASSES

Bring the fruit pulp, sugar, lemon juice, and ginger slowly to a boil. Boil for 4 hours. Pour into sterilized jars and seal.

New England Cranberry Jelly

2 quarts cranberries

1 quart water

4 cups sugar

MAKES ABOUT TEN GLASSES

Place the berries and water in a kettle. Boil for 15 minutes or until the berries pop open. Strain through cheesecloth, add the sugar, and boil until the jelly flakes around the edges of the kettle. Pour into sterilized jelly glasses and seal with paraffin.

Sweet Orange Butter

Try this tangy, sweet butter on biscuits,
cinnamon bread, or French toast.

Juice of 4 oranges plus zest
(or thin outer skin), grated

1⅓ cups confectioner's sugar

2 cups butter

MAKES ABOUT FOUR CUPS

Squeeze the oranges, straining the juice. Grate the thin outer skin of the oranges. Combine the confectioner's sugar, juice, and orange zest. Stir until as much as possible is dissolved. Add the butter and cream together until well blended. Pack the orange butter into small containers, wrap tightly in aluminum foil, and freeze until needed.

Confectioner's Sugar Frosting for Sweet Breads

1¼ cup confectioner's sugar
4 teaspoons milk

¼ teaspoon almond extract, if desired

FROSTS ONE BREAD

Beat together the sugar, flavoring, and milk, adding a bit more milk if the icing is too thick.

Lemon-Orange Frosting for Sweet Breads

1¼ cups confectioner's sugar
1 tablespoon lemon juice

1 tablespoon orange juice

FROSTS ONE BREAD

Combine ingredients and mix until smooth.

The
how-to
of
soup-making

THE STOCK is the soul of the soup. Everything goes into it ... only the essence remains. The wilted cabbage, the limp carrots and celery stalks, the half-soft tomato, all are worthy ingredients. So also are the perfect things ... peas that go "poc" when you pop their shells, round, smooth soup bones, thick leeks with manes of tangled roots, webs of dill, threads of saffron. All fall into the soup pot from your hand.

But of all these elements, the hand is the most important. You add the onion, the turnip, the parsnip, and what you add is your choice. Follow the recipe if you wish, it becomes *your* recipe. Or omit whatever you choose, that also becomes your recipe ... cooked in your kettle, stirred with your spoon. *Your* broth simmering on your stove, in front of your hearth, over your fire, evoking centuries of simmering pots and stirring spoons, producing pools of flavor, strained and clear. The backbone of the soup with the bone and the vegetables removed and the minerals and vitamins left in.

The object of making a stock is to produce a liquid brimming with flavor and nutrition. From this basic broth diverse soups can be created with the addition of other meats and vegetables. Flavor is imparted automatically through the simmering process, but to extract the maximum nutrition there are a few rules that must be carefully followed.

1. Save bits of raw vegetables, tops of scallions and celery, tender leaves of beets, tough spinach, stems of watercress and dill, limp outer leaves of lettuce and cabbage—in other words, all of the otherwise good foodstuffs you normally throw away because they are not esthetically pleasing or simply because you are accustomed to treating them as scraps. These should be well washed and refrigerated in a large jar with a lid. They can be kept up to a week and a half.

2. Freeze scraps of leftover meat in plastic containers. Meat bones and the carcasses of game birds, chickens, turkeys, or ducks may also be frozen for use in soup stocks. If poultry has been stuffed, carefully remove any remaining bits from the carcass before freezing.

3. Add leftover stuffing to soups to enhance their flavor and thicken them somewhat.

4. Bones contain no vitamins but are high in minerals, which may be extracted from the connective tissue by simmering at about 200° F. preferably for at least 1 hour.

5. After you have simmered your soup stock, don't feel guilty about straining out and discarding the bones and vegetables used to flavor it. The nutrition has passed from these ingredients into the soup liquid where they await your pleasure.

6. Simmering means cooking without letting the liquid boil. Turn your burner as low as possible and only partially cover the soup kettle to keep the soup from boiling.

7. If stocks are simmered with a tight-fitting lid, they may cloud. To overcome this and still retain the nutritional value, cover with a loose-fitting lid or leave the lid slightly ajar. (The lid *is* important, however, to keep the vitamins from being lost.)

8. Take care not to boil soups thickened with eggs or egg yolks, or the soup will curdle. While curdled soups are edible, they are certainly not attractive enough to serve to guests.

9. Cooked fresh vegetables may be frozen and used for garnishing.

Substitutions

The following ingredients may be substituted as indicated:

1. One soup stock may be substituted for another in many cases. Use your own judgment and imagination.

2. Frozen vegetables may be substituted for fresh, but *never* use soggy, devitalized, canned vegetables unless you are snow-bound in an Arctic log cabin.

3. Canned consommé, chicken broth, beef broth, and clam broth may be used in place of basic stocks or consommés.

Basic soup stocks

Simple Beef Stock

Freeze your meat bones and save your uncooked vegetable scraps in a jar to make the best beef stock you've ever tasted.

3 pounds beef or veal bones (or both)

   Any scraps of meat you have on hand

2-pound piece of lean beef

1 roast chicken carcass (optional)

4 onions

3 carrots

6 celery stalks with leaves

   Any vegetables you have been saving in your stock jar or double the amount of the vegetables listed above

4 quarts water

YIELDS TEN CUPS

Have the bones cut into small pieces. Wash and slice the vegetables. Spread the bones in a roasting pan and cover with the vegetables. Bake in a moderate oven for 50 minutes. Discard the fat. Add water and simmer on top of the stove for 4 hours, skimming off any scum that rises. Strain the stock, place in jars, and refrigerate. Remove the fat that rises to the top. Freeze in ice cube trays, if desired. Refrigerated stock will keep for 5 days; frozen stock for 2 to 3 weeks.

Beef or Brown Stock

*Freeze your meat bones and save your uncooked
vegetable scraps in a jar in the refrigerator
to make the best stock you've ever tasted.*

3 tablespoons rendered chicken fat or oil

4 pounds beef bones, cut in pieces

2 pounds veal bones, cut in pieces

4 chicken feet, cleaned and skinned

1 Roast chicken carcass, or chicken wings and necks

Any scraps of meat on hand

2 medium-sized onions

2 medium-sized carrots

6 medium-sized mushrooms

2 large leeks

3 stalks celery with leaves

5 sprigs of parsley

Any vegetables saved in stock jar

10 peppercorns

4½ quarts water

Salt to taste

MAKES EIGHT TO TEN CUPS

Heat the rendered chicken fat in a large roasting pan on top of the stove. Arrange beef and veal bones, chicken feet, roast chicken carcass, and any frozen scraps of meat, in the pan. Allow to brown on all sides. In the meanwhile, peel and slice the onions and carrots. Wash thoroughly and dry the mushrooms, leeks, and celery stalks. Chop the mushrooms coarsely. Slice the leeks and celery stalks. When the bones and meat are nicely browned, remove the roasting pan from the stove. Spread the sliced and chopped vegetables, the parsley sprigs, and any vegetables from the stock jar over the bones. Add the peppercorns and bake in an oven preheated to 350° F. for 50 minutes, stirring occasionally. Transfer all ingredients to a very deep soup kettle and cover with the water and salt to taste. Discard the fat in the roasting pan and swirl ½ cup of water around the sides, scraping the browned particles that cling to the pan. Add this liquid to the soup kettle and bring the stock to a boil. Skim off any fat rising to the surface. Cover the kettle and simmer for 4 hours. Strain the stock through several thicknesses of cheesecloth, discarding bones, meat, and vegetables. Pour into jars, cool, and refrigerate. Remove any fat that rises to the top. Refrigerated stock will keep for 5 days and frozen stock for 2 or 3 weeks.

Beef Bouillon or Broth

1½-pound piece of lean beef
   2 pounds beef bones, cut in pieces
   2 pounds veal knuckle, cut in pieces
   8 chicken feet, cleaned and skinned
   3 medium-sized onions, studded with 3 whole cloves each

3 quarts water
3 medium-sized carrots
3 large leeks
5 stalks celery with leaves
6 sprigs parsley
8 peppercorns
2 teaspoons salt

SERVES TWELVE

Arrange the beef, beef bones, veal knuckle, and chicken feet in a large soup kettle. Add the water and bring slowly to a boil, removing the scum as it rises to the surface. Meanwhile, peel the onions and stick the cloves into each. Peel and slice the carrots. Trim the leeks, discard the stems, split partially with a sharp knife, and wash thoroughly. Wash the celery. Slice the leeks and celery. Rinse the parsley. Add the vegetables, peppercorns, and salt to the boiling kettle and simmer, partially covered, over low heat for 3½ hours. Adjust the seasonings. Strain the bouillon through several thicknesses of cheesecloth. Reserve the meat for other use if desired, or discard with the bones and vegetables. Pour the bouillon into jars, cool, and refrigerate, removing any fat that rises to the top. Reheat to serve.

Beef Consommé

8 cups Beef bouillon

3 egg whites and shells

SERVES EIGHT

Place the Beef bouillon in a saucepan and bring to a boil. Beat the egg whites until they are frothy and add, together with the crushed egg shells, to the boiling soup, stirring constantly. Lower the heat slightly and continue to stir while the soup boils for 10 minutes. Remove from heat and allow to stand for 10 minutes while the particles settle to the bottom of the pan. Strain the consommé into another pan through a linen dishtowel. Reheat before serving.

Consommé Argenteuil

8 cups Beef consommé (page 68)   1 cup fresh-cooked asparagus tips

SERVES EIGHT

Heat the Beef consommé just to the boiling point. Add the cooked asparagus tips. Serve immediately.

Celery Consommé

1 large bunch celery with leaves   Salt and pepper to taste
2½ quarts Beef consommé
  (page 68)

SERVES TEN

Wash and chop the celery stalks and leaves. Add to the Beef consommé, bring to a boil, cover, and simmer over very low heat for 30 minutes to allow the celery flavor to penetrate the soup. Remove from heat, strain, season with salt and pepper to taste, and serve immediately.

Consommé Chiffonade

1 cup lettuce leaves (or   2½ quarts Beef consommé
  sorrel), finely shredded   (page 68)

SERVES EIGHT

Place the finely shredded lettuce leaves in a small saucepan. Add salted water to cover and boil for 1 minute. Drain lettuce and divide the shredded strips among 8 soup plates. Pour hot Beef consommé over and serve immediately.

Herb Consommé

2¼ quarts Beef consommé (see page 68)

¼ cup fresh parsley, finely chopped

¼ cup fresh chives, finely chopped

¼ cup fresh chervil, finely chopped

SERVES TEN

Bring the Beef consommé to a boil. Stir in the finely chopped herbs. Simmer for a few minutes to allow the flavor of the herbs to penetrate the soup. Serve hot.

Basic Consommé Madrilène

4 large tomatoes

8 cups Beef consommé (see page 68)*

1 cup port wine

½ cup fresh parsley, chives, and thyme, minced

Salt and pepper to taste

SERVES EIGHT

Cut the tomatoes in half, discarding the stems. Coarsely chop ½ of a tomato and add to the consommé in a saucepan. Bring to a boil and simmer for 5 minutes. Meanwhile, peel the remaining tomato halves. Seed them by cutting into eighths and shaking out the seeds. Chop them coarsely. Strain the consommé through a fine sieve, mashing any tomato pulp with the back of a spoon. Return the consommé to low heat, add the chopped tomatoes, and simmer for 5 minutes more. Stir in the port wine; the minced parsley, chives, and thyme; season with salt and pepper; and serve piping hot.

* If you prefer, substitute Chicken consommé (see page 75).

Jellied Madrilène in Avocado Boats

8 cups Basic consommé
  madrilène (see page 70)

3 envelopes unflavored gelatin

⅔ cup water

4 ripe avocados

Watercress

Lemon zest, cut in strips

SERVES EIGHT

Heat Basic Consommé Madrilène in a saucepan. Place the gelatin in the water and then stir the mixture into the madrilène until the gelatin dissolves. Cool and then chill. Remove the pits and slice the avocados in half. Whip the jellied madrilène lightly with a fork, and place portions of it in the avocado halves. Serve garnished with watercress and strips of lemon zest.

Consommé Julienne

½ cup onions

½ cup celery

½ cup carrots

2½ quarts Beef consommé (see
  page 68)

½ cup cooked green peas

SERVES TEN

Cut onions, celery, and carrots into 1-inch julienne strips and cook until tender. Add to the hot Beef consommé. Just before serving, stir in the cooked peas.

Mushroom Consommé

1½ pounds young fresh
  mushrooms

2 leeks

2 stalks celery with leaves

2 medium-sized carrots

4 cups water

2 quarts Beef consommé
  (see page 68)

Salt and pepper to taste

½ cup dry sherry

SERVES TEN

[71]

Rinse mushrooms and dry thoroughly. (Young fresh mushrooms do not have to be peeled.) Slice each leek down the center without cutting through, and wash thoroughly. Rinse celery stalks and peel carrots. Chop all vegetables coarsely. Place in a saucepan and cover with the water. Cover and simmer slowly for 40 minutes, or until the vegetables are cooked through. Strain the broth and discard the vegetables. Stir broth into the hot Beef consommé, and season with salt and pepper to taste. Lace consommé with sherry before serving.

Consommé Royale

1 cup milk

4 eggs

4 egg yolks

2½ quarts Beef consommé (see page 68)

Salt and freshly ground pepper to taste

SERVES TEN

Scald milk and allow to cool to lukewarm. Beat the eggs and egg yolks until frothy. Stir in the milk and season with salt and pepper. Pour the mixture into a shallow buttered pan, set the pan in hot water, and bake in a preheated 325° F. oven until the custard is firm. Cool and cut into cubes. Heat the Beef consommé. Place some custard cubes in each soup plate, pour the hot soup over, and serve immediately.

Consommé Vermicelli

8 cups Beef consommé (see page 68)

¾ cup vermicelli

SERVES EIGHT

Bring the Beef consommé to a rolling boil in a large kettle. Drop in the vermicelli, reduce heat, and simmer for 10 minutes. Serve immediately.

Consommé Vert-Pré

¼ cup quick-cooking tapioca

2½ quarts Beef consommé (see page 68)

¼ cup cooked green peas

16 cooked asparagus tips

¼ cup cooked spinach purée

¼ cup scallion tops, chives, and parsley, finely chopped

SERVES TEN

Stir the quick-cooking tapioca into cold Beef consommé. Bring just to a boil, stirring constantly. Add the vegetables and herbs, mix thoroughly, and serve immediately.

Consommé Windsor

2½ quarts Beef consommé (see page 68)

4 eggs

½ teaspoon flour

2 tablespoons heavy cream

SERVES TEN

Bring the Beef consommé to a boil. Mix the eggs with the flour and cream. Using a fine strainer, force the mixture into the boiling soup, stirring constantly and energetically. Remove from heat and serve immediately.

Double Beef Consommé

5 quarts Beef consommé (see page 68)

1 cup sherry (or 1 tablespoon brandy)

SERVES TEN

Reduce 5 quarts of Beef consommé to 2½ quarts by boiling over fairly high heat. The reduced consommé will be doubly rich and concentrated. Lace the consommé with sherry or brandy just before serving.

Tomato Bouillon

3 tablespoons butter

1 medium-sized onion

2½ cups fresh tomatoes

½ teaspoon salt

½ clove garlic

2 cups Beef consommé (see page 68)

1 cup tomato juice

¾ cup orange juice

Small bay leaf

SERVES SIX

Melt the butter in a large saucepan. Peel and dice the onion. Peel enough tomatoes to make 2½ cups. Seed them by cutting into quarters and shaking the seeds out. Chop them coarsely. Add the onion and tomatoes to the melted butter and sprinkle with the salt. Stick a toothpick in the garlic so that it can easily be located. Add to the onions and tomatoes. Stir the mixture once or twice, cover, and simmer for 30 minutes. Remove from heat and discard the garlic. Purée the mixture by forcing it through a fine sieve. Stir the Beef consommé, tomato juice, and orange juice into the purée, add the bay leaf, cover, and simmer for 30 minutes more. Remove the bay leaf before serving. This bouillon may be chilled and garnished with chopped watercress, or serve hot, sprinkled with grated orange zest.

Chicken Stock or Broth

2 calories or 1 gram of carbohydrate per serving

1 small chicken plus leftover chicken carcass with bits of chicken meat

3 quarts water

1 veal knuckle

4 chicken feet, skinned and cleaned

8 chicken necks

3 stalks celery with leaves

1 clove garlic, whole

1 bay leaf

⅛ teaspoon thyme

YIELDS TEN CUPS

Place the chicken, chicken carcass, water, veal knuckle, chicken feet, and chicken necks in a large soup kettle. Bring slowly to a low rolling boil and cook for 1 hour, skimming the scum from the surface when necessary. Wash the celery and cut into 2-inch pieces. Add the celery, garlic, bay leaf, and thyme and simmer for 2 hours. Reserve the cooked chicken for some other use; strain the stock, cool, and then chill it. Remove the fat and store the stock in the refrigerator or freeze.

Chicken Consommé

3 quarts Chicken stock (see page 74)　　　　2 egg whites and shells

SERVES EIGHT

Bring the Chicken stock to a boil in a large kettle. Continue to boil over medium heat for 1 hour, or until the stock is reduced by ⅓ and the flavor becomes more concentrated. To clarify the stock, stir in the egg whites and egg shells. Cook for 10 minutes, remove from heat, and allow the consommé to stand for an additional 10 minutes, while the egg particles sink to the bottom of the kettle. Strain the consommé through several layers of cheesecloth. Heat briefly before serving.

Double Chicken Consommé

3 quarts Chicken broth

2 small carrots

3 leeks

3 stalks of celery

1 leftover carcass of roast chicken with remaining bits of skin and meat scraps

10 chicken necks

10 chicken feet, cleaned and skinned

3 egg whites and shells, crushed

Salt to taste

SERVES SIX

Strain the chicken broth and place in a large soup kettle. Peel and chop the carrots and add. Chop the leeks and celery and add to the soup kettle. Add the carcass, skin, meat scraps, necks, and feet. Beat the egg whites lightly and add with the crushed shells. Stir the soup until it comes to a boil. Cover and continue boiling for 5 minutes. Turn the heat down very low and simmer for about 1 hour. Remove bones and pour the soup through a strainer lined with several layers of cheesecloth. Discard the vegetables and meat scraps.

Return the strained soup to the stove and cook over high heat until it is reduced by one-half. Add salt to taste. Store in jars in the refrigerator. Or you may freeze the consommé in ice cube trays. Remove and place frozen cubes in plastic bag, store in freezer, and use when needed.

Consommé Bellevue

4 cups Clam broth (see page 84)

5 cups Chicken consommé (see page 75)

½ cup heavy cream

SERVES TEN

Strain the Clam broth and stir into the Chicken consommé. Heat together over low flame. Whip the cream but do not sweeten. Serve the hot soup in small bowls, with a dollop of whipped cream in each.

Game Consommé

Leftover bones, carcasses, meat scraps, and skin of game birds

3 quarts of Beef stock (see page 68)

10 peppercorns

4 whole cloves

Bouquet garni

2 small carrots

2 medium-sized onions

½ cup sherry

2 teaspoons sugar

3 egg whites and shells

SERVES TWELVE

Place the bones, carcasses, meat scraps, and skin of the game birds; the Beef stock; the peppercorns, cloves, and Bouquet garni in a soup kettle. Peel and coarsely chop the carrots and onions and add to stock. Cover the kettle and bring the soup to a boil. Lower the heat and cook for 3½ hours. Skim the soup from time to time. Discard the bones and skin, and pour the soup through a strainer lined with several thicknesses of cheesecloth. Cool the strained broth and skim off all the surface fat. Stir in the sherry, sugar, lightly beaten egg whites, and crushed egg shells.

Return the soup to the stove and bring it to a boil over high heat. Lower the heat and cook over a very low flame for 3 or 4 minutes. Remove from stove and let stand for 45 minutes. Strain once again through cheesecloth. Reheat before serving.

Oxtail Consommé

2 small oxtails	2 cloves garlic, peeled
2 tablespoons butter	Bouquet garni
2 large onions	10 cups water
3 carrots	1 tablespoon lemon juice
3 leeks	1 tablespoon Worcestershire sauce
4 stalks celery	
1 bay leaf	Swiss cheese and dill dumplings (see page 90)
2 teaspoons salt	
10 peppercorns	

MAKES EIGHT CUPS

Have the oxtails cut into 1-inch sections. Wash the pieces well and dry them. Place in soup kettle, add butter, and brown on all sides. Add the peeled and sliced onions and carrots, the chopped leeks and celery, the spices, and the water. Boil for 5 minutes and skim the froth from the surface. Lower the heat, cover, and simmer for 3 hours. Stir in the lemon juice and the Worcestershire sauce. Strain the consommé, reserving the meat for future use, chill it, and remove the fat. Serve hot with the diced oxtail meat and Swiss cheese and dill dumplings.

Additional Consommé Variations

Many garnishes may be used to embellish the rich, clear flavor of consommé. Traditionally a spoonful of vegetables either singly or in combination are cooked in the consommé, or prepared separately and added just before serving. Raw vegetables, fresh herbs, pasta, dumplings, poached eggs, quenelles, spirits—the list is limitless. Use your imagination, or whatever you have on hand.

Vegetable Garnishes

The following may be diced or cut into julienne strips, cooked, and then added to the hot consommé just before serving. Place 1 or 2 tablespoons in each soup dish.

Brussel sprouts	*Celery*	*Tomatoes*
Carrots	*Leeks*	*Turnips*
Celeriac	*Onions*	

Small amounts of the following fresh vegetables may be stirred into the hot consommé without cooking:

Carrots, grated	*Celery, chopped*	*Mushrooms, sliced*
	Tomatoes, peeled, seeded, and chopped	

Herb Garnishes

Small amounts of the following chopped herbs may be cooked briefly in the hot consommé or added just before serving:

Chives	*Parsley*	*Tarragon*

Spirits

Cognac	*Sherry*	*Wine*

Pasta Garnishes

Cook any of the following until tender, drain, and add to hot consommé:

Noodles	*Pastina*	*Vermicelli*
Rice	*Spaghetti*	

Others

Chicken velouté (see page 85)	*Poached eggs*
Crêpes	
Finely shredded cold meats or chicken	

Quenelles, Soup Balls, and Dumplings

The following can also be used to great advantage:

Chive and basil dumplings (see page 88)	*Danish butter balls (see page 93)*
Farina dumplings (see page 87)	*Egg balls (see page 93)*
Finger dumplings (see page 88)	*Korean beef balls (see page 92)*
Fish dumplings (see page 89)	*Marrow balls (see page 93)*
Liver dumplings (see page 87)	*Parmesan cheese balls (see page 90)*
Swiss cheese and dill dumplings (see page 90)	*Parmesan meatballs (see page 92)*
Won tons	
Cream cheese-almond balls (see page 91)	*Chicken quenelles (see page 94)*
	Fish quenelles (see page 94)
Crunchy almond balls (see page 91)	

Croutons

Garlic croutons (see page 86)	*Savory croutons (see page 86)*
Pumpernickel croutons (see page 87)	

Basic Cream Soup

4 cups fresh vegetables, coarsely
   chopped
5 cups Chicken stock (see page
   74)
5 tablespoons butter

4 tablespoons flour
3 cups light cream
   Salt and pepper to taste

SERVES EIGHT

Peel the vegetable, if necessary, and chop coarsely. Place in a sauce-pan with 3 cups of the stock. Cook over medium heat until the vegetable is tender. Set aside ½ cup choice pieces of cooked vegetable to use as a garnish. Purée the remaining cooked vegetable together with the vegetable water in an electric blender, or press through a strainer. Melt the butter in a soup kettle, blend in the flour, and stir in the cream. Simmer over a low flame, stirring constantly for 3 minutes. Stir in the puréed vegetable and the remaining 2 cups of Chicken stock, and simmer for 3 minutes more. Adjust the seasonings and serve in individual bowls garnished with the reserved cooked vegetable. Serve hot or cold.

Cream of Broccoli Soup

5 cups broccoli
   Basic cream soup recipe

A pinch or two of nutmeg

SERVES TEN

Peel the stems and break broccoli into flowerets. Slice the stems. Proceed as directed in Basic cream soup recipe. Serve with nutmeg sprinkled on top.

Cream of Artichoke Soup

3½ cups cooked artichoke hearts,
   coarsely chopped, plus
   artichoke pulp scraped from
   the leaves

Basic cream soup recipe (see
page 80)
4 hard-cooked egg yolks

SERVES EIGHT

Prepare the artichokes. Proceed as directed in Basic cream soup recipe. Force the hard-cooked egg yolks through a fine sieve, and use as a garnish. Serve hot or cold.

Cream of Pimento Soup

2 cups pimento

Basic cream soup recipe (see page 80)

SERVES EIGHT

Coarsely chop the pimentos. Reserve ½ cup to use as a garnish. Proceed as directed in Basic cream soup recipe. Serve hot or cold.

Cream of Cucumber Soup

4 cups cucumbers, peeled, seeded, and diced

½ cup sour cream

Basic cream soup recipe (see page 80)

SERVES EIGHT

Reserve ½ cup diced raw cucumber to use as a garnish. Cook remaining cucumber for 8 minutes. Proceed as directed in Basic cream soup recipe. Serve hot or cold with a dollop of sour cream in the center of each bowl.

Cream of Lima Bean Soup

4 cups of lima beans

4 tablespoons crisply fried bacon, crumbled

Basic cream soup recipe (see page 80)

SERVES EIGHT

Prepare soup as directed in Basic cream soup recipe but do not reserve any lima beans. Serve hot, garnished with crumbled bacon.

Cream of Spinach Soup

4 cups spinach, coarsely chopped   2 hard-cooked egg yolks
  Basic cream soup recipe (page 80)

SERVES EIGHT

Prepare soup as directed in Basic cream soup recipe, but do not reserve any spinach. Serve hot or cold, garnished with hard-cooked egg yolks forced through a fine sieve.

Cream of Brussels Sprouts Soup

4 cups Brussels sprouts, coarsely   Pumpernickel croutons (see
  chopped   page 87)
  Basic cream soup recipe (page 80)

SERVES TEN

Prepare soup as directed in Basic cream soup recipe, but do not reserve any of the Brussels sprouts. Serve hot, garnished with Pumpernickel croutons.

Cream of Asparagus Soup

4 cups tender asparagus tips   Pumpernickel croutons (see
                                         page 87)
  Basic cream soup recipe (page 80)

SERVES EIGHT

Prepare soup as directed in Basic cream soup recipe. Garnish with reserved asparagus tips and Pumpernickel croutons. Serve hot or cold.

Cream of Cauliflower Soup

4 cups cauliflower flowerets   Paprika
  Basic cream soup recipe (page 80)

SERVES TEN

Prepare soup as directed in Basic cream soup recipe. Garnish with reserved cauliflower and a sprinkle of paprika. Serve hot or cold.

Fish Stock

6 pounds of fresh fish, including bones, head, and flesh

2 medium-sized onions

2 leeks

3 quarts water

1 cup white wine

1 small bay leaf

2 teaspoons fennel seed

1 clove

1 teaspoon salt

YIELDS TWELVE CUPS

Place all ingredients in a deep kettle and bring to a boil. Lower the heat and simmer for 45 minutes. Strain the stock, cool, and store, tightly covered, in the refrigerator.

Fish Consommé

¾ pound pike (or other white fish)

2 small onions

2 leeks

4 sprigs parsley

1 egg white

1 cup white wine

10 cups Fish stock

Salt and white pepper to taste

Sour cream

Chives. chopped

SERVES TEN

Put the fish, onions, and the white part of the leeks through a food chopper. Chop the parsley and add it, together with the egg white, to the fish mixture. Stir in the white wine and then the Fish stock. Cook over high heat, stirring constantly, until the soup comes to a boil. Lower the heat and simmer, tightly covered, for 45 minutes. *Do not stir.* Strain through an old, but clean, linen towel. Correct the seasonings. Serve with a dollop of sour cream sprinkled with chives, or use this consommé as a base for other fish soups.

Clam Broth

36 large, hard-shelled clams and
their juice
1½ quarts water
2 leeks

2 stalks celery, including leaves
Salt to taste

SERVES EIGHT

Rinse and scrub the clams thoroughly. Open them, saving the juice.
Cut the clams from their shells and chop coarsely. Place the clams,
clam juice, and water in a large saucepan. Trim the leeks, discarding
the green leaves and root; cut the white stems almost through from
top to bottom and rinse thoroughly. Wash the celery. Cut the leeks
and the celery into 1-inch pieces. Add to the clams and liquid and
simmer, covered, for 20 minutes. Remove from heat and strain
through several thicknesses of cheesecloth, discarding the clams and
vegetables. Reheat briefly, add salt to taste, and serve piping hot.

Beef and Chicken Broth

4 quarts water
2 teaspoons salt
2 pounds beef shoulder
½ capon

2 carrots, sliced
2 stalks celery, sliced
1 medium-sized onion, sliced
Salt and pepper to taste

SERVES SIXTEEN

Place the water and salt in a very large soup kettle. Add the beef
shoulder, capon, carrots, celery, and onion. Bring to a boil, reduce
the heat, and simmer, covered, for at least 3 hours. Season to taste
with salt and pepper. Remove the meat and capon, and reserve for
future use if desired. Strain the stock, discarding the vegetables.
When the soup has cooled, skim off the fat.

Chicken Velouté

2 tablespoons butter   1 cup Chicken stock (page 74)
1 tablespoon flour

MAKES ONE CUP

Melt the butter in a small pan. Stir in the flour and blend to a smooth paste. Add the Chicken stock, beating constantly until the velouté is thick and smooth. Stir into simmering beef or chicken bouillon or consommé for a taste treat.

Vegetable Stock

*81 calories or 25 grams of carbohydrate per serving**

Save parsley, watercress, and mushroom stems;
those slightly wilted outer leaves of cabbage and lettuce;
slightly soft tomatoes; onion skins; celery leaves;
and apple skins. They all enhance this rich vegetable stock.

1 tablespoon butter   5 scallions

6 onions   Any vegetables from your
                                        stock jar (if you haven't saved
2 carrots   any, double the amount of
                                        onions, carrots, and celery
10 celery stalks with leaves   listed above)
1 large bunch parsley
                                        4 quarts water
3 tomatoes

10 medium-sized mushrooms

YIELDS TEN CUPS

Melt the butter in a pan. Wash and slice the vegetables and stir them into the butter. Bake them in a moderate oven for 30 minutes. Add the water and simmer on top of the stove for 4 hours. Strain the stock, place in jars, and refrigerate. Remove the butter that rises to the top. Freeze in ice cube trays if desired. Refrigerated stock will keep for 5 to 7 days; frozen stock for 2 to 3 weeks.

* The calorie count of the stock is lower than that of the total ingredients because much of the butter and vegetable fiber is strained off.

[85]

Garnishes and Go-withs

Any simple soup may be made simply scrumptious by the addition of one or more of the following garnishes.

Corn Dodger Dumplings

2 cups white cornmeal   1½ cups boiling water
1 teaspoon salt   1 tablespoon bacon fat

MAKES SIXTEEN

Combine the cornmeal and salt in a large bowl. Add enough of the boiling water to make a batter that can be shaped with the hands. Stir in the bacon fat and refrigerate for at least 20 minutes. Bring 3 quarts of lightly salted water to a boil in a deep kettle. Form the batter into sixteen dumplings and drop into the boiling water. Cook for 20 or 30 minutes, or until the dumplings are light. Add to soup just before serving.

Garlic Croutons

3 slices of bread   ˙ 3 tablespoons butter
1 clove garlic, crushed

MAKES ONE CUP

Trim the crusts from the bread and cut the slices into cubes. Heat the butter, stir in the crushed garlic, sauté for a minute or two, and then add the bread cubes. Sauté to a golden brown, stirring constantly.

Savory Croutons

3 slices of bread   3 tablespoons butter

MAKES ONE CUP

Trim the crusts from the bread and cut the slices into cubes. Heat a small amount of butter in a skillet and fry the cubes until brown, stirring constantly. Sprinkle with garlic salt, onion salt, curry powder, marjoram, or any other seasoning desired.

Pumpernickel Croutons

6 large (or 8 medium) slices of   1½ tablespoons vegetable oil
pumpernickel bread
2½ tablespoons butter

MAKES ONE CUP

Trim the pumpernickel slices and cut into ½-inch cubes. Heat the butter and oil together in a heavy skillet. Add the bread cubes and brown on all sides, stirring frequently.

Farina Dumplings

¼ cup butter   ¼ cup fresh parsley, chopped
9 cups Beef bouillon (page 68)   2 eggs
2 cups farina

MAKES TWELVE

Melt the butter over hot water. Bring Beef bouillon to a boil. Combine farina and chopped parsley in a large bowl. Stir in the hot butter. Mix about ¼ cup of hot bouillon with the eggs, beating well, and add just enough to the farina mixture to make sure that the dumplings will hold their shape. Roll the dough into dumplings between your hands. Place the dumplings in the bouillon and let them simmer, covered, for 30 minutes. Serve with the hot soup.

Liver Dumplings

¼ cup butter   2 eggs
1 medium-sized onion   1 teaspoon salt
1 cup raw calf's liver   ½ teaspoon black pepper
1 cup dry breadcrumbs   Boiling salted water
¼ cup fresh parsley, minced

MAKES SIXTEEN

Melt the butter over hot water. Peel and grate the onion. Grind the raw calf's liver. Mix the calf's liver with the breadcrumbs and minced parsley, and add the melted butter and grated onion. Separate the eggs, setting aside the whites. Stir the yolks into the liver mixture, together with the salt and pepper. Beat the egg whites until they stand in peaks and fold them into the liver mixture. Roll into sixteen round dumplings and lower them gently into boiling salted water. Cook for 7 minutes. Add them to clear soup just before serving.

Chive and Basil Dumplings

These light, delicious dumplings perk up any beef or chicken soup.

1½ cups all-purpose or
  unbleached white flour, sifted

2 teaspoons double-acting
  baking powder

1 teaspoon salt

Freshly ground black pepper

3 teaspoons shortening

2 tablespoons fresh chives,
  chopped

1 teaspoon dried basil

¾ cup milk

MAKES SIXTEEN

Combine sifted flour, baking powder, salt, and pepper in a bowl. Using two knives, cut in the shortening until the pieces are no larger than ¼ inch in diameter. Mix in the chopped chives and basil. Add the milk, stirring only enough to moisten the dough. Bring chicken or beef soup to boiling. Shape the dumplings with a greased ice cream dipper and drop them into the soup. Cover and cook until the dumplings are firm (approximately 15 minutes).

Finger Dumplings

½ cup butter

1⅓ cups all-purpose or
  unbleached white flour

1¼ cups water

2 large eggs

½ cup chives, chopped

9 cups Beef bouillon (see page
  68)

MAKES SIXTEEN

[88]

Melt butter in a saucepan over medium heat. Stir in flour and cook, stirring constantly, pressing out any lumps with a spoon. When the mixture is smooth, add the water, stirring to blend well. Remove from the stove and mix in the eggs and chopped chives, making sure that the mixture is uniform in consistency. Allow the mixture to cool. Bring the Beef bouillon to a boil. Ladle a rounded spoonful of dumpling batter into the bouillon. If it separates in pieces, blend in as much additional flour as is needed to keep the dumplings whole. Add the rest of the batter by spoonfuls to the soup and cook for 20 minutes, or until firm. Serve immediately with the soup.

Fish Dumplings

1 large onion	2 egg yolks
2 cups fillet of sole	1/4 teaspoon ground thyme
2 tablespoons butter	Salt and pepper to taste
4 slices stale bread	Flour
2 eggs	Boiling salted water

MAKES SIXTEEN

Peel and finely chop the onion. Grind the fillet of sole. Sauté the onion slowly in the butter. Meanwhile, soak the stale bread in water. When the onion is transparent, squeeze the bread as dry as possible and sauté with the onion for a few minutes, turning the slices once. Remove from the stove. Combine with the ground sole, eggs, egg yolks, and spices in a large bowl, mixing all ingredients thoroughly. With your hands, shape the fish mixture into small dumplings, dust them with flour, and poach them gently in just enough slowly boiling salted water to cover until they are firm (about 8 to 10 minutes). Use as garnish for any fish soup.

Mushroom Dumplings

9 large mushrooms	3 eggs
6 slices fresh white bread	1 tablespoon fresh thyme
1 teaspoon onion, grated or crushed in a garlic press	1 tablespoon dry bread crumbs
	Salt and pepper to taste

MAKES SIXTEEN

Rinse the mushrooms and pat dry. Peel and chop them very fine. Soak bread slices in water, squeeze as dry as possible, and place in a large bowl. Add the grated or crushed onion and blend into the bread with the back of a spoon. Separate the eggs, reserving the whites. Stir the egg yolks into the bread mixture, along with the chopped mushrooms, thyme, breadcrumbs, salt, and pepper. The mixture should be fairly thick. (Add another tablespoon of bread-crumbs, if necessary.) Beat the egg whites until they stand in peaks and fold into the other ingredients. Grease a shallow baking pan with a little butter, carefully pour in the mushroom mixture, and bake for 20 minutes in a preheated 375° F. oven. Use a 2-inch round cookie cutter to shape the dumplings. Add them to hot soup just before serving.

Swiss Cheese and Dill Dumplings***

*These tiny golden dumplings make any plain
soup a fancy one in merely minutes.*

6 tablespoons butter

1 cup Swiss cheese, grated

¼ cup flour

2 egg yolks

1 tablespoon fresh dill, minced

MAKES SIXTEEN

Cream all ingredients together. Dust your hands with flour and shape the mixture into dumplings the size of filberts. Drop into boiling soup. When the dumplings rise to the surface, boil for one moment more. Serve immediately.

Parmesan Cheese Balls

Here's a unique way to add Parmesan to an Italian soup.

4 ounces cream cheese

½ cup Parmesan cheese, grated

½ cup parsley, minced

MAKES TWELVE

Press the cream cheese through a sieve and blend it with the grated Parmesan cheese. Form into balls the size of a small walnut. Roll the balls in minced parsley. Serve as a garnish.

Cream Cheese-Almond Balls***

To make any soup a cream soup in a matter of moments,
simply add 2 of these cream cheese balls.

8 ounces cream cheese   1 cup salted almonds, chopped

MAKES SIXTEEN

Press the cream cheese through a sieve and form into balls the size of a small walnut. Roll the balls in the chopped almonds. Serve as a garnish.

Cornmeal Beef Balls***

2 onions	2½ teaspoons salt
4 cloves garlic, crushed	½ teaspoon freshly ground black pepper
2 pounds ground chuck	
¾ cup cornmeal	1½ teaspoons crushed coriander seed
1 large, or 2 small eggs	
3 tablespoons milk	

SERVES EIGHT

Peel and finely chop the onions. Peel and crush the garlic. Combine the onions, crushed garlic, ground chuck, cornmeal, egg, milk, salt, pepper, and crushed coriander seed. Mix thoroughly. Stiffen with breadcrumbs if the mixture is too soft to shape. Form into 1-inch balls and drop into boiling soup. Simmer, uncovered, for 20 minutes.

Crunchy Almond Balls***

1 cup blanched almonds	½ teaspoon salt
⅔ cup breadcrumbs	¼ cup vegetable oil
3 egg whites	

MAKES TWELVE

Whirl the almonds in a blender until they resemble coarse meal, stopping the blender from time to time to push the nuts down onto the blades. Beat the egg whites until frothy, setting some aside for later use. Place the breadcrumbs into a small bowl; add almonds, salt, and egg whites. Shape the almond mixture into very small balls. Dip in reserved egg whites.

Heat 2 tablespoons of the vegetable oil in a medium-sized frying pan. Fry half of the balls until they are brown on all sides. Set aside on a paper towel. Add the rest of the cooking oil and fry the remaining almond balls. If necessary to reheat, place the almond balls in a medium-hot oven for a few minutes.

Korean Beef Balls

2 cloves garlic

2 green onions with 3 inches top

½ pound chuck steak, chopped

½ cup bean curd

4 tablespoons soy sauce

2 tablespoons Sesame seed powder (see page 34)

4 tablespoons sesame or vegetable oil

Pepper to taste

4 tablespoons pine nuts

4 tablespoons flour

4 eggs, beaten

MAKES SIXTEEN

Peel and finely chop the garlic and green onions. Place in a bowl with the chopped beef.

Press the bean curd with the back of a wooden spoon to remove the liquid. Add to the chopped beef along with the soy sauce, Sesame seed powder, 2 tablespoons of the sesame oil, and pepper to taste. Mix thoroughly and form into small balls. Insert pine nuts in the center of each ball. Roll in flour and dip in beaten egg. Heat the remaining sesame oil in a skillet. Brown the meat balls on all sides, adding more oil if necessary to prevent sticking. Add to hot soup.

Parmesan Meatballs

1 pound ground beef

2 large cloves garlic, peeled and crushed

3 tablespoons Parmesan cheese, grated

MAKES SIXTEEN

Mix the ground beef, garlic, and Parmesan cheese together in a bowl. Form the mixture into walnut-sized balls. Add to lightly boiling soup or stew 30 minutes before serving time. Simmer for 30 minutes. Serve hot.

Marrow Balls

½ cup beef marrow
1 cup breadcrumbs
2 teaspoons grated onion

Pinch of dry mustard
2 egg yolks
1 or 2 egg whites, beaten

MAKES TWELVE

Use your fingers to mix all the ingredients except the egg whites. Add more breadcrumbs if the mixture is too soft to form into balls. Form small balls the size of your thumbnail. Dip in beaten egg white and drop into lightly boiling soup stock. The marrow balls are ready to eat when they rise to the top of the soup.

Danish Butter Balls***

2 cups all-purpose or unbleached
  white flour
¾ teaspoon salt

¾ cup butter (at room
  temperature)
Ice water

MAKES SIXTEEN

Sift the flour and salt together. Cream the butter and work in 1½ cups of the flour. Add enough ice water to form a dough that can easily be rolled into small balls about the size of a half dollar. Roll the balls in the remaining flour. Simmer in slowly boiling soup for 10 to 15 minutes.

Egg Balls

4 hard-cooked egg yolks
2 egg whites
2 tablespoons butter (at room
  temperature)

4 tablespoons flour
¼ teaspoon salt
⅛ teaspoon white pepper

MAKES SIXTEEN

Use a spoon to force hard-cooked egg yolks through a fine strainer. Beat the egg whites. Blend the butter into the flour. Combine the egg whites, egg yolks, flour mixture, and seasonings. Form into very small balls. If they will not hold together, work in a bit more flour. The mixture should be quite pliable. Drop into lightly boiling soup and cook for about 6 minutes.

Fish Quenelles

¾ cup pike fillets

1 tablespoon Chicken velouté. chilled (see page 85)

½ egg white

Pinch of nutmeg

Salt and pepper to taste

⅓ cup heavy cream

Fish (or Chicken) stock (see pages 83 and 74)

MAKES SIXTEEN

Cut fresh pike fillets into small pieces. Put into blender along with the Chicken velouté, egg white, nutmeg, salt, and pepper. Blend at high speed for 30 seconds, stopping the blender every few seconds to force the mixture against the blades and to add the cream, a little at a time. Form into small egg-shaped balls by molding between two teaspoons. Pour lukewarm Fish stock to a depth of ¼ inch in a flat enamel pan. Arrange the quenelles in the pan, making sure their sides do not touch. Add enough additional lukewarm Fish stock to almost cover the quenelles. Poach them over low heat for 5 to 7 minutes, or until the quenelles are firm. If the pan is not large enough to hold all of them at once, repeat the procedure with the remaining quenelles. Serve at once with any fish or seafood soup.

Chicken Quenelles***

½ chicken breast

1 tablespoon Chicken velouté, chilled (see page 85)

½ egg white

Pinch of nutmeg

Salt and pepper to taste

⅓ cup heavy cream

Chicken stock (see page 74)

MAKES SIXTEEN

Bone the chicken breast, removing the skin and sinews. Cut into cubes. Place in blender along with the Chicken velouté, egg white, and spices. At high speed, blend ingredients for 30 seconds, stopping every few seconds to force the mixture against the blades. Add the cream, a little at a time. Form into small egg-shaped balls by molding between two teaspoons. Pour lukewarm Chicken stock to a depth of ¼ inch in a flat enamel pan. Arrange the quenelles in the stock, making sure their sides do not touch. Add enough additional lukewarm stock to almost cover the quenelles, and poach over low heat for 5 to 7 minutes, or until the quenelles are firm. If the pan is not large enough to hold all of them at once, repeat the procedure with the remaining quenelles. Serve at once with hot chicken bouillon or consommé, into which 1 or 2 tablespoons of Chicken velouté have been stirred.

Pistou***

*A tablespoonful of this distinctive paste
will enliven almost any soup.*

4 slices bacon
1 cup water
2 egg yolks
2 cloves garlic

1 teaspoon dried basil
6 tablespoons Parmesan cheese, grated
1 teaspoon olive oil

MAKES TEN TABLESPOONS

Boil the bacon for 3 minutes in the water. Drain and chop. Separate the eggs. Place the yolks in the blender with the bacon, garlic and basil, and blend until all ingredients are puréed. Pour the purée into a bowl. Stir in the grated Parmesan cheese and olive oil and serve.

Hushpuppies

*Fry hushpuppies and serve them with
any steaming hot fish, stew, or soup.*

1¾ cups white cornmeal
1¾ teaspoons baking powder
¾ teaspoon salt
¾ cup milk

1 small egg
¾ cup onions, finely chopped
Oil for deep frying

MAKES ABOUT TWENTY-FOUR

[95]

Sift together the dry ingredients. Stir in the milk, beaten egg, and chopped onions. Beat for 3 minutes with a wooden spoon. Add water or cornmeal if the batter is not stiff enough to drop from the spoon in small amounts. Place the oil in a deep fryer and heat till hot (375° F. on a deep-fat thermometer). Drop spoonfuls of the batter into the hot fat a few at a time. Fry until brown on all sides. Drain on paper towels and serve hot.

Fried Camembert Cakes

1 whole camembert
½ cup butter (at room
   temperature)

1½ cups breadcrumbs, sifted
¼ cup butter

MAKES SIXTEEN

Cut away the outer skin from the whole camembert. Allow to soften at room temperature. Place in a bowl with the softened butter and cream together until smooth. Shape into small cakes and roll in the breadcrumbs until thoroughly covered. Melt ¼ cup butter in a skillet and fry the patties to a golden brown, turning once. Put on a heated platter, and serve immediately with small thin slices of dark bread.

Strawberry, Lemon, or Lime Ice Cubes

*These attractive ice cubes make
a perfect garnish for cold soups.*

Strawberries, thin lemon slices,
thin lime slices

Water

Place water in ice cube trays. Tuck a strawberry or a slice of fruit in each compartment. Freeze. Serve in cold soups.

BREAD AND SOUP FROM THE NEW WORLD

American Indian

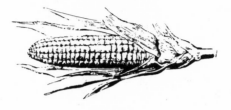

THE TRUE GREATNESS of America is not measured by the millions of miles of concrete that span it nor by the height of its towers, but by the beauty, power, and vastness of the land itself. Although few of us are related to the original Americans, we have been clothed and sheltered and nourished, as they were, by the plenty of their land. This great natural storehouse—3,000 miles across—provided the early Indians with many varieties of meats, fish, gamebirds, shellfish, fruits, vegetables, seeds, grains, spices—almost unlimited quantities of wholesome foods, their flavors undiminished by chemical additives or poison sprays. From the cool, quiet forests of the Northwest to the lush inlets of the Southeast, Indian cooks prepared a variety of subtly spiced soups and stews, cakes and breads, many of which are superb even by today's standards.

Adobe Bread***

*These fat, crusty little loaves make
bread-baking extremely satisfying.*

2 packages dry yeast
½ cup warm water
5 tablespoons melted shortening
2¼ teaspoons salt

8 cups all-purpose or
unbleached white flour
2 cups water

MAKES TWO LOAVES

In a large bowl soften the yeast in warm water. Stir in melted
shortening and salt. Sift the flour. Add to yeast mixture alternately
with the water, beating well after each addition. Knead in the last
1½ cups of flour for 10 minutes until the dough is smooth.

Form the dough into a ball and place in a greased bowl. Brush
with melted shortening. Cover with a light dry cloth. Put in a warm
place to rise for 1 hour. When doubled in bulk, punch down. Knead
on a floured board for 5 minutes.

Divide dough in half and shape into two round loaves, placing
them onto a well-greased baking tin. Cover once again with a dry
cloth and let rise for 15 minutes in a warm, draft-free place. Bake in
a 400° F. oven for 50 minutes, or until light brown. Cool on wire
racks. Serve warm or at room temperature.

Squaw Bread***

*Squaw bread is a large, round, fried bread
that is delicious with butter and jam.*

5 cups all-purpose or
unbleached white flour
2 tablespoons baking powder
1¼ teaspoons salt

1½ tablespoons melted butter
2 cups milk
Oil for frying

MAKES THREE BREADS

Measure 4 cups of the flour, the baking powder, and the salt. Sift
together into the large bowl of your electric mixer. Melt the butter
and add to the milk. Add the milk and butter mixture, a little at a

time, to the dry ingredients, beating at low speed until the dough becomes too stiff for mixer. Sprinkle the remaining cup of flour on a pastry board and knead lightly until all of the flour has been worked in. Roll the dough into three circles about ⅛ inch thick and 10 inches in diameter.

Heat 3 or 4 tablespoons of oil in a 10-inch skillet. When the oil is hot, fry each bread until crisp and light brown on both sides. Serve hot.

Buckskin Bread

4 cups flour
2¼ teaspoons baking powder

2 teaspoons salt
2 cups water

MAKES ONE BREAD

Measure the dry ingredients and sift together into a large bowl. Mix in the water briskly. Using your fingers, press the dough into a 9-inch pie pan. Bake in a preheated oven at 400° F. for 25 minutes. Cut into wedge-shaped pieces. Serve hot.

Indian Bread

Indian bread is a cornbread with a particularly crunchy texture and scrumptious flavor.

6 tablespoons honey
1 cup lukewarm water
2 packages dry active yeast
1⅓ cups cream
10 tablespoons butter
4 large eggs

1¼ cups cornmeal
5 cups all-purpose or unbleached white flour
¼ cup lukewarm water
2½ teaspoons salt

MAKES TWO LOAVES

Stir the honey into the lukewarm water. Add the yeast and stir. Allow the mixture to stand for 20 minutes. Scald the cream in a saucepan, remove it from the heat, add the butter and stir until melted. Break the eggs into a large bowl and beat them until they turn pale yellow. Stir the yeast mixture and the milk and butter mixture into the eggs. Add the cornmeal and flour. Beat with electric mixer at high speed for 3 minutes, gradually adding enough luke-warm water to make a soft, light, elastic dough. Scrape the bowl occasionally. Add the salt to the dough and beat at high speed for 3 minutes more, again scraping the bowl occasionally. Cover the bowl with a towel and allow the dough to rise in a warm, draft-free place for 1¼ hours, or until double in volume.

Punch the dough down and beat it for 5 minutes. Grease two bread pans with oil and put half the dough in each pan. Cover the pans and allow the dough to rise again in a warm, draft-free place for 1¼ hours, or until double in volume. Put the loaf pans in the oven, turn on the oven, and bake 15 minutes at 400° F. Lower the heat to 325° F. and bake 30 or 35 minutes longer.

Fiery Chili Soup

The Zuñi of the Santa Fe area favor this peppery soup.

2 tablespoons cooking oil	3 green chili peppers, sliced
2 pounds boned lamb, cut into 2-inch cubes	1 small dried hot red chili pepper, crushed
5 dried juniper berries, crushed	1½ teaspoons salt
¼ teaspoon freshly ground black pepper	2 cloves garlic, crushed
2 yellow onions	1½ teaspoons oregano
5 green peppers	¼ cup fresh parsley, minced
4½ cups canned hominy (including liquid)	5 cups water
	10 scallions, chopped

SERVES EIGHT

Heat the oil in a large heavy kettle. Sprinkle the lamb pieces with flour and sauté on all sides in the oil. Stir the crushed juniper berries and pepper into the kettle as the meat browns. Meanwhile peel and chop the onions. Remove the meat from the oil and drain on paper towels. Add the chopped onions to the kettle and sauté slowly. Discard the stems and seeds from the green peppers and cut into slices. When the onions are golden, return the meat to the kettle. Add the hominy, green chili peppers, crushed red chili pepper, salt, crushed garlic, oregano, and minced parsley. Pour in the water and simmer, covered, for 1½ hours. Sprinkle with chopped scallions. Serve immediately with Adobe bread slathered with butter.

Iroquois Soup

3 ¼-ounce packages dried mushrooms

¾ cup water

10 cups Beef consommé (see page 68)

5 tablespoons yellow cornmeal

6 medium-sized onions

3 tablespoons parsley

1 teaspoon basil

2 cloves garlic

2½ pounds haddock fillets

3 cups fresh lima beans

¾ cup dry sherry

Salt and freshly ground pepper to taste

SERVES TWELVE

Soak the dried mushrooms in water for 5 minutes. Bring to a boil the mushrooms, Beef consommé, cornmeal, coarsely chopped onion, parsley, basil, and garlic cloves, which have been peeled and finely minced. Lower the heat, cover, and simmer for 40 minutes. Add the haddock and lima beans and continue to simmer for 20 minutes, stirring from time to time. The haddock will break into small pieces. Stir in the sherry, adjust seasonings, and reheat. Serve steaming hot.

Piñon Cakes

5 cups piñon nuts

1¾ cups water

1¼ teaspoons salt

¼ cup oil for frying

MAKES SIX CAKES

Whirl the nuts in a blender until they resemble coarse meal, stopping occasionally to press the nuts down onto the blades. Mix the ground nuts, water, and salt. This will be a stiff batter. Set aside in a warm place for about 1 hour.

Heat the oil over high heat. Drop the batter into the oil with a tablespoon, forming six cakes. Lower heat and brown carefully on both sides. Remove cakes with a spatula. Serve hot.

Dried Corn Chowder***

*The Indians use dried blue and white corn
for this soup, but I find that Pennsylvania Dutch
dried corn is very good.*

1½ cups dried corn, removed
    from the cob

  8 cups water

  2 teaspoons sugar

  ½ teaspoon salt

  ½ pound salt pork

1 onion

1 green pepper

1 potato

2 cups light cream

Salt and freshly ground
pepper to taste

SERVES TEN

Measure 4 cups of the water and put in a large pan. Add corn, sugar, and salt and soak for 3 hours. Add remaining water and simmer the corn for 1 hour, or as directed on package.

Fry salt pork. Discard pork and reserve fat. Peel and chop the onion; peel, seed, and chop the green pepper; peel and chop the potato. Sauté in pork fat for 15 to 20 minutes until the potato is soft but not mushy. Add to the corn, stir in light cream, and simmer for 10 minutes. Correct the seasonings. Serve hot.

Chili-Tomato Soup

*This version of an American Indian soup is
a bit hot for my taste. but perhaps not for yours.*

  8 medium-sized tomatoes

  6 medium-sized potatoes

  4 yellow onions

2½ quarts tomato juice

  1 chili verde pepper, sliced

½ small red chili pepper.
  crushed

3 sprigs parsley

1 tablespoon salt

SERVES TWELVE

Peel and seed the tomatoes by cutting them into quarters and shaking out the seeds. Chop them coarsely. Peel the potatoes and peel and slice the onions. Place the chopped tomatoes, whole potatoes, and sliced onions in the bottom of a heavy soup kettle, add the juice and simmer, covered, until the potatoes are soft but not mushy, approximately 1 hour.

Cut the potatoes into small chunks. Slice the chili verde pepper and add it to the soup, together with the crushed red chili pepper, the parsley, and salt. Simmer for 25 minutes, covered, until the peppers are soft. Serve piping hot.

Turnip-Bean Soup

2 turnips	1 tablespoon salt
4 cloves garlic	10 peppercorns
4 cups dry pinto beans	4½ quarts water
1 lamb shank, cracked	

SERVES SIXTEEN

Peel the turnips and chop them. Peel and crush the garlic cloves. Arrange the turnips, the garlic, pinto beans, lamb shank, salt, and peppercorns (placed in a cheesecloth bag) in the bottom of a soup kettle. Cover with the water. Simmer the soup, covered, until the meat separates from the lamb shank, approximately 4 hours. Remove the lamb bone and bag of peppercorns. Serve piping hot.

Onion-Corn Soup

Juniper berries give this fresh-tasting soup
an "out-doorsy" flavor.

24 young green onions	4 cups fresh corn
12 cups Chicken stock (see page 74)	Salt and freshly ground pepper to taste
12 dried juniper berries	Sour cream

SERVES TWELVE

Peel the onions and cut into ¼-inch slices. Place the Chicken stock in a large pan, add the onions, corn and berries and bring to a boil. Lower the heat and simmer for 35 minutes. Serve hot with a dollop of sour cream.

Piñon Soup

The subtle evergreen flavor from the smooth-textured nuts of the piñon tree transforms this rich soup into a culinary adventure.

10 scallions	8 dried mint leaves
1½ pounds raw piñon nuts	¼ teaspoon pepper
1 cup chicken broth	2 quarts milk
3 coriander seeds	Chives, chopped

SERVES EIGHT

Wash, trim, and slice the scallions. Place the scallions, the piñon nuts, chicken broth, coriander seeds, mint leaves, and pepper in the bottom of a large saucepan. Add the milk and simmer, covered, for 20 to 25 minutes. Stir the soup from time to time. Then purée the soup in an electric blender. Serve hot after reheating over low flame. Or chill it and serve cold. In either case, garnish with chopped chives for a delicious experience.

Broth With Fishballs

5 tablespoons butter	2 dried bay leaves
5 tablespoons flour	2 teaspoons salt
8 cups Fish stock	10 peppercorns, in cheesecloth bag
¾ teaspoon saffron	

SERVES EIGHT

Heat the butter in a saucepan. Blend in the flour. Add the water and stir until the mixture thickens slightly. Add the saffron, dried mint leaves, salt, and peppercorns. Allow the soup to come to a boil. Drop the meatballs into the boiling soup, simmer for 20 minutes, and then discard the cheesecloth bag with the peppercorns. Serve immediately in small bowls.

Fishballs

2 onions

4 cloves garlic

2 pounds ground fish

3/4 cup cornmeal

1 egg

3 tablespoons milk

2 1/2 teaspoons salt

1/2 teaspoon freshly ground black pepper

1 1/2 teaspoons crushed coriander seed

Peel and chop the onions. Peel and crush the garlic. Combine the onions and garlic with the ground fish, cornmeal, egg, milk, salt, pepper, and coriander, and mix thoroughly. Shape into 1-inch balls and drop into the boiling saffron broth. Simmer for 20 minutes and serve hot with the soup.

Bean and Potato Soup

3 cups dried lima beans (about 1 pound)

4 1/2 quarts Chicken broth

4 yellow onions

5 tomatoes

3/4 pound salt pork

1 chili pepper, crushed

7 peeled potatoes, diced

1 1/2 tablespoons salt

SERVES TWELVE

Place the dried lima beans in a bowl, cover with 2 1/2 quarts of the broth, and soak for 6 hours. Drain the beans, rinse them, and put them in a large soup kettle. Peel and slice the onions. Peel the tomatoes. Seed them by cutting them into quarters and shaking out the seeds. Chop the tomatoes coarsely. Slice the salt pork into thin strips, 1/2x1/2x2 inches. Add the onions, tomatoes, salt pork, crushed chili pepper, potato, salt to the beans in the kettle. Pour 2 quarts of broth over these ingredients and simmer, covered, for 1 hour.

Simmer over very low heat for another hour with the cover off, stirring from time to time. Serve immediately.

Trout Chowder

8 potatoes

3 quarts Fish stock (see page 83)

3 pounds fresh trout

2 teaspoons salt

¼ teaspoon fresh ground pepper

½ teaspoon chili powder

2 tablespoons chopped chives

3 tablespoons butter

SERVES TWELVE

Peel and dice the potatoes. Put the Fish stock in large soup kettle and add the potatoes. Simmer for 20 minutes. Remove the skin and bones from the trout and cut into 1½-inch chunks. Add the fish to the kettle, together with the salt, pepper, and chili powder. Simmer for 10 minutes. Adjust the seasonings. Serve hot, garnished with chopped chives and bits of butter.

Early American

Boston Brown Bread

1 cup all-purpose or
  unbleached white flour
1 cup whole wheat flour
1½ teaspoons baking soda
1 teaspoon baking powder
1 teaspoon salt

1 cup yellow cornmeal
1½ cups raisins
¾ cup molasses
2 cups sour milk

MAKES THREE SMALL LOAVES

Sift and measure the flours. Add baking soda, baking powder, and salt, and sift again. Add the cornmeal and raisins to the flour mixture. Stir the molasses into the sour milk. Combine with the dry ingredients and mix well.

Grease three (number 2) cans and distribute the batter evenly among them. Cover each can with waxed paper or foil and tie with a string. Place 2 cups of water in a large, deep pot and stand the three cans upright in the pot. Bring the water to a boil, then lower the heat and steam the bread, covered, for about 3½ hours.

The tops of the loaves should be firm. If they are still sticky, the loaves are not done and should be steamed for 30 minutes longer.

Sally Lunn

2 cups all-purpose or unbleached
  white flower

3 teaspoons baking powder

3 tablespoons sugar

½ teaspoon salt

2 eggs, separated

½ cup milk

½ cup melted butter

MAKES ONE LOAF

Preheat the oven to 350° F. Sift and measure the flour. Add the baking powder, sugar, and salt, and sift again. Beat the egg yolks and add the milk. Combine the egg mixture with the dry ingredients. Stir lightly just to blend the two mixtures. Add the shortening. Beat the egg whites until stiff, but not dry, and fold them into the batter. Bake in a buttered 8-inch square pan for 30 minutes. Cut into 2-inch squares and serve piping hot.

Yeasted Sally Lunn

1 envelope yeast

⅓ cup light brown sugar

¼ cup water, lukewarm

¾ cup milk

2 eggs

½ cup butter

2 teaspoons salt

MAKES ONE LOAF

Add the sugar to the water, sprinkle in the yeast and allow to stand until frothy. Sift the flour. Beat the eggs and set aside. Scald the milk and stir in the butter and salt. Cool to lukewarm, add the yeast, eggs and flour. Beat for 5 minutes. Cover and allow to rise in a warm, draft-free place for 1 hour. Beat down and spoon into a well-oiled pan. Cover and allow to rise in a warm draft-free place for

1¼ hours. Place in a cold oven, turn to 400° F., bake for 10 minutes, lower heat to 350° F. and bake 30 minutes more.

Johnnycake

2 tablespoons shortening
½ cup enriched flour, sifted
2 cups yellow cornmeal
2 tablespoons sugar

2 teaspoons baking soda
1 egg
1 cup milk

MAKES ONE LOAF

Melt the shortening over hot water. Combine the sifted flour with the cornmeal, sugar, and baking soda, and sift into a large bowl. Beat the egg until light and frothy. Mix the melted shortening and milk into the egg and add to the dry ingredients. Grease an 8-inch square baking pan. Pour in the batter and bake for 25 minutes in an oven preheated to 425° F. Cut into squares after removing from oven and serve immediately.

Steamed Togus Loaf

Cornmeal makes this a truly tasty loaf from Down East.

½ cup all-purpose or unbleached
    white flour, sifted
½ teaspoon baking soda
1 teaspoon salt
1½ cups yellow cornmeal

¼ cup molasses
1½ cups milk
½ cup sour milk

MAKES ONE LOAF

Combine sifted flour with baking powder and salt, and sift again into a large bowl. Blend in the cornmeal. Mix the molasses with the milk and the sour milk. Stir into the cornmeal mixture; the batter will be thin. Grease a mold. Pour the batter into the mold; if it doesn't have a lid, cover with waxed paper or aluminum foil and tie with a string.

Set in a deep kettle, pour in boiling water to within 3 inches of the top of the mold, and boil gently for 3 hours. Add boiling water to the kettle from time to time to maintain the water level.

The top must be firm, but not sticky before it is unmolded. Carefully unmold and serve steaming hot with butter.

Kentucky Pone Bread

I was born in Kentucky, and just the thought of Southern cooking makes me feel hungry. This Pone bread is the perfect way to abate such hunger.

1 cup water
2 cups coarse cornmeal
¼ teaspoon soda

¾ cup buttermilk
1 teaspoon salt

MAKES ABOUT EIGHT PONES

Boil the water and add the cornmeal. Stir the soda into the buttermilk and add this mixture, together with the salt, to the cornmeal. Mix well. Use your fingers to shape the batter into small oval pones. Press down slightly. Place on a greased griddle and bake until brown in an oven preheated to 425° F.

Cornmeal Circles

2 cups all-purpose or unbleached
    white flour, sifted
5 teaspoons baking powder
2 teaspoons salt
¾ cup cornmeal
⅓ cup shortening

3 tablespoons fresh chives,
    chopped
1 cup milk
2 tablespoons butter, melted
½ cup cheddar cheese, grated

MAKES ONE EIGHT-INCH CIRCLE

Combine the sifted flour with the baking powder, salt, and cornmeal, and sift these ingredients together. Using two knives, cut in the shortening. When the mixture has the consistency of very small peas, stir in the chopped chives. Blend in the milk with a fork, mixing just enough to moisten all the ingredients. Dust a pastry board lightly with flour and knead the dough two or three times. Roll the dough to ⅜-inch thickness and cut into 2-inch circles.

Brush the tops of the circles with melted butter. Place the grated cheese in a small bowl. Press the circles into the cheese, and stand them on their edges, back to back in pairs, to form a circle in a well-buttered 8-inch tube mold. Top the circle with the remaining cheese. Bake 20 to 25 minutes, or until golden brown, in an oven preheated to 400° F. Remove from oven and allow to cool a few minutes. Set a plate over the mold, grip the plate tightly, and turn the mold upside down. Brush top with melted butter. Serve hot.

Fried Corn Pones

2 cups white cornmeal	1 tablespoon bacon fat
1 teaspoon salt	¼ cup milk
1 teaspoon baking powder	Bacon drippings
1–1½ cups boiling water	

MAKES EIGHTEEN

Combine the cornmeal, salt, and baking powder in a large bowl. Gradually add enough of the boiling water to make a fairly stiff batter. Blend in the bacon fat. Add as much of the milk as necessary to make a soft batter. Heat the bacon drippings on a griddle (or skillet). Drop the batter by spoonfuls onto the griddle, turning once to brown both sides. Serve hot.

Lacy Cornbread

1 cup cornmeal	A dash each of black pepper and cayenne pepper
1¾ cups water	Oil for frying
1 small onion	
2 teaspoons salt	

MAKES SIX TO EIGHT PIECES

Blend the cornmeal gradually into the water. Mince the onion and add it, together with the spices, to the cornmeal mixture, stirring well. Heat ¼ inch of oil in a large, heavy skillet to 370° F. Fry the batter by dropping rounded tablespoonfuls into the hot oil. Turn once to brown evenly. Drain on paper towels and serve crispy hot.

Corn Dodger

There once was a hungry old codger,
Who ate nothin' but steamin' Corn Dodger.
He'd fry up some bacon
As soon as he'd waken
And eat it with Dodger, this codger.

2½ tablespoons bacon drippings

½ cup all-purpose or unbleached white flour, sifted

1 cup yellow cornmeal

2 teaspoons sugar

1½ teaspoons baking powder

1 teaspoon salt

1 egg

1 cup milk

MAKES EIGHT WEDGES

Heat the bacon drippings in a small skillet. Combine the sifted flour with the cornmeal, sugar, baking powder, and salt, and sift together. Beat the egg until light and frothy and mix with the milk. Add to the dry ingredients and blend thoroughly. Add the hot bacon drippings and mix well. Place the mixture into a round baking dish that has been warmed in the oven. Bake until golden brown in a preheated 425° F. oven for about 30 minutes, or until a wooden toothpick comes out clean. Cut into wedges and serve immediately.

Fried Corn Dodgers

3 cups white cornmeal

2 teaspoons salt

2–2½ cups boiling water

1 tablespoon bacon fat

MAKES TWELVE–FIFTEEN

Combine the cornmeal and salt in a large bowl. Gradually stir in just enough boiling water so that the batter can be shaped. Mix thoroughly. Blend in the bacon fat. Preheat the oven to 450° F. Use additional bacon fat to grease a baking sheet. Allow the baking sheet to sizzle briefly in the oven, then remove it, and drop the batter by large heaping spoonfuls onto the hot sheet. Use your fingers to flatten the dodgers into 3-inch, bar-shaped mounds. Bake at 450° F. for 20 minutes; then reduce the heat to 350° F. and bake until golden brown. Split, butter, and serve warm.

Sweet Potato Biscuits

½ cup butter	1 tablespoon sugar
1 cup cooked sweet potatoes	3 teaspoons baking powder
¾ cup milk	½ teaspoon salt
1¼ cups flour, sifted	

MAKES EIGHTEEN

Melt the butter over hot water. Mash the sweet potatoes until light and fluffy, and stir in the melted butter and milk. Sift enough flour to measure 1¼ cups. Combine the flour with the sugar, baking powder, and salt and sift again into a large bowl. Blend in the sweet potato mixture, and stir until the dough comes away cleanly from the bowl. Sprinkle flour on a pastry board. Knead the dough lightly for about a minute and roll out to a ½-inch thickness. Dip the edges of a 2-inch glass in flour and cut rounds from the dough. Place on a lightly greased baking sheet and bake for 15 minutes or until lightly browned in an oven preheated to 450° F.

Parsonage Oyster Plant Soup

3 bunches oyster plant (salsify)	1½ cups light cream
	5 tablespoons butter
4 onions	Salt and pepper to taste
8½ cups milk	

SERVES TEN

Wash the oyster plant thoroughly, scrape it, and cut into thin slices. Peel and thinly slice the onions. Arrange the slices of oyster plant and onion in a large heavy skillet. Add just enough water to prevent the vegetables from burning. Cook until the vegetables are tender and the water is almost gone. Press the onions and half the slices of oyster plant through a sieve. Scald the milk and cream. Stir in the sieved vegetables, butter, salt and pepper, and the remaining slices of oyster plant. Heat, stirring occasionally, and serve piping hot.

"Necessity Mess"***

*This soup, based on a very old recipe from
Martha's Vineyard, makes a delicious and sturdy lunch
when both the larder and the stomach are empty.*

¾ *pound salt pork or slab bacon*	2 *small carrots*
4 *large onions*	12 *cups hot water*
6 *large potatoes*	¾ *teaspoon salt*
2 *small turnips*	½ *teaspoon powdered sage*

SERVES TWELVE

Cut the pork into ¼-inch slices. Peel and cut the onions, potatoes, turnips, and carrots into ½-inch slices. Add the hot water and salt, bring to a boil, lower the heat, and simmer for 25 minutes, or until the potato and turnip slices are tender. Stir in the powdered sage. Serve hot.

Connecticut Cream of Onion Soup

6½ *cups onions, peeled and thinly sliced*	5 *tablespoons flour*
8 *tablespoons chicken fat, rendered*	4½ *cups milk*
	1½ *cups light cream*
4½ *cups boiling water*	*Salt and pepper to taste*

SERVES TEN

Sauté the onions in 4 tablespoons of the chicken fat until lightly browned. Cover with boiling water. Simmer until the onion slices are tender. Force the onion mixture through a coarse sieve and re-heat. Combine the flour with the remaining chicken fat and make a paste. Add the milk and cream to the paste and stir until smooth. Cook until thickened, stirring constantly. Add the sieved onion mixture, sprinkle with salt and pepper, and serve immediately.

Old New England Clam Chowder

36 clams, shucked, and their juice

2 ounces salt pork

6 medium-sized potatoes

2 large onions

4 cups water

2 small bay leaves, crumbled

2 tablespoons butter, softened

2½ tablespoons flour

5 cups milk

3 cups light cream

Salt and freshly ground pepper to taste

SERVES TEN

Strain the clams and remove any small bits of shell. Reserve the clam juice. Mince the hard parts of the clams but keep the soft parts intact. Dice the salt pork and sauté it until it is golden brown. Peel and dice the potatoes and onion and add them, together with the water and bay leaves, to the salt pork. Boil gently until the potatoes are tender but not mushy.

Meanwhile blend the butter and flour. Add this, the milk, the cream, the clams, and their juice to the potato mixture. Stir over low heat until the soup comes to a low boil and thickens slightly. Lower the heat and simmer for 5 minutes. Serve hot.

Vermont Cabbage Soup

1 medium-sized cabbage

2 tablespoons butter

4 cups water

½ teaspoon salt

⅛ teaspoon pepper

3½ cups milk

1½ cups cream

1 cup croutons

SERVES SIX

[117]

Remove the outer leaves and hard core from the cabbage and chop coarsely (there should be about 4½ cups). Sauté the cabbage in the butter for 5 minutes. Add the water, salt, and pepper; then cover and simmer for 20 minutes. Drain off all but 1 cup of water. Add the milk and cream and heat, stirring occasionally. Correct the seasonings and serve hot with croutons.

Egg Chowder

½ cup salt pork

6 large potatoes

3 cups milk

2 tablespoons butter

6 hard-cooked eggs, sliced

1 tablespoon fresh dill, minced

Salt and pepper to taste

SERVES FIVE

Dice the salt pork. Sauté it in a deep kettle until nicely browned. Peel and slice the potatoes. Arrange them on top of the salt pork, add water to cover, and cook until the potatoes are tender, but not mushy. Scald the milk in a saucepan and add, together with the butter, the hard-cooked eggs, and dill, to the potatoes. Season with salt and pepper. Heat the soup thoroughly, stirring occasionally, but do not allow to boil. Serve immediately.

Penny-Pinching Chowder

6 slices lean bacon

3 medium-sized onions

8 frankfurters

4 large potatoes

2 cups fresh or frozen corn kernels

2½ teaspoons salt

¾ teaspoon freshly ground black pepper

1 teaspoon caraway seeds

1½ teaspoons thyme

2 beef bouillon cubes

2 cans beef broth

2 cups water

1 cup dry white wine

4 cups milk

SERVES EIGHT

Arrange the bacon in a deep, heavy kettle and sauté until brown and crisp. Meanwhile, peel and slice the onions. Slice the frankfurters. Remove the bacon from the kettle, drain on paper towels, and reserve. Brown the sliced onions and frankfurters in the bacon fat until the onions are golden. Peel the potatoes, cut them in eighths, and add to the kettle. Stir in the corn kernels, salt, pepper, caraway seeds, thyme, bouillon cubes, beef broth, and water. Bring to a boil, cover, and simmer gently for 30 minutes, or until the potatoes are tender. Stir in the wine and milk, but do not allow the soup to boil. Serve immediately, sprinkled with the reserved chopped bacon.

Cream of Parsnip Soup

Parsnips have a "homey" flavor and sweetness reminiscent of times gone by. It's easy to see why this soup was so at home in Grandmother's kitchen.

1 large onion	4½ tablespoons flour
1 cup water	1½ teaspoons salt
2 cups cooked parsnips	⅛ teaspoon pepper
7 cups milk	⅛ teaspoon paprika
6 tablespoons butter	

SERVES EIGHT

Mince the onion and boil until tender in the water. Purée the cooked parsnips and onions by forcing them through a sieve. Scald the milk in a deep kettle. Add the puréed vegetables. Blend the butter and flour and stir into the soup, continuing to stir over a low heat until the mixture is smooth and slightly thickened. Sprinkle with salt, pepper, and paprika and serve immediately.

Halleluia Soup***

*Halleluia, a popular luncheon or supper dish in old
New England, was thinned down with a little water or
broth and served as a soup when friends or
relatives dropped in unexpectedly.*

1/3-pound slab bacon or salt pork

4 large onions

4 large potatoes

5 cups hot water or Chicken
broth

2 tablespoons flour

1/3 cup cold water

1 teaspoon salt

1/8 teaspoon coarsely ground
black pepper

1/2 teaspoon sugar

1/4 teaspoon powdered sage

Butter

SERVES SIX

Slice the bacon, dice it, and brown it in a large, heavy soup pot or
skillet. Peel and slice the onions and potatoes. Add the hot water to
the soup pot and stir in the potato and onion slices. Bring to a boil,
lower the heat, and cook gently for 30 minutes, or until the potato
slices are tender. Blend together the flour, water, salt, pepper, and
sugar. Add 1/2 cup of the soup stock to the flour mixture, stir until
smooth, and mix into the soup. Bring to a boil, stirring constantly.
Serve hot, dotted with butter and sprinkled with sage.

Pennsylvania Dutch

Grumbera Twists

1 cup mashed potatoes	1 cup milk
1 tablespoon melted butter	2 eggs beaten lightly
1 tablespoon shortening	½ cup potato water
2¾ tablespoons sugar	1½ packages dry active yeast
1 teaspoon salt	6 cups flour (or more)

MAKES TWO LOAVES

Place the mashed potatoes in a large bowl, add melted butter, shortening, sugar, and salt. Scald the milk and cool to lukewarm. Add milk and lightly beaten egg to potato mixture. Dissolve the yeast thoroughly in the potato water, and add to potato mixture. Sift the flour and add, stirring rapidly until the dough no longer sticks to the sides. Cover the bowl with a dishtowel and put in a warm place for 1 hour. Place the dough on a floured board and knead until it becomes stiff. Add more flour, if necessary. Grease another bowl and put the dough into it, turning once to grease the top. Cover; put in a warm, draft-free place, and let rise 1 hour, or until double in bulk.

Knead the dough again on a floured board. Use a knife to chop through the dough several times. Place ⅓ of the dough into the greased bowl and set aside.

Divide the rest of the dough into two parts. Roll each part into three long, thin, sausage-like strips. Pinch the ends of three strips together and braid tightly. Place the two braids in greased loaf pans. Brush the tops with milk. Divide the remaining dough into six strips and make two small braids. Place a small braid on top of each of the larger braids. Coat the braided loaves with melted butter. Place the loaves in a warm, draft-free place for 1 hour, or until double in bulk. Bake in a preheated 450° F. oven until the braids are golden. Lower heat to 375° F. and bake 45 minutes longer, or until the bottom of the loaves sound hollow when tapped with a finger.

Sesame Pretzels

2 cups warm water
2 packages dry active yeast
½ cup sugar
2¼ teaspoons salt
4 tablespoons butter, softened
1 egg
7–7½ cups flour
1 egg yolk
Sesame seeds

MAKES THIRTY PRETZELS

Place water and yeast in the large bowl of electric mixer. Stir until yeast is dissolved. Add the sugar, salt, butter, egg, and 3 cups of flour. Beat at medium speed to make a smooth batter. Add enough additional flour to make a stiff dough. Cover the bowl tightly with aluminum foil and refrigerate from 4 to 6 hours.

Dust a bread board lightly with flour. Turn out the cold dough and divide in half. Cut each half into 15 pieces. Roll each piece between your hands to form pencil shapes about 18 inches long. Work fast because the dough is springy and tends to shrink. Give each piece a final stretch, shape into pretzels, and pinch the ends together. Beat the egg yolk and brush each pretzel generously with the mixture. Sprinkle sesame seeds on the side glazed with egg yolk, and arrange the pretzels on lightly greased baking sheets. Cover and let rise in a warm, draft-free place for 30 minutes. Bake for 15 minutes in an oven preheated to 400° F. When golden brown, remove from baking sheets and cool on wire racks.

Lump Soup

*I remember eating soup with "rivvels," or little lumps
of dough, when I was a child. My grandfather,
Nicholas Young, was Pennsylvania Dutch, and Lump
Soup (or Rivvel Supp) was standard fare when the
family gathered for holiday festivities. This is the
traditional way to prepare the soup, but "rivvels"
may be added to other soups as well.*

7 tablespoons flour

4 eggs

8 cups milk

1 teaspoon salt

¼ teaspoon freshly ground
pepper

2½ teaspoons butter

SERVES EIGHT

Measure flour into a small bowl. With a fork, add the beaten eggs to the flour until the dough separates into small bits. Heat the milk. Taking a small amount of dough at a time, rub through your hands into the simmering milk. Let simmer for 10 minutes. Add salt, pepper, and a small lump of butter to each bowl. Serve hot.

Onion Soup

5 tablespoons butter

3½ cups onions, chopped

9 cups Beef consommé (see
page 68)

1½ cups flour

2 eggs

Salt and freshly ground
black pepper to taste

½ cup grated cheese

SERVES TEN

Melt the butter and sauté the chopped onions until golden and transparent. Pour the consommé into a large kettle and bring it to a boil. Add the sautéed onions, lower the heat, and simmer for 10 minutes.

Meanwhile, prepare rivvels as follows: Measure the flour into a small bowl, stir in the eggs, and cut the dough into narrow pieces. Allow it to dry for 10 minutes. Rub pieces of the dough between the sides of your palms until bits break off and fall into the simmering soup. Let simmer 15 minutes. Adjust the seasonings. Serve hot, with a bowl of grated cheese on the side.

Chicken Broth with Crunchy Almond Balls***

*A rich chicken broth with chicken pieces
and crunchy almond balls.*

2½ quarts Chicken stock (see page 74)

3-pound chicken, cut into serving pieces

1 cup blanched almonds

3 egg whites

⅔ cup breadcrumbs

½ teaspoon salt

¼ cup vegetable oil

Salt and pepper to taste

2 tablespoons chives, chopped

SERVES TEN

Put the Chicken stock into a large soup kettle and add the chicken pieces. Bring to a boil, skimming frequently. Lower the heat and cover the pot. Simmer for 2 hours. Cut chicken into bite-sized pieces.

Whirl the almonds in a blender until they resemble coarse meal; stop the blender from time to time to push the nuts down into the blades. Beat the egg whites until frothy and set aside. Put the breadcrumbs into a small bowl, add the almonds and salt. Shape the almond mixture into very small balls. Dip in the reserved egg whites.

Heat 2 tablespoons of the vegetable oil in a medium-sized frying pan. Fry half of the balls until brown on all sides. Set aside on a paper towel. Add the rest of the oil and fry the remaining almond balls. If necessary to reheat the balls, place in medium oven for a few minutes.

Return the chicken to the soup, adjust the seasonings, and reheat. Place the almond balls in the soup bowls and ladle the soup over them. Sprinkle with chopped chives.

Poor Man's Soup

3 large potatoes
2½ quarts Chicken stock (see page 74)
6 eggs
4 slices white bread
¾ cup milk
4 cups mashed potatoes

1 teaspoon salt
⅛ teaspoon pepper
Flour as needed
4½ tablespoons butter
Additional salt and pepper to taste

SERVES TWELVE

Peel the potatoes and cut into 1-inch cubes. Add to the Chicken stock and simmer until the potatoes are tender. Mash the potatoes with the stock to make a thin soup.

Beat the eggs. Soak the bread in the milk and squeeze out. Mix together the eggs, bread, mashed potatoes, salt, and pepper, adding enough flour to make a fairly stiff paste. Using a spoon, drop these dumplings into the lightly boiling soup, cover, and continue to cook for 15 minutes. Adjust the seasonings. Serve immediately.

Sweet and Sour Vegetable Soup***

4 large onions
1 bunch celery, including the leaves
3 cups tomatoes
1½ pounds stewing beef
1 leftover ham bone with some meat attached
⅔ can tomato paste
1½ teaspoons peppercorns
¾ teaspoon celery seed
1 teaspoon caraway seed
1 teaspoon whole cloves

5 bay leaves
2 tablespoons Worcestershire sauce
5 tablespoons sugar
3 tablespoons lemon juice
Salt. tabasco. and freshly ground pepper to taste
2 large, ripe tomatoes
3 scallions with 3 inches of green top
Sour cream

SERVES SIXTEEN

Peel and slice the onions. Wash and dice the celery. Peel, seed, and chop the tomatoes. Place the vegetables in a large soup kettle. Add the beef, ham bone, and all of the other ingredients, *except* the turnips, parsnips, carrots, tomatoes, scallions, and sour cream.

[125]

Add enough water to cover the meat and vegetables. Cover the pot and cook at a low boil for 2½ to 3 hours. Keep the liquid at the same level by adding more water when necessary.

Strain the soup into a large bowl, forcing as much pulp as possible through the strainer with a spoon. Chop the ham. Cut the beef into small pieces. Add both meats to the strained broth.

Wash and dice the turnips, parsnips, and carrots (or other combination of fresh vegetables) along with the sugar and lemon juice. Add to the soup and cook until tender. Adjust the seasonings.

Serve the soup in individual dishes, topped with chopped fresh tomato and scallion and spoons of sour cream.

Pennsylvania Dutch Chicken and Corn-on-the-cob Soup

If you often feel "the hurrier I go, the behinder I get" when it comes to cooking, then serve this wholesome soup. It's a meal in itself.

5-pound roasting chicken, cut into 8 pieces	1 teaspoon salt
Water to cover	6 ears corn
4 stalks celery, chopped	2 hard-cooked eggs, chopped
1 large onion	2½ cups cooked ham, diced
2 carrots, peeled and chopped	3 tablespoons minced parsley
10 peppercorns	

SERVES EIGHT

Place the chicken pieces, celery, whole onion, carrots, and peppercorns in a large, deep kettle. Add water to cover, sprinkle with the salt, and simmer until the chicken is tender, approximately 1¼ hours. Remove the chicken pieces, skin them, and set aside. Boil the broth until it is reduced to 10 cups, strain, and return to low heat. Remove the shucks and silks from the corn and drop the ears into the simmering stock. Turn up the heat and boil for 10 minutes. Remove the ears; holding each one over the kettle, carefully scrape the kernels and juice into the soup. Add the chopped eggs, diced ham, and skinned chicken pieces. Reheat. Serve immediately, with a chicken piece in each bowl. Garnish with parsley.

American
plain
and
fancy

IF EVER A NATION had a great heritage upon which to build a culinary tradition, America is that land. It is simply not possible for the cuisine of a melting-pot nation to be dull or uninteresting. Those who disparage our culinary achievements are often visitors from abroad who touch down in several metropolitan areas and judge American cooking by the harried restaurant meals they consume between elevator and taxi rides.

Even Americans tend to scoff at American cooking, measuring our food by the standards of other nations. We may not prepare French food as well as the French, or German food as well as the Germans, but the merits of American cooking are not in how well we *copy* the cuisine of other nations but rather in how we adapt and change that food to make it uniquely our own.

New Orleans, Pennsylvania Dutch, Southern, and New England cooking are all worthy of plaudits. American cuisine is as delicious and diverse in its own way as that of any nation, and don't let anyone persuade you that it isn't! From the crunchy goodness of Anadama Bread to the creamy richness of Oyster Stew, America is a land of good and plenty, of plain and fancy.

Anadama Bread***

This early American bread made with cornmeal and molasses
is high and handsome as well as utterly delicious.
According to legend, it was invented by a fisherman who
had a lazy wife, and consequently had to do his own
cooking and baking. He named the bread after his wife,
"Anna, damn her." Polite society modified this to
Anadama bread. My personal feeling is that instead of
cursing his spouse, the fisherman should have blessed her
for not depriving him of the opportunity to
create something as beautiful as this.

7½–8½ cups unsifted all-purpose
    or unbleached flour
1¼ cups yellow cornmeal
2¾ teaspoons salt
  2 packages dry active
    yeast

½ cup margarine, softened
2¼ cups warm water (about
    130°F.)
¾ cup molasses (at room
    temperature)

MAKES TWO LOAVES

Combine 2½ cups of the flour with the cornmeal, salt, and yeast in a large bowl and mix thoroughly. Stir in the margarine. Add the water and molasses, a little at a time, blending well. Beat this mixture with an electric mixer at medium speed for 2 minutes, scraping the bowl occasionally. Stir in ½ cup flour and beat at high speed for 2 minutes more, scraping the bowl occasionally. Stir in enough additional flour to form a stiff dough. Turn out onto a lightly floured board. Knead the dough until it is smooth and elastic (about 8 to 10 minutes). Place the dough in a large greased bowl, turning over once to grease the top. Cover the bowl with a dishtowel, and allow the dough to rise in a warm, draft-free place until it doubles in bulk (approximately 1–1¼ hours).

Punch the dough down and divide in two equal parts. To shape the dough, roll each piece into a 14x9-inch rectangle. Roll the dough up from its short upper end and seal the sides with the fingers, folding the sealed ends under. Place the loaves, with seam sides down, in two greased 1½-pound loaf pans. Cover the pans with a dishtowel, and allow the dough to rise again in a warm, draft-free place until double in bulk (about 45 minutes). Preheat oven to 375° F. and bake the bread about 45 minutes. Remove from pans and cool on a wire rack.

Sunflower Seed Whole Wheat Bread

2½ tablespoons dry active yeast
¾ cup honey
3 cups water
¼ cup safflower oil
7½ cups unsifted whole wheat flour

¾ teaspoon sea salt
5 tablespoons dried, defatted coconut flakes
5 tablespoons sunflower seed kernels

MAKES THREE LOAVES

Have all ingredients at room temperature. Combine the yeast, honey, and water in a large mixing bowl. Let rest for 5 minutes. Add the oil, 5 cups of the flour, and the sea salt, and beat 100 strokes. Do not shirk on this process, or your bread will not be light and crunchy. Stir in the remaining 2½ cups of flour or enough to make a stiff dough. Sprinkle the coconut, sunflower seeds, and 2 tablespoons of flour on a bread board or pastry cloth. Turn the dough onto this and knead 100 times, using more flour if necessary to keep the dough from sticking. (This is the best exercise I can think of to firm the upper arms and pectoral muscles, so go at it energetically.) Oil a large bowl and place the dough in it smooth side down. Turn the greased side up, cover, and place in a warm, draft-free place. Let rise 1 hour or until double in bulk.

When the dough has doubled, punch it down to its original size, cover, and let it rise again until double in bulk. Punch it down, divide it into three equal parts, and shape into loaves. Place in generously oiled loaf pans. Cover the dough and let rise once again until it reaches the tops of the pans. Bake in an oven preheated to 350° F. for 50 minutes, or until golden brown on top. Brush lightly with butter, remove from the pans, and cool on wire racks.

Pinwheel Bread***

This whole wheat-and-white spiral is an attractive loaf.

2 cups milk

½ cup shortening

½ cup sugar

2 tablespoons salt

1 cup cold water

2 packages dry active yeast

1 cup lukewarm water

4 cups all-purpose or
unbleached white flour, sifted

Additional 3½–4 cups
enriched flour, sifted

¼ cup molasses

2½ cups whole wheat flour,
unsifted

Additional 2–2½ cups
enriched flour, sifted

MAKES THREE LOAVES

Scald the milk in a saucepan. Mix together the shortening, sugar, and salt, and blend in the milk. Add 1 cup of cold water and cool the mixture to lukewarm. Dissolve the yeast in 1 cup of lukewarm water and add to the milk mixture. Blend the mixture well. Add 4 cups of sifted flour and beat until smooth (with electric mixer, 1 minute at medium speed). Cover the dough with a dishtowel and allow it to rise in a warm, draft-free place until light and double in bulk (approximately 1 hour).

Divide the dough into two equal portions. Place each in a separate bowl. Blend 3½ to 4 cups flour into one portion to form a stiff dough. Stir the molasses into the second portion, add the whole wheat flour and as much of the 2 to 2½ cups of white flour as is necessary to form a dough that doesn't stick to your fingers.

Knead the light and dark doughs separately on a floured board until smooth and elastic (approximately 5 to 7 minutes each). Place the doughs in large greased bowls, turning over once to grease the tops. Cover with a dishtowel and allow to rise in a warm, draft-free place for 1½ hours, or until double in bulk. If the whole wheat dough has not risen sufficiently at the end of this time, allow it to rise a little longer, and proceed to shape the white dough.

Divide each dough into three parts. Roll out each part on a lightly floured board to a 12x8-inch rectangle. Place one dark rectangle on top of one light rectangle and roll up tightly, beginning with the 8-inch end. Press both doughs together firmly and tuck the ends under. Repeat the process two more times. Place each loaf in a well-greased 1-pound loaf pan. Cover with a dishtowel and let rise in a warm place until doubled in bulk (approximately 1 hour). Bake in preheated 375° F. oven for 45 to 50 minutes.

Checkerboard Bread

Divide the white dough and rye dough into three parts each. On a lightly floured board, shape each part into a strip the length of your bread pan, half the width, and about 1½ inches thick. Grease three loaf pans. Place one dark and one light strip into each pan, pressing the doughs firmly together. Cover the loaves and let rise in a warm place until doubled in bulk (about 1 hour). Bake for 45 to 50 minutes in an oven preheated to 350° F.

Onion Bread

1 package dry active yeast
¼ cup warm water
1 envelope onion soup mix
2 cups water
7 teaspoons sugar
1¼ teaspoons salt
2 tablespoons shortening

3 tablespoons Parmesan cheese, grated
5½–6½ cups all-purpose flour, sifted
Cornmeal
1 egg white
1 tablespoon water

MAKES TWO LOAVES

Sprinkle the yeast over ¼ cup warm water and allow to soften for 5 minutes. Stir the onion soup mix into 2 cups water and simmer, covered, for 12 minutes. Mix in the sugar, salt, and shortening, stir, and cool to room temperature. Stir 2 cups of sifted flour into the onion soup mixture. Add the softened yeast, stir, and add enough flour to make a moderately stiff dough.

Knead on a floured board until the dough is smooth and elastic (about 10 minutes). Place in a greased bowl, turning once to grease the top. Cover with a dishtowel and set in a warm, draft-free place until double in bulk (about 1½ to 2 hours).

Punch the dough down and divide into two parts. Place on a

lightly floured board, cover, and let rest for 15 minutes. With your hands, roll and shape each piece of dough into a long loaf, tapered at the ends. Grease a baking sheet, sprinkle it with cornmeal, and arrange the loaves so that they do not touch. Make ¼-inch-deep diagonal slashes in the tops at 3-inch intervals. Cover and set in a warm, draft-free place until double in bulk (approximately 1 hour). Preheat oven to 375° F. and bake the bread for 20 minutes. Brush the loaves with a mixture of egg white and water. Continue to bake for 15 minutes. Remove from oven and place on wire racks to cool.

Herb Bread***

½ cup milk

3 tablespoons sugar

2 teaspoons salt

3 tablespoons butter

1 package dry active yeast

1½ cups warm water
(105°–115°F.)

5½–6½ cups unsifted all-purpose
or unbleached white flour

1 cup fresh chives,
chopped

1 cup fresh parsley.
chopped

½ cup fresh dill, minced

3 tablespoons fresh chervil.
minced

MAKES FIVE SMALL LOAVES

Scald the milk. Stir in the sugar, salt, and butter, and cool to lukewarm. Dissolve the yeast in the warm water in a large warm bowl. Stir in the lukewarm milk mixture and 3 cups of the flour. Beat until smooth. Add enough additional flour to make a stiff dough. Place the dough on a lightly floured board and knead until smooth and elastic (about 8 to 10 minutes). Place the dough in a greased bowl, turning once to grease the top. Cover the bowl with a dishtowel. Allow the dough to rise in a warm, draft-free place until double in bulk (about 1–1½ hours).

Punch the dough down and turn out onto a floured board. Cover, and allow to rest 15 minutes. Divide the dough into five equal parts. Roll each part into a 12x8-inch rectangle and brush with melted butter. Combine the chives, parsley, dill, and chervil in a bowl. Sprinkle this mixture evenly over each rectangle. Roll up tightly lengthwise, pinching the seams to seal. Place the rolls 2 inches apart on greased cookie sheets and cover. Allow to rise in a warm, draft-free place until double in bulk (about 1 hour). Bake 20 to 30 minutes at 375° F.

Crackling Bread

SERVES EIGHT

Fresh cracklings are seldom available outside the Deep South. If you wish to prepare your own, proceed as follows: Chop 1½ pounds cold beef suet or salt pork coarsely until no single piece is larger than a pea. Heat a large, heavy skillet, add the chopped fat, cover, and fry, stirring occasionally until the cracklings are brown and very crisp. Drain off the fat and reserve. Remove the cracklings and drain them on paper towels. *Lightly* grease two heavy skillets with the reserved fat. Discard the remaining fat. To make the batter, use:

1 cup white cornmeal	1 cup water
2 teaspoons salt	1 cup skim milk
6 teaspoons baking powder	2 eggs

Sift the dry ingredients together. Beat the water, skim milk, and eggs lightly. Stir this into the dry ingredients and beat until smooth. Stir in the cracklings. Divide the batter between the two skillets. Bake for 30 to 35 minutes in an oven preheated to 400° F. Serve hot.

Fresh Cornbread, Southern Style

*This cornbread is made with fresh grated corn as well as
cornmeal for a doubly delicious corn-y flavor.*

2 eggs	1 cup cornmeal
1 cup corn, grated from the cob	3 teaspoons baking powder
½ cup vegetable oil (not olive oil)	1 teaspoon salt
¾ cup sour cream	

SERVES EIGHT

Beat the eggs. Mix the grated corn, oil, and sour cream, and stir into the eggs. Sift together the cornmeal, baking powder, and salt. Stir the sifted dry ingredients into the egg-corn mixture. Mix well. Pour the batter into a 9x9-inch pan and bake for about 35 minutes, or until done, in an oven preheated to 375° F.

Spicy Sweet-Potato Spoon Bread

*This mellow Southern favorite
is sweet and spicy.*

2 large sweet potatoes	½ teaspoon cinnamon
8 tablespoons butter	5 tablespoons flour
3 tablespoons sugar	¼ teaspoon salt
1½ teaspoons nutmeg	2 eggs
1½ teaspoons allspice	

SERVES EIGHT

Scrub the potatoes and boil until tender. Peel them and mash with the butter. Add the sugar, spices, flour, and salt, and mix thoroughly. Beat the eggs and stir them into the potato mixture. Pour into a buttered pan, and bake for 30 minutes in an oven preheated to 425° F.

Butterscotch Bread***

*If a moist tea bread, crunchy with nuts, is what
you're looking for, try this one.*

3 tablespoons butter, melted	2 cups sour milk
2 eggs	2 cups pecans, chopped
2 cups brown sugar	¼ cup ground (or very finely chopped) pecans
4 cups flour, sifted	¼ cup sugar
1¾ teaspoons baking powder	¼ teaspoon each nutmeg and cinnamon
1 teaspoon baking soda	
½ teaspoon salt	

MAKES TWO LOAVES

[134]

Melt the butter over hot water. Break the eggs into a large bowl and beat them until frothy. Add the brown sugar to the eggs, a little at a time, stirring well after each addition. Blend the melted butter into the egg mixture. Combine the sifted flour with the baking powder, baking soda, and salt, and sift again. Add these dry ingredients, alternately with the sour milk, to the egg mixture, stirring well after each addition. Stir in the chopped pecans. Put the batter into two greased loaf pans. Mix the ground pecans, sugar, nutmeg, and cinnamon, and sprinkle over each loaf. Bake in an oven preheated to 350° F. for 45 to 50 minutes.

Persimmon Bread, Old South

This moist, sweet bread is unusually tasty.

¾ cup ripe persimmon pulp

½ cup shortening

1 cup sugar

2 eggs

1⅔ cups all-purpose or
    unbleached white flour, sifted

1 teaspoon baking powder

1 teaspoon soda

½ teaspoon salt

¾ cup pecans, finely chopped

SERVES EIGHT

Peel the persimmons and discard the pits. Rub through a sieve. Beat the shortening until slightly softened. Gradually add the sugar, eggs, and persimmon pulp in that order. Beat for 4 or 5 minutes. Combine the sifted flour, the baking powder, soda, and salt, and sift again. Beat into the persimmon mixture. Stir in the chopped pecans and pour into an 8x11-inch pan. Bake for 45 minutes in an oven preheated to 325° F.

Buckwheat-Fruit Bread

2¼ cups buckwheat flour

1 teaspoon salt

½ teaspoon baking powder

1½ teaspoons baking soda

½ cup dried apricots

½ cup dried prunes, soaked

½ cup raisins

1½ cups buttermilk

½ cup brown sugar

MAKES ONE LOAF

[135]

Combine the buckwheat flour, salt, baking powder, and baking soda in a large bowl. Chop the dried apricots and soaked dried prunes coarsely and add, together with the raisins, to the dry ingredients. Stir the buttermilk and brown sugar together and combine with the fruits and flour mixture. Mix thoroughly. Grease a loaf pan with a small amount of oil, pour in the batter, and bake the bread for 50 or 60 minutes in an oven preheated to 325° F. Remove from pan and cool on a wire rack.

Spicy Apple Bread

2 cups all-purpose or unbleached
   white flour, sifted

1 teaspoon baking soda

1 teaspoon salt

½ teaspoon nutmeg

1 teaspoon cinnamon

¼ teaspoon cloves

¼ cup whole wheat flour

½ cup shortening

¾ cup light brown sugar (firmly
   packed)

2 eggs

1 teaspoon vanilla

1 cup grated raw apples

½ cup buttermilk

¾ cup pecans, chopped

MAKES ONE LOAF

Combine the sifted flour, the baking soda, salt, nutmeg, cinnamon, cloves, and sift together. Add the whole wheat flour. Cream the shortening and brown sugar, and beat in the eggs. Add the vanilla to the egg mixture. Grate the apples. Add the dry ingredients, alternately with the apples and buttermilk, to the egg mixture. Fold in the nuts. Put in a well-greased loaf pan and bake for 1 hour in an oven preheated to 350° F. Cool bread before slicing.

Cabbage Soup with Croutons

2 tablespoons butter

¼ pound lean salt pork, diced

3 large potatoes

4 small carrots

2 large onions

9½ cups water

1 small cabbage

2 large cloves garlic

8 croutons

SERVES EIGHT

Melt the butter in a soup kettle. Add the salt pork and brown. Peel the potatoes, carrots, and onions and cut them into large cubes. Sauté the chopped vegetables for 5 minutes. Add the water and simmer for 30 minutes. Cut the cabbage in quarters and remove the hard core. Chop the cabbage and the peeled garlic very fine and add them to the soup. Simmer for 1 hour. Mash the vegetables thoroughly and boil over high heat for 5 minutes. Serve hot over croutons.

Croutons

1½ tablespoons butter
1 clove garlic, crushed

8 slices French bread

Melt the butter in a small skillet. Add garlic and brown. Sauté the bread slices in the butter until they are golden brown on both sides.

Thick and Delicious Kidney Bean Soup***

1 cup dried kidney beans
1½ quart water
5 ounces salt pork
2 medium-sized onions
2 carrots
6 stalks celery, including leaves
9 cups water
5 peppercorns
1 bay leaf

2 teaspoons saffron
Salt and freshly ground pepper to taste
3 avocados
Lemon juice
7 scallions with 3 inches of green top
Garlic croutons (see page 86)

SERVES SIX

Place the beans in a large saucepan, cover with water, and soak overnight. Drain beans and set aside. Dice the salt pork, place in a heavy soup kettle, and fry over medium heat until crisp. Peel the onions and carrot. Chop the onions, carrot, and celery. Add to the soup kettle and sauté until onion is transparent, about 5 minutes.

Bring the water to a boil, and add to the soup kettle, together with the drained beans, peppercorns, bay leaf, and saffron. Cover the pot and simmer for 3 hours, or until the beans are tender. Purée the bean soup in a blender, a little at a time. Return the soup to the kettle and reheat. Adjust the seasonings.

Dice the avocados and sprinkle with lemon juice. Chop the scallions. Serve the soup hot, with separate bowls of avocado, scallions, and Garlic croutons.

Lima Bean, Barley, and Mushroom Soup***

1 cup large dried lima beans

3 tablespoons coarse pearl barley

2 quarts water

½ breast flank (flanken)

2 marrow bones, cut in 2-inch pieces

2 tablespoons dehydrated, sliced mushrooms

1 medium-sized onion

2 tablespoons dried parsley

½ cup celery, finely diced

1 cup carrots, finely diced

¼ teaspoon dill weed

½ teaspoon celery salt

1 tablespoon salt

SERVES EIGHT

Wash the lima beans and barley separately in cold water, and drain well. Place the beans and barley in a soup kettle. Add the 2 quarts of water and all remaining ingredients to the kettle, cover, and bring to a boil. Cook gently for about 2 hours, or until the lima beans are soft. Remove the marrow bones and breast flank. Reserve the meat for another use. Serve the soup steaming hot.

Fresh Tomato and Dill Soup

12 large tomatoes

2 medium-sized onions

4 tablespoons butter

1 teaspoon minced garlic

6 tablespoons flour

2 tablespoons tomato paste

6 cups Chicken broth (see page 74)

1 cup heavy cream

4 tablespoons fresh dill

Salt and freshly ground pepper to taste

SERVES EIGHT

[138]

Chop 4 of the tomatoes coarsely, leaving on the skins. Peel and chop the onions. Melt the butter in a soup kettle. Add onions and garlic and sauté until golden and transparent. Add the chopped tomatoes. Cook for about 3 minutes over high heat, stirring continuously. Remove the kettle from the stove and work the flour into the tomato mixture with the back of a spoon. Add tomato paste and the Chicken broth and mix well. Return kettle to stove and stir until the soup comes to a boil. Lower the heat and simmer for 10 minutes. Chop 4 of the remaining tomatoes coarsely and add to the kettle. Pour the soup through a strainer and blend in the cream. Chop the dill very fine. Peel and seed the remaining tomatoes, and cut into small pieces. Add dill and tomatoes to the soup. Reheat gently, *but do not boil.*

Cream of Tomato Soup

5 tablespoons butter	10 medium-sized ripe tomatoes
2 tablespoons olive oil	4 tablespoons tomato paste
3 medium-sized onions	1/3 cup flour
1/2 teaspoon dried thyme	6 cups Chicken stock (page 74)
3/4 teaspoon dried basil	1 1/2 teaspoons sugar
Salt and freshly ground pepper to taste	1 1/2 cups heavy cream

SERVES EIGHT

Place 3 tablespoons of the butter and the olive oil in a soup kettle and heat over a low flame. Peel and dice the onions. Sauté them, sprinkled with the thyme, basil, salt, and pepper, in the butter and oil, stirring occasionally. Meanwhile, cut the tomatoes into eighths, shake out the seeds, and chop coarsely. When the onions are soft, stir in the chopped tomatoes and tomato paste and simmer for 10 minutes. Blend the flour with 1/4 cup of Chicken stock and add to the tomatoes and onions, mixing well. Stir the rest of the Chicken stock into the mixture. Simmer the soup, covered, over low heat for 30 minutes. Using a wooden spoon, stir, scraping the bottom of the kettle occasionally, while it simmers, so that the soup does not stick.

Purée the soup by forcing it through a fine sieve. Reheat the purée and stir in the sugar and cream. Additional sugar may be used if the soup is too acid. Simmer the soup for a few minutes, stir in the remaining butter and serve immediately. The soup may be garnished with croutons (see page 86) if desired.

Apple-Vegetable Soup

2 pounds lamb cut into 2-inch cubes

3 quarts Beef consommé (see page 68)

½ cup barley

2 small turnips

6 medium-sized carrots

1 large onion

2 large McIntosh apples

4 tomatoes

2 cups lima beans, shelled

½ teaspoon white pepper

2 teaspoons salt

¼ teaspoon allspice

1 teaspoon curry powder

2 large leeks

¼ cup parsley, chopped

SERVES EIGHT GENEROUSLY

Place the meat and Beef broth into a large soup kettle. Bring to a boil. Add the barley and simmer for 1 hour. Skim off any fat. Peel and coarsely chop the turnips, carrots, onion, apples, and tomatoes, and add with the lima beans to the soup. Season with white pepper, salt, curry powder, and allspice, and simmer for 30 minutes. Wash, trim, and chop the leeks, and add with the chopped parsley to the soup. Simmer for 30 minutes more.

Black Bean Soup

2 cups black beans

8 cups cold water

3 medium-sized onions

3 stalks celery

¼ cup butter

2 bay leaves

2 tablespoons parsley, chopped

1 ham bone

½ teaspoon salt

⅛ teaspoon freshly ground black pepper

⅔ cup dry sherry

Salt and freshly ground pepper to taste

2 hard-boiled eggs

2 lemons

SERVES EIGHT

Place beans in a soup kettle. Cover with water and soak overnight. Drain beans, return to soup kettle, and simmer in 8 cups of water until soft. Peel and chop the onions. Chop the celery. Sauté onions and celery in butter until golden and transparent. Add to the soup kettle together with the bay leaves, parsley, ham bone, salt, and pepper. Continue to cook covered over medium-low heat for 3 hours, adding a bit more water from time to time if the soup becomes too thick.

Remove the bone. Whirl soup in a blender until smooth. Return to soup kettle, add sherry, and cook over low heat until hot. Adjust the seasonings.

Ladle soup into individual dishes and garnish each with slices of hard-boiled egg white and circles of lemon. Reserve egg yolks for another use.

Hardy Vegetable-Beef Soup

2 pounds beef shank. cut in pieces	1½ cups fresh whole-kernel corn
3 quarts water	8 small onions
1 large onion. diced	1 large potato
1 tablespoon salt	1 cup fresh spinach, chopped
½ teaspoon thyme	1 cup fresh green beans, broken into small pieces
½ cup split peas	1 cup fresh green peas
6 medium-sized carrots	1 cup fresh lima beans
3 cups celery	1 cup tomato ketchup
1 large green pepper	2 tablespoons fresh parsley. chopped
3 medium-sized tomatoes	

SERVES EIGHT

Arrange the pieces of beef shank in the bottom of a large kettle. Cover with the water; add the diced onion, salt, and thyme, and bring to a boil. Skim the fat from the surface of the soup as it rises. When no more scum appears, add the split peas, cover the kettle and simmer over low heat for 4 hours. Remove the shank bones. Cut the meat off the bones into small pieces and return to the kettle. Discard the bones. Peel and slice the carrots into 1-inch pieces. Cut the celery into ½-inch pieces. Wash and dice the pepper. Peel the tomatoes, quarter them, shake out the seeds, and then chop them coarsely. Scrape the corn kernels off the cobs. Peel the small onions. Peel and cube the potato. Add the carrots, celery, pepper, chopped tomatoes, corn kernels, whole onions, potato cubes, chopped fresh spinach, green beans, green peas, lima beans, ketchup, and chopped parsley to the soup. Cover and allow to simmer for 30 minutes, or until the vegetables are tender. Adjust the seasonings. Serve the soup piping hot, with plenty of hot crusty bread.

Watercress-Corn Soup

6 cups Chicken broth	½ cup watercress
2½ teaspoons parsley, chopped	2 cups heavy cream
¼ teaspoon marjoram	Salt and pepper to taste
2 cups uncooked corn kernels	8 sprigs watercress

SERVES EIGHT

Simmer the Chicken broth, parsley, and marjoram over low heat for 5 minutes. Cut and scrape the kernels from enough ears of corn to measure 2 cups, and add to the broth. Simmer for 25 minutes. Cool and press the soup through a coarse sieve, using a spoon to crush the corn well. Wash the watercress carefully, pat dry, and chop very fine. Stir the watercress, cream, and seasonings into the corn mixture and chill. Serve cold, garnished with sprigs of watercress.

Navy Bean Soup

Everybody's favorite—try it and see why.

4 cups dried navy beans	3 quarts water
1 large onion	1 cup celery
2 cloves garlic	1 cup carrots
2-pound piece of salt pork	Salt and freshly ground black pepper to taste
Crushed red peppers to taste	

SERVES TWELVE

[142]

Rinse the navy beans thoroughly. Place them in a bowl, cover with cold water, and allow them to soak overnight. Chop the onion. Peel the garlic cloves and spear them with toothpicks so that later they may be retrieved from the soup. Place the chopped onion, garlic cloves, salt pork, and crushed red peppers into a soup kettle. Add the water, cover the kettle, bring to a boil, and simmer until the salt pork is tender (approximately 1 hour). Discard the garlic cloves. Remove the salt pork, dice it, and return to the kettle. Drain the beans, add them to the soup, and simmer, covered, until the beans are soft (about 2 hours). Wash and chop the celery. Peel and grate the carrots. Add the celery and carrots to the soup, sprinkle with salt and pepper to taste, and simmer, covered, for 30 minutes more. Serve this thick, hearty soup piping hot.

Split Pea Soup

Pea soup with an unusually creamy texture equals pea soup with a difference.

2 cups green split peas	2 cups celery, chopped with leaves
2 quarts water	
1 pound smoked ham hock	3 frankfurters
1 bay leaf	2 cups Beef consommé (see page 68)
10 peppercorns	1 cup milk
2 carrots	Salt to taste
½ cup onion, chopped	

MAKES SIX TWO-CUP SERVINGS

Place the split peas and the water into a large soup kettle to soak overnight. Using the water in which they were soaked, bring the peas to a boil, add the ham hock, bay leaf, and peppercorns, and simmer, covered, for 1 hour.

Peel and dice the carrots. Add with the chopped onion and celery to the soup and simmer for 1 hour more. Remove the ham hock. Purée the soup by forcing it through a coarse sieve. Cut the meat from the ham hock into small pieces. Discard the bone. Slice the frankfurters. Reheat the soup, add the ham, frankfurter slices, consommé, and milk, and simmer for 20 minutes. Season to taste with salt just before serving piping hot.

Southern Country-Style Green Soup***

2 pounds turnip greens
1 pound spinach
1 pound mustard greens
2 1-pound ham hocks

3 quarts water
1 large onion
2 tablespoons sugar
Salt to taste

SERVES TWELVE

Cut the stalks from all the greens and wash thoroughly. (The grit can be removed by adding ¼ cup salt to the first washing.) Rinse three or four times in cold water until the water is clear. Shake the greens to remove the excess water and chop them coarsely. Rinse the salt pork and place it in a deep kettle with the water. Chop the onion and add to the kettle. Boil the water, ham hocks, and onion together for 30 minutes. Add all the greens, sugar, and salt, and simmer for 2 hours.

Cream of Carrot Soup

This nourishing soup is thick, creamy, and colorful.

4 medium-sized onions
4 cups carrots
5 tablespoons butter
4 tablespoons flour
5 cups Beef broth (see page 68)

4 whole cloves
3 cups milk
Salt and freshly ground pepper to taste
Nutmeg

SERVES EIGHT

Peel and coarsely chop the onions and carrots. Melt the butter in a soup kettle and sauté the vegetables until the onions are golden and transparent. Blend in the flour. Mix in 2 cups of the Beef broth and stir until smooth. Add remaining broth and the cloves. Simmer, covered, for 30 minutes.

Discard the cloves and whirl the soup in a blender to purée. Stir in the milk. Pour the mixture into a soup kettle and adjust the seasonings. Stir the soup until hot but not boiling. Serve sprinkled with nutmeg.

Yellow Squash Soup

*Try this chilly puréed squash soup for an unusual
summertime treat.*

5 small yellow squash

2 quarts Chicken broth (see
page 74)

1 clove garlic, peeled and
minced

⅛ teaspoon oregano

⅛ teaspoon chervil

¼ teaspoon salt

½ cup peas, fresh or frozen

½ cup sour cream

1 teaspoon fresh dill, minced

SERVES EIGHT

Wash the squash and cut them into chunks. Place the squash, broth,
minced garlic, oregano, chervil, salt, and peas in a soup kettle. Cover
and boil gently for 30 minutes, or until the vegetables are very soft.
Work the mixture through a sieve or blend in a blender. Cool to
room temperature, and stir in the sour cream until the soup is
smooth. Chill. Serve garnished with minced fresh dill.

Pepper Pot

*Serve this hearty soup with salad and bread, hot
from the oven, and you will have an extraordinarily
appetizing and robust meal. One nice thing about
Pepper pot is that it tastes even more pleasing
the day after it was cooked.*

2 pounds tripe

2 quarts water

1½ pounds marrow bones,
cracked

2 large onions

1 veal knuckle with some meat,
split

6 cups water

1 bay leaf

1 teaspoon whole allspice

½ teaspoon crushed red pepper

4 whole cloves

½ teaspoon dried thyme

3 medium-sized potatoes

1½ teaspoons marjoram

Salt and pepper to taste

Chopped parsley

SERVES TEN

Arrange the tripe in the bottom of a deep soup kettle. Pour 2 quarts
of water over it and bring to a boil. Reduce heat, cover, and simmer

[145]

until tender (approximately 6 hours). Meanwhile, cut the marrow from the cracked marrow bones and set the bones aside. Peel and chop the onions. Heat the marrow in a skillet and sauté the chopped onions until they soften. Place the veal knuckle and reserved marrow bones in a large saucepan. Cover with 6 cups of water and stir in the onions. Tie the bay leaf, allspice, red pepper, and cloves in a small cheesecloth bag, and add to the saucepan. Stir in the thyme and cook for 5 hours, or until the veal becomes tender.

Cool both the broths. Remove and chop the tripe. Remove the veal knuckle, cut the meat off and discard both the veal knuckle and marrow bones. Discard the cheesecloth bag. Keep the meats separate from the broths. Refrigerate overnight. Skim all fat from the two broths and combine in a large kettle. Add the meats and bring to a boil. Peel and dice the potatoes and stir into the combined broths. Sprinkle with marjoram and salt and pepper, stir once or twice, and simmer, covered, for 40 minutes, or until the potatoes are tender. Serve piping hot, garnished with chopped parsley.

Cream of Celery Soup

¼-*pound piece of salt pork*	*6 tablespoons flour*
1 large onion	*2 cups heavy cream*
1 large bunch celery	*⅛ teaspoon nutmeg*
1 stewing chicken	*White pepper to taste*
5 tablespoons butter	*Salt to taste*

SERVES EIGHT

Cut the salt pork into small cubes and fry until brown and crisp in a large heavy soup kettle. Use a slotted spoon to remove the salt pork from the kettle. Drain the pork on paper toweling and reserve. Chop the onion and cut the celery into 2-inch pieces. Place the stewing chicken, onion, and celery into the kettle. Add water to cover, and cook until the chicken is tender (approximately 1½ hours). Remove the chicken and reserve it for another use. Strain the stock, bring it to a boil, and continue boiling until the liquid measures about 6 cups. Cool the stock and skim off the fat.

Melt the butter in a separate pan. Blend in the flour, stir to a smooth paste, and cook until thick. Add the stock and continue to cook, stirring constantly to remove any lumps, until it boils. Cover and cook over boiling water for 20 minutes, stirring from time to time. Stir in the heavy cream, nutmeg, white pepper, and salt. Reheat the soup, but do not allow to boil. Serve hot, garnished with minced chervil and the reserved diced pork.

Oxtail Soup with Parmesan Meatballs***

*This oxtail soup with tiny Parmesan meatballs
is extraordinarily appetizing.*

1 oxtail, cut in pieces

2 chicken backs

Soup bones

¾ pound soup meat

Soup greens (1 leek or tops of 2 green onions, 1 parsnip, ½ carrot, parsley sprigs, celery leaves, all chopped, also ¼ teaspoon thyme, 2 cloves, and ¼ bay leaf, tied in cheesecloth bag)

2 large tomatoes

1 large onion

2 cups fresh (or 1 package frozen) okra

1 cup potatoes, diced

Salt and pepper to taste

2 cups lima beans

1½ cups fresh string beans, cut in pieces

1 cup fresh peas

1 cup carrots, chopped

1 8-ounce package wide noodles

SERVES EIGHT

Place the oxtail, chicken backs, soup bones, soup meat, and soup greens in a large (8 to 10-quart) soup kettle. Peel the tomatoes, seed them by cutting into quarters and shaking out the seeds, and chop them. Peel and slice the onion. Add the tomatoes and onions to the kettle, cover with water, and bring to a boil. Cover the kettle and simmer for at least 3 hours. (Longer cooking will ensure an even stronger stock.)

Remove the cheesecloth bag and discard. Remove the oxtails, chicken backs, soup bones, and soup meat from the stock. Trim all the meat from the bones. Chop the meat and return it to the stock, discarding the bones. Dice the okra. Peel and dice the potatoes. Add the okra, potatoes, and salt and pepper to the stock. Simmer the soup, covered, for 1 hour. Stir in the lima beans, string beans, peas, and chopped carrots, and simmer for 20 minutes longer, or until the vegetables are tender. Remove the soup from the heat, cool, and refrigerate. Skim off the fat, reheat, and serve with Parmesan meatballs. To serve, bring the soup to a boil, add Parmesan meatballs and simmer for 30 minutes. Ten minutes before serving, add the noodles and cook until tender. Serve piping hot.

Parmesan Meatballs

1 pound ground beef
2 small cloves garlic. crushed

3 tablespoons Parmesan cheese. grated

Mix the ground beef, crushed garlic, and grated Parmesan cheese together in a bowl. Form the mixture into walnut-sized balls. Proceed as directed above.

Curried Corn and Ham Soup

1 meaty ham bone
4 cups uncooked corn kernels
3 tablespoons onion. finely grated
½ teaspoon curry powder

3½ cups light cream
2 tablespoons butter
Salt and pepper to taste
2 tablespoons parsley. finely chopped

SERVES SIX

Place the ham bone into a soup kettle with enough water to cover (about 4 cups). Bring to a boil, skim off any foam, lower the heat, and simmer for 1½ hours. Remove the ham bone. Boil the stock and reduce it to 2 cups. Cut the meat into small pieces and reserve.

Cut and scrape the kernels from enough ears of corn to make 4 cups. Add the corn and grated onion to the stock and cook for 20 minutes, stirring from time to time. Force the mixture through a coarse sieve, crushing the corn well with the back of a spoon. Blend the curry powder with a little of the corn mixture, and stir it into the cream. Combine the cream and corn mixtures, add the butter and reserved diced ham, and season with salt and pepper. Reheat the soup, stirring occasionally. Serve hot, topped with a sprinkling of chopped parsley.

Chicken Giblet Soup

2¼ pounds chicken giblets
2 medium-sized carrots
2 medium-sized onions
1 cup celery
3 parsley sprigs

3 quarts water
½ teaspoon poultry seasoning
Salt and pepper to taste
¼ cup uncooked brown rice

SERVES EIGHT

Rinse and clean the chicken giblets, cutting away any tough membranes. Peel and slice the carrots. Peel and coarsely chop the onions. Wash and dice the celery. Arrange the giblets, carrots, onions, celery, and parsley in the bottom of a soup kettle. Cover with 3 quarts of water, add the seasonings, and bring to a boil. Cover the kettle and simmer the soup for about 1 hour. When the giblets are tender, remove from the heat and strain the soup, discarding the giblets and vegetables. Refrigerate the soup. Before reheating, remove any fat that has formed on the surface. Bring to a boil, add the uncooked brown rice, and simmer gently, covered, until the rice is tender (about 20 minutes). Serve piping hot.

Acorn Squash Soup

5 cups water
1 teaspoon salt
1¾ pounds fresh acorn squash
1 cup potatoes
5 cups heavy cream
⅔ cup fresh spinach

⅔ cup leeks
⅔ cup lettuce
4 tablespoons butter
½ cup cooked rice
2 tablespoons parsley, minced
Salt to taste

SERVES EIGHT

Bring the water to a boil and add the salt. Meanwhile, peel, seed, and slice the squash. Peel and slice the potatoes. Add these vegetables to the water and simmer until tender. Press the squash and potatoes, as well as their liquid, through a fine sieve, or purée them in an electric blender. Stir in the cream. Wash and finely chop the spinach, leeks, and lettuce. Heat the butter in a skillet. Sauté the chopped vegetables slowly over a low heat until they are wilted and all the butter has been absorbed. Add the cooked rice and minced parsley. Stir this mixture into the creamed purée, heat, stirring occasionally, and season with salt to taste. Serve immediately.

Curried Chicken-Sprout Soup***

Serve this hearty soup with a warm, crusty onion bread. a crisp green salad, and a delicate sweet, and your meal will be complete.

4-pound chicken, cut in half	2 teaspoons curry powder
3 quarts water	1½ cups tomatoes, peeled, seeded, and chopped
2 teaspoons salt	½ cup uncooked rice
4 medium-sized onions	2½ tablespoons flour
3 carrots	¼ cup water
1 teaspoon ground mace	White pepper to taste
1½ cups cooked ham	3 hard-cooked eggs
4 cups Brussels sprouts	½ cup parsley, chopped
3 tablespoons butter	

SERVES TEN

In a large kettle, bring to a boil the chicken, the water, and 1 teaspoon of salt. Peel 2 of the onions and the carrots and add, together with the mace, to the soup. Cook, covered, until the chicken is tender (approximately 1 hour). Remove the chicken from the stock, cool, and remove the skin and bones. Cut the chicken meat into large chunks. Strain the soup, cool, and skim off the fat.

Peel the remaining onions and chop. Dice the ham. Chop the Brussels sprouts coarsely. Melt the butter in a deep skillet and stir in the chicken pieces, chopped onion, ham, Brussels sprouts, the remaining teaspoon of salt, and the curry powder. Cook for 10 minutes, stirring constantly. Add the tomatoes. Stir in the rice and mix until it is well coated with butter.

Pour the chicken stock into the skillet, cover, and simmer until the rice softens (approximately 30 minutes). Blend the flour with ¼ cup water and stir into the soup, thickening it slightly. Season with pepper. Force the hard-cooked eggs through a sieve and into the soup. Pour into deep bowls and serve immediately, garnished with chopped parsley.

Chicken-and-Truffles-In-A-Pot

¾ *pound veal*

1 *veal bone*

8 *cups water*

3½ *cups white wine*

2 *cloves garlic, peeled*

1 *teaspoon salt*

1 *chicken (6 pounds), cut into serving pieces*

2 *tablespoons butter*

2 *truffles sliced, with 1 tablespoon juice from the can*

⅓ *cup brandy*

3 *tablespoons Madeira*

5 *mushrooms, washed, peeled, and sliced*

2 *leeks, washed, trimmed and cut into 1-inch pieces*

SERVES TWELVE

Place the veal, veal bone, water, wine, garlic, and salt into a large soup kettle and simmer for 2 hours. Meanwhile, brown the chicken in the butter and add it, together with the pan juices, sliced truffles and juice, brandy, Madeira, sliced mushrooms, and leeks to the strained stock. Simmer, covered, for 40 minutes. Serve hot.

Truffled Cream of Chicken Soup

2 *small onions*

2 *carrots*

1 *large leek*

2 *stalks celery, including leaves*

3 *sprigs parsley*

6 *tablespoons butter*

½ *cup flour*

10 *cups Chicken stock (see page 74)*

Salt and white pepper to taste

3 *hard-cooked eggs*

16 *green asparagus tips, cooked*

16 *small shrimp, cooked*

4 *truffles, sliced*

½ *cup green peas, cooked*

SERVES EIGHT

Peel and slice the onions. Peel and coarsely chop the carrots. Slice the leek, using only the white part. Wash and chop the celery and parsley. Melt the butter in a soup kettle, add the flour, sauté the vegetables for 5 minutes and stir constantly until the flour begins to turn a light yellow. Gradually stir in the Chicken stock and continue to stir until the sauce is smooth. Add the sautéed onions, carrots, leek, and celery. Cover and cook over low heat for about 25 minutes. Adjust the seasonings and strain the soup.

Pour the steaming hot soup into a large tureen. Peel eggs, chop and push them through a fine strainer. In individual soup bowls, place 2 asparagus tips, 2 shrimp, and 1 teaspoon sieved egg. Pour hot soup into bowls and garnish with sliced truffles and cooked green peas.

Oxtail-Vegetable Soup

4 small onions

3 carrots

2 small turnips

2 large potatoes

10 cups Oxtail consommé (see page 77)

1½ cup fresh peas

Parmesan cheese, grated

SERVES TEN

Peel and dice the onions, carrots, turnips, and potatoes. Add to the consommé, bring to a boil, lower the heat, and simmer until the vegetables are nearly tender. Add peas and cook 10 minutes longer. Serve hot with grated Parmesan cheese.

Fish Soup with Shellfish

2 medium-sized onions

2 small (or 1 large) garlic cloves

1 leek

5 scallions

1 small green pepper

3 tablespoons butter

2 tablespoons olive oil

¼ cup parsley, chopped

¼ cup dill, chopped

8 cups Fish consommé (or rich fish broth) (see page 83)

2 cups dry white wine

½ teaspoon Tabasco sauce

30 shrimps, peeled and deveined

20 bay scallops

24 oysters, shucked (retain the juice)

Garlic croutons (see page 86)

SERVES EIGHT

Peel and chop the onions and garlic. Clean and chop the leek and scallions. Remove the seeds and white pulp and chop the green pepper. Heat the butter and olive oil in a deep saucepan. Add the onions, garlic, leek, scallions, green pepper, parsley, and dill, and stir over low heat for 10 minutes. *Do not brown* the vegetables. Pour in the Fish consommé, wine and Tabasco sauce and bring to a boil. Lower the heat, and simmer for 30 minutes. Add the shrimps and scallops and boil the soup for 3 minutes. Add the oysters with their juices and turn off the flame immediately. Allow the soup to stand for 2 or 3 minutes. Serve hot with Garlic croutons.

Manhattan Clam Chowder

1½ quarts clams	½ teaspoon thyme
¾ pound salt pork	1 large bay leaf
4 small onions	3 potatoes
4 cups tomatoes	Salt and freshly ground
2½ cups celery	pepper to taste
1½ cups carrots	
3 tablespoons fresh parsley, minced	

SERVES TEN

Place clams in a soup kettle, cover with water, and steam clams open. Collect the juice of the clams and strain through several thicknesses of cheesecloth. Mince the clams very fine.

Render the salt pork in a soup kettle. Remove the residue. Peel and chop the onions and sauté in the pork fat until golden and transparent. Peel, seed, and chop the tomatoes. Add to the onions and simmer for several minutes, stirring constantly. Chop the celery. Peel and chop the carrots. Add the celery, carrots, parsley, thyme, bay leaf, and clam juice (add water to make 2½ quarts). Simmer, covered, for 1 hour.

Peel the potatoes and cut into ½-inch cubes. Add to the soup and simmer for 15 minutes. Add the minced clams and simmer 8 minutes more, or until potatoes are tender. Adjust the seasonings. Crush a handful of pilot crackers and put some in the bottom of each soup bowl. Serve the soup steaming hot.

Vegetable Clam Chowder

10 scallions, chopped

6 medium-sized potatoes, cubed

4 medium-sized carrots. diced

¼ cup butter

2 7-ounce cans minced clams

1½ cups dry white wine

2 cups Fish stock (see page 83)

1 teaspoon dill weed

Salt to taste

2 cups fresh or frozen green peas

3 cups light cream or milk

SERVES EIGHT

Clean and chop the scallions, discarding the roots. Peel and cube the potatoes. Peel the carrots and dice them. Heat the butter in a deep skillet and lightly sauté the scallions. Drain the minced clams and set aside. Add the clam liquid to the skillet, along with the wine, fish stock, potatoes, carrots, dill weed, and salt to taste. Bring to a boil, reduce the heat and simmer, covered, for 15 minutes. Stir in the green peas and continue to simmer for 10 minutes longer. Add the drained clams and the cream. Cook, stirring constantly, until the soup is heated through. Serve immediately.

Creole Gumbo***

2 large onions

3 stalks celery

1 large green pepper

5 pods okra

3 cloves garlic

4 tablespoons bacon fat

1 pound raw shrimp. peeled

1 large cooked chicken breast. boned and cubed

1 pound cooked beef. cubed

1 pound cooked ham, cubed

1 pound cooked pork. cubed

1 pound fresh or frozen crabmeat

1 quart raw oysters (optional)

3 large tomatoes

Boiling water

1 can (6 ounce) tomato paste

1 bay leaf. crumbled

¼ teaspoon thyme

Salt and pepper to taste

¼ cup chopped parsley

1 tablespoon filé powder

2 cups cooked rice

SERVES EIGHT GENEROUSLY

Peel and chop the onions very fine. Rinse the celery stalks and green pepper and chop them coarsely. Slice the okra pods. Peel and mince the garlic cloves. Heat the bacon fat in a large, deep iron kettle, and sauté all these vegetables until the onions are transparent. Stir in the raw shrimp; when they turn pink, add the cubed chicken breast, the other cubed meats, the crabmeat, and oysters. Peel and seed the tomatoes by cutting them in quarters and shaking out the seeds. Chop the tomatoes coarsely and place them in the kettle. Add just enough boiling water to cover these ingredients. Stir in the tomato paste, crumbled bay leaf, thyme, salt, and pepper. Cover the kettle and simmer the gumbo for 1 hour. Add more water if the gumbo seems too thick. Adjust the seasonings and remove from the stove. Stir in the chopped parsley and filé powder just before serving. Place 1 or 2 heaping tablespoons of fluffy cooked rice in each bowl, spoon the gumbo over, and serve immediately.

Kentucky Burgoo***

Since thick and spicy Burgoo needs extensive cooking,
why not make it in two steps? Simmer the meat and
stock one day, and the following day add the vegetables.

1 *pound each: beef, veal, and pork shanks*	1 *cup okra*
1 *pound breast of lamb*	1 *cup fresh or frozen whole corn kernels*
2 *whole chicken breasts*	1 *cup fresh or frozen lima beans*
3 *quarts water*	2 *cups tomato purée*
4 *medium-sized onions*	*Salt*
4 *medium-sized potatoes*	*Cayenne pepper*
4 *medium-sized carrots*	*Worcestershire sauce*
1 *green pepper*	*A-1 sauce*
1 *cup cabbage leaves*	*Tabasco sauce*
½ *cup celery*	½ *cup parsley, chopped*

SERVES EIGHT VERY GENEROUSLY

Arrange the meat and chicken breasts in large, heavy soup kettle. Cover with the water. Bring to a boil, cover, and simmer slowly until the meat is tender enough to fall from the bones (about 3 hours). Remove from the stove and cool. Chop the meat and chicken, discarding the bones. Strain the stock and reheat, adding the chopped meat and chicken. Peel and dice the onions, potatoes, and carrots. Coarsely chop the green pepper and cabbage leaves. Dice the celery and okra. Add these vegetables, along with the corn, lima beans, and tomato purée, to the stock. Stir in the spices and seasoning sauces; use a light touch at first since cooking the Burgoo strengthens the seasonings.

Stir occasionally while the Burgoo slowly simmers for 6 to 7 hours. After it begins to thicken, stir constantly. The Burgoo should be highly seasoned, so add more seasonings, if necessary, along with the chopped parsley, just before serving.

Oyster Stew

1 quart oysters, shucked, with their juice	½ teaspoon whole thyme
3 tablespoons butter	1½ teaspoons salt
5 cups milk	Freshly ground black pepper to taste
2½ cups heavy cream	

SERVES EIGHT

Simmer the oysters with their juice in the butter until the edges of the oysters begin to curl. Scald the milk and cream, and add, together with the thyme and salt, to the oyster mixture. Simmer for 10 minutes but do not allow to boil. Serve hot, sprinkled with pepper.

Cherrystone Clam Stew

70 cherrystone clams	2½ teaspoons Worcestershire sauce
4 cups water	
1½ cups butter	Bottled clam juice or clam broth, if needed
1½ cups celery	
1½ tablespoons onion	Salt and coarsely ground black pepper to taste

SERVES SIX

Soak the clams in several changes of water and scrub thoroughly to remove sand. Arrange them in a deep kettle, add the water, and steam until the shells open. Cool them enough to handle, then cut away the shells and hard sections. Use a fine strainer to remove any particles of shell from the clam broth. (There should be 6 cups of broth in all.) Set the whole clams aside with the broth. Heat the butter. Mince the celery and onions very fine and add, together with 1½ cups of clam broth, to the melted butter. Cook over low heat for 5 to 10 minutes. Stir in the reserved clams, the remaining broth, and the Worcestershire sauce, and simmer until the soup is heated through. Bottled clam juice may be added at this time, if necessary to thin the soup. Serve piping hot, seasoned with salt and pepper.

Clam Chowder with Wine

2 quarts fresh clams	3 cloves garlic, minced
2½ cups white wine	1 bay leaf
½ cup butter	A pinch each rosemary and thyme
2 cups onions, diced	
1½ cups celery, diced	3½ cups heavy cream
1 cup potatoes, diced	3 tablespoons fresh dill, chopped
8 tablespoons butter	
8 tablespoons flour	Tabasco sauce
Bottled clam juice	Salt and pepper to taste

SERVES TEN

Soak the clams in water for an hour to remove any sand. Scrub the shells thoroughly, place them in a saucepan with the wine, cover, and cook until the shells open. Strain the broth and set aside. Remove the clams from the shells and chop them.

Heat the ¼ cup of butter in a skillet. Sauté the diced onions and celery until the onions become transparent. Add the potatoes, brown all the vegetables, and drain them on absorbent paper. Melt the 6 tablespoons of butter in a large kettle and blend in the flour. Stir in the reserved clam broth (adding enough bottled clam juice to make a total of 8 cups) and bring the mixture to a boil, stirring constantly. Add the minced garlic, bay leaf, rosemary, and thyme, and simmer for 10 minutes. Stir in the browned vegetables and simmer until the potatoes are tender. Add the chopped clams, heavy cream, chopped dill, and a dash or two of Tabasco sauce. Bring the chowder to a boil, season with salt and pepper, and serve immediately.

Crab Soup with Fried Toast

1½ pounds cooked crabmeat

3 cups Clam broth (see page 84)

⅓ cup chili sauce

1 tablespoon Worcestershire sauce

½ teaspoon lemon juice

Celery salt and paprika to taste

4 tablespoons butter

4 cups light cream

½ cup sherry

8 slices Fried toast

1½ tablespoons chopped chives

Paprika

SERVES EIGHT

Pick over the crabmeat and discard any hard bits of shell. Place the crabmeat in a soup kettle. Add the clam broth, chili sauce, Worcestershire sauce, lemon juice, and seasonings. Dot with the butter and cook for 2 minutes until the butter melts, stirring constantly. Add the cream and sherry. Heat until the mixture just reaches the boiling point. Pour the soup over pieces of lightly toasted bread which have been fried until golden brown in butter and/or oil. Top each soup bowl with the chopped chives and a sprinkle of paprika. Serve immediately.

Curried Crab Soup

4 cups crabmeat

1½ cup dry sherry

8 tablespoons butter

2 large onions

2½ teaspoons curry powder

4 tablespoons flour, sifted

4 cups cream

4 cups milk

Salt and white pepper to taste

SERVES EIGHT

Place the crabmeat in the top of a double boiler set over hot water. Stir in the sherry and heat slowly. Melt the butter in a heavy skillet. Chop the onion very fine and sauté it gently in the butter until it becomes transparent. Add the curry powder and flour, and stir until the mixture becomes thick and smooth. Stir in the cream, milk, salt, and pepper. Cook, stirring constantly, until the mixture thickens.

Add this cream sauce to the crabmeat and sherry in the double boiler. Heat, stirring occasionally. Serve at once.

Lima Bean Chowder

Here's an easy-to-prepare, attractive, and delicious soup that's certain to please guests of all ages.

⅓ cup slab bacon, finely
   chopped

1 large onion

3 cups Chicken broth (see page
   74)

1 cup carrots, cubed

2 cups potatoes, cubed

2 cups mushrooms, sliced

1½ cups lima beans

¾ teaspoon salt

¼ teaspoon pepper

⅛ teaspoon nutmeg

1 large sprig dill weed

1 clove garlic, peeled and
   whole

1½ cups light cream

1½ tablespoons butter

Paprika

SERVES EIGHT

Fry the bacon in a large, heavy skillet until light brown. Peel and chop the onion, and sauté it in the bacon drippings until it becomes transparent. Add the broth, carrots, potatoes, mushrooms, lima beans, the spices, dill, and garlic. Cover and cook over low heat for 25 minutes. Stir in the cream and simmer for several minutes until the soup is piping hot. Remove the sprig of dill and garlic. Serve the soup hot with a bit of butter and a dash of paprika on each serving.

Oregon Cream of Filbert Soup

1 cup ground filberts

2 cups celery

2 cups onion

6 tablespoons butter

8 tablespoons flour

1 teaspoon Worcestershire
   sauce

1½ teaspoons salt

¼ teaspoon white pepper

4 cups Chicken stock (see page
   74)

4 cups milk

Croutons

SERVES EIGHT

[159]

Shell the nuts. Grind them briefly in an electric blender and reserve. Wash and dice the celery. Peel and dice the onions. Heat the butter slowly in a deep heavy skillet. Stir in the celery and onions and cook until wilted. Blend in the flour, Worcestershire sauce, salt, and white pepper. Add the Chicken stock and milk slowly, stirring constantly. Continue to stir until the soup is heated through. Strain the soup through a sieve and return to low heat. Add the ground filberts. Heat the soup, stirring frequently, but do not allow to boil. Serve piping hot, topped with croutons.

Chilled Cranberry-Claret Soup

The deep, rich color of cranberries seems to enhance the distinctive taste of this unusual soup. A small portion of this frosty favorite would be welcome at any holiday meal.

1 cup cranberries	2 tablespoons sherry
½ cup celery leaves	1 tablespoon butter
1 small onion	⅛ teaspoon each mace and marjoram
6 cups water	
1½ cups claret	Whipped cream
¼ cup cornstarch	8 sprigs parsley
2 tablespoons sugar	

SERVES EIGHT

Pick over and wash the cranberries. Put in a sauce pan with ½ cup water and the celery leaves and cook over low heat until the cranberry skins burst. With the back of a spoon, press the berries and leaves through a fine sieve. Grate the onion.

Put 6 cups of water in a saucepan and stir in the claret, cornstarch, and sugar. Bring to a boil and cook for 2 minutes, stirring constantly. Add the sieved cranberry mixture, sherry, grated onion, butter, and spices. Simmer the soup for 20 minutes, stirring once or twice. Chill the soup well. Serve chilled, garnished with whipped cream and parsley sprigs.

Mexico,
Brazil
and
islands
in the sun

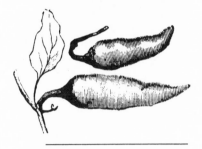

FROM THE GOLDEN VISTAS of sun-drenched Mexico to the island paradises of the lustrous Caribbean comes a wide array of temptingly piquant soups and stews.

Mexican Pan Dulce

1 package dry active yeast	½ teaspoon salt
¾ cup warm water	3 tablespoons butter
3¼ cups all-purpose flour, sifted	2 eggs
1 cup sugar	

MAKES EIGHTEEN

Mix the yeast and warm water and set aside to soften. Combine the sifted flour, sugar, and salt, and sift again into a large bowl. Melt the butter over hot water. Beat the eggs slightly. When the yeast is dissolved, add it to the dry ingredients, together with the butter and eggs. Mix thoroughly to form a smooth dough. Grease another bowl and set the dough into it, turning the dough over once to grease the top. Cover the bowl with a dishtowel and set it in a warm, draft-free place. Allow the dough to rise to double in bulk (approximately 1½ hours).

Dust a pastry board lightly with flour. With your hand, punch the dough down and turn it out onto the board. Knead for 8 to 10 minutes. The dough should be elastic and smooth to the touch. To shape the buns, divide the dough into about eighteen pieces. Roll each piece into a ball between your hands, and arrange about 2 inches apart on a buttered baking sheet. Flatten the buns by pressing each ball with the palm of your hand. Place 1 tablespoon of topping on each bun. Set the baking sheet in a warm, draft-free place, lightly covered with a dishtowel. Allow the buns to rise to double in size (approximately 30 minutes). Bake for 10 minutes in a 400° F. oven. Serve warm for breakfast or afternoon tea.

Topping

1 cup all-purpose flour	1 egg, lightly beaten
¾ cup butter	Pinch of salt
1 cup sugar	2 teaspoons cinnamon

Sift the flour. Melt the butter over hot water. Combine the flour, sugar, butter, egg, salt, and cinnamon. Arrange topping on the buns before baking.

Mexican Cornbread

*Jalapeño peppers, corn, green peppers, and cheese add
variety to this south-of-the-border skillet bread.*

3 eggs

¾ cup vegetable oil (not olive
    oil)

2 cups sour cream

2 teaspoons salt

4 teaspoons baking powder

2¼ cups cornmeal

2 jalapeño peppers

½ green pepper

¼ teaspoon chili powder

2 cups canned, creamed corn

2½ cups sharp cheddar cheese,
    grated

MAKES EIGHT PIECES

Beat the eggs in a large bowl. Add the oil, sour cream, and salt and
mix well. Sift the baking powder with the cornmeal and stir into the
egg mixture. Chop the jalapeño peppers and green pepper and add
with the chili powder and canned corn. Beat with a wooden spoon
for 2 minutes. Grease a heavy skillet and pour in half of the cornbread batter. Sprinkle with half the grated cheese. Top with the
remaining batter and the rest of the cheese. Bake for 45 minutes in
an oven preheated to 350° F.

Tortillas

*The best method for flattening tortillas is by means
of a tortilla press. However, you may use your
hands to shape them if you don't have a press. The tortilla
will not be as thin but will be exceedingly tasty anyway.*

2 cups instant masa (or Masa
    Harina)

1 teaspoon salt

1⅓ cups warm water

MAKES TWELVE

Combine all the ingredients. Mix thoroughly and set aside for
20 minutes. Wet your hands and shape the dough into twelve balls
the size of small eggs. Press the balls down into flat cakes between
two pieces of waxed paper. Fry for 2 minutes on a lightly greased

griddle. When the edges begin to lift, turn over and fry for 2 minutes on the other side. Be careful not to let them brown. Serve steaming hot.

Wheat Tortillas

2 cups all-purpose flour

1 teaspoon baking powder
(optional)

1 teaspoon salt

3 tablespoons shortening

⅔ cup water

MAKES TWELVE

Combine the flour, baking powder, and salt in a large bowl. With two knives held at right angles, cut in the shortening. Add the water, a little at a time, mixing well. The result, should be a fairly stiff dough. Mix in a few additional drops of water if the dough seems too stiff. Shape the dough into twelve small balls. Dust a pastry board lightly with flour. Flatten each ball into a thin tortilla. Fry on a lightly greased griddle for 2 minutes on each side. Turn when the edges start to lift. Be careful not to let them brown. Serve immediately.

Crusty Cuban Loaves

What could be more appetizing with soup than these crusty loaves served hot with butter?

1 package active dry yeast

2¼ cups lukewarm water

1 tablespoon sugar

1½ tablespoons salt

6–7 cups all-purpose flour

1 tablespoon cornmeal

MAKES TWO LOAVES

Dissolve the yeast in the lukewarm water. Stir in the sugar and salt, mixing well. Use a wooden spoon to blend in 1 cup of flour. Beat this mixture thoroughly with the spoon, add another cup of flour, and beat again; continue adding 1 cup of flour at a time until the dough is smooth. Knead the last cup or two of flour into the dough if it becomes too hard to work with the spoon. When the dough is smooth, knead for 5 minutes. Cover the dough and let it rise in a warm, draft-free place until it doubles in size (about 1½ hours). Lightly flour a pastry board. Place the dough on it and divide into two equal portions. Shape each half into a 14-inch tapered loaf, similar to French bread. Sprinkle a baking sheet with the cornmeal. Arrange the loaves on the baking sheet, cover, and allow to rise for 5 minutes. Use a very sharp knife to score the tops of the loaves in two or three places. Brush the tops lightly with water. Set the loaves in the oven *before* turning on the heat. Place a small pan of boiling water on the bottom of the oven. Bake at 400° F. for 45 minutes. The crust should be browned and crunchy when done. Remove the loaves from the baking sheet and cool on wire racks.

Guacamole

1 avocado	½ teaspoon chili powder
2 small ripe tomatoes	10 drops Tabasco sauce
¼ Bermuda onion	2 tablespoons lime juice
1 clove garlic	

Peel, seed, and chop the avocado and the tomatoes. Peel and mince the onion and garlic. Place in a small glass bowl. Add the chili powder, Tabasco sauce, and lime juice, and mix well. Leave the avocado pit in the center of the mixture until serving; this will prevent the Guacamole from discoloring.

Pureé of Corn Soup, Mexican Style

4 cups corn cut from the cob	1 teaspoon chili powder
1 onion	⅛ teaspoon ground cumin
1 clove garlic	Salt and freshly ground pepper to taste
2 cups water	
2 tablespoons butter	Sliced black and stuffed green olives
2 tablespoons flour	
2 cups hot milk	

SERVES EIGHT

[165]

Cut the corn from the cob. Peel and slice the onion and garlic. Place the corn, onion, and garlic in a large saucepan with the water. Cook gently until the corn is tender. Discard the garlic and work as much of the corn through a strainer as possible. Blend the butter and flour into the corn mixture. Just before serving, add the milk, chili powder, and cumin. Reheat. Adjust the seasonings to taste. Garnish with sliced olives.

Puchero

Puchero is to Mexican cooking what Pot-au-Feu is to French. The difference lies in Puchero's imaginative combination of vegetables and fruits. Since it is even more delicious the second day, this recipe will make an ample amount to serve 8 for dinner, with some left over for lunch the following day.

½ cup chickpeas (garbanzos)

¼ pound boneless lamb

¼ pound boneless beef

3-pound chicken

½ pound ham

1 large onion

3 cloves garlic

1 veal knuckle, split

1 teaspoon salt

2 quarts Chicken broth (see page 74)

½ small cabbage

2 small turnips

1 large carrot

2 small zucchini

2 small sweet potatoes

1 cup corn cut from the cob

2 white potatoes, boiled in jackets

3 barely ripe bananas

½ teaspoon coriander seeds, crushed

¼ teaspoon pepper

3 tablespoons oil (or butter)

2 pears

3 peaches

2 limes

SERVES EIGHT

Place the chick peas in a kettle, cover with broth, and soak overnight. Cut the lamb and beef into 2-inch cubes, cut the chicken into serving pieces, and dice the ham. Peel and slice the onion and garlic. Combine the drained chick peas, all the meats, the veal knuckle, onion, garlic, and salt in a large soup kettle. Cover with 2 quarts of cold water and bring to a full boil. Skim off the froth. Lower the heat, cover, and simmer for 45 minutes.

Cut the cabbage into eight wedges. Peel and slice the turnips and carrot. Slice the zucchini. Peel and slice the sweet potatoes. Cut the corn from the cob. Add the cabbage, turnips, carrot, zucchini, sweet potatoes, and corn to the kettle. Cover and simmer about 20 minutes, or until meats and vegetables are tender.

Peel the boiled white potatoes and cut into thick slices. Peel bananas and cut into 2-inch slices. Sauté potatoes, sprinkled with crushed coriander seeds and pepper in oil. Remove the potato slices with a slotted spoon. Keep warm. In the same oil sauté the bananas until golden. Keep warm with the potatoes.

Peel, core, and slice the pears and peaches. Put in a small pan with a little water and poach for 10 minutes. Do not overcook. Drain the fruit.

Adjust the seasonings. Serve each bowl of soup with the juice from one lime wedge and a tablespoon of Guacamole.

Caribbean Fish Soup***

2 medium-sized onions

2 lobster tails

2 pounds fillet of sole

½ cup olive oil

1 cup raw rice

4 medium-sized potatoes, peeled and cut in eighths

3 medium-sized tomatoes, peeled, seeded, and cut in eighths

½ medium-sized cabbage, shredded

2 pimentos, thinly sliced

2 tablespoons tomato paste

2 teaspoons salt

½ teaspoon pepper

½ teaspoon oregano

7 cups water

3 cups dry white wine

SERVES EIGHT

Peel and coarsely chop the onions. Remove the lobster tails from their shells and cut into quarters. Cut the fish fillets in 1-inch pieces. Heat the oil in a deep kettle, and gently sauté the onions until they become wilted. Stir in the fish and lobster pieces along with the rice, and cook, stirring constantly, for 5 minutes over high heat. Add the potatoes, tomatoes, cabbage, pimentos, tomato paste, salt, pepper, and oregano to the kettle. Cover with the water and wine and bring to a boil. Reduce the heat and simmer the soup, covered, until the vegetables are tender (approximately 30 minutes). Serve immediately.

Mexican Pork and Corn Soup

2 large ham hocks

2 quarts Beef broth

6 small tomatoes

4 medium-sized onions

2 cups corn cut from the cob

   Salt to taste

   Relishes:

     chopped avocado

     thinly sliced green onions

     shredded lettuce

     cubed cream cheese

     chopped chilies

     limes cut in wedges

SERVES EIGHT

Place the ham hocks into a soup kettle. Add the beef broth; the peeled, seeded, and chopped tomatoes; and the chopped onions. Simmer, covered, for 3 hours. Cool the soup. Remove the ham hocks and discard the fat and bones. Chop the meat into small pieces. Place the soup in the refrigerator, and when cold, skim off the fat. Add the meat and corn, and simmer 10 minutes. Serve with any of the relishes above.

Conch Gumbo

3 conches

12 crabs

1-pound piece of round steak

1 pound raw shrimp

1½ cups fresh lima beans

1½ cups fresh corn cut from the cob

1 pound okra, cut into thirds

1 small eggplant, cut into ¾-inch cubes

1 6-ounce can tomato paste

1 bay leaf

½ teaspoon thyme

½ teaspoon red pepper

2 cloves garlic, minced

   Salt and pepper to taste

   Water

   Fluffy cooked rice

SERVES EIGHT

Remove the thin skin from the conches and pound until the meat falls apart. Rinse and set aside. Wash the crabs, place them in a large soup kettle, cover with boiling water, and boil until the meat is white and the shells are pink (about 20 minutes). Remove the crabs and plunge them into cold water to cool. Reserve the crab stock. Pick the meat from the crabs, discarding the shells and spongy material. Reserve the crabmeat.

Cut the beef into 1½-inch cubes and add, together with the reserved crabmeat and conches, the shrimp, lima beans, corn, okra, eggplant, tomato paste, bay leaf, thyme, red pepper, garlic, salt, and pepper, to the reserved crab stock. If necessary, add enough water to cover the ingredients. Cover the kettle and simmer slowly for 1¼ hours, or until the soup has a nice consistency. Place 1 or 2 tablespoonfuls of cooked rice in each soup bowl, pour the gumbo over, and serve.

Cristobal Stew

If you are in the mood to try a really unusual recipe,
you might try this unique, thick soup containing
four kinds of meat, yellow squash, potatoes, green
bananas, lime juice, and curry powder. You
may be surprised by its savory goodness.

1½ *pounds lean pork*
1 *pound top round of beef*
½ *slice ham, ½-inch thick*
2 *small bay leaves*
2 *cloves garlic, peeled and crushed*
2 *teaspoons salt*
8 *cups water*
6 *scallions*
2 *yellow squash (about 6½ inches long)*

2 *medium-sized potatoes*
2 *limes*
1 *pound kielbasa*
1½ *tablespoons sugar*
½ *teaspoon curry powder*
¼ *teaspoon ground cloves*
¼ *teaspoon cayenne pepper*
3 *green bananas*

SERVES EIGHT

Trim the fat from the pork, beef, and ham, and cut the meat into 1-inch cubes. Place the meat, bay leaves, crushed garlic, salt, and water in a large kettle. Cover and simmer for 45 minutes. Trim and coarsely chop the scallions. Dice the squash. Peel and cube the potatoes. Squeeze the limes, reserving the juice. Cut the kielbasa into ¼-inch slices. Add half of the chopped scallions, the squash, potatoes, lime juice, kielbasa, sugar, curry powder, cloves, and cayenne pepper to the soup. Cover and boil gently until the potatoes are tender, about 20 minutes. Peel the bananas and cut them into 1-inch pieces. Stir them into the soup, cover, and simmer for 10 minutes longer. Adjust the seasonings, adding more salt or sugar as desired. Serve the stew hot, garnished with the remaining chopped scallions.

Mexican Oatmeal Soup***

This garlic-spiced oatmeal soup is unbelievably delicious.

1⅓ cups rolled oats
8 tablespoons butter
1 large onion, chopped
3 large cloves garlic, crushed

2 large tomatoes, chopped
6 cups Chicken broth
1 teaspoon salt

SERVES EIGHT

Toast the rolled oats in a large heavy skillet over medium heat, stirring frequently, until they are brown but not burned. Place the oats in a bowl and set aside. Melt the butter in the skillet, add the onion, garlic, tomatoes, chicken broth, salt, and the browned oats. Boil for 6 minutes over medium heat. Serve hot.

Guatemalan Bread Soup***

3 tablespoons butter
2 medium-sized onions. peeled and chopped
1 cup tomatoes, peeled, seeded. and chopped
¼ teaspoon sugar
1 tablespoon flour
1 cup water
4 cups Beef consommé (see page 68)

3 cups Chicken broth
1 clove garlic
3 tablespoons vegetable oil
8 slices whole wheat bread. cut in half
3 hard-cooked eggs, peeled and sliced
Grated Parmesan cheese

SERVES EIGHT

Melt the butter in a large heavy skillet. Sauté the onions and tomatoes until the onions are transparent. Sprinkle with sugar. Mix the
flour with the water and stir into the vegetables. Bring to a boil, stirring constantly. Work this sauce through a sieve, add the Beef consommé and chicken broth, and simmer for 15 minutes. Mince the
garlic and sauté in the oil. Cut the crusts from the bread and fry
in the oil until golden brown on both sides. Serve the hot soup in
individual bowls topped with the sautéed bread slices, hard-cooked
egg, and grated Parmesan cheese.

Brazilian Almond Soup

4 tablespoons butter	Cayenne pepper to taste
4 large onions, chopped	8 slices toast
3 cups blanched almonds	Grated Swiss cheese
12 cups Beef stock (see page 68)	

SERVES EIGHT

Heat the butter in a deep soup kettle. Peel and chop the onions and
sauté until golden in the butter. Meanwhile, use an electric blender
to grind the blanched almonds. Stir the Beef stock and the almonds
into the onions. Sprinkle with cayenne pepper and simmer the soup,
covered, for 15 minutes. Just before serving, put one slice of hot
toast in each soup bowl. Cover the toast with grated Swiss cheese
and add the hot almond soup.

Puerto Rican Cashew Soup

1 pound raw cashews	1 cup Chicken stock (see page 74)
7 tablespoons butter	
6 tablespoons chestnut flour	1 teaspoon lemon juice
4 cups milk	2 medium-sized green apples
1 cup light cream	

SERVES EIGHT

[171]

Use an electric blender to grind the raw cashews for 15 or 20 seconds, stopping occasionally to push the nuts down against the blades. Heat the butter in a large saucepan and stir in the ground cashews. Stir rapidly for 1 minute to allow them to brown a little. Blend in the flour. Slowly add the milk, light cream, and Chicken stock to the mixture, stirring constantly. Add the lemon juice. Keep the soup warm over low heat. Peel and thinly slice the apples. Sauté the apple slices in butter for a few minutes on each side. Serve the soup hot in small bowls. Garnish with the sautéed apple slices.

Chilled Almond-Avocado Soup***

This exquisite soup is cool green in color, with a haunting
aftertaste of almonds and avocado.

1 large ripe avocado

2 cups blanched almonds,
  coarsely chopped

5 cups Chicken stock (see page
  74)

1 teaspoon lemon juice

⅛ teaspoon nutmeg
  Salt and white pepper to taste

2 cups light cream

½ cup heavy cream, whipped

Toasted almond slivers

SERVES EIGHT

Peel, seed, and chop avocado. Place in the blender container, together with the chopped almonds and ¼ cup of Chicken stock. Blend until smooth, stopping occasionally to push the contents down against the blades. Add the remaining Chicken stock, the lemon juice, nutmeg, salt, and pepper, and stir. Put in a saucepan and bring to a boil. Lower the heat and simmer for 5 minutes. Stir in the light cream and heat over low flame until soup is hot, but not boiling. Chill for at least 2½ hours. Serve cold in small bowls garnished with a dollop of whipped cream and a sprinkling of toasted almond slivers.

Cream of Peanut Butter Soup

*This sounds strange (and is), but if you dote on peanut
butter, by all means sample this nutty soup topped
with sour cream and crumbled tostados (or Fritos).*

2 *small onions*	2 *cups heavy cream*
3 *stalks celery*	1½ *cups sour cream*
3 *tablespoons butter*	*Salt to taste*
3 *tablespoons flour*	¾ *cup coarsely crumbled*
6 *cups Chicken broth*	*tostados (or Fritos)*
¾ *cup peanut butter*	

SERVES EIGHT

Peel and mince the onions. Wash and coarsely chop the celery. Melt
the butter in a soup kettle and add the onions and celery. Sauté until
the onions are golden and transparent. Stir in the flour and cook a
few minutes longer. Gradually stir in the chicken broth, using the
back of a spoon to press out any lumps. Bring to a boil, mix in the
peanut butter, and continue to stir until the soup boils once more.

Remove the kettle from the stove and let rest for 5 minutes,
spooning off any peanut oil that rises to the top. Reheat and stir in
the cream. Add salt according to your taste. Reheat slightly over
very low heat if necessary. Ladle into individual soup bowls and
place a generous dollop of sour cream on top of each. Sprinkle with
crumbled tostados.

Bean Soup, Cuban Style

¾ *pound dried black beans*	½ *teaspoon powdered cumin*
1 *large ham bone with some meat*	1 *medium-sized tomato*
9 *cups water*	*Salt and freshly ground pepper to taste*
2 *medium-sized onions*	¾ *cup rum*
2 *green peppers*	10 *scallions*
4 *cloves garlic*	5 *hard-cooked eggs*
4 *tablespoons olive oil*	1 *avocado*

SERVES EIGHT

[173]

Cover beans with water and soak overnight. Drain beans, discard water, and place in a soup kettle along with 9 cups of water, the ham bone and diced ham. Cover and cook over very low heat until the beans are tender. Discard the ham bone.

Peel and dice the onions and green peppers. Peel and mince the garlic. Sauté the onions and the green pepper in olive oil until the onions are transparent. Add the garlic and cumin. Combine the onion mixture with the beans and ham and add the tomato, which has been peeled, seeded, and chopped. Simmer the soup gently for 30 minutes, adjust the seasonings, and stir in the rum. Serve hot in small bowls. Arrange the following garnishes in separate bowls to be added to the soup: chopped scallions, sliced hard-cooked eggs, and diced avocado sprinkled with lemon juice.

BREAD AND SOUP FROM THE ROMANTIC MEDI- TERRANEAN

Spain
and
Portugal

WHY IS A particular country considered "romantic"? A good question and one with many answers. A young man with an eye for young women might consider a country with many attractive females a "romantic" country. Strangeness of dress or exotic speech may meet another traveler's concept of romanticism, but for me, there are two important requirements. A country that has a fascinating history as well as a varied and excellent cuisine is a delectable combination that excites my imagination and arouses my taste buds. The nations that border on the Mediterranean abound in both historic and culinary feats of derring-do.

Spain is a country rich in history. Phoenicians, Romans, Goths, Moors, Greeks, Celts, Carthaginians, Iberians, and Vandals conquered Spain and each one left behind something of its cuisine.

The Phoenicians built the great city of Málaga, which in Phoenician meant "the land of salt," and Gades, one of the most important cities of the time. Gades is now called Cádiz, but the vineyards and olive groves planted by the Phoenicians still produce

—as they did in 1000 B.C.—the two most famous of all Spain's exports: excellent sherry and superlative olive oil.

So also, the Moors brought more than graceful architecture to Spain. They introduced almonds, sugar cane, rice, and spices. The saffron, cumin, cloves, and cinnamon so often found in Andalusian cooking originated in the Orient and were gifts from the Moors to their Spanish colonies.

The soups of Spain reflect this multifaceted background. They are usually lightly spiced (don't confuse Mexican cooking with Spanish) and prepared with beautifully fresh vegetables or fish. Their diversity should surprise and delight you.

Saffron Buns

These light and yellow knob-topped buns are especially good.

1 cup milk	½ cup raisins
2 tablespoons sugar	½ cup citron, chopped
½ cup butter	½ teaspoon zest (or outer skin) of lemon, grated
½ teaspoon salt	
1 package dry active yeast	Pinch of whole saffron
¼ cup lukewarm water	1 tablespoon butter, melted
4 cups flour, sifted	1 egg white
2 eggs, beaten	

MAKES TWENTY-FOUR BUNS

Scald the milk in a small saucepan. Stir in the sugar, butter, and salt, and continue to stir until the sugar dissolves. Cool to lukewarm. Dissolve the yeast in lukewarm water and add to the milk mixture. Blend in the sifted flour. Add the beaten eggs, raisins, citron, lemon zest, and saffron. Dust a board lightly with flour and knead the dough for 5 minutes, or until smooth and elastic. Put in a greased bowl. Brush the dough with melted butter. Cover with a dishtowel and allow it to rise in a warm, draft-free place. When the dough has doubled in volume (about 1 hour), punch it down. Shape the dough into twenty-four round buns. Insert small, marble-shaped pieces of dough, dipped in milk, on top of each bun. Place the buns on greased baking sheets at least 2 inches apart. Allow them to rise, uncovered, in a warm, draft-free place until they double in volume (about 45 minutes). Beat the egg white slightly, brush the buns with this mixture, and bake for 20 minutes in an oven preheated to 350° F.

Portuguese Easter Egg Breads***

Easter morning breakfast will be enhanced with these sweet bread baskets containing colorful Easter eggs. The criss-crossed handles of the little breads represent the Cross.

5½–6½ *cups flour, unsifted*	4 *tablespoons butter*
2 *packages dry active yeast*	¼ *cup water*
1¼ *cups sugar*	3 *eggs (at room temperature)*
1 *teaspoon salt*	8 *hard-cooked eggs, with decorated shells*
1 *cup milk*	

MAKES EIGHT BREAD BASKETS

Combine 2 cups of the flour, yeast, sugar, and salt in the large bowl of your electric mixer. Place the milk, butter, and water in a saucepan and heat until the mixture reaches 120°–130° F. The butter will be soft but not melted. Stir the milk mixture into the dry ingredients, a little at a time, blending well after each addition. With the electric mixer, beat for 2 minutes at medium speed, scraping the sides of the bowl from time to time. Stir in the eggs and ¾ cup of flour and beat again at high speed for 2 minutes, scraping the sides of the bowl occasionally. Make a stiff dough by blending in as much of the remaining flour as needed.

Dust a pastry board lightly with flour and knead the dough for 8 to 10 minutes, or until smooth and elastic. Grease a large bowl. Put the dough into it, turning it over once to grease the top. Cover the bowl with a dishtowel and allow the dough to rise in a warm, draft-free place until it doubles in volume (approximately 1 hour). Punch the dough down. Place on a lightly floured board and divide into eight equal pieces. Cut ¼ of the dough from each piece, divide each quarter into half, roll into 6-inch strips, and set aside. Shape the eight larger pieces of dough into flat circles ½-inch thick on greased baking sheets. A decorated Easter egg should be set in the center of each circle. Take two of the 6-inch strips and cross them over each other to form basket handles. Place the crossed strips over an Easter egg and tuck each of the four ends under the circle of dough, pressing slightly so they will stick. Repeat with the remaining 6-inch strips until eight Easter egg bread baskets have been shaped. Allow the bread baskets to rise, covered, in a warm, draft-free place until they double in size (approximately 1 hour). Preheat the oven to 350° F. and bake the bread baskets for 20 to 25 minutes. Then slide them off the baking sheets and cool on wire racks.

Portuguese Holiday Bread

This spicy-sweet bread is very similar to and
will keep as well as fruitcake. It is best served in
thin slices in the traditional Portuguese fashion.

1½ cups butter

1⅔ cups sugar

1 cup light molasses

½ cup honey

⅓ cup minus 1 tablespoon cold mashed potatoes

½ cup candied cherries, chopped

3 tablespoons candied citron, chopped

⅔ cup walnuts, quartered

5 tablespoons sweet sherry

1 teaspoon ground cloves

2½ teaspoons anise seed

2½ teaspoons cinnamon

¼ teaspoon black pepper

1 scant teaspoon baking soda

8½ cups all-purpose flour, sifted

MAKES TWO LOAVES

Place the butter, sugar, molasses, and honey in a large bowl, and cream until light and fluffy. Stir in the mashed potatoes, candied cherries, citron, walnuts, sherry, cloves, anise seed, cinnamon, pepper, and baking soda. Blend in the sifted flour and mix thoroughly. Cut waxed paper to fit the bottoms of two loaf pans. Butter the loaf pans, lay the sheets of waxed paper on the bottom, and spread butter over the sheets. Pour equal amounts of batter into each loaf pan. Bake for 3 hours in a preheated 250° F. oven. Slip the bread from the pans, remove the waxed paper, and cool on a wire rack. Serve warm, cut into thin slices. Or, when it is cold, wrap it in aluminum foil and store.

Marrow Bean Soup

HABAS CALDULDAS

2 cups marrow beans	2 marrow bones
2 medium-sized onions	1 cup tomato sauce
4 tablespoons olive oil	Salt and freshly ground
2½ quarts Beef bouillon (page 68)	pepper to taste

SERVES EIGHT

Cover the beans with water and soak overnight. Boil beans for a few minutes. Remove from the stove and let stand for 1 hour. Peel and chop the onions. Place in a soup kettle and sauté in heated olive oil, until golden and transparent. Add the bouillon, bones, beans, and tomato sauce. Cook over medium heat for about 40 minutes, or until beans are tender. Remove the bones. Adjust the seasonings. Serve hot.

Spanish White Bean Soup

CALDO GALLEGO

3½ quarts water	3 small potatoes
1½ cups white kidney beans	¾ pound smoked garlic sausage (in one piece)
2½-ounce piece of salt pork	Salt and freshly ground
¾ pound ham	pepper to taste
¾ cup onions, chopped	
¾ pound turnip greens	

SERVES EIGHT

Put the water into a soup kettle and bring to a boil over high heat. Add the beans and cook at a rolling boil for 2 minutes. Remove the kettle from heat and allow the beans to soak for about 1 hour. Meanwhile, dice the salt pork and ham. Measure 2½ quarts of water in which the beans were soaked. Combine the bean water, partially cooked beans, salt pork, ham, and onions in the kettle. Place over high heat and bring to a boil, then lower the heat and cook, covered, for about 1½ hours.

Wash the turnip greens and chop coarsely. Peel and dice the potatoes. Add the greens, potatoes, and sausage to the soup. Simmer, covered, for 30 minutes, or until the beans and potatoes are tender. Remove the salt pork and discard. Cut the sausage into ¾-inch pieces and return to the soup. Adjust the seasonings and reheat, if necessary. Serve steaming hot.

Chicken Soup with Saffron Noodles***

SOPA SCIMUNITO AZAFRANADO

A friend gave me this recipe, but she cannot remember where she got it. Because this soup is most unusual as well as delectable, I am including it here. I found it quite worth the time and effort. The gorgeous saffron-colored noodles make this otherwise ordinary chicken soup memorable.

3 teaspoons *whole saffron*
⅔ cup *water*
Pinch *salt*
4 *eggs*
2 *egg yolks*
3 cups *hard flour*
2 teaspoons *olive oil*
2 *medium-sized carrots*
2 *large celery stalks, including leaves*

4–5 sprigs *parsley*
20 *peppercorns*
2½ teaspoons *salt*
3 quarts *water*
16 *chicken wings*
Extra *chicken broth, if needed*
Freshly ground black pepper *to taste*
Minced parsley

SERVES EIGHT

Place the saffron and water in a small skillet and simmer, covered, for 15 minutes. Place the saffron and water (there should be about 3 to 4 tablespoons of liquid) into a blender. Add the pinch of salt, eggs, egg yolks, and 1½ cups of the flour. Blend for 2 minutes on high speed. The mixture should be smooth. Use a rubber spatula to scrape this paste into a large bowl. Let rest for 10 to 15 minutes. Knead in the remaining flour to form a solid ball of dough. Work in the olive oil with your fingers, shape the dough, and let stand for

10 minutes. If you have a pasta machine, set it up for use; if not, dust a pastry board and rolling pin with flour.

Form the dough into a long roll about 1 inch in diameter. Break off a 3-inch piece and, with the rolling pin, roll it out as long as possible. Roll out until the dough is quite thin, about 14 inches long and 2 inches wide. Repeat the process until all the dough is in long, thin strips. Let stand for 35 minutes to dry slightly. Cut into noodles approximately ¼-inch wide. Spread the noodles out on towels in a warm dry place for 1½ to 2 hours, or until they are brittle.

To begin the chicken soup, peel the onions and carrots and chop them into eighths. Wash and trim the celery and chop coarsely. Wash the parsley. Place these vegetables, together with the peppercorns and salt, in a large soup kettle. Cover with 3 quarts of water and bring to a boil. Add the chicken wings, lower the heat and simmer, covered, for 1½ hours. Pick the meat from the bones, chop fine, and add to the strained chicken soup.

Place 2 quarts of water in a saucepan, add the dried noodles, and boil gently for 10 minutes. Drain the noodles and add them to the chicken soup. Bring the soup and noodles to a boil, remove from the heat, and serve immediately, sprinkled with black pepper and parsley.

Spanish Vegetable Soup

MENESTRA DE VERDURAS

3 medium-sized onions ·	2 large cloves garlic, crushed
¾ pound potatoes	½ teaspoon salt
¾ cup olive oil	1½ teaspoons cumin seed
8½ cups Beef broth (see page 68)	1 teaspoon basil
4 small carrots	3 tablespoons parsley, minced
¾ pound green beans, cooked	2 hard-boiled egg yolks
¾ pound spinach	2 tablespoons water
2 small green peppers	Salt and freshly ground pepper to taste

SERVES EIGHT

Peel and chop the onions. Peel and dice the potatoes. In a soup kettle, sauté both vegetables in heated olive oil until the potatoes are brown. Add the Beef broth; the peeled and finely chopped carrots; and the cut green beans. Cook until the potatoes are tender.

Wash and chop the spinach. Dice the green peppers. Add the spinach, green peppers, garlic, salt, cumin seed, basil, and parsley to the soup kettle. Beat together the egg yolks and water to make a paste. Stir this paste into the soup and mix well. Adjust the seasonings. Simmer for 10 minutes. Serve hot.

Quarter-Hour Soup

SOPA AL CUARTO DE HORA

This shellfish and ham soup is a tasty first course
in many Spanish restaurants. Don't be misled
by its name, however. The preparation time
is well over a quarter of an hour.

9 cups Beef broth (see page 68)	½ cup long-grain rice
16 small hard-shelled clams	½ cup dry white wine
1 tablespoon garlic	1 teaspoon lemon juice
1 cup onions	¼ teaspoon whole saffron
3 tablespoons olive oil	12 large shrimp, shelled and deveined
2 small bay leaves	
½ cup smoked (or Serrano) ham	2 hard-boiled eggs, chopped
3 large tomatoes	Salt and freshly ground pepper to taste
4 tablespoons parsley	

SERVES EIGHT

Put Beef broth into a large soup kettle and bring to a boil. Add the clams and cook at a rolling boil until clams open. (Do not use any that remain closed.) Remove the clams and reserve the broth. Take the clams out of the shells and set them aside, discarding shells. Peel and chop the garlic and onions. Put olive oil in soup kettle and heat. Add garlic, onions, and bay leaves and sauté until the onions are golden and transparent.

Chop the ham and peel, seed, and chop the tomatoes. Mince the parsley. Add the ham, tomatoes, and parsley to the garlic and onions and cook quickly until the mixture holds together and the moisture has evaporated. This mixture is referred to as the "sofrito." Remove from the stove and set aside.

Strain the clam and beef broth through a strainer lined with cheesecloth. Stir the sofrito into the broth. Add rice, wine, lemon juice, and saffron. Return to the stove and bring to a boil. Turn burner down and cook over a very low heat until a grain of rice is tender when pressed between the thumb and forefinger (about 15 minutes). (This quarter hour is the source of the recipe's name.) Slice the shrimp and add to the soup, together with the eggs and the clams. Simmer until the shrimp turn pink. Adjust the seasonings. Serve hot.

Spanish Fish Soup I***

GUISADO DE PESCADOS

4 lobster tails	1 jar (8 ounce) stuffed olives
1½ pounds fresh shrimp	1½ teaspoons salt
1½ pounds fillet of sole	⅓ teaspoon black pepper
⅓ cup Spanish olive oil	¾ teaspoon basil
3 cloves garlic	8 cups Fish stock (see page 83)
⅓ cup brandy	
2 medium-sized onions	¾ cup dry white wine
4 medium-sized tomatoes	8 clams
2 cans (6 ounce) tomato paste	

SERVES EIGHT GENEROUSLY

Cut the lobster tails into quarters after removing the shells. Peel and devein the shrimp. Slice the fish fillets into 1-inch pieces. Heat the olive oil in a large, long-handled skillet and briefly sauté the garlic cloves, peeled and cut in half lengthwise. Add the lobster pieces, shrimp, and fish fillets to the skillet, and cook over medium heat for 5 minutes, or until the shellfish turn red. Sprinkle brandy over the fish and shellfish and set afire, shaking the skillet continuously. When the flames die away, remove the fish and shellfish and reserve. Discard the garlic cloves. Peel and coarsely chop the onions and sauté until lightly browned in the oil remaining in the skillet. Peel the tomatoes, seed them by cutting into quarters and shaking out the seeds, and chop them coarsely. Add the tomatoes, tomato paste, olives, salt, pepper, and basil to the onions; cover with the Fish stock and wine, and simmer, loosely covered, for 20 minutes. Carefully scrub the clams and add them to the simmering broth. When the shells open, return the reserved fish and shellfish to the skillet only long enough to heat through. Serve piping hot.

Spanish Fish Soup II

GUISADO DE PESCADOS

3 cloves garlic

2 medium-sized onions

½ cup olive oil

3 medium-sized tomatoes

2 leeks, including 3 inches green top

2 carrots

2 quarts Fish stock (see page 83)

½ teaspoon whole saffron

3 lobster tails, cut in thirds

½ pound scallops, shelled

1 pound halibut, cut in small pieces

4 small red mullets

½ pound shrimp in shell

⅓ cup pernod, or ¼ teaspoon powdered anise

⅓ cup dry white wine

Salt and freshly ground pepper to taste

Croutons (see page 86)

Mayonesa

SERVES EIGHT

Peel and mince the garlic and onions. Place in a soup kettle and sauté in ¼ cup hot olive oil until the onions are golden and transparent. Peel, seed, and chop the tomatoes. Add to the onions and garlic and cook for a few minutes.

Slice the leeks. Peel and slice the carrots. Add the leeks and carrots, along with the Fish stock and saffron to the soup kettle. Boil over high heat for 10 minutes. Using the remaining olive oil, sauté the lobster tails, scallops, halibut, and red mullets until the lobster shells turn bright red and the fish has browned lightly. Add the shrimp and continue cooking until they turn pink. Put all of the fish, shellfish, anise liqueur, and wine into the soup kettle and simmer about 5 minutes. Adjust the seasonings.

Arrange the fish attractively on a serving platter. Pour the broth into individual soup bowls, top with Croutons, and serve as a first course. Follow with the fish on the serving platter, and serve with cold Mayonesa.

Spanish Mayonnaise

MAYONESA

A slice of bread, a tablespoon of Mayonesa,
and cold, cooked, shelled shrimp, mussels,
or scallops makes an outstanding sandwich.

1½ teaspoons French mustard
2 egg yolks
½ teaspoon salt
2 cups olive oil (highest quality)

1½ teaspoons lemon juice
A pinch each cayenne and black pepper

Place the French mustard, egg yolks, and salt in a blender container and blend at low speed while you add the oil a drop at a time. Slowly, as the mayonnaise begins to thicken, add the oil in a very thin stream. When quite thick, add the lemon juice and the peppers. Continue to add the remaining olive oil. Chill well.

Spanish Vegetable Beef Soup

10 cups Beef bouillon (see page 68)
2 pounds stewing beef, cut in 1-inch pieces
1 veal knuckle
1 pound Spanish (or Italian) sausages, sliced
2 cups chick peas, partially cooked

4 cloves garlic
1 teaspoon crumbled bay leaves
1 teaspoon salt
½ teaspoon freshly ground black pepper
6 medium-sized potatoes
1 pound fresh spinach

SERVES EIGHT

Place the Beef bouillon in a deep soup kettle. Add the beef, veal knuckle, sausage, and chick peas. Peel and slice the garlic cloves. Add garlic, bay leaves, salt, and papper. Bring the bouillon to a boil, cover, and simmer for 1½ to 2 hours. Peel the potatoes and cut into quarters. Wash the spinach thoroughly. Add potatoes and spinach to the soup and continue to simmer, covered, for 20 minutes, or until the potatoes are tender. Remove the veal knuckle. Adjust the seasonings and serve piping hot.

Green Chili Soup

SOPA DE CHILIES POBLANOS

4¾ cups canned milk green
    chilies (or fresh if
    available)*

½ cup scallions with 3 inches
    of green top

8 tablespoons butter

4 tablespoons flour

4 cups Chicken stock (see page
    74)

3 cups light cream

Salt and freshly ground
    pepper to taste

SERVES EIGHT

Drain the chilies and purée in a blender. Set aside. Peel and chop the scallions very fine. Sauté the scallions in the butter and blend in the flour. Add the puréed chilies. Cook over medium heat, stirring constantly, for about 3 minutes. Blend in the Chicken stock. Stir in the light cream and cook over very low heat for about 10 minutes, stirring often. Adjust the seasonings and serve hot.

* If fresh chilies are used, use a fork and hold them over a flame so that the skins will blister. Put them in a bowl and cover with a damp cloth. When cool, peel, remove seeds, cut in chunks, and purée in blender.

Spiced Garlic Soup

SOPA DE AJO

2 tablespoons garlic

½ cup olive oil

3 cups coarse dry French (or
    Italian) breadcrumbs

1 tablespoon paprika

¼ teaspoon cayenne pepper

7½ cups Beef bouillon (page 68)

3 egg yolks

Salt and freshly ground
    pepper to taste

1 tablespoon fresh parsley

SERVES EIGHT

Peel and mince the garlic. Place the olive oil in a soup kettle and sauté the garlic until it is light yellow. Add the breadcrumbs, increase the heat, and lightly brown. Add paprika, cayenne pepper, and Beef bouillon, and cook over high heat until the soup comes to a boil. Lower the heat and cook slowly for 30 minutes more.

Beat the soup until the breadcrumbs are smooth. Add the beaten egg yolks a little at a time, stirring well after each addition. Let the soup simmer, stirring constantly for a few minutes. Do not boil or it will curdle. Adjust the seasonings. Serve hot. Chop the parsley very fine and serve as a garnish.

Tomato-Eggplant Soup

This zesty eggplant soup is garnished with meatballs!

3 small eggplants	Salt and pepper to taste
5 tablespoons butter	½ . pound veal, finely ground
5 medium-sized tomatoes	2 teaspoons onion, minced
1 large onion	⅛ teaspoon nutmeg
1½ cloves garlic, minced	Pinch of oregano
2 bay leaves, crushed	Salt and pepper to taste
Pinch of marjoram	Flour
½ cup rice	Garlic croutons (see page 86)
2½ quarts Beef stock (see page 66)	2 tablespoons chopped chives

SERVES EIGHT

Peel the eggplants and cut into 1-inch cubes. Soak the cubes in salted water for 20 minutes and then drain. Heat the butter in a large skillet, add the eggplant cubes and cook slowly, covered, for 30 minutes. Stir the eggplant occasionally to brown evenly. Peel, seed, and chop the tomatoes. Peel and chop the onion very fine. Add the tomatoes, onion, garlic, bay leaves, and marjoram to the eggplant. Cook over low heat for 15 minutes, stirring occasionally, until the tomatoes are well mixed with the eggplant.

Add the rice, Beef stock, salt, and pepper. Cover and simmer the soup for 40 minutes. Combine the ground veal with the minced onion, nutmeg, oregano, salt, and pepper. Form into tiny meatballs

[189]

and roll in flour. Force the soup through a coarse sieve, then bring it to a boil. Drop the meatballs into the soup and boil gently for 15 minutes. Serve hot, garnished with Garlic croutons and chopped chives.

Spanish XIV Century Soup

SOPA CASTELLANA SIGLIO XIV

4 *slices white bread*	1½ *teaspoons paprika*
6 *ounces ham*	8 *eggs*
3 *cloves garlic*	*Salt and freshly ground*
2 *small onions*	*pepper to taste*
½ *cup olive oil*	
8 *cups Chicken stock (see page 74)*	

SERVES EIGHT

Tear the bread into crumbs. Chop the ham very fine. Peel and chop the garlic and onions very fine. Heat the olive oil in a soup kettle and add the breadcrumbs, ham, garlic, and onions. Sauté until the onions are golden and transparent and the breadcrumbs lightly browned. Gradually add the chicken broth and paprika. Cook for 10 minutes over very low heat. Adjust the seasonings.

Pour the soup into ovenproof soup bowls. Break 1 egg into each serving of soup and bake for 10 minutes in an oven preheated to 400° F. The egg whites should be firm. Remove from the oven and serve immediately.

Portuguese Caldo Verde

½ *pound linguica (or any smoked pork sausage with garlic)*	12 *cups water*
	4 *teaspoons salt*
1 *pound kale*	*Freshly ground pepper*
6 *medium-sized potatoes*	1 *cup olive oil*

SERVES EIGHT

Prick the sausages with a fork in several places. Place in a saucepan and add enough water to cover. Bring to a boil, then lower the heat and cook for 20 minutes. Remove sausages from the pan, slice, and reserve. Pick over and wash the kale. With a sharp knife, remove the stems. Cut kale into shreds. Peel and slice the potatoes. Place the potatoes in a soup kettle and add the water. Cook over high heat until water boils. Then lower the heat and simmer until the potatoes are tender. Remove them from the liquid with a slotted spoon and mash them until smooth. Stir the mashed potatoes into the potato water and blend well. Add salt, pepper, and olive oil. Raise the heat and bring to a boil.

Put the shredded kale into the boiling soup and boil for 3 or 4 minutes. Add the sliced sausage and cook over medium heat until they are warm. Adjust the seasonings. Serve hot.

Portuguese Chicken Soup with Lemon and Mint

CANJA

4-pound stewing chicken with
   the gizzard, liver, and heart

10 cups Chicken stock (page 74)

1 cup onions

2 teaspoons salt

3 tablespoons long-grained rice

6 tablespoons lemon juice

⅔ cup fresh mint, minced

SERVES EIGHT

Quarter the chicken. Chop the gizzard, liver, and heart very fine. In a large soup kettle, combine all of the chicken parts and the chicken broth. Bring to a boil and skim off the froth from time to time. Peel and chop the onions very fine. Add onions and salt to the soup and simmer, partially covered, for 1½ to 2 hours.

Add the rice and cook over a very low heat until the rice and chicken are tender. Remove the chicken from the soup, discard the skin and bones, and cut the meat into julienne strips. Add the chicken strips and lemon juice to the soup and reheat. Place a little mint in each bowl before pouring in the soup.

Bread and Fish Soup, Malaga

4 pounds halibut	4 medium-sized tomatoes
2 tablespoons olive oil	8 cups Fish stock (see page 83)
1 cup blanched almonds	1 teaspoon paprika
2 slices white bread, quartered	Salt and pepper to taste

SERVES EIGHT

Place the halibut in a shallow pan, cover with Fish stock, and poach over a medium-low heat. Remove fish and keep warm. Strain the stock into a bowl and set 2 cups of it aside. Heat olive oil in saucepan and sauté the almonds and bread in the oil until golden. Remove from the pan and reserve. Peel, seed, and chop the tomatoes and sauté them in the same pan used for the bread and nuts, adding more oil if necessary.

Whirl the almonds, bread, and tomatoes in a blender until they become a fine powder. Stir this powder into the Fish stock and add paprika. Adjust the seasonings. Simmer soup for 3 minutes, or until hot. To serve, pour over squares of fish.

Gazpacho

2 small onions	¼ cup red wine vinegar
2 medium-sized cucumbers	5½ cups water
3 cloves garlic	1 tablespoon salt
5 medium-sized tomatoes	1 tablespoon tomato paste
1 medium-sized green pepper	3 tablespoons olive oil
3½ cups French breadcrumbs	

GARNISHES:

chopped green peppers	garlic
chopped onions	croutons
chopped cucumbers	freshly ground pepper

SERVES EIGHT

Peel and chop the onions, cucumbers, and garlic. Peel, seed, and chop the tomatoes. Wash and chop the green pepper. Remove the crusts and tear the French bread into small bits. Place the chopped vegetables, breadcrumbs, wine vinegar, water, and salt into a bowl. Add to blender, a little at a time, until it is all puréed. Return to the bowl and beat in the tomato paste and olive oil.

Place the soup, tightly covered, in the refrigerator and chill for 2 hours or more. Ladle cold soup into chilled soup bowls. Serve with any of the garnishes listed above.

France,
the
fabulous
provider

THERE IS, IN TRUTH, a longing known by every lover of good food . . . it is a yearning to visit, or to return to, France. The gourmet who has not yet visited this gastronomic paradise may daydream, while he pores over his French cookbook, that one day he can actually reach those fabled restaurant tables in Bresse or Alsace or Provence. Dreams of Périgord and Burgundy and Champagne may dance through his head like sugarplums, but this is often an ethereal yearning soon forgotten.

The longing of the visitor who has actually known France, who has experienced her wonders, is a deep and consuming one. We are gastronomic sailors with the siren song of "La Belle" luring us inexorably back to the bouquet of satisfactions that is France. It is a country of rich red and pale golden wines, of pungent cheeses, of truffles, of fabulous sauces, and of incomparable chefs, none of whom seems capable of cooking badly.

Understandably, then, the soups of France are magnificent. Stop at the most unpretentious restaurant and you will be rewarded with an excellent pot-au-feu or a bouillabaisse beyond the imagination. Even an ignominious wayfarer's stop (comparable to our "hamburger joint") may serve a Potage Saint-Germain of note along with the ever present sandwich of petit pain with jambon and Dijon mustard. And the three star restaurants . . . incredible!

Here are soup and bread recipes gleaned from my pilgrimages to the culinary parent of the world. For if an American gourmet's father is the U.S.A., his or her mother is most surely France.

French Bread***

*Hot, crusty, fine-textured French bread is a natural
accompaniment to any soup—be it hot or cold, hearty
or delicate. If your oven isn't large enough for
super-long loaves, why not bake them in semicircles
as I do? One semicircle placed inside the other
makes a very impressive, large oval loaf.*

2 packages dry active (or cakes of compressed) yeast

2½ cups warm water (105°–115°F.)

1 tablespoon salt

1 tablespoon melted butter

6½–7 cups flour, unsifted

1½ tablespoons cornmeal

1 egg white

1 tablespoon cold water

MAKES TWO LOAVES

In a large mixing bowl dissolve the yeast in warm water. Stir gently. Add the salt and butter. Stir in 2½ cups of the flour. Mix at medium speed of an electric mixer for 2 minutes until well blended. Blend in 1 more cup of flour, and mix at high speed for 2 minutes, scraping the bowl from time to time. The result will be a fairly sticky dough. Add enough of the remaining flour so that the dough becomes fairly stiff. Knead for a few minutes on a lightly floured board. Place the dough in a large greased bowl, turning it over once to grease the top. Cover with a cloth and let it rise in a warm, draft-free place until doubled in size (approximately 1 hour). To tell whether it has risen enough, press the tips of two fingers quickly into the dough (about ½ inch). If the dents stay, the dough is ready to punch down.

Punch the dough down and turn it out on a lightly floured board. Knead for a minute or two, then divide the dough in half. Shape each half into a long tapered loaf. Butter a baking sheet and sprinkle the sheet with the cornmeal. Place the loaves on the baking sheet or, if the sheet is not long enough, shape both into semicircles and place one inside the other. Cover loosely with a linen towel and set in a warm, draft-free place. Allow the loaves to double in bulk (about 1 to 1½ hours). Score the surfaces by making several diagonal cuts ¼-inch deep with a sharp knife. Brush lightly with egg white moistened with 1 tablespoon cold water. Preheat the oven to 400° F. Place a pan of hot water on the bottom of the oven, and bake the bread until crusty and golden brown (approximately 55 minutes). Remove from the oven, slide the bread from the baking sheet, and cool on a wire rack. Serve warm as a hearty accompaniment to any soup.

Croissants

1 package dry active yeast

¼ cup warm water

1½ tablespoons sugar

1 teaspoon salt

2 cups unbleached flour

2 tablespoons vegetable oil
(but not peanut, olive, or
other highly flavored oil)

⅓ cup lukewarm milk

8 tablespoons cold butter

1 egg

½ teaspoon water

MAKES TWELVE

Stir the yeast into the warm water, add ½ teaspoon of the sugar and ¼ teaspoon of the salt, and set aside to allow the yeast to soften for 5 minutes. Meanwhile, combine the flour with the remaining sugar and salt. Add the oil. Blend in the dissolved yeast and the milk. Mix thoroughly. The result will be a somewhat soft and sticky dough. If the dough seems stiff, add a bit more milk. Using your hands, push the dough into a ball and lift from the bowl. Slap it down on a pastry board, push it together again, lift it up, and continue to slap it down until the dough becomes fairly elastic. Knead the dough vigorously for a few minutes. It should be smooth and elastic. If it does not come clean from your hands, work in a little additional flour. Set the dough in a bowl, cover with a clean linen towel, and allow it to double in volume at room temperature (approximately 1–1½ hours).

Punch the dough down. Turn out on a pastry board and flatten with your hands. Wrap the dough in waxed paper and place in the refrigerator for 30 minutes to chill. Meanwhile, begin to work the cold butter into a flat cake, free from lumps and malleable. The heat of your hands may make the butter soft and runny, so work quickly. Take the cold dough from the refrigerator and flatten it with your hands into a large rectangle. Place the butter in the center of the rectangle. Fold the four sides of the dough to seal in the butter completely. Dust your rolling pin and pastry board lightly with flour. Roll the butter evenly into the dough by shaping and rolling the buttered dough into a rectangle twice as large as the original one. Take one end of the rectangle and fold it ⅓ over to the center and then fold the other end ⅓ to the center, making three layers. Turn one narrow open end of the dough toward you. Roll it out again into a long rectangle, fold it over again, and turn it so that the other narrow open end is toward you. This is a classic procedure called a "turn," which should be performed once more. Fold a final time into three layers, dust lightly with flour, and wrap in waxed paper. Refrigerate for several hours or overnight.

Divide the dough into two equal portions. Roll out each portion into a 5x15-inch rectangle about ⅛-inch thick. Cut into three 5-inch squares, and slice each square diagonally to form two triangles. Fold the point of a triangle over, then begin at the base of the triangle and roll toward the folded point. Shape the ends into crescents and place on a buttered baking sheet, pointed side down. Continue until all the dough has been used. Cover lightly with a linen towel, and allow the croissants to rise at room temperature until they are nearly double (approximately 1 to 1½ hours). Preheat the oven to 475° F. Brush the croissants with an egg mixed with ½ teaspoon of water, and bake on the middle rack of the oven for 10 to 12 minutes, or until they are a light golden brown. Remove from the oven and cool on a wire rack before serving.

Croissant dough must always be kept as cold as possible because of its high butter content. Keep any portions you are not immediately working with in the refrigerator. The dough may be frozen at any step after the butter has been added, as may the finished croissants when cooled.

Basic Brioche Dough

2 *packages dry active yeast*
½ *cup minus 2 tablespoons*
  warm water
2 *teaspoons salt*
2 *tablespoons sugar*

4 *cups all-purpose flour*
6 *large eggs*
3 *sticks cold butter (¾ pound)*

Stir the yeast into the warm water, add 1 teaspoon of the salt and 1 tablespoon of the sugar, and set aside for 5 minutes to allow the yeast to soften. Measure the flour and place in a large bowl. Add the remaining salt and sugar, the eggs, and the dissolved yeast. Mix all ingredients thoroughly to make a soft sticky dough. Lift the dough from the bowl with your hands and slap it down firmly on a pastry board. Push the dough together, then lift and slap it down again vigorously. Put it together again and continue this lifting, slapping, and pushing technique until the dough begins to stiffen and take shape. Strenuous work at this point pays dividends: your brioches will be feather light. Knead the dough energetically when it is stiff, continuing to knead until elastic and smooth enough to pull away from your hands.

Work the butter with your hands until it is malleable but still slightly cold. The butter should not be melting. Spread it smoothly on the pastry board, break off a small piece with your fingers, and incorporate it into the dough, kneading it in as thoroughly as possibile. Continue to work the butter in until it has all been used up and the dough becomes smooth and elastic again. Set the dough in a large bowl. With a sharp knife, cut a large "X" on the top surface of the dough. Cover with a slightly moistened towel from which all excess water has been squeezed. Allow the dough to rise for about 2 hours at not more than 70° F. When the dough has risen to about ⅔ of its original bulk, punch it down and turn it out of the bowl. Knead briefly. Dust the dough lightly with flour and place it back into the bowl. Cover and allow it to rise again—this time in the refrigerator—to double in volume (about 4 hours). Punch the dough down again. Use to make Petites brioches and Brioche à tête.

Petites Brioches

Basic brioche dough (see page   1 teaspoon water
198)

1 egg

MAKES SIXTEEN

Prepare the Basic brioche dough as directed. When the dough has doubled in bulk, remove it from the refrigerator and punch it down. Butter sixteen muffin tins or small pyrex baking cups. Sprinkle with flour, shaking out any excess. Divide the chilled dough into sixteen pieces. Work with only a few pieces at a time, keeping the rest chilled. Cut ¼ off each individual piece and set aside. Roll each larger piece into a ball and set it in a buttered and floured muffin tin. Roll each smaller piece into a teardrop shape. Gently poke a small hole in the exact center of each ball and insert a teardrop in each, pointed end down. Repeat until all the brioches have been shaped. Cover lightly with waxed paper and allow to rise at room temperature until almost doubled (approximately 1 hour). Mix an egg thoroughly with 1 teaspoon of water, and lightly glaze the surface of each brioche, taking care not to allow the glaze to seep down under the teardrop. Set the muffin tins on the middle rack of an oven preheated to 475° F. Bake for 15 minutes, or until golden brown. Remove from the oven and cool on a wire rack.

Brioche À Tête

Basic brioche dough (see page   1 teaspoon water
198)

1 egg

MAKES ONE LARGE BRIOCHE

Prepare the Basic brioche dough as directed. When the dough has doubled in bulk, remove it from the refrigerator and punch it down. Lightly butter and flour a 9-inch brioche mold or a very large fluted baking mold. Shape ¾ of the dough into a large ball. Set it in the mold and gently poke a 2-inch hole in the center of the ball. Roll the

[199]

remaining ¼ of the dough into a teardrop shape. Widen the hole in the larger piece at its opening and set the teardrop, pointed side down, into the hole, smoothing the dough against the teardrop. Cover lightly with waxed paper and allow to rise at room temperature until almost doubled (about 1 hour). Glaze the surface of the brioche with a mixture of 1 egg beaten lightly with 1 teaspoon of water. Take care not to let the glaze seep down where the teardrop is joined to the ball. Set the Brioche à tête on the middle rack of an oven preheated to 475° F. Bake for 20 minutes until it begins to brown; then lower the heat to 350° F. and allow to bake for an additional 30 minutes. Test for doneness by inserting a thin bladed sharp knife in the center. If the knife comes out clean, remove the brioche from oven and cool on a wire rack.

Savarin

1 package dry active yeast	8 tablespoons chilled butter
½ cup warm water	1 tablespoon sugar
1½ cups all-purpose flour, sifted	½ teaspoon salt
2 large eggs	Heavy cream, whipped
½ cup lukewarm milk	

SERVES EIGHT

Soften the yeast in the warm water for 5 minutes. Meanwhile sift and measure the flour. Place the flour in a bowl and add the yeast mixture, eggs, and ¼ cup of the lukewarm milk. Using your hand, work the mixture well until it is elastic and smooth. Stir in as much of the remaining ¼ cup of lukewarm milk as is necessary to make a soft dough. Set the dough in a warm place, cover with a linen towel, and let it rise until it is double in volume (about 45 minutes). Place the butter on a pastry board and work it until the butter is malleable but not melted. Punch the dough down after it has doubled and knead in the butter. Mix in the sugar and salt. Grease a ring mold and arrange the dough so that it half fills the mold. Cover the dough and set it in a warm, draft-free place to rise until it almost reaches the top of the mold. Preheat the oven to 425° F. and bake the Savarin for 15 to 20 minutes, or until it turns golden brown. Remove it from the oven; loosen and turn it out of the mold to cool on a wire rack. Fill the center of the mold with whipped cream, and spoon hot rum syrup over the top of the Savarin. Serve warm.

HOT RUM SYRUP

1 cup sugar	3 tablespoons rum
1 cup water	

Boil the sugar and water together for 5 minutes, stirring until the sugar dissolves. Cool a little and add the rum. Pour over the warm Savarin.

Babas

Savarin recipe (see page 200)	2 tablespoons dried currants
1 tablespoon raisins	

SERVES EIGHT

Prepare the dough as in the Savarin recipe. After the butter has been worked in, add raisins and dried currants to the dough. Proceed as directed. Babas can be baked in a ring mold or as individual Babas in popover pans.

Hearthcake

LA FOUACE

This is a truly wonderful bread. It is beautifully nutty and salty and really excellent when served warm with butter.

1 package dry active yeast	¾ cup walnuts
⅓ cup lukewarm water	½ cup sweet butter, softened
4½ cups unbleached white flour	½ cup whole wheat flour (approximately)
1¼ tablespoons salt	Cornmeal, coarse
1½ cups lukewarm milk	

MAKES ONE LOAF

Mix the yeast into the lukewarm water and allow it to soften. Meanwhile, measure the unbleached white flour into a large bowl and add the salt. Make a well in the center of the flour with your fist. Place the softened yeast into the well and add the lukewarm milk. Stir the dough thoroughly. Chop the walnuts coarsely. Blend the walnuts and softened butter into the dough. Sprinkle the whole wheat flour on a pastry board and turn the dough out onto the board. Knead in as much whole wheat flour as is necessary for the dough to hold its shape. Place the dough in a large bowl, cover it, and allow it to rise in a warm, draft-free place until it doubles in size (about 2 hours). Punch the dough down. Knead it for 5 minutes on a very lightly floured board. Shape it into a ball and place it on a baking sheet lightly sprinkled with coarse cornmeal. Press the dough down slightly to form a rounded loaf. Cover and allow it to rise for 20 minutes. Make a shallow slash in the top of the bread with a very sharp knife. Place the baking sheet on the middle shelf of an oven preheated to 425° F. Fill a pan with hot water and set it on the bottom of the oven. Bake the bread for 30 minutes at 425° F. Remove the hot water, reduce the oven temperature to 300° F., and bake 30 minutes longer. Slide the bread from the baking sheet and cool it on a wire rack.

Gougère

This deliciously rich pastry calls the French
region of Burgundy home. Serve it direct from
oven to accompany any simple soup.

⅓ cup butter

1 cup milk

¼ teaspoon salt

1 cup flour, sifted

4 large eggs

1 tablespoon heavy cream

½ cup Swiss (or Gruyère) cheese, shredded

⅛ teaspoon dry mustard

3 tablespoons Swiss (or Gruyère) cheese, diced

SERVES EIGHT

Heat the butter and milk in a large saucepan over a low flame. When the butter melts, blend in the salt and the flour, stirring constantly and energetically until the mixture comes away from the side of the pan. Beat one egg at a time into the dough. Remove the pan from the stove after adding each egg so the dough does not burn, beating constantly while on and off the stove. Thoroughly mix the heavy cream, the shredded cheese, and the dry mustard into the thick dough after removing it from the stove. Grease a 10-inch glass pie plate and mound the mixture in it. Garnish the top with the diced cheese and bake it in an oven preheated to 375° F. After 30 minutes, turn the heat down to 350° F. and bake 10 minutes longer (40 minutes in all). Serve hot with lots of butter.

Cream of Pea Soup

POTAGE SAINT-GERMAIN

1½ *pounds quick-cooking, dried split peas*

3 *quarts chicken broth*

3 *small carrots*

2 *small onions*

3 *tablespoons butter*

1 *large leek*

5 *lettuce leaves*

1½ *teaspoons sugar*

½ *teaspoon salt*

2 *cups fresh green peas, cooked*

1¼ *cups heavy cream*

1 *tablespoon butter*

Salt and pepper to taste

SERVES EIGHT

Rinse the dried split peas, drain, and place in a large soup kettle. Add 3 quarts of chicken broth, bring to a boil, and simmer, with heat reduced, for 10 minutes. Skim the froth from the top. Peel and grate the carrots and onions. Melt the butter in a skillet. Sauté the grated vegetables until golden. Wash and chop the leek and lettuce leaves very fine, and add to the sautéed vegetables. Cook over low heat for 10 minutes. Stir the vegetable mixture into the broth, together with the sugar and salt. Simmer the soup until the split peas are tender (about 2 hours). Rub the fresh-cooked peas through a fine sieve. Force the soup mixture through the same sieve. Return the mixture to the kettle and stir in the heavy cream. Heat the soup to the boiling point, stirring occasionally. Just before serving, add the butter and sprinkle with salt and pepper. Serve hot, with a garnish of hot, buttered croutons.

Cream of Lettuce Soup

SOUPE DE LAITUE

4 tablespoons butter

1½ cloves garlic, minced

4 teaspoons parsley, minced

4 teaspoons fresh tarragon, minced

1½ cup onion, chopped

2 cups tightly packed, finely shredded romaine lettuce

1½ bunches watercress, finely chopped

4 cups Beef stock (see page 67)

2 egg yolks

2 cups light cream

½ teaspoon salt

⅛ teaspoon pepper

SERVES EIGHT

Melt the butter in a heavy skillet. Sauté the garlic, parsley, tarragon, and onion until the onion is transparent. Add the lettuce and the watercress, and stir over low heat for 5 minutes. Stir in the Beef stock (or consommé) and simmer uncovered for 25 minutes. Beat the egg yolks and cream together with several tablespoons of soup. Add this to the soup and stir over a low flame until the soup is slightly thickened. Sprinkle in the salt and pepper. Serve immediately.

Vegetable Soup with Artichokes Périgourdine

Périgord is soup country. It is not unusual for Périgourdin farmers to sip soup at breakfast, as well as at lunch and dinner. Although we automatically think of foie gras and truffles in connection with this section of France, the following soup is also typical.

3 medium-sized onions, peeled and sliced

2 tablespoons bacon fat

1½ tablespoons flour

2 small garlic cloves, minced

4 medium-sized tomatoes

2 quarts water

4 artichoke bottoms, cooked

Toasted French bread

SERVES EIGHT

Sauté the onions in the bacon fat until they are lightly browned. Add the flour and minced garlic, and stir over medium heat for

5 minutes. Stir in the peeled, seeded, and chopped tomatoes and cook until soft. Mash the cooked tomatoes. Add the water, mix well, and boil gently for 30 minutes. Stir in the diced artichoke bottoms and cook 20 minutes more. Serve hot over toasted French bread.

Basque Vegetable Soup

GARBURE BASQUAISE

*One of the heartiest meals in a bowl is this meat-laden
vegetable soup from the Basque country.*

1½ cups dried white pea beans	1 red pepper
2 large onions	2 teaspoons whole dried thyme
5 large cloves garlic	2 teaspoons salt
1 medium-sized yellow turnip	1 whole Polish sausage (kielbasa)
4 carrots	½ small head cabbage
4 medium-sized potatoes	Garlic croutons (see page 86)
5 leeks	Red wine
1 large green pepper	
1-pound piece of slab bacon	
Bones and breast meat of a roast duck*	

SERVES EIGHT VERY GENEROUSLY

Soak the dried pea beans overnight. Peel and chop the onions, garlic, turnip, carrots, and potatoes. Wash and trim the leeks and cut into 1-inch pieces. Discard the seeds and white pulp from the green pepper and cut into julienne strips.

Place the pea beans, onions, garlic, turnip, carrots, potatoes, leeks, green pepper, slab bacon, duck bones and meat, whole red pepper, thyme, and salt in a large soup kettle. Add water to cover. Bring to a boil and cook until the vegetables are tender and the bacon is cooked through. Add the whole kielbasa and simmer the soup for 30 minutes. Remove the duck bones and red pepper and discard them. Reserve the meat.

Discard the core and limp outer leaves of the cabbage; shred

* The bones and meat from a small roasting chicken may be substituted, but only if absolutely necessary.

the rest. Cut the duck meat into julienne strips and add with the cabbage to the soup. Cook 10 to 15 minutes more, adding water if the soup is too thick. Ladle the hot soup over large Garlic croutons. Slice the bacon and kielbasa and serve on a separate platter. Each guest should add red wine to his or her serving as desired.

Onion Soup

This is a light, creamy onion soup, somewhat unusual, but extremely tasty.

6 large onions
3 cloves garlic
12 tablespoons butter
9 tablespoons flour
10 cups Chicken stock (page 74)

2 cups dry white wine
Salt and freshly ground black pepper to taste
Swiss cheese, grated (optional)

SERVES EIGHT

Peel and chop the onions very fine. Mince the garlic cloves. Heat the butter in a saucepan, add the vegetables, stir slowly over medium heat until the onion is golden, but not browned. Blend in the flour and stir for 3 minutes. Add the Chicken stock all at once. Raise the heat slightly and stir the soup rapidly until it comes to a boil. Add the wine and simmer the soup for 20 minutes, stirring from time to time. Serve immediately with grated Swiss cheese if desired.

Vegetable Soup Provençal

½ medium head cabbage
2 potatoes
1 carrot
1 large leek
2 small tomatoes
1 cup fresh string beans
1 cup fresh peas
2 quarts beef broth

1½ teaspoons salt
¼ teaspoon oregano
¼ teaspoon black pepper
1 teaspoon basil
Cayenne pepper to taste
½ cup macaroni
Grated Parmesan cheese

SERVES EIGHT

Remove the outer leaves and core of ½ cabbage. Shred. Peel and chop the potatoes and carrot. Wash the leek, cut off root end, and slice. Peel, seed, and chop the tomatoes. Place vegetables, beef broth, and spices in a large kettle. Bring to a boil, then lower the heat, and simmer, covered, for 20 minutes. Bring the soup to a boil and add the macaroni. Lower the heat and simmer for 15 minutes, or until the macroni is tender. Stir occasionally to prevent the macaroni from sticking. Serve hot, sprinkled with grated Parmesan cheese.

Pot-au-Feu

3½-pound rump or chuck of beef
(or 4 pounds beef plate)
Beef or veal bones
3½ quarts Brown stock (see page 67) or water
1½ tablespoons salt
2 cups water
8 small onions
8 whole cloves
8 leeks

8 medium-sized carrots
4 small white turnips
4 parsnips
2 stalks celery with leaves
1 clove garlic
5 sprigs parsley
½ bay leaf
Sprig of thyme
Salt and pepper to taste

SERVES EIGHT

Arrange the beef and bones in a large soup kettle. Cover with Brown stock, add salt, and bring to a boil, skimming the scum as it rises to the surface. When the soup reaches a rolling boil, add 2 more cups of water. This will make the scum rise faster. Continue to boil and skim the soup. When no more scum rises, lower the heat and simmer the soup, covered, for 1½ hours. Peel the onions and stud each with a whole clove. Trim the leeks, discarding the roots, and wash them thoroughly by splitting the stems almost through with a sharp knife and holding them under running water. Peel the carrots, turnips, and parsnips, and cut them into pieces. Rinse the celery and parsley and peel the garlic clove. Cut the celery into 1-inch pieces, and place the celery, garlic, and parsley in a cheesecloth bag along with the bay leaf and thyme. Add the onions, leeks, carrots, turnips, parsnips, and the cheesecloth bag to the kettle. Cover and simmer for 2 hours, then remove from heat and allow to cool. Discard the cheesecloth bag. Refrigerate the pot-au-feu for several hours or overnight to allow the fat on the surface to harden. Remove all fat and reheat the soup. Adjust the seasonings. Strain the soup as you pour it into soup bowls. Slice the meat and arrange with the vegetables on a platter. Serve the clear soup as a first course, followed or accompanied by the meat and vegetables.

Petite Marmite

*Leftover bouillon from Pot-au-feu further enriches
this renowned French soup.*

1 pound lean beef brisket, cut in pieces	4 white turnips
1 oxtail, cut in pieces	4 leeks
2 whole chicken legs, cut in sections	4 stalks celery
	8 small onions
3 quarts bouillon from Pot-au-feu (see page 207)	Butter
	Salt and pepper to taste
1 tablespoon salt	8 ½-inch marrow bones
4 carrots	Gruyère cheese, grated

SERVES EIGHT

Arrange beef, oxtail, and chicken legs in a soup kettle. Add water to cover. Parboil for 10 minutes, drain, and rinse the meat in cold water. A *marmite*, or clay casserole, is the traditional pot for cooking this soup, but a deep kettle will do. Place all the parboiled meat in the *marmite*, add the bouillon and salt, and bring to a boil. Skim the scum off as it rises to the surface while the soup simmers slowly for 2 hours with lid slightly ajar. Peel the carrots and cut them in 1-inch pieces. Peel the turnips and cut into eighths. Wash and trim the leeks and celery stalks, and cut into pieces. Peel the onions and brown them on all sides in butter. Add all vegetables to the *marmite*. Continue to simmer the soup for 2 hours and to skim if necessary. Adjust the seasonings. Arrange the marrow bones in a shallow pan. Poach them in water to cover for as long as it takes the water to boil. Arrange the marrow bones in eight deep soup bowls. Skim all fat from the surface of the soup and ladle the soup, meat, and vegetables into the bowls. Serve immediately, with grated Gruyère cheese on the side for guests to help themselves.

Soup of Touraine

*If you are searching for a straightforward, hearty
vegetable soup—without frills but with a satisfying
down-to-earth goodness—your search has ended. This
soup from the heart of the château country is your answer.*

3 white turnips

5 leeks, white parts only

2 tablespoons butter

½ pound lean slab bacon, diced

1 small head of cabbage

2½ quarts Chicken stock (see page 74)

1 cup fresh (or frozen) peas

Croutons

SERVES EIGHT

Peel and slice the turnips. Trim and wash the leeks and cut the white parts into thin slices. Sauté the turnips and leeks in the butter and diced bacon until the vegetables are slightly softened. Remove the hard core and limp outer leaves of the cabbage and cut it into eighths. Add the cabbage to the vegetables and sauté for 4 minutes more, turning each piece of cabbage once. Add the Chicken stock, cover, and cook at a low boil for 45 minutes. Add the peas and cook for 15 minutes, or until peas are tender. Serve hot over croutons.

Cabbage Soup

SOUPE AUX CHOUX

*Here is a cabbage soup in the Burgundian style
that is quite simply delicious.*

2 tablespoons butter

¼ pound lean salt pork

1 large onion

2 small carrots

½ small cabbage

9 cups water

½ teaspoon salt

⅛ teaspoon coarsely ground pepper

A generous pinch each nutmeg and cinnamon

8 croutons

1 cup heavy cream

2 egg yolks

SERVES EIGHT

[209]

Melt the butter in a soup kettle. Mince the salt pork and lightly brown it in the butter. Peel the onion and carrots and chop them very fine. Cut the cabbage in half. Discard the hard core and heavy ribs and coarsely chop the rest. Sauté the chopped vegetables for several minutes, add the water and spices, and simmer for 1 hour. Place the croutons in the bottom of a soup tureen. Pour in the heavy cream beaten with the egg yolks. Add the hot soup, stir, and serve immediately.

Chicken-in-the-Pot

POULE-AU-POT

5 pounds fowl	9 medium-sized carrots, peeled
Water to cover	8 leeks, washed and trimmed
2 chicken feet, cleaned and skinned	9 stalks celery
3½ quarts water	6 sprigs parsley
1 tablespoon salt	Salt and pepper to taste
1 large onion, studded with 1 whole clove	Cooked rice

SERVES EIGHT

Clean the fowl and truss the legs and wings. Place in a large soup kettle, add water to cover, and bring to a boil. Cook for a few minutes, then remove the fowl and discard the water. Wash the kettle and put the fowl back into it. Add the cleaned and skinned chicken feet, cover with the 4½ quarts of water, and stir in the salt. As the water comes to a boil, scum will appear on the surface. Skim off as it rises. When no more scum appears, simmer the soup, covered, for 1 hour. Peel the onion, stud with clove, and add to the soup, together with 1 of the carrots, 2 of the leeks, 2 celery stalks, and the parsley. Continue to simmer the soup, covered, for another hour. Correct the seasonings. Remove the fowl and set aside to keep warm. Using a fine sieve, strain the soup into a clean kettle, discarding the vegetables and chicken feet. Add the remaining carrots, leeks, and celery stalks (all cut in 1-inch pieces) to the kettle, and simmer the soup until the vegetables are tender. Cut the fowl into serving pieces and place in wide deep bowls. Arrange some vegetables and cooked rice in each bowl; ladle the hot soup over all. Serve immediately.

Vintner's Soup Pot***

*Serve this filling soup with a salad and a large loaf of
freshly baked bread, and you'll have an informal
meal well worth remembering. If desired,
the meat may be served on the side.*

1½-pound ham slice	1 large onion
½ pound lean slab bacon	6 leeks
2 pound pork sausages	1 small cabbage
2¾ quarts water	6 small potatoes
2 medium-sized carrots	1 cup fresh lima beans
4 white turnips	8 large toasted croutons

SERVES EIGHT

Brown the ham slice, bacon, and pork sausages in a heavy soup pot.
Add the water and simmer the meat for 1½ hours. Peel and coarsely
chop the carrots, turnips, and onion. Wash and slice the leeks. Remove the hard core, stem, and limp outer leaves from the cabbage
and cut it into four wedges. Add these vegetables to the soup and
cook until they are partially softened. Peel the potatoes and cut
them into eighths, and add them with the lima beans to the soup.
Add more water if necessary, and cook until the meat and vegetables
are tender. Slice the meat into serving pieces. Place toasted croutons
in soup bowls and pour soup into each bowl. Arrange the sliced meat
and the cabbage on a large platter. Serve with the soup. Guests may
add the meat to the soup or eat it separately with Dijon mustard.

Chicken Soup Margot

*This is delicate in the extreme—the
perfect preface to an excellent meal.*

1½ cups toasted almonds, shredded	2 egg yolks
½ cup milk	1 cup heavy cream
1½ quarts chicken broth	

SERVES EIGHT

[211]

Shred the almonds very fine. Meanwhile warm the milk slightly and pour over the almonds to cover. Soak for 30 minutes and drain, reserving the almond milk. Preheat the oven to 350° F. and toast the almonds to a golden brown, shaking occasionally to prevent burning. In a large soup kettle combine the reserved almond milk with the chicken broth and bring to just under a boil. Beat the egg yolks together with the cream. Add a little of the hot soup to this mixture and gradually add to the soup, stirring constantly so that the egg yolks will not curdle. Heat the soup for 2 minutes more, but do not allow to boil. Serve immediately, garnished with the toasted almonds.

Lobster Bisque

1 large or (2 small) lobster(s)	1 cup Fish stock (see page 83) or water
1 small carrot	1 tablespoon sherry
1 medium-sized onion	3 cups milk
8 tablespoons butter	3 cups water
5 sprigs parsley	½ cup flour
½ bay leaf	¼ cup heavy cream
Pinch of thyme	Salt and pepper to taste
¼ cup brandy	2 tablespoons brandy
½ cup dry white wine	

SERVES EIGHT

Cut the body and tail section of the lobster into pieces. Crack the claws. Peel and dice the carrot. Peel and chop the onion very fine. Heat 2 tablespoons of the butter in a skillet and sauté the vegetables a golden brown. Remove from the pan and set aside. Add the parsley and bay leaf and sprinkle a pinch of thyme over the vegetables. Melt 2 tablespoons butter in the same skillet. Arrange the lobster pieces in the skillet. Cook the lobster, shaking the pan once or twice, until it reddens. Spoon ¼ cup of brandy over the lobster pieces and set aflame. Stir in the wine and Fish stock and allow the lobster to simmer, covered, for about 20 minutes. Remove from heat and set aside. Remove the lobster from the shells, dice the meat, and sprinkle with the sherry. Reserve the shells.

Bring the milk and water to a boil. In a large saucepan, make a paste by melting 4 tablespoons of the butter and stirring in the flour. When the mixture turns golden, stir in the hot milk and water mixture, and continue to stir until the mixture thickens. Put the most tender parts of the lobster shell through a grinder. Add the ground shell and the other pieces of shell to the cream soup, along with the sautéed vegetables and Fish stock and wine liquid. Cover and simmer over low heat, stirring frequently, for 1½ hours. Remove any scum that rises to the surface. Remove the soup from the stove and press through a fine sieve, discarding the vegetables and shells. Add more milk if the mixture is not creamy enough. Return to low heat and stir in the heavy cream. A drop or two of red vegetable coloring may be added at this point if a pinker color is desired. Adjust the seasonings. Stir in 2 tablespoons brandy along with the diced lobster meat just before serving.

Potage Paysanne

3 leeks with 3 inches of green top
1 turnip, white
2 carrots
½ head Savoy cabbage
3 tablespoons butter
½ cup water
2 quarts chicken broth

½ cup green beans
¼ cup celery
1 cup peas
¾ cup lettuce, shredded
½ cup sorrel, shredded
Salt and pepper to taste
¾ cup cooked rice

SERVES EIGHT

Wash and slice the leeks. Wash and slice the turnip and carrots. Shred the Savoy cabbage. Put all of the prepared vegetables in a soup kettle. Add the butter and water. Cover the kettle and braise until vegetables are cooked.

Place the chicken broth in another soup kettle and bring to a boil. Meanwhile, wash and cut the green beans and celery into 1-inch lengths. Add to the broth along with the peas. Cover the kettle and cook over low heat until the vegetables are tender. Shred the lettuce and sorrel. Add to the soup and bring once again to a boil. Adjust the seasonings. Add the reserved steamed vegetables and heat a few minutes longer. Serve hot with a spoonful of rice in each bowl.

Bread and Cheese Bouillon***

CROÛTES AU POT DAUPHINOISE

4 tablespoons butter
6 large onions
12 stalks celery with tops
2 bay leaves
2 teaspoons whole peppercorns

1 teaspoon salt
10 cups Chicken stock (see page 74)
2 French breads
1 pound Swiss cheese

SERVES EIGHT

Melt the butter in a large saucepan. Peel and slice the onions. Cut the celery into 1-inch pieces. Sauté the vegetables and the spices for 5 minutes. Add the Chicken stock, cover, and simmer for 1 hour. Meanwhile, cut the bread into thin slices and grate the cheese. Arrange the bread slices and grated cheese in alternate layers in two casserole dishes. Strain the broth, reheating if necessary, and pour slowly into the casseroles. Cover and bake for 1 hour at 400° F. Serve immediately.

Billi Bi

3½ pounds mussels
7 medium-sized onions
6 shallots
2 sprigs parsley
2½ cups of good dry white wine
4 tablespoons butter
1 bay leaf

¾ teaspoon thyme
Pinch cayenne pepper
4 cups heavy cream
2 egg yolks
Salt and freshly ground pepper to taste

SERVES EIGHT

Squeeze the mussels several times between your thumb and fingers. Discard any mussels that do not remain closed. Scrub the mussels thoroughly with a small, stiff brush, making sure all sand and slime are removed.

Peel and coarsely chop the onions and shallots. Place the mussels, onions, shallots, parsley, wine, butter, bay leaf, thyme, and cayenne pepper into a soup kettle. Bring to a boil and cover the kettle tightly. Lower the heat and simmer 8 minutes longer. Remove mussels, discarding any that do not open.

Pour soup through several layers of cheesecloth to strain. Return soup to stove, bring to a boil, and add the cream. Bring to a boil once again. Take the soup off the stove and stir in the beaten egg yolks. Reheat over a low flame, taking care not to boil, or egg yolks will curdle. Adjust the seasonings. Place several mussels in each soup bowl and pour the hot soup over them.

Egg Bisque Biarritz

BISQUE AUX OEUFS BIARRITZ

8 cups Fish consommé (see page 83)

8 egg yolks

2 cups heavy sweet cream

A pinch each of white pepper and nutmeg

1½ cups crabmeat

2 teaspoons fresh tarragon, minced

SERVES EIGHT

Heat the Fish consommé to lukewarm. Beat the egg yolks with the cream and stir into the warm consommé. Heat over *very* low heat, stirring constantly. *Do not allow the soup to boil* or the egg yolks will curdle. Stir in the crabmeat and serve hot with a sprinkling of minced tarragon.

Vichyssoise

2 medium-sized onions

6 leeks

6 tablespoons butter

5 medium-sized potates

1¼ quarts chicken broth

1 tablespoon salt

2 cups milk

3 cups heavy cream

Salt and freshly ground pepper to taste

Minced chives

SERVES EIGHT

Peel and chop the onions. Slice the leeks using only the white part. Heat the butter in a soup kettle, and add the chopped onions and leeks. Sauté until the onions are golden and transparent. Peel and slice the potatoes very thin. Add the potatoes, together with the chicken broth and salt, to the soup kettle. Place over medium heat and cook until the potatoes are tender.

Whirl in an electric blender until smooth. Place in the refrigerator; when well chilled, add the milk and cream. Adjust the seasonings. Place icy cold soup in chilled bowls and sprinkle with minced chives. Serve at once.

French Clam Bisque

Absolutely superb! Serve with French bread and a simple tossed salad for an elegant afternoon or late-night snack.

30 *large cherrystone clams*	6 *medium-sized tomatoes*
3 *large onions*	2½ *cups good dry white wine*
3 *large cloves garlic*	1 *cup rice*
¼ *cup butter*	2 *cups milk*
1 *teaspoon whole saffron, chopped*	1 *cup heavy cream*
¾ *tablespoon fresh thyme, minced*	*Tabasco sauce, salt, and freshly ground pepper to taste*

SERVES EIGHT

Scrub the clams well and pry them open, reserving the juice. Chop the clam meat coarsely, add to the juice, and reserve. Peel and chop the onions coarsely. Peel and mince the garlic. Heat the butter in a large pan and add the onions, garlic, saffron, and thyme. Sauté the mixture until the onions are golden and transparent. Stir in the reserved clams and juice and cook over low heat for 3 or 4 minutes, stirring occasionally.

Cut the tomatoes into quarters, shake out the seeds, and chop coarsely. Add the tomatoes to the soup, together with the wine and rice. Cover the pan and simmer over very low heat for 1 hour, stirring occasionally.

Strain the liquid into a large saucepan. Place the clam-onion-tomato-rice mixture into a blender, add ½ cup of the broth, and purée until smooth. Add the puréed ingredients to the strained broth, and stir in the milk and cream. Add salt and additional heavy cream and Tabasco sauce to suit your taste. Serve hot or cold with freshly ground black pepper and a bit of minced fresh thyme.

French Fish Soup with Brandy

3 small onions

4 large cloves garlic

¼ cup olive oil

¾ teaspoon fresh thyme, minced (or 1 teaspoon dried thyme)

3 teaspoons whole saffron

2 pounds striped bass

½ teaspoon salt

¾ cup tomato purée

1 tablespoon fresh fennel, minced

1½ cups good dry white wine

6 cups water

1 cup brandy

3 cups heavy cream

Salt and freshly ground pepper to taste

SERVES EIGHT

Peel and chop the onions. Peel and mince the garlic. Warm the oil in a soup kettle and add the onions, garlic, thyme, and saffron. Sauté, stirring occasionally, until the onions are golden and transparent. Add the fish and salt. Cook for a few minutes over medium heat, breaking the fish into pieces. Blend in the tomato purée, fennel, wine, and water. Stir the soup over medium heat until it comes to a boil. Immediately lower the heat, cover, and simmer for about 20 minutes, stirring occasionally. Gradually stir in the brandy, then the cream, and boil the soup for 2 minutes. Adjust the seasonings and serve hot.

Senegalese Soup

6 cups chicken broth

6 egg yolks

2½ cups heavy cream

2½ teaspoons curry powder

Dash of cayenne pepper

Salt and pepper to taste

1 cup cooked breast of chicken, finely chopped

3 tablespoons parsley, minced

SERVES EIGHT

Heat the chicken broth to just under the boiling point in the top half of a double boiler over direct heat. Beat the egg yolks together with the cream, curry powder, and cayenne pepper. Stir 1 cup of the hot broth, a little at a time, into the egg yolks and cream mixture. Pour the mixture slowly into the hot broth, stirring constantly. Place the soup over boiling water, continuing to stir until the soup thickens slightly. Remove from heat, cool, and sprinkle with salt and pepper. Chill the soup until it is very cold. Just before serving, stir in the chopped cooked chicken. Pour into chilled soup bowls and garnish with the minced parsley.

Creamed Fish Soup

POTAGE CRÈME NORMANDE

2 onions

4 medium-sized tomatoes

1 stalk celery

1 pound sole fillets

2 bay leaves

1 cup good dry white wine

15 peppercorns

2 teaspoons fresh thyme, minced (or 1 teaspoon dried thyme)

6 cups water or Fish stock (see page 83)

1 teaspoon salt

1 slice of white bread, crusts removed

2 cups cooked shrimp, shelled

1 cup heavy cream

Nutmeg and salt to taste

2 teaspoons fresh parsley, minced

2 teaspoons fresh chives, minced

SERVES EIGHT

Peel and quarter the onions. Peel and quarter the tomatoes and shake out the seeds. Chop the celery. Place the vegetables in a large soup kettle. Add the fillet of sole, bay leaves, white wine, peppercorns, thyme, water, and salt. Cook over medium heat and bring to a boil. Lower the heat and simmer for 30 minutes. Strain the broth into a large pan. Remove the bay leaves, peppercorns, fish, and vegetables. Place the fish, vegetables, and a little broth in a blender and purée. Place in soup kettle. Crumble the bread and put in the blender, together with the cleaned shrimp and a little broth. Whirl in blender until puréed. Combine this purée with the remaining broth and the puréed fish and vegetables, return to the stove, and bring to a boil. Gradually stir in the cream. Adjust the seasonings. Reheat and ladle into individual soup bowls. Garnish with minced parsley and chives.

Chilled Cream of Watercress Soup***

CRÈME DE CRESSON GLACÉE

2 large leeks

2 medium-sized onions

2 tablespoons butter

2 large potatoes

3 cups chicken broth

1½ teaspoons salt

1 cup milk

1 cup heavy cream

2 bunches watercress (4½ ounces each), chopped

⅔ cup water

Heavy cream, whipped

SERVES EIGHT

Wash the leeks and chop, discarding the root. Peel and slice the onions. Sauté the leeks and onions in butter in a large, heavy pot until the onions are golden. Slice the potatoes very thin and add with the chicken broth and the salt to the leeks and onions. Simmer, covered, for 35 minutes, or until the potatoes are tender. Purée the soup in an electric blender. Stir the milk and cream into the puréed soup. Boil the chopped watercress in the water for 5 minutes. Purée the watercress in the blender and rub through a fine sieve. Stir the watercress into the soup and chill. Serve cold, with a dollop of whipped cream if desired.

Italian
favorites

Italian Bread

PANE CASALINGO

1 package active dry yeast	*1½ teaspoons salt*
2 cups lukewarm water	*5 cups all-purpose flour, sifted*

MAKES TWO LOAVES

Place the yeast in a small bowl. Stir in ¼ cup of the lukewarm water and set aside. When the yeast has dissolved, add it to the remaining 1¾ cups water mixed with the salt. Add the sifted flour to the yeast, salt and lukewarm water mixture, a little at a time, blending well after each addition. The result should be a fairly sticky dough that comes away clean from the side of the bowl. Dust your hands and a pastry board lightly with flour. Knead the dough for approximately 8 to 10 minutes, working in a bit more flour if the dough seems too sticky. When the dough has a smooth, elastic consistency, grease a bowl and set the dough in it, turning it over once to grease the top. Allow it to rise, covered, in a warm, draft-free place until double in volume (about 2 hours).

Test the dough by inserting two fingers into the top. If the indentations remain, the dough has risen enough. Punch the dough down and allow it to rise and double its size again, covered, in a warm, draft-free place (about 40 minutes). Place the dough on the pastry board, knead briefly, and divide into two equal portions. Make a long, fairly wide loaf from each half, and set the loaves on a greased baking sheet. Cover them lightly and allow them to rise. After 30 minutes, take a sharp knife and score the tops of the loaves diagonally, about ¼ inch deep. Sprinkle a little water over the tops. When they have doubled in size (about 30 minutes more), bake the loaves in a preheated 400° F. oven until brown and crusty (approximately 50 minutes). Serve while still warm, with or without butter.

Panettone I***

1 package dry active yeast	½ teaspoon salt
¼ cup lukewarm milk	4 tablespoons blanched almonds, shredded
8 tablespoons butter (at room temperature)	8 tablespoons seedless raisins
⅓ cup sugar	6 tablespoons citron, diced
3 eggs	1 egg yolk
3 cups all-purpose flour	1 teaspoon water

MAKES ONE LOAF

Mix the yeast with the lukewarm milk. Allow the mixture to rest until the yeast softens. Meanwhile, cream the butter with the sugar until thoroughly blended. Beat the eggs to a lemony froth. Stir the eggs into the butter-sugar mixture, a little at a time, beating 30 seconds after each addition. Measure the flour and sift together with the salt into a large bowl. First add the softened yeast and then blend in the butter-sugar-egg mixture. The result should be a soft but firm dough. Add a bit more milk if necessary. Sprinkle a pastry board lightly with flour. Turn the dough out onto it and knead until smooth (approximately 5 minutes). If the dough seems sticky, work in a bit more flour. Place the dough in a bowl that has been lightly dusted with flour. Sprinkle a dishtowel with enough water to barely moisten it, wrap the towel over the bowl, and allow the dough to rise in a warm, draft-free place until it doubles in volume (about 2 hours).

Turn the dough out and knead again for 5 minutes. Place it in the bowl, cover it, and let it rise again to double its size (about

1 hour). With a rolling pin, roll the dough out flat on the pastry board. Mix the shredded almonds, seedless raisins, and diced citron together, and distribute the mixture over the top of the dough. Bring the two ends of the dough to the center, press down, and roll out flat again. Repeat this folding and flattening process once more, then shape the dough into a ball with your hands. Set the ball into a deep buttered pan, or use the buttered top of a large double boiler. In either case, the container should be twice the size of the ball of dough. Cover the dough and allow it to double in size again (about 1 hour).

Beat the egg yolk with 1 teaspoon of water. Brush the mixture over the top of the dough. Bake in a preheated 350° F. oven for 30 to 40 minutes. When the panettone turns golden brown, remove it from oven and gently loosen it with a sharp thin knife. Turn the pan upside down and shake gently back and forth. If the bread still refuses to budge, loosen again carefully with the knife. Repeat the process without forcing until the bread comes from the pan.

Panettone II***

1 package dry active yeast

¼ cup lukewarm water

4½ cups all-purpose flour

½ cup sugar

¾ cup butter (at room temperature)

2 egg yolks

3 eggs

½ teaspoon salt

1 teaspoon vanilla

¾ cup blanched almonds, chopped

½ cup candied lemon peel, coarsely chopped

⅓ cup candied citron, coarsely chopped

½ cup seedless raisins

MAKES ONE LOAF

Stir the yeast into the lukewarm water, and add ½ cup of the flour. Set the mixture aside to rest while the yeast softens. Meanwhile, in a large bowl, cream the sugar with the softened butter until smooth. Add the egg yolks to the creamed mixture and beat in the whole eggs. When bubbles appear on the surface of the yeast mixture, stir it into the butter, sugar, and eggs. Add the salt and vanilla. Blend in enough of the remaining flour to make a soft but not sticky dough.

Divide the dough into two equal portions and set one in a deep bowl. Using a rolling pin, flatten the other piece of dough; distribute the almonds, candied lemon peel, citron, and raisins over the surface, and work the fruit and nuts into the dough by kneading thoroughly. Put the fruit and nut-filled dough into a second deep bowl, cover both bowls, and allow both doughs to rise in a warm, draft-free place until double in bulk (about 1½ to 2 hours).

Punch both doughs down. Dust a pastry board very lightly with flour. Turn out each dough separately and knead for 4 minutes. Roll out the plain dough and form a large triangle. Roll out the fruit and nut-filled dough into a triangle of equal size and set it on top of the plain dough. Begin at the widest end of the triangle, and roll the combined dough toward the point. Butter the sides and bottom of a tube pan, sprinkle sugar over the butter, and shake out any excess. Squeeze the rolled dough with your hands, if necessary, to lengthen it so that both ends meet in the tube pan. Place the dough in the pan and allow to rise, covered, for 1½ to 2 hours, or until it doubles in bulk. Preheat the oven to 400° F. and bake the panettone for 10 minutes, then lower to 350° F. and bake for 50 minutes longer. When puffy and golden, remove the panettone from the oven and cool.

Bread Sticks

1 package dry active yeast
½ cup lukewarm water
3 tablespoons shortening
½ cup hot water

3 cups sifted all-purpose or
   unbleached white flour
2 egg whites, beaten until stiff

MAKES SIXTEEN

Dissolve the yeast in the lukewarm water. Melt the shortening in the hot water and add to the yeast. Beat in 1 cup of the sifted flour until the dough is smooth. Fold in the egg whites. Add the remaining flour, and knead for 5 minutes until the dough is smooth and elastic. Place the dough in a greased bowl, turning it so that it is greased on all sides. Cover the dough lightly with a damp towel and let it rise in a warm, draft-free place until double in volume (about 1 hour). Punch the dough down, cover, and let it rise again in a warm, draft-free place until double in bulk (about 45 minutes). Again, punch the dough down and let it rest for 15 minutes.

Divide the dough into two equal pieces and roll each piece on a floured pastry board into a rectangle about ⅓ inch thick. Cut the rectangles into 2-inch squares. Using your palms, roll each piece of dough into a narrow, pencil-shaped stick. Place them on a greased baking sheet, cover with a damp towel, and let the dough rise for 30 minutes in a warm, draft-free place. Bake at 350° F. until golden brown (about 12 to 15 minutes).

Minestrone

A minestrone with an interestingly different flavor—
a hearty Italian soup.

11 cups water	1 clove garlic, minced
1½ cups dried navy beans	3½ cups fresh tomatoes
1 tablespoon salt	¼ cup parsley
4 peppercorns	3½ cups cabbage
½ cup olive oil	1 zucchini
1 cup celery with leaves, chopped	2 cups elbow macaroni
1 cup onion, finely chopped	Grated Parmesan cheese

SERVES EIGHT

Pour the water into a large kettle and soak the beans overnight. Bring the water and beans to the boiling point, add the salt and peppercorns, and simmer, covered, for 1 hour. Meanwhile, heat the olive oil in a heavy skillet and sauté the celery, onion, and garlic until the vegetables are browned. Peel the tomatoes, cut them into quarters, shake out the seeds, and chop coarsely. Wash and chop the parsley. Stir the sautéed vegetables and the chopped tomatoes and parsley into the beans. Simmer the soup, covered, 1 hour longer. Shred the cabbage, discarding the core and limp outer leaves. Wash and slice the zucchini thinly. Add the cabbage, zucchini, and elbow macaroni to the soup. Simmer, uncovered, for 15 minutes. Pour into soup bowls and serve with a dish of grated Parmesan cheese on the side, so that guests may help themselves.

Broccoli Soup

¾ pound pork rind
3 quarts Beef broth
3 cloves garlic
2 small onions
2½ tablespoons olive oil
1 pound smoked ham
3 teaspoons salt

6 cups fresh broccoli, chopped
½ pound macaroni, broken into 2-inch pieces
Salt and freshly ground pepper to taste
1½ cups Parmesan cheese, grated

SERVES EIGHT

Cover the pork rind with broth and boil for 2 hours. Strain it into a bowl, set the liquid aside, and cut the rind into thin strips. (The liquid should measure about 2 quarts; add water if necessary.) Peel and mince the garlic. Peel and chop the onions. Heat the oil in a soup kettle and sauté the garlic and onions until the onions are golden and transparent. Chop the ham and add it, together with the pork rind, the reserved liquid, and the salt. Place over medium-high heat and bring the mixture to a boil. Lower the heat and cook for 25 minutes.

Cover the broccoli with some of the liquid and cook until tender. *Do not overcook.* Drain and keep warm. Bring the soup to a rolling boil and add the macaroni. When the macaroni is almost done, add the broccoli and cook until heated through. Adjust the seasonings. Serve with a bowl of grated Parmesan cheese.

Zucchini Soup

⅓ pound ham fat
4 small onions
2 stalks celery
3 tablespoons olive oil
1½ cups white rice
3 quarts Beef bouillon (see page 68)

⅓ pound prosciutto
5 small zucchini
3 tablespoons chives
Salt and freshly ground pepper to taste
1½ cups Parmesan cheese, grated

SERVES EIGHT

[225]

Chop the ham fat, peel and chop the onions, and chop the celery. In a soup kettle sauté the ham fat, onions, and celery in the heated olive oil until the onions are golden and transparent. Add the rice and stir for 3 minutes over low heat. Add the beef bouillon, bring the mixture to a boil, and cook over medium heat for about 25 minutes or until a grain of rice is tender when pressed between the thumb and forefinger.

Cut the prosciutto into thin strips and reserve. Cut the unpeeled zucchini into thin slices and add it, together with the prosciutto and chives, to the hot soup and cook, covered, for 5 minutes. Remove the soup kettle from the stove and allow it to rest for 5 minutes more. Adjust the seasonings. Serve hot with a bowl of grated Parmesan cheese.

Bean Soup Borghese

1½ pounds white, navy, or cannellini beans

¾ pound prosciutto, unsliced

¾ pound fresh pork, lean

2½ quarts Beef broth

1½ teaspoons salt

¼ teaspoon pepper

3 ounces ham fat

1½ pounds beets

3 tomatoes

2 celery hearts

4 carrots

2 small onions

2 cloves

3 cloves garlic

4 sprigs fresh rosemary

Salt and freshly ground pepper to taste

32 slices French bread, cut thin

3 tablespoons butter

1½ cups Parmesan cheese, grated

SERVES EIGHT

Cover the beans with water and soak overnight. Drain and place in a large soup kettle, together with the prosciutto, fresh pork, broth, salt, and pepper. Place the kettle on medium-high heat and bring to a boil. Skim off the film until the liquid is clear.

Chop the ham fat and reserve. Peel and slice the beets. Dice the tomato, celery hearts, and carrots. Add these vegetables to the soup, together with the onions (stick one clove in each onion), the garlic, and rosemary. Simmer for 1½ to 2 hours. Remove the meats from the soup, chop coarsely, and return to the soup. Adjust the seasonings. Reheat.

Remove the crusts from the French bread and sauté in the butter until golden. Place 4 pieces of bread in each soup bowl, pour the hot soup over, and serve with grated Parmesan cheese.

Cioppino

1 pint raw clams	7 medium tomatoes
1 pint raw mussels*	¾ cup olive oil
10 cups water	1 cup tomato purée
8 tablespoons dried mushrooms	3½ cups red wine
3 medium-sized onions	Salt and pepper to taste
2 green peppers	1 medium sea bass
1 cup spinach	3 small live lobsters
5 cloves garlic	1 pound large raw shrimp
1 teaspoon salt	

SERVES EIGHT

Arrange the raw clams and mussels in their shells in a large bowl. Cover with the water. Allow to soak for 3 hours, changing the water several times. Chop the dried mushrooms, cover with water, and soak for 1 hour.

Meanwhile, peel the onions and chop them very fine. Rinse the peppers, discard the stems and seeds, and chop very fine. Wash and chop the spinach. Peel and chop the garlic cloves. In a small cup, mix the chopped garlic with the salt, pressing the salt in with the back of a spoon. Peel the tomatoes, seed them by cutting into eighths and shaking out the seeds, and chop them coarsely. Drain the clams and mussels. Scrub the shells thoroughly. Place them in a saucepan with 1½ cups of water, and steam them until they open. Strain and reserve the liquid.

Heat the olive oil in a deep soup kettle. Drain the dried mush-

* Discovering a few fresh mussels whose shells have opened after you buy them needn't be a cause of alarm. Squeeze both sides of the shell together firmly. Any mussels that do not stay shut should be discarded.

rooms and add them, together with the onions, peppers, spinach, and the garlic-salt mixture, to the hot oil. Sauté for 5 minutes over low heat, stirring occasionally. Add the chopped tomatoes, the reserved liquid from the clams and mussels, the tomato purée, and the wine. Sprinkle with salt and pepper to taste, bring to a boil, reduce the heat, and allow the soup to simmer, covered, for 30 minutes.

While the soup is simmering, slice the sea bass into 2-inch pieces. Cut up the live lobsters. Shell the shrimp and devein them. Add the bass, lobster pieces, and whole shrimp to the soup. Cook for 10 minutes, or until the lobster turns a bright red. Add the clams and mussels in their shells and cook just long enough to heat through. Serve immediately with hot, buttered, crusty Italian bread.

Cheese Soup

Begin your Italian dinner with appetizing Zuppa parmigiana con pepperoni or, served with thick slices of Italian bread, it makes a nourishing lunch.

3 quarts Chicken stock (see page 74)	*8 eggs*
1 pound pepperoni	*2 cups Parmesan cheese, grated*
1 medium-sized potato	*1 teaspoon oregano*
1 cup dry white Italian wine	*2 tablespoons thyme, chopped*

SERVES EIGHT

Place the Chicken stock in a large saucepan and bring it to a boil. Cut the pepperoni into quarters lengthwise, and cut each piece into ¼-inch slices. Peel the potato, cut it into quarters, and add with the pepperoni and wine to the boiling stock. (The potato helps to reduce the saltiness if the pepperoni is not the highest grade.) Cover the soup and allow the pepperoni to simmer for 20 to 25 minutes. Beat the eggs briskly in a large bowl. Stir the grated cheese and oregano into the eggs, a little at a time. Blend well after each addition to make sure the cheese dissolves. Discard the potato quarters and bring the soup to a boil. Remove the soup from the stove and immediately stir in the egg-cheese mixture with a wire whisk, beating constantly and vigorously. Return the soup to a very low flame and continue to beat until the soup is the consistency of heavy cream. Do not allow the soup to boil or the egg-cheese mixture will separate. Adjust the seasonings if necessary. Serve immediately, topped with chopped thyme.

Bean Soup with Macaroni

MINESTRA DI FAGIOLI CON PASTA

1½ pounds dried cranberry beans	12 cups Beef broth
¾ pound ham fat	¼ teaspoon cinnamon
2 small onions	1 teaspoon salt
¾-pound leftover ham bone with some of the meat left on	¾ pound macaroni, broken into 1-inch pieces
¾ pound fresh pork rind	Salt and freshly ground pepper to taste
2 tablespoons olive oil	

SERVES EIGHT

Cover the beans with water and soak overnight. Drain. Place in a large soup kettle, together with the chopped ham fat and the peeled and chopped onions. Add the ham bone, pork rind, olive oil, broth, cinnamon, and salt. Bring to a boil, then lower the heat, and simmer for 2 hours, or until beans are tender. Remove the ham bone and pork rind. Cut the ham meat into small pieces and return to the pot. Bring the soup to a boil once more, add the macaroni, and cook over medium heat until they are tender but not overcooked. Adjust the seasonings. Serve hot with grated Parmesan cheese.

Cream of Spinach Soup Florentine

2½ pounds spinach, washed	2 cups heavy cream
¾ cup water	7 egg yolks
½ teaspoon salt	1 cup ham, cooked
9 cups chicken broth	Croutons

SERVES EIGHT

Cook the spinach in water and salt over medium heat for 10 minutes, adding more water if necessary to keep from burning. Rub the spinach through a fine sieve. Place the spinach and the chicken broth in a large saucepan and boil 7 minutes. Beat together the cream, egg yolks, and ham. Add a small amount of the hot spinach soup to the egg and cream mixture. Stir. Add to hot soup and cook over medium heat, stirring constantly, until the soup thickens. Do not overcook, or yolks will curdle. Serve hot or chilled with croutons.

Cheese Pancakes in Broth

The Italians make thin pancakes similar to French crêpes suzettes. They fill these pancakes with cheese and ladle hot soup over them. Unusual but extremely pleasing.

3 cups all-purpose or
   unbleached white flour
9 eggs
¾ teaspoon salt
3½ cups Parmesan cheese,
   grated

Cinnamon
Beef and veal broth (see
   page 370)
¼ cup chives, minced

SERVES EIGHT

Measure the flour and set aside. Break the eggs into a medium-sized bowl and add the salt. Beat the eggs and add the flour, a little at a time, until the batter is smooth and has the consistency of heavy cream (add a little water if necessary).

Lightly grease a 7- to 9-inch skillet and place over low heat. Spoon just enough batter into the pan to cover the bottom. (The pancakes must be very thin.) Cook on one side until light brown. Gently loosen pancake, turn, and cook on other side until light brown. As pancakes are finished, stack on top of the stove with pieces of aluminum foil in between. When ready to serve, place 1 tablespoon Parmesan cheese in the center of each. Sprinkle with cinnamon and roll up.

Place 5 rolled pancakes in each bowl, 3 across the bottom and 2 on top. Ladle the hot veal and beef broth over them. Serve hot with additional Parmesan cheese, if desired. Garnish with chives.

Bread Soup

9 slices of thinly sliced prosciutto	¼ teaspoon freshly ground pepper
5-pound chicken, cooked	1½ loaves Italian bread
6 tablespoons beef marrow	9 tablespoons butter
4 eggs	3 quarts Beef bouillon (see page 68)
1 cup Parmesan cheese, grated	
¾ teaspoon salt	Grated Parmesan cheese

SERVES EIGHT

Chop prosciutto very fine and set aside. Remove the meat from the chicken and chop very fine. Combine prosciutto, chicken, and marrow. Add the beaten eggs, 5 tablespoons of Parmesan cheese, salt, and pepper. Mix all ingredients thoroughly. Remove the crusts from the bread and cut into rounds. Spread half of the rounds with the meat mixture. Top with the remaining rounds, making little sandwiches. Press the edges together firmly so that they will not come apart. Sauté the stuffed bread sandwiches in butter until they are a light brown.

Heat the bouillon. When ready to serve, put several of the sautéed sandwiches in each soup bowl and pour hot soup over them. Serve with a bowl of grated Parmesan cheese.

Italian Wedding Soup

4 cups all-purpose or unbleached white flour	1 tablespoon oregano, chopped
4 large eggs	1½ teaspoons salt
¾ tablespoon olive oil	¾ teaspoon pepper
¾ teaspoon salt	⅓ cup Chicken stock (see page 74)
¾ pound ground beef	Fat for frying
1 pound ground veal	10 cups Chicken stock (see page 74)
1 cup fine breadcrumbs	
3 small eggs	Salt and pepper to taste

SERVES EIGHT

In a large bowl, mix the flour, 3 eggs, olive oil, and salt. Form into a noodle dough by kneading with your hands until the dough is smooth and elastic. Allow the dough to rest for 30 minutes. Meanwhile, combine the beef, veal, breadcrumbs, 2 small eggs, oregano, salt, and pepper with the ⅓ cup Chicken stock, and mix well. Form the meat mixture into tiny balls. Heat the fat (390° F.) in a deep skillet and fry the meat balls until they are brown. Drain them thoroughly on paper toweling. Pinch off tiny pieces of noodle dough. Form them into balls, and deep-fry in the hot fat. When brown, drain them on paper toweling. Heat 10 cups of Chicken stock and stir in the meat and noodle balls. Simmer the soup for 30 minutes, adjust the seasonings, and serve piping hot.

Sausage Soup

⅓ pound ham fat	1½ cups white rice
2 small onions	4 tablespoons butter
1½ pound sweet Italian sausage	2 cups fresh Parmesan cheese, grated
4 tomatoes	1½ tablespoons parsley, chopped
3 quarts Beef bouillon (see page 68)	Salt and pepper to taste

SERVES EIGHT

Chop the ham fat and onions very fine. Place them in a soup kettle and sauté until lightly browned. Set aside. Cover the sausage with water and cook over medium-high heat for 15 minutes. Drain off the water and slice the sausage into 1¼-inch sections. Set aside. Peel and dice the tomato, cover with water, and cook over medium-high heat until they are soft when tested with a fork. Add the sausage and tomato to the soup kettle and stir in the Beef bouillon. When the soup reaches a rolling boil, stir in the rice. Cook over medium heat for 25 minutes or until the rice is tender. Remove from the stove and blend in the butter, Parmesan cheese, and parsley. Adjust the seasonings. Serve hot, with extra grated Parmesan cheese in a separate bowl.

Countries
around the
Mediterranean

Challah

5½–6½ cups flour, unsifted	1 cup warm water (120–130°F.)
3 tablespoons sugar	
1½ teaspoons salt	4 eggs (at room temperature)
1 package dry active yeast	
½ cup butter (or margarine), softened	1 teaspoon cold water
	½ teaspoon poppy seeds
Pinch powdered saffron	

MAKES TWO LOAVES

Combine 1¼ cups flour, sugar, salt, and yeast in a large bowl. Mix in the softened butter. Stir the saffron into the warm water until it dissolves. Add a little at a time to the flour mixture and blend thoroughly. Beat for 2 minutes with electric mixer at medium speed, scraping the bowl occasionally. Separate the yolk and white of 1 egg. Blend the single egg white and the other 3 whole eggs into the batter. Reserve the single egg yolk. Stir ½ cup of flour into the batter and beat at high speed for 2 minutes, scraping the bowl occasionally.

Blend in enough additional flour to make a soft dough. Knead the dough on a lightly floured board about 8 to 10 minutes, or until it is smooth and elastic. Place the dough in a greased bowl, turning it once to grease the top. Cover and allow the dough to rise in a warm, draft-free place until double in bulk (approximately 1 hour).

Flour a pastry board lightly and set the dough on it. Divide the dough into two equal portions. Divide each portion into two pieces, using ⅓ of the dough for one piece and ⅔ of the dough for the other. Divide the larger piece into three equal portions. Roll each of these into 12-inch lengths. Braid the lengths together tightly, using the fingers to press the dough together at the ends. Divide the smaller piece into three equal portions. Roll each of these into 10-inch lengths and braid tightly. Place the smaller braid on top of the larger one and seal the ends.

Place both braided loaves on a greased baking sheet. Mix the reserved single egg yolk with 1 teaspoon cold water and brush the tops of the loaves with this mixture. Sprinkle with the poppy seeds, and let the loaves rise until double in bulk in a warm, draft-free place (approximately 1 hour). Bake in a preheated 400° F. oven for 20 to 25 minutes. Remove from the oven and cool on wire racks.

Greek Christmas Bread***

CHRISTOPSOMO

½ cup milk less 2 tablespoons	1 teaspoon salt
¾ cup butter	2½ teaspoons anise seed, crushed
2 packages dry active yeast	7 cups all-purpose flour
½ cup warm water less 2 tablespoons	8 candied cherries
	1 walnut half
4 eggs	1 egg white
1 cup sugar	

MAKES ONE LOAF

Scald the milk and set it aside to cool. Melt the butter over hot water and cool to lukewarm. Mix the yeast with warm water in a large bowl. Allow it to rest for 5 minutes. When the yeast is dissolved, beat the eggs lightly and add to the yeast. Blend in the milk, butter, sugar, salt, and crushed anise seed, and mix thoroughly. Add the flour, a little at a time, mixing well after each addition. The dough will be soft. Dust a pastry board lightly with flour. Knead the dough to a smooth, elastic consistency (approximately 8 to 10 minutes). Grease a large bowl and place the dough in it, turning it once to grease the top. Allow the dough to rise, covered, in a warm, draft-free place until doubled in size (approximately 2 hours).

Punch the dough down and place on an unfloured board. Using your fingers, pull off two small pieces of dough, shape into 3-inch balls, and set aside. Smooth the large piece of dough into a rounded shape by kneading it slightly. Grease a baking sheet, set the rounded dough on it, and pat it down until it forms a circle 9 or 10 inches wide. Roll each of the smaller pieces of dough between the hands to form a 15-inch rope. With a sharp knife, make a 5-inch cut into the ends of each rope. Set one rope across the center of the flattened round bread and separate the cut ends. Curl the cut ends into circles going in opposite directions. Lay the remaining length of dough on top of the other to form a cross and curl the cut ends similarly. *Do not press the ropes down.*

Center a candied cherry in each curl. Lay the walnut half on the center of the cross. Beat an egg white slightly and brush over the top and sides of the loaf. Allow the loaf to rise, covered, until it doubles in volume (approximately 1 hour). Preheat the oven to 350° F. and bake the bread for about 45 minutes. The loaf is done when a toothpick inserted in the center comes out clean. Remove from oven, slide from baking sheet, and cool on a wire rack. This anise-flavored bread may be served warm, accompanied by sweet butter.

Potato Kephtides***

These golden brown potato cakes, soft and creamy on the inside and crisp and tasty on the outside, provide a filling accompaniment to any hearty soup.

2 tablespoons butter	½ cup flour
2 scallions	Salt and pepper to taste
2 large tomatoes	Oil for frying
1 pound cold mashed potatoes	

MAKES TWELVE CAKES

Melt the butter over hot water. Chop the scallions very fine. Peel the tomatoes, quarter them, shake out the seeds, and chop finely. Force the mashed potatoes through a sieve and mix thoroughly with the melted butter and chopped vegetables. Stir in the flour; use enough to make a soft, but not sticky, dough. Season the mixture with salt and pepper. Knead for a few minutes, roll out to ¾-inch thickness, and cut into 3-inch rounds. Fry the rounds in *very* hot oil to a golden brown, turning once.

Iranian Yoghurt Pancakes

1½ cups flour

2 tablespoons sugar

2 tablespoons baking soda

1 teaspoon salt

¾ cup butter

3 eggs

2 cups plain yoghurt

MAKES TWELVE PANCAKES

Combine the flour, sugar, baking soda, and salt. Sift together. Melt butter over hot water. Separate the eggs and set the whites aside. Beat the yolks slightly and mix with the yoghurt. Blend the dry ingredients into the yoghurt mixture. Beat the egg whites until they stand in peaks. Fold into the batter. Drop the batter by spoonfuls onto a hot greased griddle. Fry over medium heat, turning once.

Traditional Greek Soupa Lakhanika

3 small onions

⅓ cup olive oil

5 tomatoes

10 cups chicken broth

1 medium-sized head of cabbage

5 ounces vermicelli

Salt and freshly ground pepper to taste

SERVES EIGHT

Peel and chop the onions very fine. Place in a soup kettle and sauté in heated olive oil until golden and transparent. Peel, seed, and chop the tomatoes. Add to the onions, along with the chicken broth. Place over a high heat and bring to a boil. Cover the kettle. Turn the burner down and cook over very low heat for about 1¾ hours.

Cut the cabbage into quarters and remove the core and limp outer leaves. With a sharp knife, slice the cabbage into thin shreds. Add the shredded cabbage to the soup, together with the vermicelli, which has been broken into 1½-inch pieces. Stir the soup thoroughly and cook gently for about 15 minutes, or until the vermicelli is done. Adjust the seasonings. Serve hot with Greek cheeses and olives.

Greek Soup À La Reine

AVGOLEMONO

12 cups chicken broth	12 egg yolks
5 tablespoons lemon juice	Salt and freshly ground white pepper to taste
Zest (grated outer peel) of 1 lemon	Lemon slices

SERVES EIGHT

Heat the chicken broth until it is scalding hot. Add the lemon juice and the zest. Beat the egg yolks and mix with a little hot broth. Add this mixture gradually to the remaining broth, lower the heat, and stir constantly so that the soup will not curdle. Adjust the seasonings. Serve immediately, garnished with thin lemon slices.

Greek Seafood Stew

9 lobster tails	3 cups Fish stock (see page 83)
¼ cup good quality olive oil	30 small clams
8 cloves garlic, finely chopped	36 shrimp, shelled, with tails intact
4½ large tomatoes	2 bay leaves
3 cups tomato juice	½ cup parsley, finely chopped
4 cups white wine	

SERVES EIGHT

[237]

Completely thaw the lobster tails and remove the meat from the shells. Cut each tail into four pieces. Heat the olive oil in a heavy skillet. Sauté the lobster pieces and garlic for 3 or 4 minutes, turning the lobster meat once or twice. Peel, seed, and chop the tomatoes, and add them, together with the tomato juice, wine, and Fish stock, to the skillet. Bring the mixture to a boil. Carefully wash and scrub the clams and add them to the boiling soup. Cover and cook for about 10 minutes, or until the shells begin to open. Stir in the shrimp, bay leaves, and parsley, and cook for several minutes more, covered, until the shrimp turn pink. Heat eight soup bowls and serve at once—with hot, crunchy French bread.

Turkish Wedding Soup

2 onions

7 carrots

4 pounds lamb neck bones

10 cups Beef broth

1½ teaspoons salt

½ pound butter

1 cup flour

6 egg yolks

2 tablespoons lemon juice

Freshly ground pepper to taste

¼ teaspoon cayenne pepper

3½ teaspoons paprika

Croutons

SERVES EIGHT

Peel the onions and carrots, cut into quarters, and put into a soup kettle with the lamb bones, broth, and salt. Simmer, covered, for 1 hour, or until the meat is soft. Strain the broth into a bowl. Remove the meat from the bones and cut into thin strips. Add the meat to the broth.

Melt 12 tablespoons butter and work in the flour. Add 1 cup of the warm broth, a little at a time, and mix well. Gradually stir this butter-flour mixture into the rest of the soup. Bring the soup to a boil, stirring constantly. Lower the heat and cook for about 10 minutes. Keep the soup warm. Beat the egg yolks with a fork and mix in the lemon juice. Add 4 tablespoons of hot soup. Stir this mixture briskly into the rest of the soup. Reheat over a very low flame. *Do not boil.* Adjust the seasonings.

Melt 4 tablespoons of butter, and add cayenne pepper and

paprika. Pour the soup into individual soup bowls. Float spoonfuls of this spiced butter over the top of each. Serve hot, with croutons.

Turkish Almond Soup

1 pound dry blanched almonds	*2 teaspoons salt*
6 bitter almonds	*10 cups Beef and veal stock (see page 370)*
10 hard-cooked egg yolks	
2 teaspoons lemon zest (thin outer skin), grated	*2 cups heavy cream*
	½ cup fresh mint, minced (optional)
2 teaspoons coriander seeds	

SERVES EIGHT

With your electric blender, reduce the blanched and bitter almonds to a fine powder. Remove about ½ the almonds from the blender jar and reserve. Place the egg yolks, grated lemon zest, and coriander seeds in the blender jar and blend at high speed for 15 seconds. Mix with the reserved almond powder. Add the salt to 6 cups of the stock and bring to a boil. Stir the remaining stock into the egg and almond paste and add it to the boiling stock. Reduce the heat and simmer, covered, for 10 minutes. Whip the heavy cream. Stir it into the soup and heat briefly. Continue to stir but do not allow the soup to boil. Garnish with minced mint leaves, if available.

Turkish Lentil Soup

2 medium-sized onions	*¼ cup flour*
6 tablespoons butter	*4 egg yolks, beaten*
¾ pound red lentils	*3 cups milk*
4 cups water	*Salt and red pepper to taste*
6 cups Beef consommé (see page 68)	*Croutons*

SERVES EIGHT

Peel and chop the onions. Melt 2 tablespoons of the butter in a large, heavy soup kettle. Sauté the onions until they are golden and transparent. Add the lentils and water. Simmer 20 to 30 minutes, or until the lentils are cooked. Stir occasionally. *Do not boil.* Heat the consommé and add to the soup. Purée in an electric blender.

Melt the remaining butter in a small pan and stir in the flour. Cook over low heat for about 5 minutes, stirring constantly so that the flour will not burn. Remove the pan from the stove and gradually add the beaten egg yolks, stirring until smooth. Beat in the milk and stir the puréed mixture into the soup, a little at a time adding enough extra milk to thin the soup if necessary. Adjust the seasonings. Reheat and serve with croutons.

Yemenite Soup

2 *pounds boneless veal, cut in 1-inch cubes*	½ *teaspoon salt*
2 *quarts water*	½ *teaspoon pepper*
6 *small onions, cut in quarters*	2 *teaspoons each ground coriander, cumin, fenugreek, and turmeric*
1 *green onion*	
2 *medium-sized tomatoes, peeled, seeded and cut in quarters*	2 *medium-sized zucchini*
	3 *medium-sized carrots, cut in 1 inch pieces*
1 *parsley root*	4 *medium-sized potatoes, cut in eighths*
1 *clove garlic, minced*	
1 *cup spinach, minced*	½ *cup raw rice*

SERVES EIGHT

Arrange the veal in the bottom of a deep kettle and cover with 2 quarts of water. Bring to a boil and simmer, covered, for 30 minutes. Meanwhile, peel and quarter the onions. Peel the green onion. Peel the tomatoes, cut into quarters, and seed by shaking the quarters. Scrape and wash the parsley root. Peel and mince the garlic. Add the quartered onions, whole green onion, tomatoes, the spinach and minced garlic to the kettle, along with the minced parsley and spices. Cover again and simmer the soup for 20 minutes. Rinse the zucchini and cut each into 4 pieces. Peel and cut the carrots into 1-inch pieces. Peel the potatoes and cut them in eighths. Add the zucchini, carrots, potatoes and raw rice to the kettle and continue to simmer the soup, covered, for 25 minutes, or until the vegetables and rice are tender. Serve immediately.

Turkish Turquoise

*Try small bowls of this lovely cold cucumber and
yoghurt soup before any summer meal.*

4 medium-sized cucumbers	8 tablespoons olive oil
Salt	3 pints plain yoghurt
6 small cloves of garlic	2 tablespoons water
4 tablespoons vinegar	Salt and freshly ground pepper
6 tablespoons fresh mint, minced	to taste
8 tablespoons fresh dill, minced	

SERVES EIGHT

Peel and grate the cucumbers very fine, sprinkle with salt, and mix lightly. Rub a bowl thoroughly with the garlic cloves and put the vinegar into it. Let rest for a few minutes.

Combine the cucumbers, mint, dill, oil, and yoghurt, and stir until smooth. Add the water and stir well. Adjust the seasonings. Pour the soup into the seasoned bowl and put into the refrigerator, covered, until well chilled.

Turkish Cucumber Soup

*This delicate hot weather soup is very often followed
by various broiled meats.*

1½ pints plain yoghurt	9 cups tomato juice
3 tablespoons olive oil	3 cucumbers, peeled and
6 tablespoons lemon juice	chopped
1½ tablespoons curry	6 tablespoons parsley, chopped
6 tablespoons vinegar	Salt and pepper to taste

SERVES EIGHT

[241]

Beat the yoghurt in a large bowl until smooth. Add the olive oil, lemon juice, curry, and vinegar. Stir in the tomato juice, cucumber and seasonings. Cover and refrigerate about 4 hours. Ladle the soup into bowls and sprinkle with chopped parsley.

Turkish Fall Soup

2 medium-sized onions
7 large fresh tomatoes
5 green peppers
¾ cup white rice
1½ tablespoons butter
9 cups beef broth

2 cups milk
2 teaspoons fresh parsley and chives, minced
Salt and freshly ground pepper to taste
Croutons

SERVES EIGHT

Peel and grate the onions. Seed and chop the tomatoes and peppers. Place the rice in a soup kettle and add the onions, tomatoes, peppers, and butter. Stir in the beef broth and cook over medium-low heat for 50 minutes. Gradually stir in the milk, and continue cooking over low heat until the rice is tender, about 25 minutes. About 5 minutes before the rice is soft, stir in the chives and parsley. Adjust the seasonings. If a thinner soup is desired, add a little more broth. Ladle into individual soup bowls and garnish with croutons.

Turkish Farina Soup

7 medium-sized fresh tomatoes
¾ cup water
1 cup farina
6 tablespoons butter
10 cups Chicken stock (see page 74)

5 eggs
1¼ cups milk
Salt and freshly ground pepper to taste

SERVES EIGHT

Peel, seed, and chop the tomatoes; place in a soup kettle together with the water. Cook over medium-low heat until the tomatoes are cooked to a pulp.

Sauté the farina in the butter, stirring constantly for 3 or 4 minutes. Stir in the Chicken stock. Simmer for 15 minutes. Add the tomatoes and simmer for 10 minutes more. Beat together the eggs and the milk. Beat in ½ cup of the hot soup. Gradually add 3 more cups of the soup, stirring constantly. When the mixture is smooth, add to the rest of the hot soup. Stir thoroughly. Adjust the seasonings. Ladle the soup into bowls and serve at once.

Armenian Barley and Yoghurt Soup

1 cup barley
6 cups chicken broth
1 cup onion
¼ cup butter
3 tablespoons fresh (or 1 tablespoon dried) mint

2 tablespoons fresh parsley, minced
Salt and freshly ground pepper to taste
1 quart yoghurt

SERVES EIGHT

Place the barley and the broth in a soup kettle and cook for a few minutes. Peel and chop the onion; sauté in butter until it is golden and transparent. Add to the soup kettle, together with the mint, parsley, salt, and pepper. Simmer the soup until the barley is soft. Stir in the yoghurt and continue to simmer for about 5 minutes. This soup can be served either hot or icy cold in small decorative bowls.

Moroccan Bean and Almond Soup

1 cup navy beans
6 cups Chicken stock (see page 74)
1½ cups blanched almonds
4 leeks, white part only
5 cloves garlic

¾ teaspoon salt
1 cup grape juice
White pepper to taste
1 teaspoon sugar
Additional blanched almonds

SERVES EIGHT

Wash the navy beans, cover with water, and soak overnight. Drain the beans and cook in the Chicken stock until the beans are very tender. Purée. Place the almonds in the blender container with ½ cup purée. Purée again. Stir the almond purée into the cooked beans. Carefully wash the leeks, discarding the roots and tops; chop the white parts very fine. Crush the garlic cloves to a paste and mix with the salt. Add the leeks, garlic paste, grape juice, white pepper, and sugar to the soup, and simmer until the leeks are soft. Rub the soup through a fine sieve. Chill for several hours. Serve cold, topped with a few blanched almonds on each serving.

Hannah's Sweet and Sour Cabbage Soup***

Slices of warm onion rye bread thickly spread with cold butter are a must with this old-world favorite.

2-pound head of cabbage

9 cups water

1½ cups onions, finely diced

½ cup carrots, finely diced

¼ cup celery, finely diced

1 can (28 ounces) tomatoes

8 ginger snaps, crumbled

2 teaspoons salt

½ teaspoon celery salt

½ teaspoon dill weed, dried

¾ cup sugar

¼ cup light brown sugar

1 teaspoon sour salt (citric acid)

Freshly ground pepper to taste

SERVES EIGHT

Cut the cabbage into quarters, remove the core and any limp outer leaves, and shred. Bring the water to a boil and add all the ingredients except the sugars and sour salt. Cover and simmer for 2¼ hours. Add the sugars and sour salt and cook over medium heat for 15 minutes longer. Add more sugar, sour salt, and salt, if necessary, to suit your taste. Sprinkle with pepper. Serve hot.

Lamb Soup of the Middle East

4 tablespoons butter

4 tablespoons olive oil

2 large onions

3 pounds lamb stew, cut in
1-inch pieces

1 tablespoon sugar

1 cup dry white wine

2 cans (12-ounce) tomato
sauce

2 teaspoons salt

½ teaspoon white pepper

1½ pounds fresh green beans

4 beef bouillon cubes

¼ teaspoon ground cumin

7 cups water

SERVES EIGHT

Heat the butter and oil together in a deep heavy skillet. Peel and
chop the onions and sauté slowly until golden. Brown the lamb
pieces with the onion, stirring frequently to ensure even browning.
Stir in the sugar, white wine, tomato sauce, salt, and pepper. Cover
and simmer for 45 minutes. When the meat is tender, add the green
beans and bouillon cubes. Sprinkle with ground cumin and stir in
the water. Cook over low heat, covered, for 30 minutes, or until the
beans are tender. Serve immediately. Thin wedges of Greek feta
cheese atop pieces of melba toast make a tasty complement to this
distinctively different soup.

Turkish Hittite Soup

5 cups Beef consommé (see
page 68)

1½ cups red lentils

3 medium-sized onions

5 tablespoons butter

3 tablespoons flour

6 cups tomato juice

Cayenne pepper

Salt and freshly ground
pepper to taste

Croutons (see page 86)

SERVES EIGHT

Put the Beef consommé into a soup kettle, add the lentils, and simmer until the lentils are tender. Peel and chop the onions. Melt the
butter in another soup kettle and sauté the onion until it is golden
and transparent. Stir in the flour and continue to cook and stir for

5 minutes more. Gradually add the tomato juice, stirring constantly. Bring the soup to a boil and add the lentils and cayenne pepper. Lower the heat and simmer for 30 minutes. Adjust the seasonings. A little more consommé may be added if a thinner soup is desired. Serve hot with croutons.

Tunisian Sorrel Soup

12 cups water

2 pounds sorrel (or 1½ pounds of sorrel and ½ pound of spinach)

2 teaspoons salt

8 scallions with 3 inches of green top

1 cucumber

2 hard-boiled eggs

Freshly ground pepper to taste

Sour cream

SERVES EIGHT

Put the water in a soup kettle and bring to a boil. Wash the sorrel thoroughly, drain, and cut off the stems. Add to the boiling water, together with the salt, and boil for about 3 minutes. Strain the sorrel and reserve the broth. Chop the sorrel and scallions coarsely. Peel and chop the cucumber coarsely. Mash the eggs very fine and add to the broth, together with the sorrel, scallions, and cucumber. Adjust the seasonings. Serve hot, with liberal amounts of sour cream.

BREAD AND SOUP FROM NORTHERN EUROPE

Scotland,
Ireland
and
England

ENGLISH COOKING HAS, perhaps rightly, been called "impoverished." The cooking of Ireland and Wales is only slightly more creative. But the history and cuisine of Scotland captured both my heart and my palate. I must apologize, therefore, for devoting myself almost entirely to soups from this lovely land.

If ever a country's soups typified the characteristics of its people, Scotland is that country. The soups of Scotland are a hearty lot—warm, honest, straightforward, wholesome, healthful, and classically economical. True, there are a few frivolous soups among the more sensible ones, most of them inspired by the French who came to Scotland during the period of the Auld Alliance. But, for the most part, Scottish soups reflect Scotland's early history of poverty due to foreign invasions and domestic clan warfare.

True, food was at times in meager supply and the cattle were kept for milk, butter, and cheese. But Scottish cooking was never impoverished. Delicious soups and broths and stews became staples rather than steaks and rib roasts. Wholesome oats and barley; wild vegetables and game; sorrel, leeks, cabbage, turnips, kale, and potatoes—cooked in hearty broths of lamb, chicken, mutton, and fish— provided excellent and nourishing soups in country kitchens across the land.

The Scots will retain their love of soups and stews. Although the modern housewife may substitute canned bouillon, broth, or consommé for the time-consuming fresh stocks of more placid times, a rich soup, chocked with bits of meat or poultry, and thick with pearl barley, carrots, turnips, and leeks remains an important staple.

Irish Soda Bread

4 tablespoons butter (at room temperature)

4 cups all-purpose flour

1 tablespoon sugar

3 teaspoons baking soda

1 teaspoon salt

1¼ cups currants (optional)

1 egg

1¾ cups buttermilk

MAKES TWO LOAVES

Work the butter into the flour with your fingers. Add the sugar, baking powder, baking soda, and salt, still mixing with your fingers. When the mixture resembles coarse meal, beat the egg lightly with the buttermilk, and add to the other ingredients. Stir with a wooden spoon until well blended. The dough should be soft. Dust your hands lightly with flour and shape the dough into a ball. Place the ball on a flour-sprinkled pastry board and knead for 3 minutes. The dough should become smooth. Cut into two equal portions. Shape each portion into a ball and set both balls on a greased baking sheet. Gently press the dough with your palms until slightly flattened. With a very sharp knife dusted with flour, make ¼-inch deep criss-cross slashes on the top of each loaf. Bake in a preheated 375° F. oven for 35 minutes, or until golden and crusty. Slide the loaves from the baking sheet and cool on a wire rack.

(For a sweeter Irish soda bread, add currants to the flour mixture before stirring in the egg and buttermilk.)

Scottish Oatcakes

1 cup rolled oats	1 teaspoon salt
1 cup all-purpose or unbleached white flour	½ cup vegetable shortening
1 cup sugar	3 tablespoons cold water, approximately
1 teaspoon baking soda	Additional rolled oats

MAKES EIGHTEEN

Place the rolled oats, flour, sugar, baking soda, and salt into a large bowl. With two knives, cut the shortening into the dry ingredients. When the mixture resembles coarse meal, add the cold water, a little at a time, blending well after each addition. The dough should be stiff. Cover a pastry board with additional rolled oats. Turn the dough out and roll very thin. Using the edge of a drinking glass, cut the dough into 3-inch cakes. Arrange them on baking sheets. Bake until slightly browned in an oven preheated to 375° F. (about 15 minutes). Slide the cakes from the baking sheets and cool on wire racks.

Oatmeal Scones

A crunchy scone is a wonderful accompaniment to any hearty soup.

1½ cups all-purpose or unbleached white flour	2 tablespoons butter (at room temperature)
1 teaspoon baking soda	⅔ cups rolled oats
2 teaspoons cream of tartar	½ cup milk
¼ teaspoon salt	1 egg yolk

MAKES SIXTEEN

Sift together into a large bowl the flour, baking soda, cream of tartar, and salt. With your fingers, blend in the butter and rolled oats. Add the milk and mix thoroughly until the dough has a soft consistency. Turn out on a lightly floured board. Knead the dough quickly until it is smooth and elastic. Roll out to ½-inch thickness and cut into

2-inch circles. Place on a lightly greased cookie sheet. Brush the tops with the egg yolk mixed with 1 teaspoon of water. Bake in an oven preheated to 425° F. for 10 minutes, or until brown on top. Cool on a wire rack, or butter immediately and serve hot.

Cream Scones

½ cup butter

4 cups all-purpose or unbleached white flour, sifted

2¾ teaspoons cream of tartar

1½ teaspoons baking soda

1 egg

6 tablespoons sugar

1 cup sour milk

MAKES SIXTEEN

Melt the butter over hot water. Combine the sifted flour, the cream of tartar, and baking soda, and sift together. Beat the egg in a large bowl and stir in the sugar and sour milk. Blend in the dry ingredients and mix together thoroughly. Add the melted butter, a little at a time, beating the dough after each addition. Dust a pastry board lightly with flour and roll the dough out to ¼-inch thickness. Using the edge of a drinking glass, cut the dough into 3-inch circles. Slice each circle into eight wedges and dust with a light sprinkling of flour. Cook on a hot griddle for 10 minutes, or until golden brown on each side.

Irish Sweet Bread

½ cup shortening

¼ cup sugar

¼ cup molasses

1 egg

3 cups all-purpose or unbleached white flour, sifted

¾ teaspoon baking soda

1½ teaspoons salt

1½ cups sour milk

1 cup raisins

¼ cup citron

1½ cups currants

MAKES TWO LOAVES

[252]

Combine the shortening, sugar, and molasses in a large bowl, and cream thoroughly. Add the egg and blend well. Combine the sifted flour, the baking soda, and salt, and sift together. Add the dry ingredients alternately with the sour milk to the creamed mixture, a little at a time, blending well after each addition. Chop the raisins and citron and add, together with the currants, to the batter. Grease two loaf pans and put equal amounts of batter into each. Bake in a preheated 325° F. oven for 1 hour and 20 minutes.

Irish Barmbrack***

*Tradition has it that the lucky Irishman or woman who
comes across a ring, coin, or button while eating
a slice of sweet Irish Barmbrack baked on Halloween
will have good fortune the rest of the year.*

1 cup milk	½ cup currants
2 packages dry active yeast	¾ cup seedless raisins
½ cup warm water	½ cup candied lemon peel, finely chopped
4 cups all-purpose flour, sifted	1 ring or coin wrapped in aluminum foil (optional)
¾ cup sugar	
2¼ teaspoons salt	2 tablespoons sugar
1 teaspoon ground allspice	1 tablespoon water
⅓ cup butter (at room temperature)	

MAKES ONE LOAF

Scald the milk and set it aside to cool. Add the yeast to the warm water and allow it to rest for 5 minutes until it softens. Combine 2 cups of the sifted flour, the sugar, salt, and allspice, and sift together into a large mixing bowl. Blend in the milk, yeast, and butter. Using an electric mixer, beat for 2 minutes at medium speed. Let the dough rise, covered, in a warm, draft-free place for 30 minutes. When it has doubled in bulk, add 1 cup of the flour and beat with the electric mixer for 1 minute at low speed, until the flour is well blended. Repeat with the remaining cup of flour.

Dust a pastry board with flour. Place the dough on it and knead for 8 minutes, kneading in the currants, raisins, and lemon peel at the same time. Grease a bowl, set the dough in it, and turn it over once to grease the top. Allow it to rise, covered, in a warm, draft-free place for about 1¾ hours, or until double in volume. Push the dough down, using a stirring motion with your hand. If desired, add a ring or coin wrapped in aluminum foil. Pat the dough into a round loaf, set the loaf on a greased baking sheet, and allow it to rise again, covered, until it is just about double in size (about 1½ to 2 hours). Bake for 45 minutes in an oven preheated to 350° F. Combine the sugar and water, and brush this mixture over the top and sides of the loaf. Return to the oven for 5 minutes. Remove from the oven and slide onto a wire rack to cool.

Popovers

1 cup all-purpose flour, sifted   *2 eggs*
½ teaspoon salt   *1 cup milk*

MAKES EIGHT

Combine the sifted flour with the salt, and sift again into a large bowl. Beat the eggs slightly and add the milk; blend the liquid thoroughly with the flour and salt. Preheat the oven to 450° F. and set the popover pans inside to heat briefly. Butter the hot popover cups well and pour batter into each cup, filling only ½ full. Bake the popovers for 20 minutes at 450° F. Lower the heat to 375° F. and bake for about 25 minutes longer, or until the popovers are nicely browned. Serve hot, with lavish helpings of butter.

Cheese Popovers

Basic popover batter   *¼ cup cheddar cheese, grated*

MAKES EIGHT

Combine the sifted flour with the salt, and sift again into a large bowl. Add the cheddar cheese. Proceed as directed.

English Cobblestone Bread

1½ packages dry active yeast	1 teaspoon salt
½ cup warm water	4 tablespoons sugar
½ cup milk	3½ cups all-purpose flour, sifted
½ cup butter, melted	Melted butter

MAKES ONE LOAF

Dissolve the yeast in the warm water. Scald the milk and cool to lukewarm. Combine the yeast, milk, and melted butter. Add the remaining *dry* ingredients and beat well. Knead for 2 or 3 minutes. Place the dough in a greased bowl, turning it over once to grease the top. Cover with a damp towel and set in a warm, draft-free place until doubled in bulk (about 1½ hours).

Punch the dough down, turn it out on a lightly floured board, and pat it into a ½-inch thick rectangle. Cut the dough into diamonds 2½ inches long. Dip each one in melted butter. Overlap the pieces of dough in a 9-inch ring mold. It will be approximately half full. Cover with a damp towel and let the dough rise in a warm, draft-free place until doubled in bulk, or until the ring mold is full. Bake in a preheated 400° F. oven until the bread is a golden brown (about 25 minutes). Remove from pan and cool on a wire rack, being careful not to separate the pieces.

Crumpets

½ cup milk	1¾ cups flour
½ cup plus 2 tablespoons water	1 teaspoon salt
1 package dry active yeast	¾ teaspoon baking soda
1 teaspoon sugar	3 tablespoons hot water

MAKES TWELVE

Place the milk and water in a small saucepan and heat to lukewarm. Remove from the heat, sprinkle with yeast and sugar, and let stand for 10 minutes. Sift the flour and salt together and stir into the yeast mixture. Allow the batter to rise in a warm place until bubbly and double in bulk (about 1 hour). Mix the baking soda with the hot water and stir into the batter. Allow to rise in a warm place until it doubles in bulk again (about 45 minutes).

Heat a griddle to medium hot and place twelve muffin rings on top. Spoon equal amounts of the batter into each ring, and cook until the crumpets are golden brown on the bottom. Turn to brown for a minute or two on the other side. To serve, split the crumpets, toast and spread thickly with butter and jam.

Yorkshire Pudding

Scrumptious with roast beef or simply luscious with jam—either way, by all means try Yorkshire pudding.

2 cups all-purpose flour, sifted

1 teaspoon salt

1 cup milk

1 cup light cream

4 eggs

8 tablespoons butter or pan drippings from roast beef*

SERVES EIGHT

Combine the sifted flour and salt, and sift again. With an egg beater, gradually blend in the milk and cream, beating after each addition until the mixture is smooth. Add the eggs, one at a time, beating at least 1 minute for each. Set the liquid batter in the refrigerator, covered with a cloth or aluminum foil, for at least 2 hours. Preheat the oven to 450° F. Melt the butter in a shallow baking pan and place it in the oven. Beat the batter again briefly with an egg beater and pour over the sizzling butter to a depth of ½ inch. Bake for 15 minutes at 450° F., or until the pudding rises; then lower the temperature to 375° F. and bake for 10 to 15 minutes. When the pudding turns crispy brown and light in texture, cut into squares and serve immediately.

* If the Yorkshire Pudding is to be served with jam use butter; if it is to be served with roast beef, use the pan drippings.

Cheddar Cheese Circles

1½ cups sharp cheddar cheese, grated

4½ tablespoons butter, softened

1 cup all-purpose or unbleached white flour

2½ cups breadcrumbs, finely ground

½ teaspoon salt

½ teaspoon cayenne pepper

2½ cups milk

MAKES SIXTEEN

Cream the grated cheddar cheese into the softened butter. Mix in the flour, breadcrumbs, salt, cayenne pepper, and milk. Blend all ingredients well. Dust a pastry board lightly with flour. Turn out the dough and knead until it becomes smooth and elastic (about 8 to 10 minutes). Dust the board with flour again. Roll out the dough to ½-inch thickness. Use a drinking glass to cut 2-inch circles. Grease baking sheets and place the circles on them. Bake in a preheated 400° F. oven until slightly browned (approximately 10 minutes).

Cock-a-Leekie Soup

This traditional Scottish soup may be traced back to the days of friendship between France and Scotland. It is at once delicate and filling, and I recommend it highly to anyone who likes chicken soup in any form. One-half cup of rice may be added, if desired, but I prefer it "as is."

1 small roasting chicken

2½ quarts chicken broth or water

8 white peppercorns

1½ teaspoons salt

2 cloves

6 leeks

6 dried prunes

6 dried apricots

2 tablespoons parsley, chopped

SERVES EIGHT

Rinse and dry the chicken. Place the whole chicken, together with its giblets, in a large soup kettle. Add the chicken broth, peppercorns, salt, and cloves. Cover and simmer until the chicken is tender (approximately 2 hours). Turn the chicken every 30 minutes to assure even cooking, Skim off the excess fat. Remove the chicken, peppercorns, and cloves from the soup. Wash the leeks thoroughly and cut into 1-inch pieces. Add the leeks, prunes, and apricots, and simmer for 20 minutes. Cut the chicken into 1-inch cubes, and discard the skin and bones. Return the chicken meat to the kettle, reheat, and serve the soup hot, garnished with parsley.

Kail Brose***

Unusual and tasty in the extreme is this traditional
Scotch curly kale soup thickened with rolled oats.

1 ham bone with some meat

2 quarts water

1½ pounds curly kale

8 tablespoons quick-cooking rolled oats

Salt and freshly ground black pepper to taste

SERVES EIGHT

Place the ham bone and water in a soup kettle, bring to a boil, skim off the froth, lower the heat, cover, and simmer for 2 hours. Remove the ham bone and chop the meat. Wash the kale, chop very fine, and add to the stock. Cover and boil gently for 20 minutes. Add the oats and chopped ham and boil for 10 minutes more. Adjust the seasonings and serve piping hot.

Cullen Skink

1 medium-sized finnan haddie

Water

1 large onion, peeled and chopped

3½ cups buttermilk, warmed

1 tablespoon butter

1 cup mashed potatoes

Salt and freshly ground pepper to taste

3 tablespoons chopped parsley

SERVES EIGHT

Place the finnan haddie in a soup kettle and cover with water. Cover and bring to a boil. Take the finnan haddie from the kettle and remove the skin. Return the fish to the soup kettle, and when the liquid boils, add the chopped onion. Turn the heat down and cook gently until the fish flakes. Once again remove the fish from the stock and, with a fork, flake the fish from the bones and set aside. Put the fish bones back into the stock, and simmer, covered, for about 1 hour. Strain the soup stock through several thicknesses of cheesecloth. Pour it back into the soup kettle.

Bring the stock to a low boil, then reduce the heat and add the flaked fish, warmed buttermilk, and butter. Mix in enough mashed potatoes to make the soup the consistency of heavy cream. Adjust seasonings. Pour soup into bowls; sprinkle with parsley. Serve hot.

Feather Fowlie

*Every Scottish cook has a favorite recipe for traditional
Feather fowlie. As a matter of fact, so do many
non-Scottish cooks. Here's mine.*

5-pound roasting chicken

10-ounce slice of lean ham

2 medium-sized onions, peeled and sliced

3 small carrots, peeled and sliced

2 stalks celery, washed

2 tablespoons parsley, minced

10 cups water

Several sprigs thyme

A blade of mace

1 teaspoon salt

5 egg yolks

3 tablespoons heavy cream

SERVES EIGHT

Remove the skin from the chicken and cut into serving pieces. Soak in salt water for 20 minutes. Pour off the water and rinse the chicken pieces. Place the chicken and ham, the sliced onions and carrots, the celery, parsley, and water in a soup kettle. Bring nearly to a boil and skim off the froth. Add the thyme, mace, and salt. Cover and cook over medium-low flame for 2 hours. Strain the broth and remove the fat. Chop the chicken and return to the broth. Discard the bones. Beat the egg yolks, heavy cream, and ½ cup of the hot broth. Stir this into the soup and heat over a very low flame for a few minutes, stirring constantly. *Do not boil*, or the egg yolks will curdle.

Scotch Broth***

This recipe for Scotch broth is extremely good.
It produces a thick soup with succulent pieces
of lamb. I heartily recommend it.

2-pound piece of leg of lamb

3 medium-sized carrots, peeled
and diced

3 small turnips, peeled and diced

3 large leeks, washed, trimmed,
and chopped

3 tablespoons pearl barley

3 tablespoons dried split peas

¼ teaspoon pepper

1 teaspoon salt

10 cups water

1 carrot, peeled and grated

5 tablespoons kale, chopped

1 tablespoon parsley, chopped

SERVES EIGHT

Rinse the meat and place it in a large soup kettle; add the carrots, turnips, and leeks. Wash the barley. Rinse the peas and parboil them for 5 minutes in 1½ cups water. Discard the water from the peas and add them, together with the barley, pepper, salt, and 8 cups of water, to the kettle. Bring to a boil, skim off the foam, cover tightly, and simmer for 3 to 4 hours, adding a little water from time to time if the soup becomes too thick. Cool to room temperature and remove any excess fat. Cut the meat into ¾-inch cubes and return to the soup, adding the grated carrot and chopped kale. Cook over low heat for 15 minutes, adding a bit of water if necessary. Serve very hot, garnished with the chopped parsley.

Scottish Potato and Milk Soup

Here's a simple soup that's warm and comforting
on a bleak winter's day.

2 large soup bones (or the
carcass of a large roast
chicken)

2 large onions

1 teaspoon salt

1½ quarts water

3 large potatoes

3 large carrots

2 cups milk

2 tablespoons parsley, chopped

Black pepper to taste

SERVES EIGHT

Rinse the bones and place them in a large kettle; add the peeled whole onions, the salt, and the water. Cover and simmer for 1 hour. Peel the potatoes and cut them into ½-inch cubes. Peel and grate the carrots. Add the vegetables to the soup, cover, and simmer for 1 more hour. Remove the onions and the bones. Add enough milk to make a hearty soup. Adjust the salt if necessary. Reheat. Garnish with parsley and sprinkle with pepper. Serve hot.

Irish Leek Soup

20 leeks, white parts only	1 bay leaf
2½ tablespoons butter	¾ teaspoon ground mace
2½ tablespoons flour	4 egg yolks
4 cups milk	1 cup heavy cream
4 cups Chicken stock (see page 74)	Salt and freshly ground white pepper to taste

SERVES EIGHT

Cut the white part of the leeks into thin slices and sauté in the butter until pale yellow and translucent. Stir in the flour and the milk all at once. Mash out any lumps with the back of a spoon. Bring to a boil over a low flame, stirring constantly. Add the Chicken stock, bay leaf, and ground mace. Stir. Cover and simmer until the leeks are tender. Beat the egg yolks with the heavy cream, and pour into the bottom of a soup tureen. Ladle in the hot soup, adjust the seasonings, stir, and serve hot.

Scottish Shepherd's Stew

This is called a stew, although it is really a soup—warm and filling enough to keep a shepherd well protected from the chilling breezes of Scotland.

2 pounds lamb's neck	1 teaspoon salt
1½ cups carrots, chopped	¼ teaspoon pepper
2 cups onions, chopped	⅔ cup barley
2½ quarts water	

SERVES EIGHT

Place the lamb's neck, carrots, onions, water, salt, and pepper in a large pot. Bring to a boil and then simmer for 1 hour, or until the meat is tender. Do not overcook or the meat will be stringy. Cool the meat, broth, and vegetables. Skim off all fat. Remove the meat from the bones, chop it into 1-inch pieces, and set aside. Add the barley to the broth and simmer until tender, stirring occasionally. Stir in the meat and heat, but do not allow to come to a boil. Serve hot.

Sheep's Head Broth

*Not everyone will be tempted to try this rather
difficult recipe, but if you happen to have a
sheep's head handy, it's worth the effort.*

1 young sheep's head (with brain and tongue), split	2 stalks celery
Water	3 leeks
3 tablespoons vinegar	2 small carrots
3 ounces pearl barley	2 small turnips
1 teaspoon salt	2 large onions
⅛ teaspoon pepper	2 tablespoons parsley, minced
3 sprigs parsley	

SERVES EIGHT GENEROUSLY

Wash the head and soak it for 3 hours in cold water to cover. Remove the brains and place them in a bowl. Sprinkle with vinegar; turn them over once. Drain the head and place it with the rinsed barley, salt, pepper, and parsley in a deep kettle with water to cover. Bring the water to a boil, skim off the foam, reduce the heat, and simmer, covered, for 2 hours. Wash, trim, and chop the celery and leeks coarsely. Peel and chop the carrots, turnips, and onions. Add the vegetables to the sheep's head, cover, and simmer for 1½ hours longer.

Cover the brains with cold water and bring to a slow boil, lower the heat, and simmer for 10 minutes. Drain, clean, chop, and add to the broth. Remove the head from the broth and slice the meat. Skin the tongue and cut into ½-inch slices. Keep the meat warm and serve with parsley sauce. Serve broth hot, sprinkled with minced parsley.

PARSLEY SAUCE

¼ cup parsley, minced   ½ cup sheeps head broth
½ cup milk   1 tablespoon butter

Simmer all ingredients together for 7 minutes.

Irish Jerusalem Artichoke Soup

6 large Jerusalem artichokes
4 medium-sized onions
4 medium-sized potatoes
2½ tablespoons butter
4 cloves garlic
2 bay leaves

10 cups Chicken consommé (see page 74)
½ cup heavy cream
¾ teaspoon nutmeg
Salt and freshly ground pepper to taste

SERVES EIGHT

Peel and chop the artichokes. Peel and chop the onions and potatoes. In a soup kettle, sauté all of the vegetables in butter until the onions are transparent.

Peel and chop the garlic and add to kettle, together with the bay leaf and Chicken consommé. Cover and cook over very low heat for 30 minutes. Pour the soup through a strainer. Adjust the seasonings. Serve hot, adding 1 tablespoon of hot heavy cream to each bowl of soup. Sprinkle with nutmeg.

Welsh Buttermilk Soup

2 pounds lamb bones
1-pound piece of lean lamb
2 stalks celery with leaves
2 leeks
2 small turnips
2 onions

2½ quarts water
2½ cups buttermilk
4 tablespoons butter
4 tablespoons flour
Salt and pepper to taste
2 tablespoons parsley, minced

SERVES EIGHT

Rinse the lamb bones and meat and place in a soup kettle with the well-washed, chopped celery and leeks, the peeled and quartered turnips and onions, and the water. Bring slowly to a boil, skimming frequently. Lower the heat and simmer, uncovered, for 2 hours. Remove the bones and set them aside. Remove the piece of lamb, chop it, and set aside. Strain the soup and discard the vegetables. Return the bones to the kettle with the strained broth and simmer until it is reduced to 5½ cups.

Bring the buttermilk to room temperature. Melt the butter in a large skillet. Stir in the flour, add the buttermilk, and stir constantly until the sauce is thick and smooth. Add the lamb broth, 1 cup at a time, stirring well after each addition. Adjust the seasonings. Stir in the reserved lamb and simmer for 8 to 10 minutes. Serve hot, sprinkled with minced parsley.

Mulligatawny***

Chicken and apple and curry in a soup? Absolutely!
And this Scottish version is particularly wonderful.

4-*pound chicken, cut into*
  serving pieces

3 *tablespoons butter*

2 *sour green apples, peeled and*
  chopped

½ *cup onion, chopped*

½ *cup green pepper, chopped*

¼ *cup carrots, chopped*

2 *tablespoons flour*

2 *teaspoons curry powder*

3 *quarts Chicken stock (see*
  page 74)

½ *cup shredded coconut*

4 *cloves, whole*

1 *tablespoon parsley, minced*

1 *tablespoon sugar*

2 *teaspoons salt*

3 *small tomatoes*

  Boiled rice

SERVES EIGHT

In a large soup kettle, brown the chicken in the butter. Add the apples, onion, green pepper, and carrots, and brown lightly, stirring occasionally. Stir in the flour and curry powder, and blend well. Add the Chicken stock and coconut, and stir over low heat for 5 minutes. Add the cloves, parsley, sugar, and salt, and simmer until the chicken is tender. Peel the tomatoes, shake out the seeds, and chop coarsely. Add to the soup and cook at a low boil for 15 minutes. Remove the chicken pieces, discard the skin and bones, and cut the meat into small cubes. Strain the soup and use a spoon to force the vegetables through a sieve into the soup. Add the chicken, reheat, and serve with spoons of boiled rice.

Scottish Brown Soup

2 medium-sized onions

1 pound lean ground round steak

2 tablespoons butter

2 medium-sized turnips

2 medium-sized carrots

3 stalks celery

8½ cups Beef stock (see page 67) or Beef consommé (see page 68)

½ teaspoon pepper

½ teaspoon caraway seeds

1 teaspoon Bovril

Salt to taste

1 cup red wine

SERVES EIGHT

Peel and chop the onions. Sauté the onions and ground steak in the butter in a large, heavy Dutch oven until the meat is lightly browned. Peel and chop the turnips and carrots. Trim and chop the celery. Add the chopped vegetables, Beef stock, pepper, and caraway seeds to the sautéed meat and bring to a boil. Lower the heat and simmer, covered, for 1 hour, or until the vegetables are soft. Stir in the Bovril, salt, and wine. Serve piping hot.

Cheddar Cheese Soup

1 medium-sized onion

4 tablespoons butter

1½ quarts milk

4 egg yolks, beaten

2 cups light cream

6 ounces cheddar cheese, grated

Salt and freshly ground pepper to taste

Freshly grated nutmeg

SERVES EIGHT

Peel and mince the onion. Melt the butter in a large saucepan, add the minced onion, and sauté until golden and transparent. Pour in the milk and bring to a boil. Remove from the stove. Combine the beaten egg yolks with the light cream. Blend in the egg mixture, the grated cheese, salt, and freshly ground pepper to taste. Cook over low heat, stirring constantly until hot and fairly thick. Do not boil or the eggs will curdle. Sprinkle with freshly grated nutmeg and serve hot in small bowls.

Scottish Bread Soup***

*If bread soup sounds to you as if it is more suited
for beggars than kings, you really should sample
this tasty old standby.*

3½ cups bread cubes (I usually
   use French bread, but slices
   of rye, cubed, are superb)

6 tablespoons butter

5 medium-sized onions

10 cups beef broth or beef
   consommé (see pages 67, 68)

3 cups lima beans, fresh or
   frozen

1½ teaspoons sugar

½ teaspoon salt

¼ teaspoon pepper

½ cup dry sherry

SERVES EIGHT

Toast the bread cubes in a medium oven. In a heavy Dutch oven, sauté them in the butter for 5 minutes. Peel and chop the onions, and add them to the bread. Sauté 5 minutes more. Place the sautéed bread cubes and onions in a bowl and set aside. Place the beef broth in the Dutch oven, bring it to a boil, and add the lima beans. Simmer until the beans are tender. Add the bread cubes and onions, the sugar, salt, and pepper. Simmer for 5 minutes without boiling. Stir in the sherry and serve immediately.

Germany, Austria and Holland

GERMAN AND AUSTRIAN cooking is hearty, filling, and surprisingly varied. Although we tend to think strictly in terms of sausage in seemingly infinite variety, of dumplings and winekraut and venison, the cooking of these two countries ranges from the delicate to the super-rich. Their soups in particular are superb—full-bodied, diverse, and certainly worthy of your best culinary efforts.

Muenster Cheese Loaf

6½–7½ cups flour, unsifted

2 packages dry active yeast

1½ teaspoons sugar

1¼ tablespoons salt

1 cup plain yoghurt

2½ tablespoons butter

½ cup water

6 eggs (at room temperature)

¾ pound Muenster cheese, shredded

1 egg

1 tablespoon milk

MAKES TWO LOAVES

Combine 1½ cups of the flour with the yeast, sugar, and salt in a large bowl, and mix thoroughly. Combine the yoghurt, butter, and water together in a small saucepan, and heat over low flame to the scalding point. It is not necessary to melt the butter. Add the yoghurt mixture, a little at a time, to the dry ingredients, mixing thoroughly after each addition. Beat for 2 minutes with an electric mixer at medium speed. Scrape the bowl occasionally. Add the 6 eggs, ½ cup of the shredded Muenster, and 1 cup of the flour to the ingredients in the bowl. Beat for 2 minutes at high speed. Scrape the bowl occasionally. Add as much flour as is needed to make a stiff dough. Dust a board lightly with flour, and knead the dough until it is smooth and elastic (about 8 to 10 minutes). Place the dough in a greased bowl, turning it once to grease the top. Cover the bowl and allow the dough to rise in a warm, draft-free place until it is double in bulk (approximately 1 hour).

Punch the dough down and divide it into two equal pieces. Pat the dough lightly until each piece is slightly rounded in shape. Place on greased baking sheets, cover, and allow to rise again in a warm, draft-free place until double in bulk (approximately 1 hour). Beat the single egg. Mix with the milk and brush over the loaves. Top the loaves with the remaining shredded Muenster. Bake at 350 F. until the loaves are golden (approximately 30 minutes). Remove the bread from the oven, and set the loaves on wire racks to cool.

Soft Pretzels***

These are soft, soft pretzels—actually more like rolls—
and make a wonderful "go-with" for any hearty soup.

2¼ cups warm water	7-7½ cups all-purpose or unbleached white flour
2 packages dry active yeast	
⅓ cup sugar	1 egg yolk
2¼ teaspoons salt	1 tablespoon water
5 tablespoons butter, softened	Coarse or kosher salt
1 egg	

MAKES THIRTY

Place the water and yeast in the large bowl of an electric mixer. Stir until the yeast is dissolved. Stir in the sugar, salt, butter, egg, and 3 cups of the flour. Beat at medium speed until the batter is smooth.

Add the remaining flour to make a stiff dough. Cover the bowl tightly with aluminum foil and refrigerate from 4 to 6 hours.

Dust a bread board lightly with flour and turn the cold dough out onto it. Divide the dough in half and cut each half into fifteen pieces. Roll each piece between your hands to form pencil shapes about 18 inches long. Work fast because this procedure is not as easy as it may sound. The dough is springy and tends to shrink up into shorter lengths. Give each piece a final stretch before forming it into a pretzel shape. Place the pretzels on lightly greased baking sheets. Beat the egg yolk and water together, and brush the pretzels generously with this mixture. Sprinkle liberally with salt, cover, and let rise in a warm, draft-free place for 30 minutes. Bake in an oven preheated to 400° F. for 15 minutes, or until golden brown. Remove the pretzels from the baking sheets and cool on wire racks.

Kügelhopf

½ cup milk	1 teaspoon salt
1 package dry active yeast	4 cups all-purpose flour, sifted
½ cup warm water	¾ cup almonds, slivered
½ cup butter (at room temperature)	1 cup golden raisins
⅓ cup sugar	2 teaspoons lemon zest (thin outer skin), grated
4 eggs (at room temperature)	½ cup almonds, finely chopped

MAKES ONE

Scald the milk in a saucepan and cool to lukewarm. Soften the yeast in the warm water until dissolved, and stir in the lukewarm milk. Cream the butter and sugar together in a large bowl until fluffy. With an electric mixer on low speed, beat the eggs into the creamed mixture one at a time, blending well after each addition. At low speed, beat in the yeast mixture, blending well. Combine the salt with the sifted flour, and sift together into the other ingredients. Beat at low speed to make a smooth batter. Then add the slivered almonds, raisins, and grated lemon zest to the batter. Set the bowl in a warm, draft-free place. Allow the batter to rise, covered with a linen towel, until it doubles in size (about 2 hours).

If you are the proud possessor of a Kügelhopf mold, now is the time to use it. Otherwise, any 10-cup tube mold will serve nicely.

Butter the sides and bottom of the mold generously, and sprinkle with finely chopped almonds. Punch the batter down, and then arrange it in the mold. Cover the mold lightly, and allow the batter to rise again. When it nearly reaches the top of the mold, put it in a preheated 375° F. oven to bake for 50 to 60 minutes, or until a toothpick inserted in the top comes out clean. Cool the bread by inverting the tube mold over a wire rack. The fruit- and nut-filled Kügelhopf goes especially well with tea or coffee.

Viennese Striesel

2½–3½ cups all-purpose or
    unbleached white flour,
    unsifted
  1 package dry active yeast
  ⅓ cup sugar
  ¾ teaspoon salt
  ½ cup milk
  ¼ cup water
  4½ tablespoons butter

1 egg
¼ cup candied orange peel,
    chopped
¾ cup currants
⅓ cup candied cherries,
    chopped
1 cup confectioner's sugar
1 tablespoon milk

MAKES ONE

Mix ¾ cup of the flour, the yeast, sugar, and salt together in a large bowl. Combine the milk, water, and butter in a saucepan, and heat slowly until the liquid reaches about 130° F. It is not necessary to melt the butter. Pour the milk mixture, a little at a time, into the dry ingredients, blending well after each addition. With an electric mixer, beat 2 minutes at medium speed, scraping the bowl occasionally. Mix in the egg and ½ cup flour and beat for 2 minutes at high speed, scraping the bowl occasionally. Blend in enough of the additional flour to make a soft dough. Place the dough on a lightly floured board and knead it for 8 to 10 minutes. When the dough is smooth and elastic, put it in a greased bowl, turn it over once to grease the top, and cover. Allow to rise in a warm, draft-free place until double in volume (approximately 1 hour).

    Punch the dough down and put it on a lightly floured board. Knead in the orange peel, currants, and cherries. Divide the dough into nine equal portions. Roll each one into 15-inch lengths. Place four of the rolled lengths on a lightly greased baking sheet and braid them together, using the two center lengths as one piece. Indent the center of the braid with the side of your hand, forming a slight depression in the dough. Braid three more lengths and lay this braid on top of the center depression. Loosely twist the two remaining lengths, place on top of the loaf, and tuck the ends under the loaf to seal. Toothpicks may be used to keep the loaf together. Cover the loaf and allow it to rise in a warm, draft-free place until double in volume (approximately 1 hour).

Bake for 30 minutes in an oven preheated to 350° F. Remove the loaf from the pan, take out the toothpicks, and cool on a wire rack. Combine the confectioner's sugar with the milk; dribble this frosting over the top of the loaf. Slice and enjoy with afternoon tea.

Cream Cheese Soup***

*Austrian cheese soup is unusually creamy
and pleasantly satisfying.*

4 *stalks celery*	2 *8-ounce packages cream cheese (at room temperature)*
6 *large leeks, white parts only*	
5½ *tablespoons butter*	2 *cups plain yoghurt*
6 *tablespoons white flour*	4 *egg yolks*
4½ *cups chicken broth*	*White pepper to taste*
3 *cups water*	½ *cup leek tops, minced*
1¼ *teaspoons salt*	

SERVES EIGHT

Peel and chop the celery. Wash and chop the white part of the leeks. Sauté the chopped celery and leeks in the butter, stirring occasionally, until the leeks are transparent. Do not brown the vegetables. Blend in the flour, broth, water, and salt. Cook over high heat, stirring constantly, until the mixture comes to a boil. Simmer for 15 minutes.

Meanwhile, cream together the cream cheese, yoghurt, and egg yolks. Remove the soup from the stove and cool for 5 minutes. Stir in the cream cheese mixture, mashing any lumps with the back of the spoon. Simmer, stirring constantly, until the soup is hot. *Do not*

[271]

boil, or the egg yolks will curdle. Season with white pepper and additional salt, if desired. Serve hot, sprinkled with chopped chives.

Cream Cheese-Potato Soup***

This chunky potato soup originally from the Adriatic
is speckled with green—dill, chervil, chives, mint, and
parsley—and enriched with sieved cream cheese.

8 *large potatoes*	2 *teaspoons mint, minced*
2 *large onions*	4 *teaspoons dill, minced*
2½ *teaspoons salt*	2 *8-ounce packages cream cheese*
9 *cups water*	
6 *tablespoons butter*	2 *tablespoons parsley, chopped*
4 *tablespoons flour*	4 *teaspoons chives, chopped*
3 *teaspoons chervil, minced*	

SERVES EIGHT

Peel the potatoes and cut them into large cubes. Peel and chop the onion. Put the vegetables, salt, and water into a large pan, and cook until the potatoes are barely tender. Melt the butter in a large, heavy skillet. Stir in the flour; add the potatoes, onions, and potato water, and cook, stirring constantly, until the soup has thickened. Add the chervil, mint, and dill, and simmer for 5 minutes. With a spoon, sieve equal amounts of cream cheese into eight soup bowls. Spoon the hot soup over the sieved cheese, sprinkle with parsley and chives, and serve immediately.

Tyrolean Cheese Soup

8 *tablespoons butter*	4 *cups Swiss cheese, grated*
1 *cup flour*	½ *teaspoon salt*
8½ *cups milk*	8 *tablespoons shallots, minced*
2 *cups water*	

SERVES EIGHT

Melt the butter in a heavy skillet. Stir in the flour and blend until smooth. Add the milk and water and stir until the sauce begins to thicken. Cover lightly and cook over very low heat for 10 minutes, stirring occasionally. Just before serving, stir in the cheese and salt. Garnish with chopped shallots. Serve immediately, with thick slices of pumpernickel bread.

Old-Fashioned German Mushroom Soup

3 medium-sized onions	4½ teaspoons Worcestershire sauce
¾ cup butter	
3 tablespoons flour	¼ teaspoon nutmeg
2½ pounds mushrooms	Salt and pepper to taste
10 cups beef broth	Garlic croutons (see page 86)

SERVES EIGHT

Chop the onions coarsely. Heat the butter in a deep kettle and sauté the onions slowly until transparent. Blend in the flour and cook the mixture for 1 minute. Brush or rinse the sand from the mushrooms, cut into small cubes, and add with the beef broth, Worcestershire sauce, and spices to the onion mixture. Simmer the soup, covered, for 10 to 15 minutes. Serve immediately, garnished with Garlic croutons in each bowl.

German Salsify Soup

3 cups salsify	6 tablespoons butter
11 cups Chicken stock (page 74)	¼ cup flour
3 tablespoons vinegar	Salt and white pepper to taste
3 tablespoons flour	4 egg yolks
1 teaspoon salt	4 tablespoons cold water

SERVES EIGHT

Wash and peel the salsify. Put it into a soup kettle and cover at once with the Chicken stock. Mix ½ cup stock, vinegar, flour, and salt until smooth. Stir into the soup kettle. Cut the salsify into 1-inch pieces and return immediately to the stock. Cook over medium-low heat until tender when tested with a fork. Strain into a bowl, reserving both the liquid and the salsify.

Melt the butter in the soup kettle, add ¼ cup flour, and stir until smooth and slightly golden. Gradually add this mixture to the reserved liquid, stirring constantly so that no lumps will form. Bring to a boil once again and then lower heat. Simmer for 15 minutes. Adjust the seasonings. Beat the egg yolks thoroughly with the cold water and stir into the hot soup. Add the reserved salsify. Serve immediately without reheating.

Cream Cheese and Leek Soup with Ham***

This smooth and creamy soup is absolutely exquisite
served alone or as a preamble
to a relatively simple meal.

5 tablespoons butter	Salt and white pepper to taste
1 pound spinach, chopped	
4 large leeks, white part only	2 cups yoghurt
6 tablespoons flour	4 egg yolks
4½ cups chicken broth	2 cups cooked ham, coarsely chopped
4½ cups water	1 cup chives, finely chopped
1 teaspoon salt	
2 8-ounce packages cream cheese (at room temperature)	

SERVES EIGHT

Heat 2½ tablespoons of the butter in a heavy soup kettle. Chop the spinach and the white part of the leeks, and cook gently in the melted butter. When the vegetables are soft, sprinkle in the flour, and cook for 2 minutes over medium-high heat, stirring constantly. Remove the kettle from the stove and add the chicken broth, water, and salt. Return to low heat and continue to stir until the mixture thickens slightly. Simmer for 15 minutes. Mash the cream cheese in a small bowl. Sprinkle with salt and white pepper to taste, and stir in the yoghurt and egg yolks. Beat the mixture until smooth. Sauté the ham in the remaining butter. Carefully stir the cheese mixture into the soup and cook over low heat for 5 minutes, stirring constantly. Add the ham. Serve the soup piping hot, garnished with chopped chives.

German Fresh Green Pea Soup

3 cups fresh green peas

6 tablespoons butter

⅓ cup flour

11 cups Brown stock (see page 67)

Salt and freshly ground pepper to taste

2 tablespoons parsley, minced

SERVES EIGHT

Shell the peas and place in a soup kettle. Sauté the peas in butter, add the flour, and continue to cook for several minutes, stirring occasionally. Gradually stir in the Brown stock. Bring to a boil, then lower the heat and cook slowly until the peas are quite soft. Adjust the seasonings. Serve hot. Garnish with fresh minced parsley and, if desired, small meatballs.

Tyrolean Vegetable Soup

¼ cup butter

1 medium-sized onion

3 slices bacon

2 carrots, sliced

2 cups Brussels sprouts, sliced

3 celery stalks, chopped

1 clove garlic, chopped

9 mushrooms, chopped

2 leeks (white part only), sliced

3 small tomatoes

2 tablespoons tomato paste

2 quarts Chicken stock (see page 74)

½ cup dried white beans

1½ cups salted water

½ cup macaroni

½ cup parsley, chopped

Salt and pepper to taste

Grated Parmesan cheese

SERVES EIGHT

[275]

Melt the butter in a heavy saucepan. Dice the onion and the bacon slices, and sauté them in the butter. Stir in the carrots, Brussels sprouts, celery, garlic, mushrooms, and leeks, and simmer slowly for 10 minutes, or until the vegetables are wilted. Peel, seed, and chop the tomatoes. Add the tomatoes and tomato paste and cook for 5 minutes. Stir in the Chicken stock and simmer for 2 hours. In a separate saucepan boil the dried white beans in the salted water for 1½ hours, adding more water if necessary to keep from scorching. Break the macaroni into short lengths and add to the soup 30 minutes before serving time. Stir the parsley, salt, pepper, beans, and bean liquid into the soup. Serve hot, with grated Parmesan cheese on the side.

Pumpernickel Soup

5 tablespoons butter

5 medium-sized onions

7 medium-sized potatoes

2 quarts beef broth

10 slices dark pumpernickel bread

4 stalks celery

3 scallions

2 small carrots

1 large bay leaf

Salt and freshly ground pepper to taste

1 cup sour cream

2 tablespoons chopped chives

Pumpernickel croutons (see page 87)

SERVES EIGHT

Place the butter in a large pan. Peel and chop the onions coarsely. Sauté them in the butter for 5 or 10 minutes, stirring frequently. Peel the potatoes, cube them, and add to the onions. Pour in the beef broth. Cover and cook gently for 10 minutes.

Trim the crusts from the pumpernickel bread and cut into cubes. Chop the celery and scallions. Peel and chop the carrots. Add the cubed pumpernickel, celery, scallions, carrots, and bay leaf to the soup. Simmer for 20 minutes. Purée the soup in a blender or press through a sieve. Adjust the seasonings. Stir in ½ cup of the sour cream, reserving the rest for garnish. Reheat the soup. Serve hot, in small bowls, with 1 tablespoon of sour cream, chopped chives, and pumpernickel croutons garnishing each serving.

German Cauliflower Soup

1 large head cauliflower	2½ cups milk
8 cups boiling water	3 egg yolks
2 teaspoons salt	4 tablespoons cold water
6 tablespoons butter	Salt and freshly ground
¼ cup flour	pepper to taste

Wash the cauliflower and separate it into flowerets. Place in a soup kettle and add the boiling water and salt. Simmer until the cauliflower is tender. Strain the cauliflower water into a large bowl. Reserve the cooked cauliflower flowerets.

Melt the butter in the soup kettle and stir in the flour. Cook, stirring constantly, until the flour takes on a creamy color. Gradually add the cauliflower liquid and the milk, stirring constantly so that lumps will not form. Simmer for 10 minutes. Gently stir in the cooked cauliflower. Beat the egg yolks, add the water, and heat again. *Do not boil.* Mix with 1 cup of the soup and then gradually add this mixture to the soup kettle. Adjust the seasonings. Serve immediately.

Potato Soup***

Unusual flavor marks this creamy soup—its surprising tang is much like hot German potato salad!

7 slices lean bacon	6 large potatoes
3 large onions finely chopped	3 egg yolks
6 mushrooms, finely chopped	1½ cups sour cream
4½ tablespoons flour	2 tablespoons parsley, minced
9 cups beef bouillon (see page 68)	2 tablespoons dried basil

SERVES EIGHT

Dice the bacon and sauté it in a deep kettle for 5 minutes. Stir in the chopped onions and mushrooms, and sauté until the vegetables are soft (approximately 5 minutes). Blend in the flour and gradually add the bouillon, stirring constantly. Peel and slice the potatoes very thin; add them to the simmering bouillon and cook for 1 hour.

Beat the egg yolks and mix with the sour cream. Stir ½ cup of the hot soup slowly into the egg yolk mixture. Add this mixture to the soup and simmer for 10 minutes, stirring constantly. Serve immediately, sprinkled with minced parsley and dried basil.

Austrian Creamed Potato Soup

10 cups Brown stock (see page 67)

1½ teaspoons cumin seed

1 teaspoon salt

1 cup dry white wine

2 cups sour cream

1½ tablespoons flour

7 potatoes, cooked, peeled, and diced

1½ cups heavy cream

Salt and freshly ground pepper to taste

SERVES EIGHT

Put the Brown stock in a soup kettle, together with the cumin, salt, and wine. Place over medium-high heat and boil for 10 minutes. Measure the sour cream into a small bowl and blend in the flour. Stir in 1 cup of the hot stock. Gradually add this mixture to the soup, beating thoroughly with a wire whisk. Add the diced potatoes and gently stir in the heavy cream. Adjust the seasonings. Cook over low heat until the soup is hot.

Calf's Brain Soup

3 tablespoons butter

1 medium-sized onion, sliced

3 tablespoons flour

9 cups chicken broth

1 calf's brain

4 egg yolks

2½ cups cream

Salt and freshly ground pepper to taste

Croutons

6 tablespoons fresh parsley and chives, minced

SERVES EIGHT

Melt the butter in a soup kettle, add the onion slices, and sauté until the onion is golden and transparent. Mix the flour thoroughly into the butter and onions. Gradually pour in the chicken broth, stirring well to avoid lumps, and continue stirring until the soup has started to thicken. Cover and simmer for 15 minutes.

Wash the calf's brain, pull away the thin outer skin, remove all membranes, rinse, and cut into chunks. Put the brain into the soup and cook over low heat for 15 minutes. Strain the soup into a bowl, pressing the calf's brain through with the back of a spoon. Beat the egg yolks with a fork, stir in the heavy cream, and add to soup. Adjust the seasonings. Pour the soup back into the soup kettle and heat over a low flame just until hot. Serve in individual bowls, sprinkled with croutons and minced parsley and chives.

Sauerkraut Soup***

*Thick, rich soup, spiked with slices of barenwurst
sausage and flavored with caraway and fennel
seeds, is sure to be a conversation piece, whether
served alone or as part of a German meal. I have
found it to be perfectly reheatable for a quick
meal. Serve it warm with freshly baked soft pretzels
and cold butter. Delicious.*

1¾ pounds sauerkraut (I use the delicatessen style)	½ teaspoon fennel seeds
9½ cups Beef stock (see page 67)	½ teaspoon caraway seeds
3 large onions	1 teaspoon paprika
6 slices slab bacon	½ teaspoon salt
3 medium-sized potatoes	2 barenwurst
1 tablespoon tomato paste	½ cup baked or boiled ham

SERVES EIGHT

Drain the sauerkraut and simmer it in the Beef stock for 30 minutes. Meanwhile, peel and chop the onions; dice the bacon; and sauté these until the onions are transparent. Peel and grate the potatoes and soak them for 5 minutes in cold water. Add the sautéed onions and bacon, the drained potatoes, the tomato paste, fennel seeds, caraway seeds, paprika, and salt to the sauerkraut mixture. Cover and boil gently for 30 minutes more.

Ten minutes before serving, peel and slice the barenwurst, dice the ham, and add both to the boiling soup. Serve hot.

Cream of Brussels Sprouts Soup

6 tablespoons butter	⅛ teaspoon white pepper
4½ tablespoons flour	6 cups Brussels sprouts, cooked
1½ cups milk	6 cups chicken broth
3 teaspoons chives, chopped	Sour cream
½ teaspoon salt	1 cup hard-cooked egg, minced

SERVES EIGHT

Melt the butter in a heavy soup pot over low heat. Stir in the flour and add the milk, a little at a time, stirring constantly. When the mixture is thick and smooth, add the chives, salt, and pepper. Chop the Brussels sprouts very fine and add to the chicken broth. Stir the broth with the sprouts slowly into the sauce, stirring constantly. Simmer the soup for 10 minutes. Serve piping hot, garnished with a dollop of sour cream and hard-cooked egg.

Dutch Chervil Soup

6 tablespoons butter	6 egg yolks
8 tablespoons flour	Salt and pepper to taste
8 cups beef and veal stock	
5 tablespoons fresh chervil, chopped	

SERVES EIGHT

Melt the butter in a soup kettle. Blend in the flour to make a smooth paste. Add the meat stock, 1 cup at a time, stirring after each addition. Continue to stir the soup for 10 minutes over medium heat. Mix in the chervil, stir once or twice, and remove from heat.

Separate the egg yolks into a large bowl. Beat well. Stir in a little of the hot soup and mix thoroughly. Continue to add the remainder of the hot soup, mixing well after each addition. Pour the soup back into the kettle and heat over *very* low flame. Do not allow the soup to boil, or the eggs will curdle. Serve hot in small bowls.

Tomato Soup with Cheese***

Fresh tomato soup, creamy with cheese, makes a wonderful introduction to any meal.

10 *small tomatoes*

2 *tablespoons butter*

1 *medium-sized onion, chopped*

1 *cup mushrooms, chopped*

2 *tablespoons flour*

2 *teaspoons sugar*

8 *cups Beef stock (see page 67)*

2 *cloves garlic*

½ *teaspoon each: basil, rosemary, and thyme*

  Salt and white pepper to taste

3-*ounce package of cream cheese, softened*

2 *tablespoons fresh parsley, chopped*

1 *tablespoon fresh mint, chopped*

SERVES EIGHT

Peel the tomatoes, shake out the seeds, and chop them coarsely. Place in a lightly buttered casserole, cover, and bake in a preheated oven at 325° F. for 20 minutes. Meanwhile, heat the butter in a large soup kettle and add the onions and mushrooms. Sauté these for five minutes, stirring. Sprinkle the flour and sugar over the mixture, and stir until the flour is absorbed. Add the Beef stock, garlic cloves, basil, rosemary, and thyme, and continue to stir until the soup comes to a boil. Add the baked tomatoes, cover, reduce the heat, and simmer for 30 minutes. Mix the salt and white pepper with the softened cream cheese, and sieve the mixture into the soup. Serve the soup piping hot, sprinkled with chopped fresh parsley and mint.

Waterzooi

2 chickens (2½–3½ pounds each)

5 tablespoons butter

5 leeks, washed and chopped

8 stalks celery, cut into 2-inch pieces

3 carrots, sliced

3 small onions

1 bay leaf

¼ teaspoon thyme

⅛ teaspoon nutmeg

15 peppercorns

5 whole cloves

10 cups Chicken stock (see page 74)

2 lemons

3 tablespoons parsley, finely chopped

6 egg yolks

½ cup heavy cream

Salt and pepper to taste

SERVES EIGHT

Cut the chickens into serving pieces. Melt the butter in a large, heavy soup pot and brown the chickens on all sides. Add the leeks, celery, carrots, onions, bay leaf, thyme, nutmeg, peppercorns, cloves, and Chicken stock, and bring to a boil. Lower the heat and simmer, covered, until the chickens are tender. Strain the stock and set aside. Remove the skin and bones from the chicken pieces. Keep warm. Squeeze 1 lemon and thinly slice the other. Add the lemon juice and the parsley to the strained stock. Heat the soup until it is hot but not boiling. Beat the egg yolks lightly into the cream. Stir ½ cup of the soup into the egg and cream mixture and add to the soup. Stir constantly over low heat until the soup thickens slightly. Take care not to boil, or the eggs will curdle. Serve hot, with pieces of boned chicken and a lemon slice in each serving dish.

Scandinavia
and
Finland

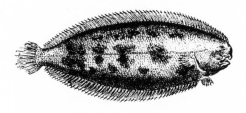

Danish Sour Bread

1½ cups whole wheat flour

¾ cup rye flour

½ cup rice flour

1 tablespoon salt

1 tablespoon ground caraway
seeds

1 cup Sourdough starter (see
page 24), at room
temperature

¼ cup butter (at room
temperature)

1 package dry active yeast

1⅓ cups warm water

¾ cup whole wheat flour

Caraway seeds

MAKES ONE LARGE LOAF

Combine the whole wheat, rye, and rice flours in a large bowl. Stir
in the salt and ground caraway seeds. With your fist, make a well in
the center of the dry ingredients, and place the starter, butter, and
yeast in the well. Add warm water gradually, stirring well after each
addition, and mix the ingredients together thoroughly (mix at least
8 minutes). Cover the dough with a linen towel, set it in a warm,
draft-free place, and let it rise until it doubles in size (approximately
1 hour). Stir the dough down with a wooden spoon and incorporate
enough of the additional whole wheat flour to stiffen the dough.

[283]

When the flour has been well worked in, sprinkle caraway seeds on the board and coat the dough by rolling it in the seeds. Set the loaf on a greased baking sheet, cover loosely with a linen towel, and allow to rise again in a warm, draft-free place until it doubles in bulk (about 30 minutes). Preheat the oven and bake at 425° F. for 15 minutes. Then reduce the heat to 300° F. and bake for 45 minutes more, or until the crust is well browned. Remove from the oven and slide from the baking sheet. Cool on a wire rack.

Finnish Easter Crown Bread***

*Add the crowning touch to your Easter dinner with
this rich and pungent high-rising bread!*

2 cups heavy cream	2 teaspoons fresh ground cardamom
1 cup milk	
3 packages dry active yeast	4 tablespoons orange zest (thin outer skin), grated
¾ cup warm water	
9½ cups all-purpose flour	2 teaspoons lemon zest (thin outer skin), grated
½ cup light cream	
1½ cups butter	2 cups golden raisins
7 egg yolks	1 cup blanched almonds, chopped
1¾ cup sugar	
2 teaspoons salt	3 cups rye flour

MAKES ONE VERY LARGE BREAD

Scald the heavy cream and milk in a saucepan, and cool to luke-warm. Stir the yeast into the warm water. When the yeast softens, add the cooled cream and milk. Blend 2 cups of the flour into the yeast mixture, reserving the rest. When the yeast and flour mixture is smooth, cover the bowl and set in a warm, draft-free place. Allow to rise until double in bulk (approximately 2 hours). Scald the light cream in a saucepan. Melt the butter over hot water. Allow both to cool. When the dough has risen, stir in the butter, egg yolks, sugar, salt, cardamom, grated orange and lemon zest, raisins, and almonds. Combine the cooled light cream with the rye flour and add both to the dough, stirring well. Stiffen the dough by adding 4 more cups of the flour and mixing thoroughly. Spread the remaining ½ cup of flour on a pastry board. Work this flour into the dough by kneading for 8 to 10 minutes, or until the dough is smooth and elastic.

Set the dough in a greased bowl, turning it once to grease the top. Allow it to rise, covered, in a warm, draft-free place for approximately 2 hours. When it has doubled in bulk, punch it down. Shape it into a smooth ball with your hands and set it into a deep 4-quart kettle or pail that has been well greased. Press down slightly to flatten the bottom of the dough, cover, and allow to rise again in a warm, draft-free place until the dough almost reaches the top of the kettle (about 2 hours). Bake in an oven preheated to 350° F. for 1½ hours, or until a long toothpick inserted in the top comes out clean. Remove from the oven, brush the top with melted butter, and cool for 30 minutes before removing from the kettle. Serve warm or cold, with butter or slices of cheese—or both.

Finnish Bread

Surprisingly easy—delectable too!

2 *cups water*	1½ *package dry active yeast*
4 *tablespoons butter*	¾ *cup warm water*
4 *tablespoons sugar*	4½ *cups rye flour*
3 *teaspoons salt*	4 *cups all-purpose flour*

MAKES TWO LOAVES

Heat the water in a small saucepan. Place the butter, sugar, and salt in a large bowl. Pour the hot water over these ingredients, and stir briefly. Cool to lukewarm. Sprinkle the yeast into a small bowl, mix with ½ cup warm water, and set aside for 5 minutes. When the yeast has softened, stir it into the butter and sugar mixture. Using a wooden spoon, beat in the rye flour. When this flour has been fully incorporated, mix in 2 cups of the all-purpose flour. Stir until both flours are well blended. Sprinkle a pastry board with ½ cup of all-purpose flour. Work this flour into the dough by kneading for 8 to 10 minutes until the dough is smooth and shiny. If the dough seems sticky, add more flour. Grease a large bowl and set the dough in it. Coat the top surface lightly with melted butter. Cover with a linen towel that has been slightly moistened with water and squeezed out.

Set the bowl in a warm, draft-free place and allow the dough to rise until it is just about double in size (about 1 hour).

Punch the dough down. Turn out onto a pastry board and knead for 3 or 4 minutes. Divide into two equal portions and roll each portion into a ball. Grease a baking sheet lightly. Set the balls of dough on it and flatten them with your hands to 1-inch thickness. Allow them to rise, covered, until nearly double (about 45 minutes). Preheat the oven to 400° F. Bake for 25 to 30 minutes to a golden brown. Remove from baking sheet and cool on a wire rack. To serve in the traditional Finnish way, cut in wedges and spread thickly with butter.

Finnish Easter Bread

6½–7½ cups all-purpose or unbleached white flour, unsifted

¾ cup sugar

2½ packages dry active yeast

3 tablespoons orange zest (thin outer skin), grated

1 teaspoon lemon zest (thin outer skin), grated

⅔ teaspoon salt

1 teaspoon ground cardamom

⅔ cup butter

1¼ cup milk

½ cup water

3 eggs (at room temperature)

½ cup raisins

¾ cup blanched almonds, chopped

Sugar icing (see page 62)

Dried apricots

Currants

MAKES TWO LOAVES

Combine 2½ cups of the flour with the sugar, yeast, grated orange and lemon zest, salt, and cardamom, and mix in a large bowl. Heat the butter, milk, and water together over a low flame to a temperature of 120°–130° F. The butter should be softened but not melted. Add the liquids to the dry ingredients, a little at a time, mixing well after each addition. Beat together with an electric mixer for 2 minutes at medium speed, scraping the bowl from time to time. Stir in the eggs and 1 cup of flour, and beat at high speed for 2 minutes, scraping the bowl occasionally. Stir in enough additional flour to make a soft dough. Knead the dough on a lightly floured board for 8 to 10 minutes, or until the dough is smooth and elastic.

Grease a bowl and put the dough into it, turning it once to grease the top. Cover the bowl and allow the dough to rise in a warm, draft-free place until it has doubled in volume (approximately 1 hour). Punch the dough down. Place it on a lightly floured board and knead in the raisins and chopped almonds. This process requires a great deal of patience, for the fruit tends to pop out. Shape the dough into two balls of equal size. Grease two 8-inch cake pans. Place one ball in each cake pan, cover, and allow them to rise in a warm, draft-free place until double in volume (approximately 1 hour). Bake in a preheated 375° F. oven for 40 minutes, or until done. Remove from the pans and cool on a wire rack. When cool, cover with Sugar icing. Decorate with "flowers"—wedge-shaped dried apricot "petals" and currant centers.

Swedish Limpa***

*The best among loaves is this orange and anise-flavored
rye bread. Definitely one to try!*

4 cups water	1 package dry active yeast
1 cup brown sugar	6–6½ cups all-purpose or unbleached white flour, sifted
2 tablespoons shortening	
2 teaspoons caraway seeds	2 teaspoons salt
1 tablespoon orange zest (thin outer skin), grated	4–4½ cups 100% rye flour
1 tablespoon anise seeds	

MAKES TWO LOAVES

Combine in a saucepan: the water, brown sugar, shortening, caraway seeds, grated orange zest, and anise seeds. Boil for 3 minutes. Remove from the stove and allow to cool slightly. When the mixture becomes lukewarm, add the yeast and stir thoroughly. Add enough of the sifted flour to the mixture to make a soft dough. Place the dough in a warm place. Cover and allow to rise for 1½ to 2 hours. Add the salt and enough of the rye flour to make a stiff dough. Divide into two equal portions. Put in separate bowls, cover, and allow to rise again for 2 hours in a warm, draft-free place.

Knead each portion for 5 minutes until smooth and elastic.

Shape into loaves and place in greased loaf pans. Cover and let rise again for 30 minutes. Bake in a preheated 350° F. oven for 1 hour. Remove immediately, turn out of the pans, and cool on a wire rack.

Swedish Rusks

⅓ cup orange juice

1½ teaspoons butter

½ package dry active yeast

1½ teaspoons sugar

2½ tablespoons lukewarm water

½ cup all-purpose flour

¾ cup rye flour

1 teaspoon salt

1 teaspoon ground fennel

2 tablespoons butter (at room temperature)

2 tablespoons light brown sugar

MAKES ABOUT FIFTY

Heat the orange juice to lukewarm and add 1½ teaspoons of butter to melt. Meanwhile, mix the yeast with the sugar. Stir in the luke-warm water; let the yeast mixture soften. Place the white and rye flours, the salt, and ground fennel in a large bowl. With your fist, make a well in the center of the dry ingredients. Combine the yeast and orange juice mixtures and pour into the well. Stir thoroughly for several minutes until the dough becomes quite stiff. Cover the bowl and allow the dough to rise until double in bulk (approximately 1 hour). Cream until smooth the 2 tablespoons of butter and light brown sugar. With the back of a large spoon, work this mixture into the dough after it has risen. Knead until the butter-sugar mixture has been thoroughly incorporated into the dough. Break up the dough into about twenty-five equal pieces. Roll each piece into a ball between the palms, place on lightly oiled baking sheets, and press each down slightly. Cover the baking sheets and allow the balls to rise in a warm, draft-free place until they double in size (about 20 minutes). Do not turn on the oven until the baking sheets are arranged on the oven racks. Bake at 400° F. for 12 minutes. Reduce the temperature to 350° F. and bake the rusks 15 minutes longer. Remove from the oven and cool on wire racks. When cool, slice them in half. Toast the rusks to a golden brown for 15 minutes in an oven preheated to 275° F. After cooling once more, store in tight containers.

Rieska

*The barley flour called for in traditional Finnish Rieska
is available in health food stores.*

3 tablespoons butter	3 teaspoons baking powder
3 cups barley flour	1 teaspoon salt
5 teaspoons sugar	1½ cups light cream

MAKES ONE LOAF

Melt the butter over hot water. Place the barley flour, sugar, baking powder, and salt in a large bowl. Blend in the melted butter and light cream. The result should be a smooth dough. Grease a baking sheet well with butter. With floured hands, set the dough on the baking sheet and shape it into a ball. Lightly press down on the ball with the hand and flatten it to a ½-inch thickness. Prick the top surface lightly with a fork. Bake in a preheated 450° F. oven until crisp and golden. Slide it from the baking sheet and allow to cool briefly. Serve it in the Finnish way—cut in wedges and spread thickly with butter.

Danish Wine Soup with Butter Balls

3 pounds beef knuckles	½ cup white wine
7½ cups beef broth	⅓ teaspoon salt
2 small onions	1 cup heavy cream
2 medium-sized carrots	3 tablespoons parsley, finely chopped
3 stalks celery	
1 bay leaf	
Butter balls (see page 93)	

SERVES EIGHT

Rinse the beef knuckles and dry with paper towels. Cut some of the meat from the bones and place the meat and bones in a soup kettle. Add the beef broth. Peel and chop the onions and carrots and add them to the kettle, together with the celery and bay leaf. Place over high heat and bring to boil. Lower the heat and simmer for 3 or 4 hours. Pour the soup through a strainer. Place in the refrigerator and, when cold, skim off all the fat.

Twenty minutes before serving, bring the soup to a low boil, add the Danish butter balls, and boil for 10 minutes. With a slotted spoon, remove the butter balls from the soup and place in soup bowls. Keep warm. Add the white wine, salt, and heavy cream to the soup. Heat gently. Pour the soup over the butter balls and sprinkle with chopped parsley. Serve immediately. (If your heat has been too high, the beef broth may have been reduced too much. If the soup tastes too strong or there is not enough to serve 8, add more beef broth.)

Danish Cabbage Soup***

*Have a bowl of this hearty soup with slices of
black bread spread with sweet butter.*

2½ pounds brisket of beef
1 pound oxtails
2½ quarts water
10 whole peppercorns
½ teaspoon salt
1 teaspoon caraway seed
½ teaspoon dill seed
1 teaspoon basil
4 medium-sized carrots, cut in
1-inch pieces

4 large potatoes, cut in quarters
2 leeks, cut in 1-inch pieces
8 small white onions
2 medium-sized white cabbages, cut in eighths
2 tablespoons fresh parsley, minced

SERVES EIGHT

Arrange beef brisket and oxtails in a kettle and cover with 2½ quarts of water. Tie 10 whole peppercorns in a cheesecloth bag and add to the kettle along with the spices. Bring the water to a boil, cover, and simmer for 2 hours. Peel the carrots and cut into 1-inch pieces. Peel and quarter the potatoes. Thoroughly wash and slice the leeks. Peel the whole onions. Discard the core and limp outer leaves of the cabbages and slice into eighths. Remove the oxtails and peppercorns from the soup and discard. Add the carrots, potatoes, leeks, whole onions, cabbage wedges and minced fresh parsley to the kettle and continue to simmer, covered, for 45 minutes. When the meat is tender, remove and slice it. Serve the soup immediately, accompanied by slices of meat and buttered black bread attractively arranged on a separate platter.

Danish Chicken Soup with Beef Balls and Dumplings

For your pleasure—a meal in itself!

2 stewing chickens (3 pounds
    each), cut in serving pieces

4 teaspoons salt

1 teaspoon white pepper

1 teaspoon sweet basil

1 teaspoon thyme

3 quarts chicken broth

5 medium-sized carrots

6 leeks

SERVES EIGHT VERY GENEROUSLY

Arrange the chicken pieces in a deep soup kettle. Sprinkle with salt, white pepper, basil, and thyme. Cover with the chicken broth and allow the soup to simmer, covered, until the chicken is tender (approximately 1½ hours). Meanwhile, peel and cut the carrots into 2-inch pieces. Discard the roots of the leeks and wash the leaves thoroughly. Cut into 2-inch pieces. When the chicken is tender, remove the pieces from the kettle and reserve. Allow the broth to cool a little and skim off the fat. Bring to a boil and add the carrots and leeks. Drop rounded beef balls into the broth and continue to simmer, covered, for 45 minutes. Add the dumplings during the last 10 minutes, and simmer the soup uncovered. Just before serving, return the chicken pieces to the soup, and heat through. There will be additional soup and chicken for luncheon the following day.

BEEF BALLS

2 medium-sized onions

2 pounds beef, ground twice

1½ cups milk

⅔ cup flour

2 eggs

2 teaspoons salt

½ teaspoon pepper

Peel and grate the onions. Mix with the beef, milk, flour, eggs, salt, and pepper, and form into walnut-sized balls. Drop into the simmering soup 45 minutes before serving.

DUMPLINGS

4 tablespoons melted butter	1½ teaspoons salt
3 cups all-purpose flour, sifted	½ teaspoon ground cardamom
2 tablespoons sugar	2 eggs
2 teaspoons baking powder	2 cups milk

Melt the butter over hot water. In the meantime, combine the sifted flour, the sugar, baking powder, salt, and cardamom. Beat the eggs until they are light and frothy. Mix the eggs with the melted butter and milk. Stir this mixture into the dry ingredients, pressing out any lumps with the back of a spoon. Ten minutes before serving, round off small amounts of the batter with a tablespoon, and drop them into the simmering soup. The soup should simmer uncovered while the dumplings cook.

Danish Chilled Sweet Buttermilk Soup

2 lemons	⅔ cup sugar
8 cups buttermilk	2 teaspoons vanilla
6 egg yolks	1 cup heavy cream, whipped

SERVES EIGHT

Squeeze the lemons and strain the juice. Beat the buttermilk with a wire whisk for several minutes. Beat together the strained lemon juice, egg yolks, sugar, and vanilla. Stir the egg mixture into the buttermilk, a little bit at a time. Chill well. Serve icy cold, in small bowls topped with mounds of chilled whipped cream.

Norwegian Wine Soup

5 cups water	9 tablespoons sugar
2½ ounces sago	1 lemon
¾ cup raisins	3½ cups sweet wine
5 egg yolks	Salt and pepper to taste

SERVES EIGHT

Place water in a soup kettle and bring to a boil. Stir in the sago and cook over medium-low heat until the sago is tender. Add the raisins to the soup and cook until they are plump. Beat the egg yolks with a fork, add sugar, and mix well. Gradually stir the egg mixture into the soup. Add the juice and rind of the lemon and the wine. Simmer a few minutes longer. Serve hot in small bowls.

Danish Dark Bread and Beer Soup

¾ pound whole wheat bread

¾ pound pumpernickel bread

7½ cups water

    Zest (or thin outer peel) of 1 lemon, grated

⅓ teaspoon salt

9 tablespoons sugar

2 sticks cinnamon

7½ cups dark beer

1 cup heavy cream, whipped

SERVES EIGHT GENEROUSLY

Cut the breads into slices and put into a heavy bean pot or casserole. Add the water, cover, and let soak overnight. Put the bread mixture in a soup kettle, cover, and cook slowly until it becomes thick. Add the grated lemon zest, the salt, sugar, and cinnamon. Stir in the beer, bring to a boil, and remove from heat immediately. Serve hot, garnished with dollops of unsweetened whipped cream.

Danish Queen's Soup***

4 egg yolks

2 cups heavy cream

½ cup sherry

9 cups chicken broth (page 74)

    Crunchy almond balls (see page 91)

SERVES EIGHT

Beat the egg yolks until light and lemon-colored. Gradually add the cream and sherry. Place in a warmed soup tureen. Heat the chicken broth to the boiling point and pour it into the tureen, stirring constantly. The chicken broth must be *really hot*. Serve with Crunchy almond dumplings.

Danish Dried Fruit Soup

¾ cup dried apples	1 cup plus 2 tablespoons sugar
¾ cup dried apricots	½ cup quick-cooking tapioca
¾ cup dried pears	4 cups water
¾ cup dried pitted prunes	1 stick cinnamon
¾ cup dried peaches	½ cup lemon juice
¾ cup golden raisins	¾ cup grape jelly
4 whole cloves	2 cups grape juice

SERVES EIGHT

Put each dried fruit into a separate bowl. Add 1½ cups of water to each of the six bowls. Drain the fruits and place all of the liquid in a large soup kettle. Dice the fruit and add to the kettle along with the cloves. Cook over low heat until the fruits are tender.

Pour the liquid through a strainer into a saucepan, add the sugar, tapioca, water, and cinnamon. Return to stove and boil for 30 minutes, stirring occasionally, until the soup is clear. Lower the heat and stir in the lemon juice and jelly. Cook until the jelly melts. Add the fruits and a little more lemon juice if soup is too sweet for your taste. Stir in grape juice. Reheat and serve hot.

Swedish Yellow Pea Soup with Pork

Serve with the traditional Scandinavian aquavit and chilled beer to fully enjoy this unusual soup.

3 quarts water	3 teaspoons salt
2½ cups quick-cooking, dried yellow split peas	¾ teaspoon pepper
1 large bay leaf	3 leeks
2 medium-sized onions	1 celeriac (or 1 celery stalk)
2 pounds boned pork shoulder	2 medium-sized potatoes
¾ teaspoon dill weed	

SERVES EIGHT

Bring the water to a brisk boil in a deep soup kettle. Rinse the yellow split peas thoroughly, and add with the bay leaf to the boiling water. Lower the heat and simmer, covered, for 1 hour. Stir the peas from time to time. Peel and chop the onions. Add the onions, pork shoulder, dill weed, salt, and pepper to the peas. Simmer for 1 more hour, covered, stirring occasionally. Wash the leeks thoroughly and discard the roots. Slice into 1-inch pieces. Wash, peel, and cube the celeriac. Peel the potatoes and cut in eighths. Add the vegetables to the soup and simmer, covered, until tender (about 45 minutes), stirring occasionally. Before serving, discard the bay leaf and remove the pork shoulder from the kettle. Slice the meat, arrange on a serving plate, and surround with very thin slices of Swedish rye or pumpernickel spread with butter. Serve with the hot soup.

Finnish Klimp Soup

*Little dumplings or "klimps" make this rich broth
a good light-supper soup.*

12 cups beef broth	1/3 teaspoon salt
3 eggs	1/2 teaspoon nutmeg
1 1/2 cups flour	3/4 cup milk

SERVES TEN

Put the beef broth into a soup kettle and bring to a boil. Beat the eggs lightly with a fork. Put the flour into a bowl, add salt and nutmeg, and stir in the beaten eggs and milk to produce a smooth batter.

Lower the heat and, when the broth is simmering, drop in the dumpling batter—a teaspoon at a time. Cover the kettle and cook for 12 to 15 minutes, or until the dumplings are cooked through. Serve steaming hot.

Cream Cheese and Smoked Salmon Soup

2 1/2 quarts Fish stock (page 83)	8 scallions with 3 inches of green top
2 pounds smoked salmon, sliced	4 ounces cream cheese
1/8 teaspoon fresh ground pepper	
2 1/2 cups small, tender spinach leaves	

SERVES EIGHT

Pour the Fish stock into a soup kettle. Cut the salmon into small pieces and add to stock with the pepper. Simmer gently for 15 minutes, stirring from time to time.

Wash the spinach and chop the scallions. Add the spinach and half of the chopped scallions to the soup and simmer for 5 minutes. Mix the cream cheese with ¼ cup hot soup until smooth. Stir the cheese mixture into the soup and reheat. Serve hot, garnished with the reserved chopped scallions.

Lapland Fool

Wondering what to do with those left-over meats?
Do as the Laplanders do—try Lapland fool!

5 cups leftover meat or
   combination of meats

6 slices bacon

8 whole allspice

6 whole peppercorns

2 bay leaves

5 cups mashed potatoes

10 cups beef broth

   Salt and freshly ground
   pepper to taste

SERVES EIGHT

Grind or coarsely chop the leftover meat and the bacon. Place in a soup kettle together with the spices. Stir the mashed potatoes into the beef broth, pressing out any lumps with the back of a spoon. Stir the potato mixture into the soup. Place over medium heat and bring soup to a boil, stirring to avoid sticking. Adjust the seasonings. Turn stove off, cover the kettle, and let rest for about 10 minutes. Serve hot.

Finnish Cabbage Soup

½ medium-sized head of cabbage

4½ cups water

1 teaspoon salt

2½ tablespoons flour

6 cups milk

1 teaspoon sugar

1 tablespoon butter

1 teaspoon curry powder

SERVES EIGHT

Shred the cabbage, discarding the core and limp outer leaves. Place the shredded cabbage in a soup kettle and add the water (the cabbage should be covered with water). Add the salt and cook over medium heat until tender. Mix the flour and the milk, blending with the back of a spoon until free from lumps. Stir the flour mixture into cabbage and water and bring to a boil, stirring constantly. Lower heat to medium and cook, covered, for 15 to 20 minutes. Add sugar, butter, and curry. Stir well and serve piping hot.

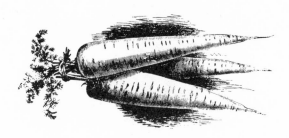

Finnish Carrot Soup

This is a light, delicious, rich milk broth.

8 *carrots*	1½ *teaspoons salt*
2 *cups water*	4 *tablespoons flour*
8 *cups milk*	2 *tablespoons water*
2 *tablespoons sugar*	2½ *tablespoons butter*
2 *tablespoons fresh dill, minced*	2 *cups cooked ham, warm*

SERVES EIGHT

Peel and slice the carrots and place them in a saucepan. Add the water and simmer, covered, until tender when pierced with a fork. Remove the carrots with a slotted spoon and set them aside. Boil the carrot water until it is reduced to ½ cup. Place the carrot water and milk in a saucepan. Stir in the sugar, dill, and salt. Combine the flour and water until free from lumps, and gradually stir it into the soup. Bring to a boil, stirring constantly, until the soup thickens. Add the carrot slices and cook a few minutes longer. Spoon ½ cup of ham in each bowl, pour soup over, float one teaspoon butter on each.

Finnish Sauerkraut Soup

*In Finland, this rich, spicy soup is very often
served for supper, accompanied with
little meat pies called "purakkaa."*

1½ pounds very lean pork, cubed

1 ham bone

5 cups sauerkraut

12 cups beef broth

10 whole allspice

Salt and freshly ground
pepper to taste

Sour cream

SERVES EIGHT

Trim all fat from the pork cubes. Place in a soup kettle, together
with the ham bone, sauerkraut, broth, and allspice. Cook over
medium-low heat for about 2½ hours. Adjust the seasonings. Serve
hot, garnished with sour cream. Serve with rye bread and a sharp,
country-style cheese.

Finnish Beer Soup

*A favorite Finnish soup, prepared in many ways
all over Finland.*

3½ cups dark beer

6 cups milk

8 tablespoons flour

8 tablespoons water

1¼ teaspoons ground ginger

3½ tablespoons sugar

1 teaspoon salt

Croutons (see page 86)

SERVES EIGHT

Place the beer and milk in separate saucepans and heat. Combine
the flour and water to make a smooth paste, and stir into the milk.
Add the ginger, sugar, and salt to the beer. Remove the two pots
from stove and beat the hot milk mixture into the beer, a little bit
at a time. The soup should be frothy. Serve at once in small bowls.
Top with croutons.

BREAD AND SOUP FROM EASTERN EUROPE

Russia
and
Czechoslovakia

SAY "RUSSIA" AND THE mind's eye immediately flashes images of droshkies gliding through the snow, fanciful towers of the Kremlin rising over forbidding walls, and the frozen steppes of Siberia stretching off into the infinite Russian night. Russia is all of these things and more—a vast and mysterious land of hearty, hardworking vital people with a predilection for great literature, food, and vodka. The cooking of Russia is also as we imagine it to be—as solid, substantial, and earthy as Mother Russia herself. Huge loaves of heavy black bread, hearty cabbage soups so thick they could be eaten with a fork, beautiful cold soups pink with beets and crunchy with cucumbers—the expected and the unexpected combine to make Russian cuisine unusually delightful.

Black Bread

Black bread with its coarse grainy texture and thick crust
makes a robust accompaniment to hearty soups
In making the dough, use dark breadcrumbs, if available.
These give the loaf a richer, darker color.

3 cups dark breadcrumbs, finely
   ground
½ cup warm water
3 packages dry active yeast
¼ teaspoon ground ginger
1 cup bran cereal
2 cups water
3 teaspoons instant coffee

4 tablespoons dark molasses
2 cups rye flour
¼ cup melted butter
2 teaspoons salt
2 cups all-purpose flour
1 teaspoon instant coffee

MAKES ONE LOAF

Toast the dark breadcrumbs in the oven until they turn even darker, but be careful not to burn them. Pour the warm water into a small bowl, stir in the yeast, add 1 teaspoon of molasses, the ginger, and stir. Allow this mixture to rest for 15 minutes. Meanwhile, heat 2 cups of water in a saucepan. In a large bowl, mix the water with the instant coffee. Add the molasses and stir in the toasted breadcrumbs. Allow the crumbs to soak while the mixture cools to luke-warm.

Combine the yeast mixture with the bran and breadcrumb mixture. Stir in the rye flour and blend thoroughly. Add the melted butter and the salt, and stir well. Arrange the all-purpose flour on a pastry board. Place the dough in the center of the flour. Turn the bowl it was mixed in upside down over the dough for 15 minutes. Uncover and knead the all-purpose flour into the dough until it becomes smooth and stiff, about 8 to 10 minutes. Place in a greased bowl, turning it over once to grease the top. Allow to rise, covered, in a warm, draft-free place until double in volume (about 1½ hours).

Dust the pastry board with flour. Set the dough on it and knead lightly for a few minutes. Shape into a long oval loaf. Place on a greased baking sheet and allow to rise again, covered, for approximately 30 minutes. Preheat the oven to 400° F. Mix 1 teaspoon instant coffee with hot water and brush the top surface of the bread with it. Bake for 40 to 45 minutes. Slide from baking sheet and cool on a wire rack.

Kulich

Russians celebrate the arrival of Easter by baking this
glorious cylindrical fruit-filled coffeecake, its
towering top festively crowned with icing.

¾ cup dark rum

1 teaspoon saffron

½ cup toasted almonds

3 bitter almonds

½ cup candied cherries

½ cup candied citron

5–6 cups all-purpose flour,
   sifted

¼ cup water

3 packages dry active yeast

1 cup plus 2 tablespoons light
   brown sugar

1 cup light cream

¾ cup butter

3 eggs (at room temperature)

1 teaspoon almond extract

1 teaspoon anise extract

MAKES ONE COFFEECAKE

Pour the rum over the saffron, mix well, and set aside for 1 hour or longer. Meanwhile, with an electric blender, grind the toasted and bitter almonds together for a few seconds. Chop the candied cherries and citron. Mix the ground almonds and candied fruits into 1 cup of the sifted flour. Heat the water to lukewarm, pour it into a small bowl in which the yeast and 2 tablespoons of the brown sugar have been mixed, and allow the yeast to soften. Heat the light cream until it is just warm. Cream the butter and the remaining 1 cup of brown sugar in a large bowl until thoroughly blended. Separate the eggs, reserving the whites. Stir the yolks into the creamed mixture, together with the warm light cream and the almond and anise extracts. When bubbles appear on the surface of the yeast mixture, add it to the butter-sugar mixture. With an electric mixer, blend in the remaining flour at medium speed until the dough is smooth and elastic. Cover the dough, and allow it to rise in a warm, draft-free place about 1 hour. Beat the dough down. Beat the egg whites until they stand in peaks. Add to the dough the saffron and rum mixture, the cup of flour containing the candied fruits and nuts, and then fold in the stiffened egg whites. Cover the dough again, and allow to rise in a warm, draft-free place about 1 hour.

Butter a large cylindrical mold or 9-inch tube mold generously. Arrange the dough so that the mold is at least ⅔ full. Cover again and let the dough rise in a warm, draft-free place until it reaches the top of the mold (approximately 2 hours). Bake in an oven preheated to 375° F. for 20 minutes. Reduce the temperature to 325° F., and bake until golden (about 40 minutes more). Turn out to cool on a wire rack. While still warm, frost or sprinkle with powdered confectioner's sugar.

FROSTING

1 egg white

2 cups confectioner's sugar

1 teaspoon fresh lemon juice

1 teaspoon almond extract

Beat the egg white until it stands in peaks. Beat in the sugar. Add the lemon juice and almond extract. Trickle the frosting over the top and down the sides of the Kulich.

Czechoslovakian Fruit Buns

¼ cup butter

¾ cup milk

¼ cup water

3–4 cups all-purpose or
    unbleached white flour

1 package dry active yeast

⅓ cup sugar

1 teaspoon salt

1 egg (at room temperature)

    Oil for frying (not olive oil)

2 cups prepared canned fruit
    pie filling

MAKES EIGHTEEN

Heat the butter, milk, and water together in a saucepan over a low flame until the mixture reaches a temperature of 120°–130° F. The butter will be soft but not melted. Meanwhile, mix 1 cup of the flour together with the yeast, sugar, and salt. Stir the warm milk mixture into the dry ingredients, and beat with an electric mixer for 2 minutes at medium speed, scraping the bowl from time to time. Blend in ½ cup of flour and the egg. At high speed, beat for 2 minutes more, scraping the bowl from time to time. Make a soft dough by blending in enough additional flour. Knead the dough on a lightly floured board until smooth and elastic (approximately 8 to 10 minutes).

    Grease a large bowl and put the dough into it, turning it over once to grease the top. Cover the bowl and allow the dough to rise in a warm, draft-free place until it is double in bulk (approximately

1 hour). Punch the dough down and place it on a lightly floured board. Roll the dough out until it is about ½-inch thick. Cut 3-inch buns from the dough, arrange them on greased baking sheets, and cover with a towel. Allow the buns to rise in a warm, draft-free place until they have doubled in volume (approximately 1 hour).

Heat cooking oil to 375° F. in a deep skillet or fryer. Do not handle the buns too much, or the dough will fall. Drop each bun into the oil and fry for a few minutes until browned on both sides. Carefully remove the buns from the oil and allow to drain on paper towels. When cool, cut away the center of each bun. Spoon fruit pie filling into these holes, top the buns with whipped cream or powdered sugar, and serve as a luscious luncheon dessert.

Czechoslovakian Christmas Twist

VÁNOČKA

8 cups all-purpose or unbleached white flour, sifted

¼ teaspoon mace

2 teaspoons powdered anise

1 lemon zest (thin outer skin), grated

½ cup sweet butter (at room temperature)

2 packages dry active yeast

1 cup plus 2 tablespoons brown sugar

¼ cup lukewarm water

½ cup heavy cream

4 egg yolks

1½ cups milk

1 cup currants

½ cup toasted almonds, sliced

Egg yolk

2 tablespoons light cream

MAKES TWO LOAVES

Combine the sifted flour with the mace and anise, and sift together into a large bowl. Add the lemon zest. Using two knives, cut in the butter until the mixture resembles coarse meal. Stir the yeast and 2 tablespoons of the brown sugar into the lukewarm water. While the yeast is softening, heat the heavy cream slightly. Beat the egg yolks and add them, together with the remaining brown sugar, to the warm cream. Form a well in the flour mixture. Pour both the yeast mixture and the warm cream mixture into this well. Blend all these ingredients thoroughly. To make a very stiff dough, heat the milk slightly and add as much as necessary. Knead the dough thirty times. Place the dough in a bowl, cover with a linen towel, and put the bowl in an oven preheated to 200° F. and then turned off. Allow the dough to rise until double in bulk (approximately 1½ to 2 hours).

Punch the dough down. Turn out on a lightly floured board and knead in the currants and sliced almonds. Divide the dough into ten long rolls. Cover with linen towel and allow the rolls to rise for 20 minutes. Cut and butter enough parchment paper to line two loaf pans. Braid three long rolls together and place in a loaf pan lined with the buttered paper. Take two more rolls, twist them loosely around each other and lay them on the braided loaf. Repeat this procedure with the five remaining long rolls to form another braided loaf in the second pan. Cover the braided loaves and allow to rise in a warm, draft-free place for 1½ hours. Bake in an oven preheated to 375° F. After 40 minutes, brush the tops of the loaves with a mixture of egg yolk and 2 tablespoons light cream. Return the loaves to the oven to bake 10 minutes longer. Remove the loaves from the pans and cool on a wire rack.

Meatless Borscht***

*Chill this wonderfully refreshing sweet and sour beet
soup, and serve it with a dollop of sour cream
for a summertime treat. Or try it piping hot served
with dark bread in the frosty winter-time.
Either way, it's a delight.*

9 cups water	4½ tablespoons lemon juice
8 medium-sized beets, peeled and grated	7½ tablespoons sugar
1½ large onions, chopped	2 teaspoons salt
4 tomatoes, chopped	3 eggs
4½ tablespoons tomato paste	Sour cream

SERVES EIGHT

Place water, beets, onion, and tomato in a soup kettle. Simmer for 1 hour. Add tomato paste, lemon juice, sugar, and salt. Simmer for 30 minutes and cool to room temperature. Beat the eggs with 2 cups of the soup, then add to the soup in the pot. Heat over a very low flame, stirring constantly, until the soup thickens slightly. Do not boil, or the eggs will curdle. Serve hot or chilled, with a dollop of sour cream in each bowl.

Borscht with Beer***

Serve this very different and delicious meat and beer soup with thick slices of home-baked buttered rye bread.

2 slices lean bacon

½ pound stewing beef, cut in 1-inch pieces

½ pound stewing lamb, cut in 1-inch pieces

2 medium-sized beets, peeled and diced

1 medium-sized carrot, diced

1 medium-sized onion, diced

1 cup celery, diced

2 medium-sized tomatoes, peeled, seeded and chopped

1½ teaspoons flour

1 tablespoon fresh parsley, minced

7 cups beef broth

1 teaspoon salt

½ teaspoon ground nutmeg

4 medium-sized potatoes, cut in eighths

1 cup cabbage leaves, shredded

1 egg yolk

8 ounces light beer

4 slices rye bread

SERVES EIGHT

Sauté bacon in a small skillet until crisp and set aside. Arrange beef and lamb pieces in a soup kettle. Peel and dice the beets, carrot, and onion. Wash and dice enough celery to measure 1 cup. Peel the tomatoes, seed them by cutting into quarters and shaking out the seeds, and chop them coarsely. Place the diced and chopped vegetables in the kettle with the meat. Mince the sautéed bacon. Mix with the flour and parsley until well blended, and add this mixture to the kettle. Cover with 7 cups of beef broth, sprinkle with salt and nutmeg, and bring to a boil. Simmer the soup, covered, for 2 hours, add the peeled potatoes cut in eighths and the shredded cabbage, and continue to simmer until the potatoes are tender, approximately 30 minutes. Just before serving, beat an egg yolk slightly in a large bowl and mix with 4 tablespoons of hot soup. Stir in the beer and blend this mixture slowly into the soup as it cooks over low heat, together with crumbled slices of rye bread. Do not allow the soup to

[307]

boil. Heat through thoroughly. Serve dolloped with sour cream, accompanied by a surfeit of cold beer and additional buttered slices of rye bread.

Russian Strawberry Soup

4½ cups ripe strawberries

1¾ cups confectioner's sugar

2 cups sour cream

3 cups claret wine

3 cups cold water

8 whole strawberries with leaves

SERVES EIGHT

Rub the strawberries through a fine sieve. Stir in the sugar and sour cream. Add the wine and water. Simmer over *very* low heat, stirring constantly with a wooden spoon. *Do not allow to boil.* Serve the soup cold, garnished with whole berries. (I sprinkle a bit of powdered sugar on the top before decorating with the whole berry. This is attractive but not typically Russian.)

Pearl Barley Soup***

*Simple fare but plainly delicious is this
thick barley and mushroom soup.*

¾ cup pearl barley

3 cups water

2½ quarts Beef stock (see page 67) or Beef consommé (see page 68)

2 medium-sized onions

1 large carrot

6 large mushrooms

Salt and pepper to taste

2 egg yolks

¾ cup sour cream

SERVES EIGHT

Soak the barley overnight in the water. One hour before serving, drain the barley and discard the water. Place the barley and Beef stock in a large soup kettle and bring to a boil. Peel and chop the onions and carrot and slice the mushrooms. Add the vegetables, the salt, and the pepper to the boiling stock, lower the heat, and simmer for 45 minutes, or until the barley and vegetables are tender. Mix ½ cup of the hot soup with the beaten egg yolks and sour cream. Stir this mixture into the soup. Reheat the soup, stirring constantly, but do not boil, or the eggs will curdle. Serve hot with extra sour cream, if desired.

Fish Soup with Cucumber

5 medium-sized onions, chopped	3 medium-sized tomatoes
10 cups water	2 small cucumbers
¼ cup parsley, minced	2 tablespoons lemon juice
4½ teaspoons salt	¼ cup fresh dill, minced
2 bay leaves	3 tablespoons parsley, minced
3¾ pounds haddock steaks	24 black olives, pitted
6 medium-sized onions, sliced	Salt and white pepper to taste
6 tablespoons butter	

SERVES EIGHT GENEROUSLY

Peel and chop 5 onions. Place in a large soup kettle, together with the water, parsley, salt, and bay leaves. Cook over high heat until the liquid comes to a boil. Add the fish to the kettle and cook gently over low heat for 5 minutes. Do not overcook. Remove the fish from the soup kettle, discard the skin and bones, and cut the fish into bite-sized pieces. Strain the liquid into a bowl and reserve.

Place the 6 sliced onions in the soup kettle and sauté in butter until golden and transparent. Peel, seed, and chop the tomatoes coarsely. Peel the cucumbers, discard the seeds, and cut into thin slices. Add the tomatoes and the cucumbers to the onions and sauté for about 8 minutes. Stir in the reserved fish liquid and add the fish. Reheat. Remove from the stove and add the lemon juice, the dill, minced parsley, and olives. Stir gently. Adjust the seasonings. Serve hot.

Russian Fish Chowder

1½ pounds haddock fillets

2 cups water

8 thin slices smoked salmon

1 cup tomato juice

4 tablespoons butter

¼ cup flour

10 cups Clam broth (see page 84) or bottled clam juice

2 small sour gherkins, minced

2 tablespoons capers

1 cup cooked shrimp, chopped

2 cups heavy cream

Salt and pepper to taste

¼ cup fresh parsley, chopped

1 cup hard-cooked eggs, chopped

SERVES EIGHT GENEROUSLY

Place the haddock fillets in a large soup kettle. Cover with the water and simmer gently for 5 minutes, or just long enough to poach the fillets. Remove the fish from the water and set aside. Poach the smoked salmon in the kettle for 1 minute, then remove and reserve with the fish fillets. Cut the salmon and fillets into bite-sized pieces. Stir the tomato juice into the water simmering in the kettle, add the butter, and blend in the flour. When the mixture is slightly thickened, add the Clam broth, minced gherkins, capers, and the reserved fillet and salmon pieces. Heat thoroughly, then add the chopped shrimp and heavy cream. Season to taste with salt and pepper. Serve hot, sprinkled with fresh chopped parsley and hard-cooked eggs.

Rassolnik Soup with Barley***

*If kidney soup flavored with dill pickles does not sound
like your cup of soup, sample this unique
Russian favorite and be pleasantly surprised.*

3 tablespoons pearl barley

1½ cups water

3 cups potatoes, diced

10 cups beef broth

2 medium-sized onions

2 cups carrots, peeled

8 lamb kidneys

1½ tablespoons flour

3 small dill pickles

1 cup sour cream

3 tablespoons parsley, minced

Coarsely ground black pepper to taste

SERVES EIGHT

[310]

Cook the pearl barley in the water until soft. Meanwhile, simmer the diced potatoes and carrots in the beef broth until they are soft. Drain the barley and add to the broth. Keep the broth hot. Chop the onions and sauté them in the butter. Discard the fat from the kidneys and cut them into ¼-inch slices. Add the kidney slices to the onions and sauté for 2 minutes, stirring once or twice. Blend the flour into the kidneys and onions, and cook for 2 minutes more. Reduce the heat, cover, and simmer for 10 minutes. Add 1 cup of the broth and allow to come to a boil. Peel the dill pickles and cut into long strips. Squeeze the pickle juice into the broth containing the potatoes and barley. Discard the seeds and chop the pickles. Add them, together with the kidney and onion mixture, to the broth. Simmer the soup for 10 minutes. Place the sour cream at the bottom of a soup tureen. Add ½ cup of the hot soup, stirring well so that the sour cream does not curdle. Pour in the remaining soup, sprinkle with parsley and black pepper, and serve at once.

Sturgeon and Champagne Soup

If matters financial do not deter you when
a new and unique recipe presents itself, you may
want to attempt the following—

2½ *pounds haddock*	2½ *quarts water*
1½ *pounds fish heads and bones, preferably cod*	1½ *pounds fresh sturgeon, trimmed and cut into 8 slices*
4 *large onions, chopped*	3 *cups dry champagne*
1 *small Russian parsley root*	10 *scallions, trimmed and chopped*
1 *teaspoon salt*	1 *lemon, cut into 8 wedges*
6 *white peppercorns*	
1 *bay leaf*	
¼ *cup celery with leaves, chopped*	

SERVES EIGHT

Place the haddock, fish heads and bones, chopped onion, parsley root, salt, peppercorns, bay leaf, celery, leaves, and water in a large soup kettle. Bring to a high boil, skim off any surface scum, lower the heat to medium, and cook for 15 minutes. Skim the surface again, lower the heat a bit more, and cook, covered, for 1½ to 2 hours. Skim the fish stock once more and strain it through a fine sieve lined with a clean dishtowel dipped in hot water. Wash the sturgeon pieces and poach them in the hot stock for 25 minutes. Heat the champagne in a small saucepan and add it to the soup after the fish is tender. To serve, carefully place one piece of sturgeon in each soup bowl. Ladle the soup over the fish and serve at once. Arrange the chopped scallions and lemon wedges attractively on a plate and pass around for guests to help themselves.

Russian Meat Soup with Cucumber

1 pound bottom round beef, cubed

¾ pound ham, cubed

12 cups Beef bouillon (see page 68)

1 teaspoon salt

¼ teaspoon pepper

6 medium-sized onions

6 tablespoons butter

3 cucumbers

3 large tomatoes

1 cup mushrooms, cut in small pieces and sautéed in butter

5 frankfurters, thinly sliced

24 black olives, pitted

2 small lemons

Salt and freshly ground pepper to taste

SERVES EIGHT

Place the meats, Beef bouillon, salt, and pepper into a soup kettle. Bring to a boil and skim off the film several times until the broth is clear. Lower the heat, cover, and cook the meat until tender (about 2 hours).

Peel and slice the onions. Place in a skillet and sauté in the butter until golden and transparent. Peel the cucumbers, discard the seeds, and cut into thin slices. Peel, seed, and chop the tomatoes. Add the cucumbers to the onions and sauté for 2 minutes. Add the tomatoes and continue cooking for about 8 to 10 minutes. Combine the sautéed vegetables with the broth, and add the frankfurters. Reheat.

Cover the olives with water and boil for several minutes. Drain and add to the soup. Adjust the seasonings. Garnish with thin lemon slices.

Beef Soup with Apricots

2½ pound piece of chuck steak
2 small onions
6 tablespoons butter
5 medium-sized tomatoes
2 quarts Beef stock (see page 67)

6 medium-sized potatoes
1 cup apricots, cut in quarters
3 tablespoons fresh coriander, minced
Salt and freshly ground pepper to taste

Cover the chuck steak with water, add salt and pepper, and cook over medium-low heat until tender, skimming off froth and fat. Remove the meat from the pot and cut into bite-sized pieces. Reserve. Peel and chop onions. Place them in a soup kettle and sauté in butter until golden and transparent. Peel, seed, and chop the tomatoes. Add them to the onions, and continue to cook until the liquid from the tomatoes has disappeared. Add the Beef stock.

Wash, peel, and dice the potatoes and add them to the soup along with the apricots. Stir well. Bring to a boil, lower the heat, and simmer for 15 minutes, or until the potatoes are tender but not mushy. Ten minutes before the potatoes are done, add the reserved meat. Adjust the seasonings. Serve hot. Use minced coriander as a garnish.

Hlodnik***

Here gorgeous pink, chilled beet soup is garnished with hard-cooked eggs and lemon slices. Its flavor is further enhanced with chopped shrimp, cucumbers, and ham.

8 small beets
½ cup young beet tops
1½ cups water
5 tablespoons scallions, minced
1 tablespoon fresh dill, minced
1¼ cups sour cream
¼ cup lemon juice
2 teaspoons vinegar

1½ teaspoons salt
5 cups chicken broth
1 cup cooked shrimp
2 medium-sized cucumbers
1½ cups cooked ham
Freshly ground black pepper
5 hard-cooked eggs
8 thin slices lemon

SERVES EIGHT

[313]

Peel the beets and slice them. Wash the beet tops thoroughly and mince them. Place the beets and beet tops in a saucepan. Add the water and cook for 20 minutes, or until the beets are tender. Cool the beets, reserving the cooking water, and chop them very fine. Stir the chopped beets into the beet water, and add the scallions, dill, sour cream, lemon juice, vinegar, salt, and chicken broth. Refrigerate for 3 hours or longer. Place soup bowls in the refrigerator. Chop the shrimp. Peel and chop the cucumbers. Dice the cooked ham. Chill well. Stir the shrimp, cucumbers, and ham into the cold soup.

To serve, put 1 tablespoon of crushed ice in each chilled bowl and pour the soup over it. Sprinkle with the black pepper and garnish with the hard-cooked eggs, cut in eighths, and lemon slices.

Ukrainian Borscht

1 cup navy beans	1 teaspoon salt
1½-pound piece of lean beef	10 beets
1-pound piece of lean fresh pork	2 cups cabbage
	2 large leeks
½-pound piece of slab bacon	3 medium-sized potatoes
10 cups cold water	6 tomatoes
1 bay leaf	1 tablespoon tomato purée
8 whole peppercorns	3 tablespoons vinegar
1 clove garlic	4 tablespoons sugar
4 sprigs parsley	1 pound kielbasa
1 carrot	2 tablespoons flour
1 celery stalk	1 tablespoon butter
1 large onion	

SERVES EIGHT

Soak the navy beans overnight. Cook until tender and drain. Place the beef, pork, and slab bacon in a large soup kettle. Cover with the cold water and bring to a boil. Skim the fat from the surface, and add the bay leaf, peppercorns, garlic, parsley, carrot, celery, onion, and salt. Cover and simmer over low heat for 1½ hours.

Carefully scrub the beets, reserving the 2 smallest for grating. Cook 8 beets in 4 cups of boiling salted water until tender (approximately 45 minutes). Drain and discard the water. Peel and cut each beet into eighths. Peel the 2 remaining raw beets, grate them, and cover with ½ cup cold water to soak. Shred the cabbage. Wash and slice the leeks carefully. Peel the potatoes and cut into eighths. Peel and quarter the tomatoes and shake out the seeds.

Remove the meat from the soup and set aside. Strain the soup into another pot, and add the cooked beets, cabbage, leeks, potatoes, tomatoes, tomato purée, vinegar, sugar, and meat. Bring to a boil and simmer for 45 minutes. Cut the kielbasa in 1-inch pieces and add, with the cooked navy beans, to the soup. Boil gently for 20 minutes more.

Mix the flour and butter together to form a paste. Stir this into the soup to thicken slightly. Squeeze the raw beets and add the liquid to the soup. Discard these beets. Additional sugar or vinegar may be added if you wish a more pronounced sweet or sour flavor. Slice the meat, and arrange it in soup bowls. Pour the hot soup and vegetables over the meat and serve immediately.

Iced Fish, Meat, and Cucumber Soup***

OKROCHKA

Beautifully white and creamy is this chilled cucumber soup laced with chicken, shrimp, and fennel.

4 cups plain yoghurt	6 tablespoons parsley, minced
4 cups milk	2½ tablespoons fresh fennel, minced
1½ large cucumbers, peeled and chopped	
	1 large leek, washed and minced
3 small dill pickles, peeled and chopped	
	3 tablespoons lemon juice
1½ cups cooked shrimp, chopped	Salt and pepper to taste
1½ cups cooked chicken, chopped	6 hard-cooked eggs

SERVES EIGHT

Stir the yoghurt and milk together. Add the cucumbers, pickles, shrimp, chicken, parsley, fennel, and leek. Stir in the lemon juice, salt, and pepper, and chill the soup for at least 4 hours. Serve cold, garnished with sliced hard-cooked eggs.

Russian Fruit Soup

*Gooseberries are difficult to obtain and raspberries are
usually incredibly expensive, but if these two lovely
berries are available, do try this Russian favorite.*

2 cups raspberries	4 cups claret wine
2 cups gooseberries	2½ cups water
1¾ cups sugar	Sour cream
2 cups sour cream	Grated orange rind

SERVES EIGHT

Rub the berries through a fine sieve. Mix in the sugar and then the
sour cream. Stir in the wine and water. Simmer, stirring constantly
with a wooden spoon, until the soup is hot and the sugar is dissolved. *Do not allow to boil.* Serve cold, garnished with a small
dollop of sour cream and grated orange rind.

Poland, Hungary and Roumania

Hungarian Goulash Soup

½ pound slab bacon

5 medium-sized onions

1½ pounds lean beef chuck, cut
    in 1-inch cubes

5 cloves garlic

½ teaspoon caraway seeds

3½ teaspoons paprika

⅛ teaspoon marjoram

9 cups Beef stock (see page 67)

4 cups tomatoes, chopped

½ cup dry red wine

1½ teaspoons salt

1 cup tomato juice

3½ teaspoons sugar

5 medium-sized potatoes

6 beef frankfurters, sliced

1¼ cups water

⅓ cup flour

    Lemon slices (optional)

    Red wine (optional)

    Salt and freshly ground
    pepper to taste

SERVES EIGHT GENEROUSLY

Cut the bacon into ½-inch cubes, place in soup kettle, and fry until
transparent, stirring from time to time. Remove the bacon and set
aside. Peel and chop the onions. Stir into the soup kettle with the
beef cubes, and cook until the onion is golden and the beef slightly

[317]

browned. Peel and mince the garlic and add to kettle with the caraway seeds, paprika, and marjoram. Stir for 2 minutes over low heat. Add the Beef stock, cover, and simmer for 25 minutes. Peel, seed, and chop the tomatoes, and add them to the soup. Stir in the wine, salt, tomato juice, and sugar. Bring soup to a boil, lower heat, cover, and simmer for 25 minutes more.

Peel and dice the potatoes. Add to the soup, together with the sliced frankfurters, and simmer until the potatoes are tender. Blend the water and flour until free from lumps. Add 1 cup of soup and mix well. Stir this mixture slowly into the hot soup and continue cooking, stirring constantly, over low heat until the soup thickens.

If you like the taste of wine in your soup stir a quantity in to your taste. Add salt and pepper if necessary, cook 5 minutes longer, and serve steaming hot.

Fish Soup with Garlic

¾ *pound halibut*
9½ *cups Fish stock (see page 83)*
3 *pounds halibut steaks*
4 *cloves garlic*
¾ *teaspoon salt*

1½ *medium-sized cucumbers*
3 *tablespoons white vinegar*
Salt and freshly ground
pepper to taste

SERVES EIGHT

Remove the skin and bones and chop a ¾ pound piece of halibut coarsely. Place Fish stock and chopped fish in a large soup kettle, and slowly bring to a boil, stirring now and then. Lower the heat and cook gently for 15 minutes. Whirl in a blender to purée. Lay halibut steaks in the bottom of the soup kettle and pour puréed fish over them. Simmer for 15 minutes with the lid slightly off. The fish should be completely cooked, but not falling off the bones.

Peel and mince the garlic and work into a smooth paste with the salt. Beat this mixture into 1 cup of hot soup until smooth. Keep warm. Peel, seed, and dice the cucumbers and set aside. Place the halibut steaks in individual, ovenproof soup bowls, and keep warm in a moderate oven. Add the vinegar and diced cucumbers to the remaining hot soup. Adjust the seasonings and pour over the fish steaks. Serve with warm garlic sauce on the side.

Roumanian Ciorba with Meatballs***

*This traditional Roumanian soup improves with time
as the exotic combination of ingredients permeates the soup.**

3½ pounds veal and pork bones
2½ quarts water
  3 stalks celery, including the leaves
  3 large carrots
  4 tomatoes
⅓ cup fresh parsley, chopped
  4 cups sauerkraut juice
  3 large leeks with 4 inches of green top
  2 stalks celery
  1 knob fennel with green top
  5 tablespoons rice

⅓ cup fresh parsley, chopped
  2 sprigs tarragon
½ teaspoon thyme
¼ teaspoon dried red pepper
  4 egg yolks
  2 cups sour cream
  1 tablespoon flour
  3 tablespoons water
    Additional sour cream
  1 tablespoon fresh dill, chopped
    Salt and freshly ground pepper to taste

SERVES EIGHT GENEROUSLY

Put the bones and water into a soup kettle and bring to a boil. Chop the celery. Peel and chop the carrots. Peel, seed, and chop the tomatoes. Add the celery, carrots, tomatoes, and parsley to the soup kettle. Cover and cook over medium heat until the vegetables are nearly tender but not soft. Stir in the sauerkraut juice. Raise the heat and bring to a boil. Adjust the seasonings. Remove soup from the stove and let it rest while you prepare the meatballs.

Strain the soup; it should taste quite tart. Add more sauerkraut juice if more tartness is desired; add more water if a milder flavor is preferred. Pour the soup back into the soup kettle and bring it to a rolling boil. Cut the leeks into thick slices. Chop the celery. Peel and chop the fennel, using part of the green top.

Wash the rice and add to the boiling soup. Carefully add the meatballs, together with the leeks, chopped celery, fennel, parsley, and tarragon. Add the thyme and red pepper. Cook until the rice is tender.

Beat the egg yolks with a fork and mix in the sour cream. Add the flour and water and stir constantly while the soup boils 15 to

* Several ingredients are repeated because they are used in different steps of the recipe.

20 minutes longer. Gradually stir the egg mixture into the hot soup. Serve hot. Place a dollop of sour cream on top each serving and sprinkle with chopped dill. This soup improves with age and can be stored, covered, in the refrigerator or frozen.

MEATBALLS

¾ pound fresh lean pork	Salt and pepper to taste
½ pound veal	2 tablespoons rice, cooked
1 small onion	1 egg
2 teaspoons fresh parsley, chopped	Flour
1 teaspoon fresh thyme	

Chop the pork and veal coarsely and then grind very fine in a food grinder. Peel and chop the onion very fine. Add to the meat, along with the parsley, thyme, salt, pepper, rice, and egg. Mix all ingredients together thoroughly. Make small meatballs and roll them in flour. Refrigerate.

Traditional Transylvanian Peasant Soup

2 medium-sized onions	5 tablespoons flour
2½ tablespoons bacon fat	3 cups red wine
2 tablespoons butter	2 large red peppers
8 tablespoons paprika	2 pounds small potatoes
3¾ pounds chuck, cut in ½-inch cubes	Salt and freshly ground pepper to taste
1 pound calf's liver, sliced	

SERVES EIGHT

Peel and chop the onions. Place in a soup kettle and sauté in bacon fat and butter until golden and transparent. Mix in 1 tablespoon of paprika. Add the beef and brown on all sides. Add the sliced liver and brown evenly. Stir in the flour, add the wine, and stir again to mix. Lower the heat, cover the kettle, and simmer for about 1 hour.

    Remove and discard the seeds from the red peppers. Chop the

liver and peppers very fine, add to the soup, and cook over very low heat until the beef is soft (about 1¼ hours).

Peel and cube the potatoes, place in a small pan, cover with water, and cook until nearly tender. Add the potatoes to the soup, along with the remaining paprika. Stir in enough of the potato water to make the soup as thick or thin as you desire. Adjust the seasonings. Serve hot.

Polish Blackberry Soup

3 pints blackberries	*1½ cups sugar*
4 cups light sweet wine	*3 cloves*
2-inch stick of cinnamon	*3 cups sour cream, chilled*

SERVES EIGHT

Pick over the berries, discard any bad ones, and set aside ½ cup of the largest ones to use as a garnish. Place the remainder in a strainer and run cold water through them. Pour the washed berries into a soup kettle and add the wine, cinnamon, sugar, and cloves. Place over medium-high heat and bring slowly to a boil. Lower the heat and cook gently for about 5 to 8 minutes. Strain the soup into a bowl, pressing as many of the berries through the strainer as possible. Refrigerate overnight, or for at least 4 hours. When ready to serve, fold in the chilled sour cream. Serve at once.

BREAD AND SOUP FROM THE NEAR AND FAR EAST

India

Indian Lentil Soup

2 medium-sized anions

2 teaspoons vegetable shortening

8 cups water

2 cups red lentils

¼ teaspoon turmeric

3 large cloves garlic

Salt and freshly ground pepper to taste

Heavy cream

SERVES EIGHT

Peel and chop onions. Sauté them in the shortening until golden brown. Reserve. Pour the water into a soup kettle and add the lentils, turmeric, and garlic. Cook over very low heat, covered, for about 1½ hours. Strain the soup into a bowl, pressing the lentils through the strainer. Add the onion and salt. Cook for a few minutes over a very low heat. Adjust the seasonings. Thin the soup to desired consistency with heavy cream. Reheat if necessary. Serve hot.

Indian Cumin Soup

*Very, very strange to Western taste is this super-spicy,
sour Indian soup. Serve in small bowls.*

8 cups of water	½ teaspoon cayenne
5 tablespoons cumin seeds	1½ teaspoons freshly ground
2 small lemons	pepper
3 tablespoons coriander seeds	Salt

SERVES EIGHT

Put the water into a soup kettle. Add the cumin seeds and place in a warm place for 8 to 10 hours or overnight. With a sharp knifè, cut the skin and pith from the lemons. Remove the lemon pulp from the membranes and set aside.

Strain the cumin broth into a bowl and reserve. Place the soaked cumin seeds, coriander, cayenne, freshly ground pepper, the lemon pulp and 2 cups of cumin broth into a blender. Whirl for about 3 minutes. Pour into a pan. Place over high heat and boil for 3 or 4 minutes. Add the remaining cumin broth. Remove from the stove and add salt. Allow the soup to rest for 1 hour in a warm place. Pour through a strainer once more. The soup may be served hot or cold.

Indian Curried Potato Soup***

8 cups raw potatoes	½ cup Chinese parsley
1½ cups onions	4 tablespoons butter
2 large cloves garlic	6 cups milk
6 cups Beef broth (see page 67)	½ teaspoon each black pepper and salt
3½ teaspoons curry powder	

SERVES EIGHT

Peel and dice the potatoes and onions. Peel and mince the garlic cloves. Put the potatoes, onions, garlic, broth, parsley, curry powder, and salt into a large soup kettle. Cook, tightly covered, over a medium-low heat about 40 minutes, or until the potatoes are soft.

With a wooden spoon, press the soup through a strainer. Add the butter, milk, and pepper. Adjust the seasonings. Return to the stove and reheat. Serve hot.

Indian Ginger Soup

8 cups water

8 teaspoons ginger, ground

5½ tablespoons honey

⅔ cup lime juice

1 teaspoon freshly ground pepper

2½ cups cooked rice

8 thin lime slices

SERVES EIGHT

Put the water into a soup kettle and bring to a boil. Add the ground ginger. Cook over a medium-low heat for 3 or 4 minutes. Add the honey, lime juice, pepper, and cooked rice. Stir well. Serve hot.

Indian Lime Soup

10 cups boiling water

2 cloves garlic, finely minced

5 teaspoons dark brown sugar

1½ teaspoons salt

1 teaspoon freshly ground pepper

½ cup Chinese parsley

1½ cups lime juice

SERVES EIGHT

Put the water into an ovenproof soup kettle and bring it to a boil. Add garlic, sugar, salt, and pepper. Wash and chop the parsley and add to the soup. Cook over medium heat for 7 or 8 minutes. Stir in the lime juice. Remove from the stove. Set oven at 200° F. Place the covered soup kettle in the oven and steep for 1 hour. Serve hot or cold.

Oriental
wisdom
in a
bowl

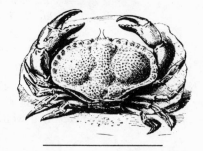

THE COOKING OF THE ORIENT is multifaceted and gem-like in its brilliance. Its sauces are triumphs, its stocks inscrutably clear—each bit of meat, fish, or vegetable a masterwork of cutting or slicing. The soups that follow range from the simplest Japanese Tofu Soup to complex Korean concoctions, so fascinating to me that I couldn't resist including many of them here. You most certainly will not be able to conquer Oriental cooking the first time you try, but you will surely produce results superior to those of the average Chinese restaurant in America. So be not faint of heart, for faint heart ne'er fair Won Ton won.

Shark's Fin Soup

1½ packages (8 ounces)
    prepared shark's fin

7½ cups Chicken consommé
    (see page 75)

5½ tablespoons soy sauce

  2 tablespoons sugar

1½ teaspoons salt

2½ teaspoons sesame oil

  2 teaspoons monosodium
    glutamate

⅓ cup peanut oil

1 pound crabmeat, cooked

1 pound chicken, cooked

9 tablespoons cornstarch

½ cup water

  Roe of 6 crabs

2 eggs

  Salt and freshly ground
  pepper to taste

SERVES EIGHT

Cover the shark's fin with warm water for 25 minutes. Drain and reserve 2 cups. Mix together the Chicken consommé, soy sauce, sugar, salt, sesame oil, and monosodium glutamate. Place the peanut oil in a soup kettle and heat. Add the shark's fin and sauté for 5 minutes. Blend cornstarch with water and stir into the Chicken consommé. Add remaining ingredients and bring to a boil stirring constantly. Cover and simmer for 15 minutes. Serve hot.

Chinese Winter Melon Soup

4-pound chicken, with skin and
  bones removed

½ cup ham, diced

½ cup fresh mushrooms, diced

1 cup Chinese dried mushrooms,
  soaked

8 cups chicken broth

1 can lotus seeds

½ teaspoon salt

  Freshly ground pepper to
  taste

1 winter melon (about 7
  pounds)

SERVES EIGHT

Cut the chicken into ½-inch cubes. Dice the ham and both the mushrooms. Place the chicken and ham in a soup kettle together with the fresh and dried mushrooms, the chicken broth, lotus seeds, salt, and pepper. Bring to a boil and adjust the seasonings. Wash and dry the melon and cut off the top, several inches down. Remove all of the seeds and scoop out some of the melon meat so that the soup may be added.

Place the melon, cut side up, in a Pyrex bowl. A circle of crumpled aluminum foil may be placed around the bottom of the melon to support it. Place the bowl on a rack in a deep soup kettle. Add 2 inches of hot water to the kettle. Pour the soup into the melon and cover. If the lid of the kettle will not fit, cover tightly with aluminum foil tied with a string. Steam for about 3 hours and adjust the seasonings. Ladle the soup into individual bowls, making sure to place some of the melon meat in each serving.

Won Ton Soup***

Preparing your own won tons at home can be fun. These soft, meat-filled dumplings are easy to make and—best of all—should boost your reputation as a versatile cook!

8 cups chicken bouillon
  Filled won tons
2 tablespoons green onions,
  chopped

Soy sauce

SERVES EIGHT

Place the chicken bouillon in a large kettle. Bring to a boil and add a few filled won tons at a time, as the bouillon simmers. Cook the won tons until they rise to the surface (approximately 5 minutes). Remove the won tons with a slotted spoon and set them aside to keep warm. When all the won tons have been cooked, return them to the bouillon to heat through. Place an equal number of won tons in each serving bowl, pour the soup over them, sprinkle with the chopped green onions, and let the guests help themselves to soy sauce.

WON TON DOUGH

2 cups all-purpose or
  unbleached white flour
1 teaspoon salt

1 egg
⅓ cup plus 3 tablespoons
  lukewarm water

MAKES TWENTY-FOUR WON TONS

Sift the flour and salt together. Beat the egg lightly and mix thoroughly with the dry ingredients. Stir the lukewarm water into the flour mixture, a little at a time, blending well after each addition. When the dough reaches the right consistency for rolling, place it on a lightly floured board. Knead until smooth and elastic, then cover with a towel for 20 minutes. Roll out into a very thin rectangle, at least 6x24 inches. Cut into 2-inch squares. Place a spoonful of won ton filling in the center of each square. Bring each corner up over the filling and gently press the edges together, sealing with a few drops of water. Any excess dough may be rolled again and cut into thin noodles to be cooked with the won tons.

WON TON FILLING

2 pounds pork, finely ground   2 tablespoons soy sauce
2 eggs   Freshly ground black pepper

Sauté the pork until it is no longer pink. Beat the eggs lightly and add to the pork, together with the soy sauce and pepper. Mix together thoroughly and place by spoonfuls in the center of each square of won ton dough.

Chinese Cabbage Soup

2 teaspoons shrimp paste   1¼ teaspoons laos powder
3 cloves garlic   4 ears fresh corn
1 small onion   1 head Chinese cabbage
6 cups chicken broth   Salt and freshly ground
1½ chili peppers, chopped   pepper to taste
1¼ teaspoons turmeric

SERVES EIGHT

Fry the shrimp paste in a small skillet. When cool, reduce it to a powder. Peel and mince the garlic. Peel and chop the onion. Place the chicken broth in a soup kettle. Add the shrimp paste, garlic, onion, chili peppers, turmeric, and laos powder. Cook over medium-high heat until the soup boils, then lower the heat and simmer for

4 to 5 minutes. Add the corn, cut from the cob, and cook until tender. Finally, place the washed and coarsely chopped Chinese cabbage into the soup and cook for 3 minutes more. Adjust the seasonings. Serve hot.

Chinese Watermelon Soup

½ pound lean fresh pork, diced

1 roasting chicken (boned)

1 small duck (boned)

½ pound spring lamb, diced

2 cups abalone, diced, (substitute fresh or canned clams if necessary)

½ pound smoked ham, diced

1 cup dried mushrooms, diced

1 cup fresh mushrooms, diced

3 onions

8 stalks Chinese cabbage, cut in 1½-inch pieces

8 stalks celery, cut in 1½-inch pieces

1½ cups bean sprouts

1 tablespoon sugar

2 tablespoons dry mustard

2 tablespoons soy sauce

1 tablespoon caraway seeds

1 quart chicken broth (with fat removed)

1 underripe watermelon (about 2 feet long)

½ bunch watercress, coarsely chopped

4 small cooked lobster tails, with shells removed

Salt and freshly ground pepper to taste

SERVES EIGHT

Put the pork into a large soup kettle, cover with water, and cook at a low boil for slightly over 1 hour. Remove the pork. Reserve the broth and refrigerate. Skim off the fat. Use the broth to thin the soup, if necessary.

Place the remaining ingredients (except the watermelon, watercress, and lobster) in a large soup kettle. Cover the kettle and simmer for about 2 hours.

Cut an oval slice, 1 foot long, from one side of the melon. Scoop out about half of the flesh, leaving the walls approximately 3 inches thick. All of the seeds should be discarded. Place the whole watermelon in a roasting pan, cut side up. A circle of crushed aluminum foil may be placed around the bottom of the melon for support. Fill the pan with about 2 inches of water. Pour the soup into the melon adding reserved broth if desired. Cover with a lid or aluminum foil, and cook for 1 hour in an oven preheated to 450° F.

When ready to serve, adjust the seasonings and add the watercress and lobster meat, cut into ½-inch pieces. Float fresh flowers on top of the soup. Serve hot. Ladle the soup into individual dishes, scooping out some of the melon flesh to place in each bowl.

Cream of Crab Soup

3 tablespoons vegetable oil

3 slices ginger, chopped

3 scallions, cut into 1-inch pieces

1½ cup crabmeat, flaked

1½ tablespoons sherry

6 cups chicken broth

3 egg whites

4 tablespoons heavy cream

3 teaspoons cornstarch

Salt to taste

SERVES EIGHT

Heat the vegetable oil in a heavy skillet. Add the ginger and scallions. Stir over high heat for 1 minute. Add the crabmeat and sherry, and cook 1 minute more, stirring constantly. Pour in 5½ cups of the chicken broth and bring the soup to a boil. Lower the heat and continue cooking for 5 minutes.

Meanwhile, beat the egg whites until they are frothy and mix in the heavy cream. Add this mixture to the hot soup and stir for 1 minute. Blend the cornstarch with the remaining ½ cup of chicken broth and add this to the soup, stirring constantly, until the mixture begins to bubble and thicken. Simmer for several minutes. Serve hot.

Japanese Tofu Soup

10 cups beef broth

1 pound tofu

4 teaspoons soy sauce

2 teaspoons ginger root, peeled and minced

Salt to taste

10 scallions

16 carrot slices, each cut to resemble a flower

SERVES EIGHT

Put the broth into a soup kettle and bring it to a boil. Cut the tofu into ½-inch cubes and add to the broth, together with soy sauce and ginger root. Cook until the soup is very hot. Adjust the seasonings. Wash and slice the scallions, and add to the hot soup. Serve immediately garnished with carrot slices.

Japanese Shrimp Miso***

10 cups chicken stock (see
   page 74)
2 pounds shrimp, cooked and
   shelled
1½ cups white miso

1 pound tofu
1 cup spinach, cooked and
   chopped
Togarashi

SERVES EIGHT

Put the stock into a soup kettle and bring it to a boil. Clean and chop the shrimp coarsely, and add to the soup kettle. Combine the miso with 1 cup of the hot soup. Gradually stir the mixture into the soup. Chop the tofu and add. Cook for 3 minutes longer. Add the cooked and chopped spinach and a few drops of togarashi. Serve hot.

Japanese Pumpkin Soup

1½ pounds pumpkin
1 large potato
1 teaspoon salt
5 cups water
4 cups heavy cream
⅓ cup sorrel, chopped
½ cup spinach, chopped

1 cup lettuce, chopped
1 leek, trimmed
3 tablespoons butter
½ cup rice, cooked
1 cup young fresh shelled peas
2 tablespoons parsley, minced

SERVES EIGHT

Peel and slice the pumpkin and potato. Put these in a saucepan, and add the water and salt. Simmer until tender. Purée these vegetables and their liquid in a blender. Stir in the heavy cream. Sauté the sorrel, spinach, lettuce, and leek in the butter until the leek is transparent. Do not brown. Stir the sautéed vegetables into the pumpkin mixture along with the rice and peas. Simmer for 10 minutes. Serve hot, sprinkled with the minced parsley.

Japanese Cucumber and Beef Slice Soup

½ pound flank steak, sliced paper thin

1 tablespoon sherry

2 inches ginger root, minced

½ teaspoon sugar

1 tablespoon vegetable oil

Salt and freshly ground pepper

2 large cucumbers, sliced

8 cups beef broth

Soy sauce

SERVES EIGHT

With your fingers, work the sherry, ginger root, sugar, vegetable oil, salt, and pepper into the sliced flank steak. Marinate for 1 hour. Place the cucumbers and the beef broth in a large soup kettle and bring to a boil. Reduce heat, cover, and simmer for 45 minutes. Add the beef and marinade to the soup and simmer for 2 minutes more. Skim off any fat. Serve immediately with soy sauce.

Japanese Ham Soup

2 cups ham (with fat left on), cubed

3 medium-sized onions

11 cups water

7 medium-sized potatoes

4 carrots

Salt and freshly ground pepper to taste

1 cup spinach leaves, well washed

½ cup fresh peas

Soy sauce

SERVES EIGHT

Place the ham in a soup kettle and cook over medium heat until most of the fat has cooked out of the meat. Peel and chop the onions; add them to the kettle and cook over low heat until they are golden and transparent. Pour in the water slowly. Raise the heat to medium high and bring the stock to a boil. Then turn the heat down and simmer for 20 to 25 minutes. Peel and chop the potatoes; add them to the kettle and cook until they fall apart. Peel and chop the carrots; add them to the soup and cook gently until they are tender. Adjust the seasonings. A few minutes before the carrots become soft, add the spinach, peas, and soy sauce. Serve hot.

Japanese Clam Soup

24 clams in shell	4 tablespoons soy sauce
10 cups clam broth	Togarashi (or crushed red pepper)
8 scallions with 3 inches green top	
4 sprigs parsley	Salt and freshly ground pepper to taste
2 teaspoons sugar	14 dry mushrooms, cooked

SERVES EIGHT

Wash the clams thoroughly and place in a soup kettle. Add the broth and cook over low heat until the clams open. Chop the scallions. Mince the parsley and add to the soup, together with the scallions, sugar, sauce, and a few drops of togarashi. Boil for several minutes. Adjust the seasonings. Serve hot with chopped mushrooms.

Korean Sesame Seed Soup

3½–4 pound chicken	3 tablespoons sesame oil
Hot water, or chicken broth	1½ cup mushrooms, quartered
10 medium-sized green onions with tops	Korean decorative eggs (see page 341)
½ tablespoon ginger root	4 pears, partially ripe
8 tablespoons soy sauce	9 tablespoons pine nuts
4 cups sesame seeds	Salt and pepper to taste
6 cucumbers	⅓ cup parsley, minced

SERVES EIGHT

Remove the gizzard, liver, and heart from the chicken and save for another use. Place the chicken in a soup kettle, cover with hot water, and cook over low heat until tender but not falling from the bone. Remove the chicken from the kettle. Discard the skin and bones and cut into thin slices about 2 inches long. Peel and chop the green onions. Mince the ginger root and add to chicken broth along with the onions and soy sauce. Place in the refrigerator; when congealed, skim off all of the fat.

Wash and pick over the sesame seeds. Place in a saucepan, cover with water and soak for about 2 hours. Rub off the outside skin of the seeds. Cover with water and discard the hulls when they rise to the top. Drain and place the seeds in a heavy skillet. Cook over low heat, stirring constantly, until the seeds smell hot but are not brown. Remove the seeds from the fire, add a small amount of water, and mash well. Strain into a bowl, mashing the seeds through the strainer with the back of a spoon. Add the sesame liquid to the chicken broth.

Cut the cucumbers into thin wedges, leaving on the peel, and sprinkle with salt. Set aside for 7 or 8 minutes and drain well. Sauté the cucumber wedges in hot sesame oil for 2 minutes, stirring constantly. Sauté the mushrooms until golden in the remaining oil (adding more if necessary). Reserve. Prepare the Korean decorative eggs. Cut each egg round into 1-inch diamonds. Reserve. Peel the pears; cut in 1-inch cubes. Place in a little salted water; set aside.

Combine the sliced chicken, cucumbers, mushrooms, egg diamonds, and pear cubes in soup bowls, and pour the chilled sesame seed-chicken soup over these ingredients. Adjust the seasonings. Garnish with pine nuts and parsley. Serve cold.

Korean Egg Soup

1 pound partially frozen flank steak

6 tablespoons Sesame seed powder (see page 341)

2 tablespoons vegetable oil

8 tablespoons soy sauce

12 cups beef broth

12 green onion tops

6 eggs

Salt and freshly ground pepper to taste

SERVES EIGHT

[337]

Use a sharp knife to cut the beef into very thin slices. Cut these slices into 1-inch squares. Mix the meat squares with the Sesame seed powder, the vegetable oil, and 4 tablespoons of the soy sauce in a large soup kettle. Sear the meat, remove it from the pan and set aside. Add the remaining soy sauce and beef broth to the pan. Place over medium-low heat and cook for 20 minutes.

Cut the onion tops into approximately 1-inch lengths, add to the kettle, and cook 5 minutes more. Beat the eggs until the yolks and the whites are well blended. Stir the eggs briskly into the hot soup, and continue beating for 5 minutes over very low heat. Adjust the seasonings. Add reserved meat, stir and serve immediately.

Korean Eggplant Soup***

5 cloves garlic

10 medium-sized green onions with tops

½ pound flank steak, partially frozen

6 tablespoons Sesame seed powder (see page 341)

6 tablespoons soy sauce

12 cups beef broth

3 small eggplants

8 tablespoons flour

4 eggs, beaten

4 tablespoons vegetable oil

3½ teaspoons salt

Salt and freshly ground pepper to taste

SERVES EIGHT

Peel and chop the garlic and onions coarsely. With a sharp knife, cut the partially frozen beef into very thin 1-inch square slices. Mix together the meat, garlic, onions, Sesame seed powder, and 4 tablespoons of the soy sauce. Turn into a large soup kettle and sear the meat. Set meat aside. Add remaining soy sauce and broth to the pan. Place over medium-low heat and cook until the meat is tender (about 25 minutes).

Peel the eggplants and cut into pieces about 2½ inches long and ⅓-inch thick. Roll in the flour and dip in the beaten eggs. Heat the vegetable oil in a skillet and cook the eggplants until lightly browned on all sides. Sprinkle the salt over the eggplants. Just before serving, add the eggplant pieces to the soup along with the meat. Serve hot.

Korean Beef Ball Soup

4 *cloves garlic*

8 *green onions with tops*

1 *pound flank steak, partially frozen*

8 *tablespoons soy sauce*

6 *tablespoons Sesame seed powder (see page 341)*

2 *tablespoons sesame oil*

1 *cup mushrooms, thinly sliced*

12 *cups beef broth*

Salt and freshly ground pepper to taste

¼ *cup parsley, minced*

SERVES EIGHT

Peel and chop the garlic and green onions. Cut the green onion tops into 1¾-inch pieces and reserve. Cube the flank steak. Combine the garlic, onions, meat cubes, 4 tablespoons of the soy sauce, Sesame seed powder, vegetable oil, and mushrooms. Put into a large soup kettle and sear the meat on all sides. Add the remaining soy sauce and the water. Cook over medium-low heat until the meat is tender (about 45 minutes). Add the Beef balls to the soup and cook 10 minutes. Five minutes before the soup is ready, add the onion tops. Adjust the seasonings. Serve hot garnished with parsley.

BEEF BALLS

3 *cloves garlic*

2 *green onions with tops*

½ *pound chuck, chopped*

½ *cup bean curd*

4 *tablespoons soy sauce*

6 *tablespoons Sesame seed powder (see page 341)*

4 *tablespoons sesame oil*

4 *tablespoons pine nuts*

4 *tablespoons flour*

5 *eggs, beaten*

Salt and freshly ground pepper to taste

Peel and chop the garlic and green onions very fine. Place in a bowl with the chopped beef. Press the bean curd with the back of a wooden spoon to remove the liquid. Add it to the chopped beef, together with the soy sauce, Sesame seed powder, and 2 tablespoons of the vegetable oil. Mix the ingredients thoroughly and form small balls with 2 pine nuts in the center of each. Roll in the flour and dip in the beaten eggs. Heat the rest of the vegetable oil in a skillet. Add the beef balls and brown lightly, adding more oil if necessary. Add to the hot soup.

Korean Summer Meat Dumplings

4-*pound stewing chicken, cut*
 in quarters
 Chicken broth
3 *cucumbers*
 Salt
1 *tablespoon vegetable oil*
2 *onions*
1 *carrot*

½ *cup water*
1 *cup ham, cooked*
¾ *cup mushrooms*
2 *tablespoons vegetable oil*
 Meat filling
 Dumpling dough
 Korean decorative eggs
 (see page 341)

SERVES EIGHT

Cover the chicken pieces with chicken broth and cook over medium-low heat until the chicken is tender. Remove the chicken from the broth, cut the meat into thin strips and place it in a bowl. Put the broth in the refrigerator; when congealed, skim all the fat off.

Cut the cucumbers in julienne strips, leaving the peeling on. Sprinkle liberally with salt and let rest for a few minutes. Drain well and sauté in the vegetable oil for only a few minutes so that the color will be preserved. Set aside. Peel the onions and dice very fine. Peel the carrot and cut into julienne strips. Place the water in a saucepan and bring to a boil. Add carrot strips and cook for 2 or 3 minutes. Drain, dice, and reserve. Dice the ham and mushrooms and sauté in a small amount of oil in a skillet. Add the onions, carrot pieces, celery, and mushrooms, and sauté until the onions are golden and transparent and the carrot pieces tender. Add the chicken meat and cucumbers. Adjust the seasonings and set aside.

Place 2 or 3 dumplings in each soup bowl and pour the chilled chicken broth over them. Cut Korean decorative eggs in small shapes and use as a garnish for the soup.

MEAT FILLING

Chicken meat, cut in thin
strips
3 *tablespoons Sesame seed*
 powder (see page 341)

3 *tablespoons soy sauce*
¼ *teaspoon black pepper*

Combine all ingredients and mix thoroughly.

DUMPLING DOUGH

4½ cups flour
1½ cups water

3 tablespoons pine nuts

Combine the flour and water. Knead for 5 or 6 minutes. Divide dough in half, and roll out each half very thin. Cut dough in 2½-inch squares. Put about a teaspoon of meat filling and 2 or 3 pine nuts on each square. Bring the four points together and twist firmly, squeezing together all the open seams.

Bring 1 cup of water to a rolling boil. Carefully slide the dumplings into the water. After they rise to the surface, cook for several minutes. Remove them from water with a slotted spoon and cool.

Korean Decorative Eggs

4 eggs

Separate the eggs. Beat the egg whites slightly. Oil a skillet lightly. Spread a very thin layer of the egg white over the bottom of the skillet. When cooked, gently turn over and cook briefly on the other side. Set aside. Cook the egg yolks in the same way. Follow the directions in the recipe calling for decorative eggs.

Sesame Seed Powder***

2 cups sesame seeds, white

3 teaspoons salt

Pick over sesame seeds. Place in a strainer and run water through the seeds thoroughly.

Place in a cast iron (or other heavy) skillet over low heat. Stir the seeds constantly for about 4 minutes to ensure even browning and plumping. Do not burn the seeds. Remove from stove and sprinkle with salt. Pound, mash, or blend the seeds until they become a fine powder.

The
South
Pacific

NATIVE SOUTH PACIFIC COOKING is directly related to the somewhat limited resources of the islands—coconut, fish, a few vegetables, but little in the way of fresh meat. The larger islands have a greater variety of foods, and their cooking tends to reflect—at least to some extent—their parent nation. In Tahiti, for example, the cuisine is French, although native dishes still prevail. In Australia and New Zealand the dishes are essentially—although not exclusively—British-oriented. In Hawaii the polygot population—Polynesian, Chinese, Japanese, and American—reflects as many cooking styles.

Some of the soup recipes that follow are Polynesian in origin. I think you will find them especially interesting and quite unusual.

Australian Busters***

These soft, thin cheese biscuits are absolutely
superb with vegetable soup or, in fact, with any
soup that isn't creamy or cheese-y.

8 tablespoons butter	6-7 tablespoons water
2 cups flour, unsifted	A pinch or two of cayenne
3½ cups grated cheddar, loosely	pepper
packed	

MAKES TWELVE

With your fingers, rub the butter into the flour until the particles
are very small. Once again, using your fingers, lightly mix in the
grated cheese. Stir in the water and cayenne pepper with a fork.
Roll the dough out to ¼-inch thickness, cut into 3-inch rounds,
prick each biscuit ten times with a fork, and place on a greased baking sheet. Bake for 15 minutes in an oven preheated to 450° F.

Australian Cream of Lobster Soup

2 large onions	4 cups milk
1 large cauliflower	4 tablespoons flour
4 cups water	4 cups lobster, cooked
2 bay leaves	Fresh parsley, minced
Salt, freshly ground pepper,	Whipped cream
and nutmeg to taste	

SERVES EIGHT

Peel and chop the onions. Wash, trim, and chop the cauliflower.
Place the water into a soup kettle along with the onion, cauliflower,
and bay leaves. Simmer for 20 minutes or until cauliflower is tender.
Strain the soup into a bowl, pressing as much of the onion and
cauliflower through as possible. Add salt, pepper, and nutmeg. Pour
the soup back into the kettle. Return to the stove and bring the soup
to a boil.

Take about 1 cup of the milk, add the flour, and mix until all
the lumps have disappeared. Take out 1½ cups of the hot soup,

combine it with the flour mixture, and return to the rest of the soup. Stir in the remainder of the milk and cook 10 minutes longer.

Chop the lobster coarsely and add it to the soup. Cook until the lobster is heated through. Ladle the soup into a tureen and sprinkle with minced parsley. Top with whipped cream.

Spicy Chicken Soup

4-pound roasting chicken
10 cups water
8 green onions, sliced
1 curry leaf
1 teaspoon salt
1 teaspoon shrimp paste
9 tablespoons yellow onions
2 small cloves garlic

2 tablespoons coconut oil
3 thin slices green ginger, peeled
9 macadamia nuts, crushed
½ teaspoon coriander seeds, ground
¾ teaspoon turmeric
Salt and freshly ground pepper to taste

SERVES EIGHT

Clean the chicken and place in a soup kettle with 7½ cups of water, the green onions, curry leaf, and salt. Place over medium-high heat and bring to a boil. Turn the heat down, cover, and cook gently until chicken is done. Remove the chicken from the broth and set aside. Fry the shrimp paste in a small skillet, mash with the back of a spoon and set aside. Peel and slice the yellow onions, and peel and chop the garlic. Heat coconut oil in a skillet and sauté the onions, garlic, ginger, and crushed nuts until the onion is golden and transparent. Add the onion mixture to the broth, together with the shrimp paste, coriander, and turmeric. Cook over low heat for about 30 minutes. Adjust the seasonings. Cut the chicken away from the bones and into slivers.

Prepare bowls of:

Slivered chicken
Cooked rice
Diced green onions
New potatoes, cooked and sliced
Diced celery

Chinese vermicelli, cooked
Hard-cooked eggs, sliced
Lemon slices
Onion flakes

TO SERVE: Place the broth and a large bowl of rice in the center of the table. Arrange the other bowls around them. Each guest places a bit of chicken, vermicelli, vegetables, and egg in his or her bowl. The broth is spooned over this. Onion flakes and lemon slices are used as a garnish. Serve hot.

Australian Gems

Just as hot crumpets soak up melted butter like little sponges, so do these Australian Gems.

2 tablespoons butter

¼ cup sugar

1 egg

1½ cups flour, sifted

¾ cup milk

MAKES SIXTEEN

Cream together the butter and sugar. Beat in the egg; add the flour and milk alternately, beating well after each addition. Spoon into patty tins and bake for 15 minutes in an oven preheated to 450° F. Serve hot with butter.

Chicken Soup Delight

3½-pound roasting chicken

1 teaspoon salt

⅛ teaspoon freshly ground pepper

2 medium-sized onions

½-inch slice green ginger, peeled

8 macadamia nuts

1 tablespoon coconut or peanut oil

1½ teaspoons turmeric

1 tablespoon coconut or peanut oil

SERVES EIGHT

Rinse the chicken and discard the gizzard, heart, and liver. Place in a soup kettle, add salt and pepper, and cover with water. Peel and chop the onions; chop the ginger and nuts. Place coconut or peanut oil in a small skillet and heat; add the onions, ginger, and nuts, and cook until the onions are golden. Add to chicken along with the turmeric. Cook gently over low heat until the chicken is tender (about 1½ hours).

Remove the whole chicken from the soup kettle and drain the liquid into a saucepan. Adjust the seasonings. Keep the broth warm. Brown the chicken in coconut or peanut oil on all sides. Cut the meat away from the bones and into thin strips.

Prepare large bowls of:

Chicken meat

Cooked rice

Bean sprouts, scalded and drained

Hard-cooked eggs, sliced

Cabbage, shredded and cooked for a few minutes

Chinese noodles, soaked in water, drained, and then fried in oil for 2 minutes

Prepare small bowls of:

Onion flakes

Thin lemon slices

Sambal*

TO SERVE: Place the broth and a large bowl of rice in the center of the table. Arrange the other bowls around them. Each guest places a bit of chicken, bean sprouts, hard-cooked eggs, cabbage, and Chinese noodles in his or her bowl. The broth is spooned over this. Onion flakes, lemon slices, and sambal are used as garnishes. Serve hot.

* To prepare sambal, mince fresh red chilies and a small piece of green ginger. Add a little white vinegar and a small amount of chicken broth.

Hawaiian Pineapple-Pumpkin Soup

2 medium-sized onions

6 tablespoons butter

2 tablespoons fresh parsley, finely chopped

3 cans crushed pineapple with the juice

3 cans (1 pound, 2 ounces each) pumpkin

⅛ teaspoon each: cinnamon, nutmeg, and allspice

1 cup water

6 tablespoons cornstarch

3 cups milk

3 cups light cream

Salt to taste

¾ cup heavy cream, whipped

SERVES EIGHT

Peel and chop the onions. Heat the butter in a soup kettle, add the onions and parsley, and sauté until the onions are golden and transparent. Stir in the pineapple, pumpkin, and the spices. Simmer for 15 minutes, stirring occasionally. Add the water and simmer, covered, for 40 minutes. Blend the cornstarch and the milk until smooth. Add 1 cup of the hot soup to the cornstarch mixture. Stir this into the rest of the soup and cook, stirring constantly, until the soup boils. Lower the heat and stir in the cream. Adjust the seasonings. Serve hot, with a dollop of whipped cream on each serving.

Eggplant Soup

3 medium-sized onions

3 small cloves garlic

4 tablespoons coconut or peanut oil

14 macadamia nuts

½ teaspoon cumin seeds

¾ teaspoon turmeric

1 tablespoon ground chili

1½ teaspoons coriander seeds

2 thin slices green ginger, peeled and chopped

¾ teaspoon salt

1 cup raw chicken meat, chopped

4 curry leaves

¾ teaspoon laos powder

8 cups coconut milk

4 small eggplants

Salt and freshly ground pepper to taste

8 tablespoons lime juice

SERVES EIGHT

[347]

Peel and chop the onions and garlic. Heat the oil in a soup kettle and sauté the onions and garlic until the onions are golden and transparent. Put the nuts, cumin seeds, turmeric, ground chili, and coriander seeds into a blender and blend until pulverized. Add pulverized mixture, chopped ginger, salt, and chicken meat to the soup kettle. Cover with water. Place over medium-high heat and bring to a boil. Add curry leaves and laos powder to the soup, and simmer for 20 minutes. Stir in the coconut milk and cook over low heat for 8 to 10 minutes. Peel and chop the eggplants, add to the soup, and simmer until tender but not soft. Adjust the seasonings. Just before serving, stir in the lime juice. Serve hot.

Hawaiian Welcome Soup

½ pound mushrooms	6 cups Chicken stock (page 74)
1 cup celery	1 large bay leaf
2 tablespoons onion	1 teaspoon whole saffron
2 cloves garlic	½ teaspoon green ginger, peeled and minced
2 green peppers	
4 leeks	2 tablespoons lemon juice
4 tablespoons butter	1 cup water
1 pound prawns	2 tablespoons cornstarch
8 medium-sized tomatoes	Salt and freshly ground pepper to taste

SERVES EIGHT

Wash and cube the mushrooms. Wash and chop the celery. Peel and chop the onion and garlic very fine. Remove the seeds and membranes from the peppers and cube. Wash and slice the leeks. Heat the butter in a soup kettle, add the vegetables, and cook over a low flame until the onions are golden and transparent. Clean and chop the prawns. Peel, seed, and chop the tomatoes. Stir both the prawns and the tomatoes into the soup. Add the Chicken stock, bay leaf, saffron, ginger, and lemon juice. Stir thoroughly over medium-high heat, and bring to a boil. Mix the water and cornstarch, and blend to smooth paste. Gradually stir this mixture into the boiling soup. Turn the burner down and cook gently for about 25 minutes. Adjust the seasonings. Remove the bay leaf and serve hot.

SPECIAL
BREADS
AND
SOUPS

Sweet breads and soups

Sweet soups and breads may be found in other parts of this book. There are some, however, that do not fit into any special category. Since they are too delicious to resist, I am including them here.

Applesauce Bread

1¼ cups sweetened applesauce
⅓ cup sugar
¼ cup dark brown sugar
1 large egg
⅓ cup melted butter
2¼ cups all-purpose flour

⅔ teaspoon baking soda
1 teaspoon nutmeg
1 teaspoon cinnamon
1 cup pecans, coarsely chopped
¾ cup raisins

MAKES ONE LOAF

Place the applesauce, sugar, brown sugar, egg, and melted butter in a large bowl. Beat until the brown sugar is dissolved, pressing any lumps against the bowl with the back of the spoon. Mix together the flour, baking soda, nutmeg, and cinnamon. Add the dry ingredients to the butter mixture, a little at a time, stirring well after each addition. Stir until the batter is smooth. Fold in the chopped nuts and raisins, and spoon the batter into a well-greased, fluted mold. Preheat the oven to 350° F. Bake for 1 hour and 10 minutes, or until a toothpick inserted in the thickest part comes out clean. Cool for 10 minutes. Loosen the edges with a sharp thin knife and turn out onto a cake plate. Sprinkle with confectioner's sugar, if desired. Serve warm.

Lemon and Lime Bread***

1 cup sugar

½ cup shortening

2 eggs

1¼ cups all-purpose flour, sifted

1 teaspoon baking powder

½ teaspoon salt

½ cup milk

¾ cup raw cashews or walnuts, finely chopped

Zest (thin outer skin) of 1 lemon, grated

Zest (thin outer skin) of 1 lime, grated

2 tablespoons fresh lemon juice

2 tablespoons fresh lime juice

5 tablespoons sugar

MAKES ONE LOAF

Place the sugar in a large bowl, add the shortening, and cream together. Beat the eggs lightly and add to the butter and sugar mixture. Combine the sifted flour, baking powder, and salt, and sift all together. Alternately add the dry ingredients and the milk to the sugar, shortening, and eggs. Stir well after each addition. Stir the chopped nuts into the batter along with the grated lemon and lime zest.

Grease a loaf pan. Pour in the batter and bake for 1 hour in an oven preheated to 350° F. Remove the bread from oven and cool for 10 minutes in the pan. Mix the lemon and lime juice with the sugar. Invert the loaf on a serving plate. Using a sharp knife, slice 1 inch off the top of the loaf, pour the sugared juices over the rest of the loaf, and replace the top. Cool before serving.

Orange Juice Bread

*What could be better with orange juice and coffee than
a moist slice of Orange juice bread?*

½ cup sweet butter

1¼ cups sugar

2 large eggs

1½ cups all-purpose or
unbleached white flour

1 teaspoon baking powder

¼ teaspoon salt

¼ cup orange juice

¼ cup milk

1 lemon zest (thin outer skin),
grated

1 orange zest (thin outer
skin), grated

1 tablespoon lemon juice

1 tablespoon orange juice

⅓ cup sugar

MAKES ONE LOAF

Cream the butter with the sugar in a large bowl. Beat the eggs and
add to the creamed mixture. Sift the flour, baking powder, and salt
together. Mix the orange juice and milk. Add the liquids alternately
with the sifted dry ingredients to the creamed mixture, a little at a
time, beating well after each addition. Stir the lemon and orange
zest into the batter. Butter a loaf pan 11x4x3 inches. Line the bottom of the pan with waxed paper and butter the paper. Smooth the
batter over the waxed paper and bake in an oven preheated to
325° F. for 45 minutes, or until the bread springs back lightly when
touched in the center. Combine the lemon and orange juice with the
sugar in a small saucepan. Cook over medium heat until the sugar
dissolves, stirring constantly. Brush the bread with this icing as soon
as it is taken from the oven. Cool in the pan. Orange juice bread is
especially good for breakfast, or spread with thick butter for afternoon tea.

Cranberry Nut Bread

1 egg, well beaten

1 cup milk

2 tablespoons butter, melted

3 cups sifted all-purpose flour

½ cup sugar

1 teaspoon salt

4 teaspoons baking powder

1 cup cranberries

½ cup pecans, chopped

1 teaspoon vanilla

MAKES ONE LOAF

[353]

Mix the egg with the milk and butter. Sift together the flour, ¼ cup of the sugar, salt, and baking powder. Add the liquid to the flour mixture and blend. Chop the cranberries very fine and add the remaining ¼ cup of sugar. Fold the cranberries, pecans, and vanilla into the batter. Pour into a greased loaf pan and bake at 350° F. for approximately 1 hour.

Orange-Honey Bread

2½ cups sifted all-purpose or
    unbleached white flour
½ teaspoon baking soda
½ teaspoon salt
2½ teaspoons baking powder
 2 tablespoons butter

1 cup honey
1 egg, well beaten
¾ cup orange juice
¾ cup nuts, broken

MAKES ONE LOAF

Sift the dry ingredients together. Cream the butter with the honey and blend well. Add the beaten egg. Add the sifted dry ingredients to the butter and honey mixture alternately with the orange juice, blending only until the flour is moistened. Fold in the nuts. Pour into a greased 9-inch loaf pan and bake for 1 hour and 10 minutes. (If desired, use a 13-inch loaf pan and bake for only 1 hour.)

Brazil Nut Tea Loaf

2 cups sifted all-purpose flour
2 cups whole wheat flour
½ cup sugar
1 teaspoon baking soda
1 teaspoon salt

½ cup unsulphured molasses
1 cup buttermilk
1 cup seedless raisins
1 cup Brazil nuts, chopped

MAKES TWO SMALL LOAVES

Sift together the flours, sugar, baking soda, and salt. Add the molasses and buttermilk, and blend well. Fold in the raisins and nuts.

Pour into two small greased loaf pans, and bake at 350° F. for about 1 hour, or until a toothpick inserted in the center of the loaf comes out clean. Cool the loaves on a wire rack.

Moist Pineapple-Bran Bread

½ cup crushed pineapple, drained

⅔ cup pineapple syrup

⅔ cup whole bran cereal

2 cups all-purpose or unbleached white flour

¼ teaspoon baking soda

2 teaspoons baking powder

1 teaspoon salt

½ cup sugar

¾ cup blanched almonds, chopped

1 egg, beaten

2 tablespoons butter, melted

MAKES ONE LOAF

Drain the pineapple and reserve the fruit. Measure ⅔ cup of syrup (adding orange juice or water if necessary). Place the bran in a small bowl, pour the pineapple syrup over it, and let soften for 15 minutes. Combine the sifted flour, baking soda, baking powder, salt, and sugar, and sift again. Add the pineapple, almonds, egg, and butter to the bran. Stir in the dry ingredients, using only enough strokes to blend. Grease a loaf pan, spoon the batter into it, and bake for 1¼ hours in a preheated 350° F. oven.

Apple-Cheese Loaf

½ cup butter

⅔ cup sugar

2 eggs

½ cup mild cheddar cheese, grated

1 cup ground apples with liquid

¾ cup nut meats, coarsely chopped

2 cups sifted all-purpose or unbleached white flour

1 teaspoon salt

1 teaspoon baking powder

½ teaspoon baking soda

¼ teaspoon nutmeg

MAKES ONE LOAF

[355]

Cream the butter. Gradually add the sugar and mix until pale yellow and fluffy. Add each egg separately, beating approximately 1 minute after each addition. Mix in the cheese, apples, and nuts until well blended. Sift together the dry ingredients and add half at a time to the apple-cheese mixture, blending only until the flour is moistened.

Pour the batter into a greased 9-inch loaf pan. Push the batter to the sides and into the corners of the pan leaving the middle of the pan slightly depressed. Bake in a preheated 350° F. oven for 1 hour, or until the loaf tests done when a wooden toothpick is inserted. (A 13x4½-inch loaf pan may also be used, but reduce the baking time to about 45 minutes.)

Cinnamon-Oatmeal Bread

These cinnamon-and-sugar-twirled oatmeal loaves
are sweet enough for toasting or eating plain,
spread with cold butter.

3 cups milk

2 packages dry active yeast

½ cup warm water (115° F.)

1½ cups quick-cooking rolled oats

½ cup sugar

1 tablespoon salt

½ cup shortening

1½ cups dried apricots, finely chopped

½ cup currants

7–7½ cups all-purpose or unbleached white flour, sifted

2 eggs

3 tablespoons cinnamon

¼ cup sugar

MAKES THREE LOAVES

Scald the milk in a saucepan. Dissolve the yeast in the warm water. Combine the scalded milk with the rolled oats, ½ cup sugar, salt, shortening, and dried fruits in a large bowl. Mix and cool to lukewarm. Blend in 3½ cups of the sifted flour. Beat the eggs and add with the yeast to the milk and flour mixture. Stir in enough additional sifted flour to make a stiff dough. Knead on a lightly floured board until smooth and elastic (about 10 minutes). Roll the dough into a ball, place in a greased bowl, turning once to grease the top. Cover with a dishtowel and let rise in a warm, draft-free place until double in bulk (about 2 hours). Punch down, turn over, cover, and let rise again until double in bulk (approximately 1 hour). Punch it down again and divide into three parts. Roll each part into a ball, cover, and allow to rest for 10 minutes.

Flatten each ball into a long rectangle. Slap each rectangle with the back of the hand to break any bubbles. Mix the cinnamon and ¼ cup sugar and divide the mixture among the three rectangles. Roll up each rectangle along the width. Seal the edges, and place in three lightly greased bread pans with the seams underneath. Brush lightly with melted butter. Cover with a dishtowel and let rise until double in bulk (about 1½ hours). Bake for 40 to 50 minutes in an oven preheated to 375° F., or until the bread is brown and begins to leave the sides of the pan.

Chocolate-Cinnamon Tea Bread

1 package (4 ounces) German
   Sweet Chocolate

2½ cups minus 2 tablespoons
   all-purpose flour, sifted

1¾ cups sugar

1 teaspoon salt

½ teaspoon soda

¼ teaspoon cinnamon

¾ teaspoon cream of tartar

1 cup soft butter

¾ cups milk

1 teaspoon vanilla

3 whole eggs

1 egg yolk

MAKES ONE LOAF

Partially melt the chocolate in the top of a double boiler. Remove from heat and stir rapidly until totally melted. Combine the sifted flour, sugar, salt, soda, cinnamon, and cream of tartar, and sift together. Cream the butter and add the dry ingredients, milk, and vanilla. Mix only enough to moisten. Beat with an electric mixer at medium speed for 1½ minutes. Add the eggs, egg yolk, and melted chocolate, and beat again for 1 minute.

Pour the batter into a greased and lightly floured (9- or 10-inch) tube pan, lined with waxed paper on the bottom. Bake about 65 minutes at 350° F., or until the bread comes free from the edge of pan. Cool for 15 minutes and then turn out onto serving plate. Ice with chocolate glaze and serve.

CHOCOLATE GLAZE

1 package (4 ounces) German Sweet Chocolate

1 cup sifted confectioner's sugar

¼ cup water

Pinch of salt

1½ tablespoons butter

½ teaspoon vanilla

Place chocolate, water, and butter in a saucepan over low heat and mix, stirring constantly, until chocolate is melted. Combine the dry ingredients. Gradually add the chocolate, blending well. Stir in the vanilla. Pour the glaze over the bread.

Fig and Apricot Bread***

1 cup all-purpose or unbleached white flour

½ cup hickory nuts (if not available, use walnuts)

1 teaspoon baking soda

½ cup dried figs, chopped

½ teaspoon salt

½ cup dried apricots, chopped

1 egg

1 tablespoon orange zest (thin outer skin), grated

½ cup dark brown sugar

1 cup buttermilk

⅓ cup butter, melted

1 cup rolled oats

MAKES ONE LOAF

Combine the sifted flour, baking soda, and salt, and sift again. Set aside. In a large bowl beat the egg until it is frothy. Add the brown sugar, a little at a time, and continue beating until it is light and frothy. Add the buttermilk alternately with the dry ingredients, stirring only enough to mix.

Carefully fold in the rolled oats, nuts, figs, apricots, grated orange zest, and the melted butter. Put in a greased, paper-lined loaf pan and bake at 350° F. for 55 minutes, or until a toothpick comes out clean. When cool, ice with lemon-orange frosting, allowing it to drip down the sides of the bread. Decorate with dried apricot pieces arranged as stars.

1¼ cups confectioner's sugar   1 tablespoon orange juice
 1 tablespoon lemon juice

Combine the ingredients and mix until smooth.

Fruit and Buckwheat Bread

2¼ cups buckwheat flour

1 teaspoon salt

½ teaspoon baking powder

1½ teaspoons baking soda

½ cup dried apricots

½ cup dried prunes, soaked

½ cup raisins

1½ cups buttermilk

½ cup brown sugar

MAKES ONE LOAF

Combine the buckwheat flour, salt, baking powder and baking soda in a large bowl. Chop the dried apricots and soaked dried prunes coarsely and add, with the raisins, to the dry ingredients. Stir the buttermilk and sugar together and combine with the fruits and flour mixture. Mix thoroughly. Grease a loaf pan with a small amount of oil, pour in the batter and bake the bread for 50 or 60 minutes in an oven heated to 325° F. Remove from pan and cool on a wire rack.

Carrot Bread

1¾ cups sifted cake flour (or 1½ cups all-purpose flour), sifted

1 teaspoon ground cinnamon

1 teaspoon baking powder

¾ teaspoon salt

½ teaspoon baking soda

1 cup sugar

¾ cup salad oil

1 cup raw carrots, finely grated

2 eggs

½ cup pecans, finely chopped

MAKES TWO LOAVES

Combine the sifted flour, cinnamon, baking powder, salt, and baking soda. Sift together and set aside. Combine the sugar and salad oil and beat with an electric mixer at medium speed about 2 minutes, or until smooth and well blended. Fold in the grated carrots with their juice. Add the eggs, one at a time, beating well after each addition. Stir in the chopped nuts. Add the dry ingredients and mix well.

Grease and dust with flour two 8x4x3-inch loaf pans. Pour in the batter and bake in a preheated 350° F. oven for 55 to 60 minutes. Cool. Serve warm or wrap and store in refrigerator for up to 1 week (this improves the flavor and makes the bread more moist).

Spicy Sweet Potato Spoon Bread

Sweet and spicy is this mellow Southern favorite.

2 large sweet potatoes	1½ teaspoons allspice
8 tablespoons butter or margarine	½ teaspoon cinnamon
3 tablespoons sugar	5 tablespoons flour
1½ teaspoons nutmeg	¼ teaspoon salt
	2 eggs

SERVES EIGHT

Scrub the potatoes and boil until tender. Peel them and mash with the butter. Add the sugar, spices and flour and mix thoroughly. Beat the eggs and stir them into the potato mixture. Pour all ingredients into a buttered pan, and bake for 30 minutes in an oven preheated to 425° F.

Chocolate Nut Tea Bread

3 cups cake flour, sifted	1 egg
1½ teaspoons baking soda	1¼ cups sour milk
½ cup cocoa	⅓ cup shortening
1 cup sugar	¾ cup pecans, chopped
1 teaspoon salt	

MAKES ONE LOAF

Combine the sifted flour, baking soda, cocoa, sugar, and salt, and sift again. Beat the egg and blend it into the sour milk along with the melted shortening. Add the dry ingredients to the egg mixture all at once, stirring briskly until the batter is smooth. Fold in the chopped nuts. Put in a greased loaf pan and bake in 350° F. preheated oven for 1 hour. Allow this tea bread to cool before slicing.

German Elderberry Soup

2½ pounds elderberries   6 tablespoons cold water
9 cups water   2 tablespoons lemon juice
Lemon rind   ¾ cup sugar
4 tablespoons cornstarch

SERVES EIGHT

Wash berries and place in a soup kettle. Add water and a twist or two of lemon rind. Cook until the berries are soft. Strain into a bowl, pushing through as much of the pulp as possible. Return the liquid to the kettle, bring to a boil, and remove the kettle from the stove.

Combine the cornstarch, cold water, and lemon juice, pressing out all the lumps. Add to the soup, together with the sugar, and stir thoroughly. Place over medium-low heat and cook, stirring constantly, until thick and clear. Adjust the sugar and lemon to suit your taste. Serve hot or cold.

Orange Soup

1 cup sugar   2½ cups white wine
1 quart water   10 oranges
1 large stick cinnamon   Ground cinnamon
2½ cups orange juice

SERVES EIGHT

Place the sugar, water, and cinnamon in a large saucepan, bring to a boil, and continue boiling until it becomes light and syrupy. Do not overcook. Remove from stove and stir in the orange juice and wine. Chill for 1 hour. Peel the oranges with a very sharp knife; cut through and remove the white underskin. Cut each orange section from the membranes, discarding any seeds. Remove the cinnamon stick from the soup. Place a few orange sections in each bowl and pour the soup over them. Serve cold, in small bowls sprinkled lightly with ground cinnamon.

Chilled Strawberry Soup

1½ pounds fresh ripe strawberries

5 cups port wine

1¼ cups water

⅓ cup sugar

Pinch of salt

3½ tablespoons arrowroot

¼ cup water

Sour cream

SERVES EIGHT

Wash and hull the strawberries. In a medium-sized saucepan, combine the strawberries, port, and water. Bring to a boil over medium heat, and add the sugar and salt. Blend the arrowroot with the ¼ cup water, and mix it into the soup, stirring constantly until thick and smooth. Chill the soup. To serve, top each portion with a dollop of sour cream. Serve in small bowls for a summer brunch, lunch, or after-theater snack.

Rhubarb Soup

4 pounds rhubarb

2 quarts water

2½ tablespoons cornstarch

¼ cup water

Sugar to taste

1 cup heavy cream

2 egg yolks

SERVES EIGHT

Wash rhubarb and cut into 2-inch lengths. Place in a soup kettle, add the water, and cook until tender. Strain into a bowl. Reserve rhubarb and pour liquid back into the kettle. Place over medium heat. Mix the cornstarch and water thoroughly. Add 1 cup of the hot soup and mix well. Stir this mixture into the rest of the soup, and cook over low heat until slightly thickened and clear. Add sugar to taste. Whip the cream and fold the egg yolk into it. Gently stir this mixture into the hot soup and serve immediately.

Chilled Cantaloupe and Honeydew Soup

3 cups ripe cantaloupe, finely chopped

3 cups ripe honeydew melon, finely chopped

2 cups fresh orange juice, strained

⅓ cup fresh lime juice

3 tablespoons honey

2 cups sparkling white wine, chilled

½ cup heavy cream, whipped

Peppermint leaves

SERVES EIGHT

Reserve and chill ½ cup chopped cantaloupe and ½ cup chopped honeydew melon. Purée the remaining chopped melons by forcing them through a sieve. Stir the orange juice and lime juice into the purée. Add the honey and stir in the reserved chopped melons. Refrigerate for at least 4 hours. Just before serving, stir in the sparkling wine. Garnish each bowl of soup with a dollop of whipped cream and 2 peppermint leaves.

Chilled Casaba Soup

1 casaba melon

⅓ cup butter

Grated rind of 1 lemon

1 tablespoon sugar

Salt

4 cups milk

SERVES EIGHT

Peel the rind of the melon, discard the seeds, and chop the meat. Reserve 1 cup for garnish. Heat the butter in a soup kettle, add the rest of the chopped melon, lemon rind, sugar, and a little salt. Cook 2 or 3 minutes.

Stir in the milk, bring to a boil, lower the heat, and cook gently for about 15 minutes. Whirl the soup in a blender until smooth. Place in the refrigerator. Serve chilled soup in small bowls garnished with reserved melon.

Chocolate Soup with Whipped Cream***

Satisfy your sweet tooth with this rich and creamy Chocolate soup.

5¾ cups milk

½ pound semisweet chocolate, grated

2 teaspoons flour

⅔ cup sugar

4 egg yolks

1 cup heavy cream

Chocolate or mint cordial

SERVES EIGHT

Bring the milk and grated chocolate to a boil in a large saucepan. Mix 1 or 2 tablespoons of the hot chocolate milk with the flour, and add to the soup as it boils. Stir in the sugar and remove from the stove. Add the egg yolks, stirring constantly, and return to low heat only long enough to warm the soup.

Serve hot or cold in small bowls as a special dessert, with a dollop of whipped cream and a few sprinkles of chocolate or mint cordial.

Restaurant
SOUPS

OF COURSE, THERE ARE exceptions, but for the most part the professionals do it better, whatever it happens to be, and in the realm of cooking, this is surely true. After all, who knows more about the culinary arts than a really first-rate chef? And where are the really first-rate chefs to be found if not in the first-rate restaurants?

It is little wonder, then, that in the course of dining out, I rarely fail to start the meal with a soup. I have quite naturally run across examples that I have found especially intriguing for one reason or another. Usually an inquiry to the chef succeeds in eliciting the recipe, so that in this section I am happy to be able to present a number of recipes for some really fine soups. These are printed exactly as they were presented to me and I hope you will enjoy them as much as I have.

[365]

Soupe À la Bière

from Lutèce, New York City

*Soupe à la bière and Potage aux grenouilles are two
Alsatian gourmet soups from the world-renowned
restaurant Lutèce located at 249 East 50 Street.
These recipes were generously provided by its gracious
propriètaire, André Surmain.*

2 quarts chicken broth	Pepper
2 cups beer	Nutmeg, ground
8 ounces mie de pain (the soft insides of bread)	½ cup heavy cream
Salt	

SERVES EIGHT

Bring the chicken broth to a boil, add the beer and the bread, and
cook for 20 minutes. Strain. Season to taste with salt, pepper, and a
sprinkle of ground nutmeg. At the last moment blend in the heavy
cream and serve.

Frog's Legs Soup

POTAGE AUX GRENOUILLES

from Lutèce, New York City

1 ounce shallots, finely chopped	2 ounces flour
8 tablespoons butter	½ cup milk
12 pairs of frog's legs	3 ounces watercress
½ cup white wine	2 eggs
1 quart Fish stock (see page 83)	½ cup heavy cream
Salt	Nutmeg, ground
Pepper, freshly ground	

SERVES EIGHT

Cook the shallots gently in 4 tablespoons of the butter until they
turn blond. Add the frog's legs and cook for 2 minutes over medium
heat without browning. Add the white wine and then the Fish stock;

season to taste with salt and pepper. Cook for 10 minutes over medium heat. Remove the frog's legs from the liquid and set aside. Mix the flour and cold milk until smooth, and add to the liquid, making sure it is well blended. Cook for 25 minutes.

Cut the watercress in strips (chiffonade) and cook 3 minutes in a little water. Bone the frog's legs and cut into cubes. At the last moment place the eggs and heavy cream into the upper part of a stainless steel double boiler (the water must be very hot, nearly boiling) and stir vigorously with a whip to obtain a mousseline; it should be quite light and equal to about four times the original volume. Strain the soup through a fine sieve. Add the watercress and the egg-cream mixture. Adjust the seasonings again and sprinkle with ground nutmeg. With the whip, blend in the rest of the butter. Add the frog's legs and serve.

Sopa Castilla La Vieja

*Here is a unique, very Spanish, and extremely popular
soup, created originally by F. Martinez de Montino,
head chef of the court during the reign of Charles V.
It is now an outstanding specialty of the Spanish
Pavilion Restaurant, 475 Park Avenue in New York
City. Home made beef consommé is a must in this
case; canned beef broth will change the taste of the soup.*

1 cup blanched almonds
⅔ cup Spanish olive oil
8 cups Beef consommé
   (see page 68)
Salt to taste

3 cups toasted French bread,
   cut in ⅛-inch slivers
1½ cups blanched almonds,
   sliced and toasted

SERVES EIGHT

Whirl the blanched almonds in your electric blender until finely ground. Heat the olive oil in a frying pan, add the ground almonds, and sauté them until lightly golden. Pour the entire contents of the frying pan into the blender and purée. This should yield approximately 1⅓ cups of purée. Thoroughly heat the consommé in a saucepan. Add salt to taste. Pour 1 cup of consommé into each of eight earthenware crocks. Top each with toasted bread slivers and 2 tablespoons of almond purée. Place the crocks under the broiler until the almond purée is lightly browned and bubbly. Remove from broiler. Sprinkle each with sliced, toasted almonds. Serve immediately.

The New York area probably has more Italian restaurants per square mile than any other type. And little wonder. Italian food is hearty and relatively inexpensive but, alas, often undistinguished. No wonder, then, that Mona's Trattoria in Croton Falls, New York stands out like a rare jewel among rhinestones, for this is perhaps the finest of northern Italian cooking—Bolognese to be precise. And not just Bolognese but Bolognese prepared by Mona Martelli herself. Tiny tortellinis, delicate and deftly made, floating in a rich broth . . . minestrone, delectable beyond description—but why take my word? Try them for yourself. If you are not within commuting distance of Mona's, prepare the following recipes with the loving care Mona would lavish on them, and your rewards will be immediate and unbelievably delicious.

Il Minestrone Di Mona

1 cup butter

1 medium-sized onion

4 medium-sized carrots

2 leeks

2 stalks celery

1 clove garlic, minced

1 thin slice lard

1 small can peeled tomatoes

2 tablespoons fresh Italian parsley, finely chopped

2 large potatoes

4 zucchini

1 cup dried lentils

1 pound fresh white beans, or 1 can white beans

1 pound fresh green peas, or 1 can baby peas

3 quarts water

2 beef bouillon cubes

Salt and pepper to taste

½ cup rice or pastina

8 croutons

Imported Parmesan cheese (Parmigiano), grated

SERVES EIGHT

Heat the butter in a deep soup kettle. Peel and chop the onion and carrots very fine. Thoroughly wash the leeks and celery, chop them very fine, and add them, together with the onion, carrots, and minced garlic to the hot butter. Sauté the vegetables very gently until the onions turn golden. Chop the slice of lard. Slice the canned tomatoes. Stir the lard cubes, tomatoes, and chopped Italian parsley into the onion mixture. Cook for 5 minutes, stirring once or twice. Peel and dice the potatoes, wash and dice the zucchini, and add them, together with the lentils and beans, to the other vegetables in the kettle. Simmer for 20 minutes over very low heat, covered, stirring the mixture from time to time.

Add the water, beef bouillon cubes, and salt and pepper to taste. Bring to a boil and allow the soup to boil for 5 minutes. Lower the heat, cover the kettle, and let simmer for 2 hours, stirring once in a while. If too much water evaporates during the cooking, a bit more may be added. Rice or pastina may also be cooked in the minestrone. Thirty minutes before the soup is ready, add rice or pastina and let it simmer. Croutons may be used to embellish the minestrone. Serve the soup piping hot, sprinkled with imported grated Parmesan cheese.

Zuppa Regina***

1 whole chicken, roasted or boiled, or 1 small cooked boneless veal roast

1 cup blanched almonds

1 hard-cooked egg yolk

4 slices bread, trimmed

2 quarts Chicken and Beef broth

Croutons

Parmesan cheese (Parmigiano), grated

SERVES EIGHT

Skin, bone, and chop the chicken (or cut the veal in pieces). Grind the meat with the blanched almonds. Mash the egg yolk with a fork and add to the ground meat mixture. Trim the crusts from the bread. Heat the broth to simmering. Pour a little of the hot broth over the bread slices. When the bread is well soaked, add to the meat mixture. Mix all ingredients thoroughly and place in the bottom of a large soup tureen. Ladle a little hot soup into the tureen. Arrange croutons, which have been browned in oil, in the soup tureen over the meat mixture, and fill with the remaining hot broth. Serve piping hot, accompanied by a large bowl of grated Parmesan cheese so that guests may help themselves.

Basic Broth

BRODO

1½ pounds beef shoulder
1 pound veal
½ capon
2 carrots
2 stalks celery

1 medium-sized onion
4 quarts water
2 teaspoons salt
Salt and pepper to taste

SERVES EIGHT

Arrange the beef shoulder, capon, carrots, celery, and onion in a deep soup kettle. Cover with the water, add the salt, and bring to a boil. Simmer, covered, for 3 hours. Season with salt and pepper to taste. Remove the beef and capon, reserving for another use. Strain the stock and discard the vegetables. After the stock has cooled, skim off the fat. Use as much or as little of this stock as you need at one time.

Soup Royale

*This delectable, elegant and very delicate soup deserves
only the best, so imported Parmesan cheese is a must.
It's available at Italian specialty stores.*

8 heaping tablespoons flour
8 heaping tablespoons Parmesan
(Parmigiano) cheese, grated
Pinch of salt
Pinch of freshly grated
nutmeg

3 eggs, beaten
6 tablespoons butter
10 cups Chicken and Beef broth

SERVES EIGHT

Combine the flour, grated Parmesan cheese, salt, and freshly ground nutmeg in a large bowl. Stir in the lightly beaten eggs. Cut the butter into small pieces and add to the mixture. Wet a cloth napkin, squeeze out, and spread it out flat. Spoon the cheese mixture into the middle of the napkin, bring up the ends of the napkin, and tie together to form a tight bag. Place the bag into a soup kettle with 10 cups Chicken and Beef broth. Bring to a boil, cover, and simmer for 2 hours.

Remove the bag from the broth. Let it cool to room temperature. Untie the bag, remove the now-hardened mixture from the napkin, and cut into ½-inch slices. Cut these slices into cubes. Reheat the broth to a boil, add the cubes, and continue to boil 10 minutes longer. Serve piping hot.

Tortellini***

INGREDIENTS FOR TORTELLINI DOUGH

1 pound flour   *4 eggs*

DIRECTIONS FOR TORTELLINI DOUGH: Place flour in a large bowl, mix in the eggs, and work together with your hand to make a stiff dough. Turn the dough out on a floured pastry board and knead until smooth. Roll the dough as thin as possible and cut into squares. Place a tablespoon of stuffing in the center of each square. Starting at one end of a tortellini, bring a corner up to form the tortellini into a triangle. Then, with both corners of the base or widest end of the triangle secured, wrap the tortellini around a finger and tuck one corner into the other. The apex or point of the triangle should remain upright, and the tortellini should fit your finger like a ring. A little practice will produce a perfect tortellini, an inspiration to behold.

INGREDIENTS FOR TORTELLINI STUFFING

2 tablespoons butter

¼ pound pork loin, boned

2 ounces chicken breast, boned

¼ pound mortadella (Italian cold cut)

1 ounce very lean Prosciutto ham

2 egg yolks

¼ pound imported Parmesan cheese (Parmigiano), grated

Pinch each of salt and nutmeg

[371]

DIRECTIONS FOR TORTELLINI STUFFING: Heat the butter in a large skillet. Add the pork loin and chicken breast and sauté for 10 minutes. Place the mortadella and Prosciutto in the skillet and sauté all the meat for 5 minutes more. Cool slightly, and grind all the meat together 2 or 3 times in the meat grinder. Stir the egg yolks, imported Parmigiano, salt and nutmeg into the ground meat mixture. Put all ingredients together in the grinder and grind once more. Arrange a tablespoon of meat stuffing on each tortellini square of dough. Shape the tortellini as directed.

INGREDIENTS FOR SOUP

9 cups Brodo (see page 370)   Stuffed tortellini

SERVES EIGHT

DIRECTIONS FOR SOUP: Bring 9 cups of Brodo to a boil in a large kettle. Drop stuffed tortellini into the broth, reduce to very low heat and simmer for 5 minutes, or until the tortellini are cooked through. Spoon some tortellini into each soup plate, pour the broth over them, and serve immediately.

Passatelli

Absolutely essential to creating Passatelli in the Italian manner is a special ricer called "Ferra da Passatelli," available from any of the Italian specialty supply stores. Passatelli is a delightfully different and well-loved dish from Bologna. The version given here is from Mona's Trattoria, Croton Falls, New York.

	Pinch of nutmeg
6 *tablespoons unflavored breadcrumbs, finely ground*	4 *tablespoons flour*
12 *tablespoons imported Parmesan cheese (Parmigiano), grated*	4 *eggs*
	8 *cups Beef and Chicken broth*
Salt to taste	

SERVES EIGHT

Combine breadcrumbs, grated Parmesan, salt, nutmeg, and flour in a large bowl. Add the eggs and knead the mixture as if preparing regular dough. The mixture should be soft. Stir in another egg if the dough seems too hard. Bring the Beef and Chicken broth to a boil in a large saucepan. Put a little dough in the "Ferra da Passatelli," squeeze the ricer over the boiling soup, and cut the dough into 1-inch cylinders with a sharp knife as it emerges from the ricer. Repeat with the remaining dough until all has been squeezed through the ricer and cut into the soup. Reduce heat to very low and simmer the Passatelli in the soup for 5 minutes. Serve piping hot.

Onion Soup Brasserie

Brasserie, New York City

1 large onion	Pinch of thyme
1 tablespoon cooking oil	Salt and pepper to taste
1 quart chicken bouillon	½ glass dry white wine
1 bay leaf	7 ounces Gruyère cheese, grated

SERVES FOUR

Slice the onion (fairly thin) and sauté in a skillet coated with hot cooking oil. When the onion is golden, pour in the bouillon and allow to simmer for 10 minutes. Stir occasionally. Add bay leaf, thyme, salt, and pepper. Then, stirring slowly, add the wine. Sprinkle each serving with grated Gruyère cheese.

Cold Mulligatawny

Four Seasons Restaurant, New York City

1 medium-sized onion, sliced	1 tablespoon cornstarch
4 tablespoons butter	Salt and pepper to taste
1 teaspoon curry powder	6 tablespoons diced cooked chicken breast
10 dried apricots, finely chopped	1 cup heavy cream, chilled
2 quarts Chicken stock (see page 74)	

SERVES SIX

Cook the onion in butter until soft but not brown. Mix in the curry and dried apricots. Pour in Chicken stock. Simmer for 15 minutes. Add cornstarch, salt, and pepper. Strain, and add chicken. Chill. Blend in cream just before serving.

Chili Bean Soup***

El Parador Safe, 325 East 34 Street, New York City, is an outstanding restaurant in a city of outstanding restaurants. The Mexican-Spanish specialties are prepared with a very light hand and served with loving care, under the guidance of the warm and charming host, Carlos Jacott. This spicy Mexican soup is served topped with grated mild cheese and chopped onions. It may also be used as a stock for cooking shellfish.

½ cup peanut oil	1 teaspoon oregano
2 cups onions, finely chopped	4–6 bay leaves
½ cup medium-hot red peppers, chopped, or a small amount of canned jalapeños or chile serranos (caution: these chiles are fiery hot)	2 cans (6-ounce) tomato paste
	5 cups fresh or canned beef broth
	Salt to taste
2 tablespoons garlic, chopped	1 tablespoon cornstarch
½ cup mushrooms, finely chopped	2 cans (15-ounce) black or pink chili beans
¾ cup green peppers, finely chopped	¼ pound mild cheddar cheese, grated
1½ tablespoons flour	Raw onion, chopped
2 cups cold water	

SERVES EIGHT

Heat the oil in a large stove-top casserole or Dutch oven. Add the onions, red peppers, garlic, mushrooms, and green peppers. Cook, stirring frequently, until the onions are golden brown. Stir in the flour, cold water, oregano, bay leaves, tomato paste, and beef broth. Bring to a boil, cover, and continue to simmer for 2 hours, stirring occasionally. Season to taste with salt. The soup may be thickened with cornstarch blended with a little water, if desired. Heat canned black or pink chili beans in a separate saucepan. Pour 1 cup of the soup into each serving bowl, and stir in 2 or 3 spoonfuls of beans.

Top with a handful of grated cheddar cheese. Sprinkle raw chopped onion over the cheese for an authentic Mexican touch.

Chilled Minted Pea Soup

The Tower Suite, New York City

1 pound onions

1 pound romaine lettuce

1 pound bacon

½ quart chicken broth

2½ pounds green peas, frozen

1 small bunch fresh mint, chopped

2 cups light cream

2 cups heavy cream

½ teaspoon sugar

Salt and pepper to taste

⅛ cup arrowroot

2 egg yolks

1 ounce green crème de menthe liqueur

½ pound spinach, finely chopped

SERVES SIX

Put onions, lettuce, and bacon through a food chopper. Place in saucepan, together with chicken broth, and bring to a boil. Add peas, chopped mint, light and heavy creams, sugar, salt, and pepper. Cook for 1 hour. If necessary to bind, use arrowroot and egg yolks. After cooking add crème de menthe and spinach. Strain, chill, and serve.

Charley O's Bean Soup

Charley O's Restaurant, New York City

2 cups dry white beans

1 shallot, finely chopped

6 slices Irish bacon, or ¼ pound Irish ham, cut in small strips

1 onion stuck with 2 cloves

1 stalk of celery

2 carrots

2 leeks

1 bay leaf

Salt and pepper to taste

2 quarts water

Parsley, chopped

Bacon, cooked and crumbled

Heavy cream (optional)

SERVES SIX

Wash the beans thoroughly and soak overnight in water to cover. Drain and place the beans in a large saucepan. Add the shallot, Irish bacon, vegetables, and seasonings. Add the water and bring to a boil. Reduce the heat and simmer, covered, until the beans are soft and the other ingredients well blended. Remove the onion, celery, carrots, leeks, and bay leaf. You may either purée the beans or leave them whole. Adjust the seasonings. Serve with a garnish of chopped parsley and, if you wish, crumbled crisp bacon. If the beans are puréed, add warm heavy cream just before serving.

Cold Senegalese Soup

Four Seasons Restaurant, New York City

5 tablespoons butter
1 small onion, coarsely chopped
1 carrot, coarsely chopped
1 stalk celery, coarsely chopped
1 heaping teaspoon curry powder
3 small sticks cinnamon
2 bay leaves
1 teaspoon whole cloves
5 cups strong chicken broth

1 tablespoon tomato purée
2 heaping tablespoons almond paste
1 tablespoon red currant jelly
3 tablespoons flour
Salt
Freshly ground white pepper
2 cups heavy cream
Toasted coconut

SERVES SIX–EIGHT

Melt 2 tablespoons of the butter in a heavy saucepan. Add the vegetables. Cook over moderate heat, stirring occasionally, until the vegetables have taken on a little color. Stir in the curry powder until well blended. Add cinnamon sticks, bay leaves, cloves, chicken broth, tomato purée, almond paste, and jelly. Mix well, bring to a boil, and simmer for 1 hour. Skim off any foam that rises to the surface. Knead the remaining butter together with the flour. Add, little by little, to the soup, stirring until well blended. Cook for 5 to 6 minutes, or until the soup has thickened slightly. Strain, adjust the seasonings, cool, and refrigerate. Just before serving, add the heavy cream. Serve in well-chilled soup cups with a sprinkling of toasted coconut.

Ground Floor Café Cheese Soup with Bourbon

*The following are six delectable recipes from Restaurant
Associates Restaurants (Executive chef: Joseph
Renggli). This one is from the Ground Floor Café,
51 West 52nd Street, New York City.*

1 cup flour
½ onion, finely chopped
1 cup dry red wine (e.g.
  California Louis Matini or
  Mountain Red)
3 cups cold water
5 cups Beef stock (see page 67)

1 bay leaf
2 ounces bourbon
  Salt and pepper to taste
2 slices white bread
5 tablespoons grated Swiss
  cheese

SERVES FIVE

Put the flour in a skillet and heat over low flame, stirring constantly
until golden brown. In another pot, combine the onion and wine,
heat, and reduce the wine by half. Mix cold water with the browned
flour until smooth. Add to Beef stock, together with bay leaf and
bourbon, and simmer for 45 minutes. Cut the bread into small cubes
and sauté until golden brown. Strain the soup into soup bowls.
Sprinkle each serving with 1 tablespoon grated Swiss cheese and the
croutons. Serve very hot.

Fresh Eel Soup

Luchow's, New York City

4 ounces dried mushrooms
3-pound fresh eel, skinned and
  cleaned
1 teaspoon salt
1 pint sour cream

¼ teaspoon freshly ground black
  pepper
¼ teaspoon paprika
2 teaspoons rye flour
3 tablespoons fresh dill, chopped

SERVES SIX

Cut eel in 2-inch pieces. Wash mushrooms, drain; cover with cold
water, let stand 24 hours. Drain water and pour it over eel, add

additional cold water to cover, about 1½ quarts of liquid all together; add salt, cover. Bring to a boil, then lower heat and cook slowly until eel is tender, 25 to 35 minutes. Add mushrooms and stir. Remove eel from the soup.

Add sour cream slowly to soup, stirring steadily. Add pepper and paprika. Mix flour with a spoonful of hot soup and stir into the kettle. Stir until soup boils, add eel; bring to a boil again. Serve with chopped dill sprinkled on top.

Dallas Cowboy Bean Soup

*Here's a peerless bean soup, courtesy of the Dallas
Cowboy Restaurant in New York City. It's especially
tasty when reheated after a day's refrigeration.*

1 pound dried white pea beans
   (the smallest size)

3 quarts water

¼ pound smoked bacon

1 large onion

1 carrot

2 cups celery

½ small green pepper

1½ cloves garlic

3 quarts water

½ pound ham, diced

½ teaspoon Tabasco sauce

1 teaspoon Lawry's Seasoned
   Salt

½ cup tomato ketchup

1 tablespoon sugar

1 tablespoon fresh parsley,
   finely chopped

1½ teaspoons salt

½ teaspoon paprika

SERVES EIGHT

Cover the dried white pea beans with water and soak overnight. Dice the smoked bacon and sauté in a large soup pot for 5 minutes over low heat. Peel and chop the onion and carrot. Chop the celery, green pepper, and garlic very fine. Add to the bacon and cook over low heat until the vegetables are wilted. Add 3 quarts of water, the drained pea beans, ham, Tabasco sauce, Lawry's Seasoned Salt, ketchup, sugar, parsley, salt, and paprika. Bring all ingredients to a boil and simmer, covered, for 2½ to 3 hours, or until the beans are tender. Correct the seasonings. If desired, thicken the soup with 2 or 3 tablespoons of leftover or instant mashed potatoes, mixed with a little soup before stirring in. Serve immediately, or refrigerate overnight and reheat the following day.

Luchow's Liver Biscuits

Luchow's, New York City

Rich biscuit dough, or puff pastry   *Cooked chicken livers, chopped*
Melted butter

Roll dough ¼-inch thick; cut with small round cutter. Brush with melted butter: add 1 teaspoon livers. Cover with another round of dough; crimp edges together. Bake in hot oven (450° F). until biscuits are light and brown, (about 12 minutes). Serve with soup.

Barley Soup with Giblets

GRAUPENSUPPE MIT HÜHNERKLEIN

*This full-bodied and delicious soup is reprinted from
the marvelous Luchow's Cookbook.*

1 cup pearl barley   *¼ teaspoon grated nutmeg*
  Boiling water   *Chopped chicken giblets*
1 tablespoon butter   *Salt and pepper*
2 quarts beef or chicken   *2 tablespoons chopped parsley*
  bouillon
*2 cups broth in which giblets
  were cooked*

SERVES SIX

Wash barley, drain. Pour boiling water over it twice and drain. Heat butter, cook barley 2 or 3 minutes. Place barley, bouillon, broth from giblets, and nutmeg in soup kettle. Boil slowly 1½ hours. Add giblets for last 20 minutes of cooking. If seasoning is needed, add salt and pepper. Add parsley before serving.

COOKED GIBLETS

  Chicken giblets   *½ teaspoon salt*
1 cup white wine   *¼ teaspoon pepper*
1½ cups Chicken stock or   *¼ teaspoon grated nutmeg*
  bouillon

[379]

Wash giblets, drain; split and clean gizzard. Add wine, Chicken stock, and seasonings. Cover and cook slowly until all giblets are tender, 20 minutes or longer. Drain, chop giblets. Save broth and use as described above.

Luchow's Venison Soup

ST. HUBERTUS OR WILDBRET SUPPE
Luchow's, New York City

1 shoulder venison, boned	2 leeks, chopped
Salt	2 sprigs parsley
2 tablespoons butter	½ teaspoon thyme
2 tablespoons flour	1 bay leaf
¼ cup sausage meat	2 cups water
1 partridge, cleaned, dressed, and boned	Salt and pepper to taste
	Toast triangles
2 slices lean bacon	2–3 cups stock or bouillon
4 carrots, chopped	
2 onions, chopped	

SERVES SIX

Cut venison in large pieces, season with salt, and dredge with flour. Brown meat in butter on all sides. Place venison in soup kettle or soup casserole. Add water to cover. Cook slowly for about 50 minutes.

Rinse the partridge inside and out; pat dry. Fill with sausage meat; skewer opening tightly with toothpicks. Cut bacon in small pieces and heat in frying pan. Cook partridge and vegetables in fat until golden and tender. Add herbs and water. Cover pan, simmer 10 minutes. Add vegetables, partridge, and liquid in which they cooked to venison kettle. Cover and let boil gently 25 minutes. Skim top. Lower heat and simmer 2 hours.

When venison is done, place in a warmed soup tureen and keep hot. Remove partridge and take sausage stuffing out of it. Chop or grind partridge. Mix stuffing and partridge, season with salt and pepper, if needed; spread on toast triangles to serve with soup. Strain the soup. Add bouillon as needed to make 6 large servings. Reheat. Pour over venison in tureen.

Quick
and
easy
SOUPS

WOULD YOU BELIEVE a lovely, utterly delectable cold Gazpacho in less time then it takes to perk a good cup of coffee? Or a fabulous onion soup guaranteed to please the most dyed-in-the-wool gourmet? Or a hearty corn chowder so zesty and delicious friends and family will beg for more . . . all the fruits of just 10 minutes effort?

What's the secret? Substitution! You simply take advantage of the enormous variety of canned and frozen and pre-packed and pre-prepared and pre-everything foods! With a flick of the wrist and a flash of the can opener you can make lunches sparkle, you can make suppers a delight. You can enhance dinner parties and intrigue guests with a delightful variety of really superb dishes. Here are some examples of quick cuisine.

Rice and Chicken Soup

¼ cup butter
½ cup celery, chopped
½ cup onions, chopped
⅓ cup flour
5 cups rich chicken stock
3 cups light cream

3 hard-cooked eggs
1 cup cooked rice
1 cup cooked chicken, diced
¾ cup stuffed olives, sliced
Salt and pepper to taste

SERVES EIGHT

Melt the butter in a deep kettle and sauté the celery and onions over low heat until they are transparent. Blend in the flour, stirring to remove any lumps, and cook for 3 minutes more. Stir in the chicken stock and light cream. Continue to cook over low heat for 15 minutes, stirring occasionally. Do not allow the mixture to boil. Coarsely chop the hard-cooked eggs and mix into the soup along with the cooked rice, diced cooked chicken and ¾ cup of sliced stuffed olives. Season with salt and pepper to taste and heat the soup for 5 minutes more. Serve immediately garnished with minced scallions and a sprinkle of paprika.

Avocado Soup***

*Few soups are as lovely and delectable
as creamy Avocado Soup.*

3 large ripe avocados
6 cups chicken broth
(see page 74)
1½ teaspoons lemon juice

1¾ cups heavy cream
Salt and white pepper to
taste

SERVES EIGHT

Peel, seed and cut avocados in cubes. Place in blender container with ½ cup chicken broth. Blend until smooth, stopping once or twice to push the avocado cubes down against the blades. Mix in the remaining broth and lemon juice and stir. Pour into a glass or enamel pot and bring to a boil. Lower the flame immediately and simmer over very low flame for 4 minutes. Stir in cream, salt and pepper and reheat. Serve immediately.

Marinated Beef Slice Soup with Asparagus

*Chinese-y and easy but not quite authentic is this soup
with a chicken broth base, tender and deliciously
flavored marinated beef slices, and bright green
asparagus tips. The final step in making this soup
must be carried out immediately prior to serving,
so arrange your time accordingly.*

MARINADE

1 tablespoon sugar	3 tablespoons sherry
½ teaspoon salt	4 tablespoons soy sauce
1½ tablespoons cornstarch	2 slices ginger, minced

SOUP

¾ pound flank steak	3 scallions
½ pound fresh asparagus	8 cups chicken broth
4 tablespoons oil	

SERVES EIGHT

Mix sugar, salt, cornstarch, sherry, soy sauce and ginger in a bowl. Cut the steak into paper-thin slices across the grain. Use your fingers to work the marinade into the meat slices. Marinate for 30 minutes (or longer).

Meanwhile wash the asparagus, cut away the fibrous outer part of the stems, and slice very thinly. Heat 2 tablespoons oil in a frying pan and when it is very hot, add the asparagus. Stir over high heat for 2 minutes. Remove the asparagus from the pan and sprinkle with salt.

Trim the scallions and cut them into 1-inch sections. Bring the remaining oil to a high heat and add scallions and meat. Stir over high heat for 30 seconds. Add the chicken broth and stir for 30 seconds more. Remove the meat and scallions and set aside.

Stir the soup until it boils briskly. Add the meat and the asparagus. Stir. Serve hot. Do not plan to reheat this soup or the steak will become tough.

Cold Buttermilk Soup with Cucumber

5 cups buttermilk

2½ cups sour cream

5 tablespoons parsley, chopped

1½ teaspoons salt

Tabasco

1 large cucumber

1 hard-cooked egg yolk

SERVES EIGHT

Stir the buttermilk and sour cream together until well blended. Chop the parsley and add to the soup, along with the salt and a dash of Tabasco. Peel the cucumber, cut it in quarters, and scoop out the seeds. Slice the cucumber thinly and add to the buttermilk mixture. Chill the soup, and serve garnished with thin whole slices of unpeeled cucumber and sieved egg yolk.

Quick Oyster Chowder

*Quick, easy, colorful and delicious. This
oyster chowder has everything!*

2 medium-sized onions

1 stalk celery

1½ pounds potatoes

½ cup fresh parsley, minced

¼ cup butter

½ teaspoon sugar

1 teaspoon salt

¼ teaspoon black freshly
ground pepper

3 cups water

1 cup clam juice

1 package frozen cream-style
corn

2½ cups milk

1 small jar pimentos, drained

1½ pints fresh oysters with
liquor

SERVES EIGHT

Peel and chop onions. Chop celery. Peel and cut potatoes into ½-inch cubes. Mince parsley. Heat the butter in a heavy soup kettle, add chopped onions and celery and cook until onions are golden and transparent. Measure in the water and clam juice. Add the cubed potatoes, parsley, sugar, salt and pepper. Cover pot and cook at a low boil for 15 minutes. Add the corn and simmer for 5 minutes.

Drain pimentos and cut into ½-inch squares. Add to soup along with the milk, the oysters and oyster liquor. Bring just to a boil, lower heat and cook gently until oysters plump up and edges curl. Do not overcook or oysters will be tough. Adjust the seasonings and serve at once from the soup kettle.

Sour Cream Soup with Mushrooms

1 pound young fresh
  mushrooms
1 leek
3 tablespoons butter
1½ teaspoons lemon juice
1 cup sour cream

Salt and pepper to taste
2½ cups milk
2½ cups heavy cream
Several dashes of Tabasco
  sauce
1 tablespoon chopped chives

SERVES EIGHT

Rinse mushrooms and slice them lengthwise. Melt the butter in a large heavy skillet or kettle. Sauté the mushrooms in the butter for 3 minutes over moderate heat, stirring constantly. Lower the heat slightly, cover the mushrooms and cook for 10 minutes, stirring occasionally. Remove from the heat and stir in the lemon juice and sour cream. Cook over very low heat, but do not boil. Stir in the milk, cream and Tabasco sauce. Heat, but do not allow to come to a boil. Correct the seasonings and serve hot, sprinkled with chopped chives.

Cream of Almond Soup

*The delicate flavor of almonds accents this
creamy, smooth-textured soup.*

2⅓ cups blanched almonds
3 lumps sugar
5 cups chicken consommé
  (see page 75)
1 cup milk

1½ cups heavy cream
⅛ teaspoon ground cardamom
  Salt and white pepper to
  taste

SERVES EIGHT

[385]

Using an electric blender, finely chop 2⅓ cups almonds and 3 lumps of sugar. Turn off the blender every few seconds and gradually add 3 tablespoons of cold water. Place the consommé in a saucepan. Add the almond-sugar mixture and simmer the soup, covered, for 10 minutes. Heat the milk in a separate saucepan. Remove the soup from the heat, stir in the hot milk, add the cream, cardamom and salt and pepper to taste, and return to very low heat for a minute or two to heat through. The soup may also be chilled and served cold.

Cold Guacamole Soup***

My penchant for using leftovers resulted in this
out-of-the-ordinary avocado soup. All the ingredients
contained in guacamole are here plus
a generous supply of rich heavy cream.

2 *large ripe avocados*

5 *cups chicken broth*

1½ *tablespoons mayonnaise*

2 *cups heavy cream*

¾ *cup ripe tomatoes, peeled,*
seeded and coarsely chopped

¼ *cup Bermuda onion, peeled*
and finely chopped

1 *teaspoon chili powder*

10 *drops Tabasco sauce*

2 *tablespoons lemon juice*

SERVES EIGHT

Peel, seed and chop avocados. Reserve ¾ cup. Place pit and lemon juice in the cup and refrigerate. Place remaining chopped avocado in blender container with ¼ cup chicken broth. Blend until smooth, stopping occasionally to push contents down against the blades. Add the remaining chicken broth and mix thoroughly. Place in a glass or enamel pot and bring slowly to a boil. Lower flame immediately and simmer over very low flame for 5 minutes. Cool. Meanwhile peel, seed and chop the tomatoes and peel and chop onion. Refrigerate. In a small bowl add the cream, a bit at a time, to the mayonnaise, stirring until smooth. Add the mayonnaise-cream mixture to the cooled avocado soup and chill well. Just prior to serving, stir in remaining ingredients including reserved chopped avocado with pit removed. Serve very cold, ganished with a Lemon Ice Cube (see page 96).

Gazpacho*** ,

4 cups cold canned tomato juice	4 ice cubes
4 cups undiluted cold canned beef consommé	4 large tomatoes
	2 large cucumbers, peeled
¼ teaspoon Tabasco sauce	2 large green peppers, with stem, pith and seeds removed
4 tablespoons olive oil	
1 teaspoon salt	10 green onions, cleaned
8 tablespoons lemon juice	½ cup parsley, minced
4 large garlic cloves, peeled	

SERVES EIGHT

Place tomato juice, consommé, Tabasco sauce, olive oil, salt, lemon juice, garlic cloves and ice cubes in blender container. Cover and blend on high speed for 1 minute. Dip the tomatoes in scalding water for 1 minute and pull off the skins. Cut the tomatoes in quarters and shake out the seeds. Cut tomatoes, cucumber, green peppers, and green onions separately into ½-inch dice. Serve soup icy cold with individual bowls of tomato, cucumber, green pepper, green onions and parsley which guests may spoon into soup as they wish.

Quick and Delicious French Onion Soup***

4 medium-sized onions, peeled	3 tablespoons olive oil
2 large cloves garlic, peeled	½ cup brandy
8 tablespoons butter	8 slices French bread
4 10½-ounce cans beef consommé	1½ cups grated Swiss cheese
2 soup cans water	

SERVES EIGHT

Cut the onions into thin slices and mince the garlic. Sauté in 6 tablespoons butter, stirring occasionally, until onions are soft but not brown. Sprinkle the flour over the onions and stir well. Add one can consommé and one can water and bring the mixture to a boil, stirring constantly. Add the remaining consommé and water and the

[387]

brandy. Stir until the soup is smooth and steaming hot. Heat the remaining butter and the olive oil in a skillet. Sauté the bread until the slices are brown. Place 1 slice sautéed bread in the bottom of each serving bowl and fill with hot soup. Sprinkle with grated cheese and serve immediately.

Quick and Hearty Frankfurter-Bean Soup

5 frankfurters	2½ cups milk
2 tablespoons butter	1¼ cups light cream
2 cans green pea soup	Salt and freshly ground
2 cans bean with bacon soup	pepper to taste

SERVES EIGHT

Cut frankfurters into ¼-inch slices, sauté in 2 tablespoons butter and place in soup kettle. Add the green pea and bean soups.

Stir in the milk a little at a time until hot and free from lumps. Blend in cream. Reheat but do not boil. Adjust seasonings and serve hot.

Garlic Consommé with Poached Eggs

6 medium-sized cloves garlic	4 cups water
8 tablespoons butter or vegetable oil (or 4 tablespoons of each)	8 eggs
4 slices pumpernickel bread	3 tablespoons fresh dill, chopped
4 cans beef consommé	Freshly ground black pepper to taste

SERVES EIGHT

Peel the garlic and crush them into a large skillet. Add the butter or oil and heat until frothy. Meanwhile trim the crusts from the bread and cut the slices into quarters. Toss the bread squares into the hot fat and sauté until brown on both sides. Set aside these croutons and keep them warm. Pour the consommé and the water into the skillet and bring to a very low boil. Break the eggs into a bowl and slip them carefully into the consommé. Spoon the lightly bubbling liquid over the eggs for 3 minutes (or a little longer if you prefer firm eggs). Trim any ragged edges from the egg whites and place one egg and two croutons in each soup dish. Strain the soup over the eggs and croutons, sprinkle with dill and black pepper. Serve at once.

Quick Sweet Pumpkin Soup

1 pint light cream

1¾ pound can pumpkin purée

5 tablespoons honey

2 tablespoons butter

¼ teaspoon nutmeg

¼ teaspoon cinnamon

¼ teaspoon mace

1 teaspoon salt

1 tablespoon light brown sugar

2 tablespoons maple syrup

1 orange, juice and zest

SERVES EIGHT

Put light cream, pumpkin purée, honey and butter in a medium-sized pot. Stir over low heat until warm.

Measure together nutmeg, cinnamon, mace, salt and light brown sugar. Add to pumpkin mixture and simmer gently without allowing to boil.

Squeeze and strain the juice from the orange and grate the outer skin, making sure not to include any of the bitter white underskin. Add the orange juice slowly to the soup stirring well. Allow to simmer for 10 minutes. Cool to room temperature.

Add one pint of light cream and chill well. Serve with dollops of whipped cream if desired.

Health and diet soups

I CONSIDER NEARLY all of the bread recipes in this book to be health breads. None contain preservatives and organically grown wheat, rye and whole wheat flours may be substituted for their grocery store counterparts wherever you wish.

So also are most home-simmered soups brimming with nourishment, in particular these made from a stock of vegetables and bones.

The following are a few of my favorites which did not seem to fit elsewhere in the book.

Spring Herb Soup

6 tablespoons fresh herbs
(chives, tarragon, dill, thyme,
etc.), minced

6 tablespoons butter

4 tablespoons flour

¼ cup rice, uncooked

9 cups Beef stock (see page 67)
Salt and pepper to taste

2 egg yolks

4 tablespoons sour cream

SERVES EIGHT

Place 4 tablespoons of the minced herbs in a soup kettle and sauté in the butter. Mix in the flour and rice, and stir for several minutes until all of the rice kernels are coated with butter. Gradually stir in the Beef stock. Bring to a boil and then immediately lower the heat and simmer until the rice is tender. Adjust the seasonings. Beat the egg yolks, add the sour cream, and beat again. Add the egg yolk mixture to 1 cup of the soup, blend, and stir into the hot soup in the kettle. Serve immediately, sprinkled with the remaining 2 tablespoons of fresh herbs.

Bean Sprout Soup

To adjust Korean recipes to American taste, it is better to use beef broth instead of water in these soups.

2 *cloves garlic*	6 *tablespoons soy sauce*
4 *medium-sized green onions*	6 *cups fresh bean sprouts**
½ *pound partially frozen flank steak, sliced*	12 *cups water or beef broth*
1 *tablespoon Sesame seed powder (see page 341)*	*Salt and freshly ground pepper to taste*

SERVES EIGHT

Peel and mince the garlic and green onions. Cut the green onion tops into 1¾-inch pieces and reserve. With a sharp knife, cut the partially frozen beef into paper-thin slices; cut these slices into 1-inch squares. Combine the meat, garlic, green onions, Sesame seed powder, and 4 tablespoons of the soy sauce. Put into a large soup kettle and sear the meat on both sides.

Remove the wispy ends from the bean sprouts, wash thoroughly, add to the meat, and simmer for a few minutes. Add the remaining soy sauce and the water. Place the soup kettle over medium-low heat and cook until the meat and sprouts are done (about 25 minutes). Five minutes before the soup is ready, add the green onion tops. Adjust the seasonings. Serve hot.

* If canned bean sprouts are used, drain and simmer with the meat for a few minutes.

Belgian Herb Soup

*This delicate green herb soup is as nutritious
as it is satisfying.*

4 tablespoons butter

4 tablespoons parsley, chopped

1 cup green onion tops,
chopped

¾ cup watercress leaves,
chopped

1½ cups lettuce leaves, shredded

1 cup spinach, shredded

2½ teaspoons sweet basil,
chopped

1½ teaspoons salt

1 small bay leaf

6 cups chicken broth

3 tablespoons chives, chopped

1½ cups whipped cream

SERVES EIGHT

Melt the butter in a deep, heavy skillet. Add the parsley, green
onion tops, watercress, lettuce, spinach, sweet basil, salt, and bay
leaf. Cover and cook over low heat for 10 minutes. Add the chicken
broth. Cover the soup and simmer 25 minutes. Adjust seasonings.
Fold the chives into the whipped cream. Serve soup hot with whipped
cream in a separate bowl so that each guest may add a dollop as
desired.

Dandelion Soup

1½ pounds tender dandelion
leaves

3 quarts Chicken consommé
(see page 75)

8 egg yolks

1 cup Romano cheese, grated

Salt and freshly ground
pepper to taste

SERVES EIGHT

Parboil the dandelion leaves. Drain, chop, and set aside. Place the
Chicken consommé in a soup kettle and bring it to a rolling boil.
Add the chopped dandelion leaves and boil for 10 minutes.

Beat the egg yolks, add the grated Romano cheese, and blend
well. Remove the soup from the stove and add the cheese mixture
gradually, stirring until the soup thickens slightly, Adjust the seasonings. Serve hot.

Chicken Soup with Lemon and Mint

4-pound roasting chicken

4 quarts water

3 teaspoons salt

4 medium-sized onions

6 tablespoons white rice

½ cup lemon juice

Salt and freshly ground pepper to taste

8 tablespoons minced fresh mint

SERVES EIGHT

Clean the chicken and put into a large soup kettle, together with the gizzard, liver, and heart—which have been chopped into small pieces. Add the water and salt. Place the kettle over medium-high heat and bring to a boil. Skim off the scum from time to time until the soup is clear. Peel and chop the onions and add to the kettle. Turn the heat down and cook gently, partially covered, for 2 hours. Wash the rice and add to the soup. Cook over low heat until the rice is tender.

Remove the chicken from the soup and set the broth aside. Cut the chicken meat into thin strips. Discard the skin and bones. Return the chicken meat to the broth, add the lemon juice, and adjust the seasonings. Reheat. Put 1 tablespoon of mint into each soup bowl and ladle the soup over it.

Corn Chowder***

⅓ cup salt pork, diced

1 small onion

4 sprigs parsley

1 bay leaf

½ teaspoon salt

2 cups water

2 medium-sized potatoes, diced

2 cups corn

3 tablespoons flour

⅓ cup water

1½ cups milk

1½ cups light cream

2 egg yolks

1 tablespoon butter

SERVES EIGHT

Brown the salt pork lightly. Peel and slice the onion, and sauté for 3 minutes. Add the whole parsley, bay leaf, salt, 2 cups of water, and potatoes. Simmer for 10 minutes. Add corn and simmer until potatoes are tender. Blend flour and ⅓ cup of water into a smooth paste. Remove the pan from the stove and stir in the flour and water. Add the milk and stir. Cook over medium heat, stirring constantly, until the soup thickens. Beat together the cream and egg yolks and mix with ½ cup of the soup. Stir this mixture into the hot soup. Remove the bay leaf and parsley. Serve immediately with a bit of butter in each soup bowl.

Dried Beef Soup

1 jar dried beef (5 ounces)	1½ cups green pepper, chopped
9 ears sweet corn	3 teaspoons sugar
1¾ quarts water	2½ cups heavy cream
8 scallions with 3 inches of green top	Black pepper to taste

SERVES EIGHT

Soak the dried beef in 1 cup water for 5 minutes. Drain. Cut the corn from the cob, scraping all the milk from the cob. Stir the corn, corn milk, and 1¾ quarts water together in a small soup kettle. Simmer over low heat for 30 minutes. Wash the scallions and slice them. Add the dried beef and chopped green pepper to the soup. Simmer 20 minutes longer. Five minutes before serving, stir in the scallions and sugar and heavy cream. Reheat and serve hot, sprinkled with freshly ground pepper.

White Bean and Spinach Soup

8 cups white beans	Salt and freshly ground pepper to taste
2 cups cooked rice	
2 cups beef broth	2 cups spinach leaves, without stems
2 cups tomato sauce, canned	Butter
2 teaspoons lemon juice	

SERVES EIGHT

Soak the beans in water to cover overnight. Cook until tender and drain. Cook the rice according to directions on the package. Whirl the beans and the beef broth together in a blender until smooth. Transfer to a soup kettle and add tomato sauce, cooked rice, and lemon juice. Bring to a boil and adjust the seasonings. Lower heat, stir in the washed and drained spinach leaves, and cook for a few minutes over medium heat. Serve hot with a teaspoon of butter on top of each serving.

Buttermilk Soup

5½ cups buttermilk
3½ cups milk
3 tablespoons tapioca
¾ cup sugar

1 tablespoon lemon juice
1 stick cinnamon
Sprinkle of salt

SERVES EIGHT

Put milks, tapioca, lemon juice, and cinnamon stick in a soup kettle. Simmer for one hour. It is important to stir this soup frequently to prevent burning. Stir in the sugar and salt while the soup is still hot. Remove cinnamon stick and serve immediately.

Beef Soup with Apricots

1½ pound piece chuck steak
1 small onion
6 tablespoons butter
3 medium-sized tomatoes
1½ quarts Beef stock (see page 67)
1½ pounds white potatoes

½ cup apricots
2 teaspoons salt
3 tablespoons fresh coriander, minced

Salt and freshly ground pepper to taste

SERVES EIGHT

[395]

Cover chuck with water, add salt and pepper and cook on medium low heat until tender. Remove from pot and cut into bite-sized pieces. Reserve.

Peel and chop the onions. Place them in a soup kettle and sauté in butter until golden and transparent. Peel, seed and chop the tomatoes. Add them to the onions, and continue to cook until the liquid from the tomatoes has disappeared. Measure in the Beef stock.

Wash, peel and dice the potatoes and add to the soup along with the apricots. Stir well. Bring to a boil, lower heat and simmer for 15 minutes or until the potatoes are tender but not mushy. Ten minutes before potatoes are done add the reserved meat. Adjust seasonings. Serve hot. Use minced coriander as a garnish.

Dried Mushroom Soup***

3 1/4-ounce packages dried mushrooms

10 cups Beef consommé (see page 68)

5 tablespoons yellow cornmeal

6 medium-sized onions

3 tablespoons parsley

1 teaspoon basil

2 cloves garlic

3 cups fresh lima beans

3/4 cup dry sherry

Salt and freshly ground pepper to taste

Garlic croutons (see page 86)

SERVES EIGHT

Soak the dried mushrooms in 3/4 cup of water for 5 minutes. Bring to a boil the mushrooms, consommé, cornmeal, coarsely chopped onion, parsley, basil and garlic cloves which have been peeled and finely minced.

Add the lima beans and continue to simmer for 20 minutes, stirring from time to time.

Adjust for seasoning. Stir in the sherry and reheat. Serve steaming hot with garlic croutons.

Wild Rice Soup

2 cups wild rice

3½ pounds shoulder of lamb with no fat

2½ quarts Beef broth (see page 67)

5 small onions

Salt and freshly ground pepper to taste

SERVES EIGHT

Wash rice in cold water and set aside. Peel and chop onions. In a soup kettle, place the lamb, onion and water. Simmer without a cover for 2½ hours. Meat should be tender.

Add the wild rice, salt and pepper. Cover and simmer for 20 minutes. Stir for 1 minute then continue to simmer 20 minutes longer without cover, or until rice is tender. Serve hot with additional Beef broth if a thinner soup is desired.

Chinese Cabbage Soup

2 teaspoons shrimp paste

3 cloves garlic

1 small onion

6 cups Chicken broth (see page 74)

1½ chili peppers, chopped

1¼ teaspoons turmeric

1¼ teaspoons laos powder

4 ears fresh corn

1 head Chinese cabbage

Salt and freshly ground pepper to taste

SERVES EIGHT

Fry the shrimp paste in a small skillet and when cool, reduce it to a powder. Peel and mince the garlic. Peel and chop the onion. Place the broth in a soup kettle. Add the shrimp paste, garlic, onion, chili, turmeric, laos powder. Cook over medium high heat until soup boils then lower heat and simmer for 4 to 5 minutes. Add the corn, cut from the cob, and cook until tender. Finally, place the washed and coarsely chopped Chinese cabbage into the soup and cook for 3 minutes more. Adjust seasonings. Serve hot.

Carrot Soup

282 calories per serving

*This rich and nourishing soup is filling enough to take
the place of lunch or to make a gourmet
dinner even more special.*

1 tablespoon butter

4 medium-sized carrots

2 small tomatoes

1 cup Chicken stock
(see page 74)

½ cup water

½ teaspoon nutritional yeast

½ teaspoon natural organic
sugar

Pinch of sea salt

2 cups milk

1 teaspoon parsley, finely
chopped

2 teaspoons alfalfa sprouts

SERVES TWO

Melt the butter in a skillet. Peel the carrots and slice them thinly.
Sauté the carrots in the butter over low heat for 5 minutes. Chop the
tomato, add to the carrots, and sauté for 2 minutes. Heat the Chicken
stock with the water, yeast, sugar, and salt. Pour into the carrot mixture, cover, and simmer for 30 minutes. Stir in the milk, reheat, top
with the parsley and alfalfa sprouts, and serve immediately.

Watercress Soup

153 calories per serving

1 bunch watercress

2 small potatoes

2 small onions

4 cups Chicken stock
(see page 74)

2 tablespoons whole wheat flour

4 teaspoons yoghurt

¼ teaspoon sea salt

Pinch of nutmeg

SERVES TWO

While you wash the watercress, keep an eye open for snails. They
seem to love this nutritious plant as much as we do. Discard the
dark, wilted leaves and any presumptuous snails. Peel and slice the
potato and onion, and cook in the Chicken stock until tender. Chop

the watercress and add to the vegetables and stock. Cook for 15 minutes. Rub the soup through a sieve (or blend and then strain it). Mix the flour with a little water, the yoghurt, and spices. Blend this mixture into the soup. Stir over medium heat until thick. Serve hot.

Buttermilk Soup

128 calories per serving

1 cucumber

2 cups buttermilk

1 teaspoon lemon juice

2 teaspoons honey

1 teaspoon fresh dill

¼ teaspoon sea salt

2 teaspoons fresh mint leaves

SERVES TWO

Peel and chop the cucumber. Place all ingredients in a blender and blend until smooth. Chill. Serve cold, topped with a mint leaf or two.

Cabbage Soup

88 calories per serving

This takes rather a long time to cook but requires very little work. Still, if you are devoting the time to it, why not make at least a double portion? It chills well.

4 cups water

½ head cabbage, with hard stem removed

2 small onions, chopped

¼ teaspoon sea salt

3 teaspoons sesame butter*

SERVES TWO

Bring the water to a boil. Add the cabbage, onion, and salt. Reduce the heat and simmer, partially covered, for 50 to 60 minutes, or until the cabbage is tender. Stir in the sesame butter. Serve hot.

* Make sure the sesame butter is not rancid before you stir it into the soup. For some reason, this does not keep too well.

Goat's Cheese Soup

4½ grams of carbohydrate per serving

2 teaspoons butter
½ cup heavy cream
½ cup light cream
1 cup goat's cheese, grated
½ teaspoon nutritional yeast
¼ teaspoon vegetable salt
 seasoning

Generous pinch of nutmeg
1 garlic clove, crushed
2 egg yolks
½ teaspoon mustard sprouts,
 chopped

SERVES TWO

Place all ingredients except the egg yolks, 2 tablespoons of light cream, and the mustard sprouts into the top of a double boiler. Stir over boiling water until the cheese is melted. Beat the egg yolks with remaining tablespoon of cream, and gradually stir this into the cheese mixture. Lower the heat and stir for 1 or 2 minutes, or until the soup thickens slightly *but does not boil.*

Serve immediately sprinkled with mustard sprouts.

Hot Cucumber Soup

62 calories per serving

2 teaspoons butter
1 cucumber
2 cups Chicken stock
 (see page 74)
2 scallions with 3 inches green
 top

½ teaspoon vegetable salt
 seasoning
Pinch of nutmeg
2 tablespoons yoghurt
2 teaspoons mint leaves,
 chopped

SERVES TWO

Melt butter in pan. Peel cucumber and cut in half lengthwise. Remove the seeds and cut into thin slices. Sauté for 2 minutes. Chop the scallion and add it, together with the Chicken stock and spices, to the pan. Simmer for 5 minutes. Serve hot, topped with yoghurt and chopped mint.

Healthy Onion Soup

79 calories per serving

2 *small onions*
2 *teaspoons butter*
2 *cups Beef stock (see page 67)*
1 *teaspoon nutritional yeast*

1 *clove garlic, crushed*
  2-inch cube goat's cheese,
  grated

SERVES TWO

Peel the onion and cut into ¼-inch slices. Separate the slices into rings. Melt the butter in a skillet and sauté the onion rings until tender. Add the Beef stock, yeast, and garlic, and boil for several minutes. Place the soup in a bowl, top with grated cheese, and serve immediately.

Chicken Soup with Cheese Squares

5 grams of carbohydrate per serving

*Italian in origin, this interesting soup
is both tasty and healthful.*

8 *tablespoons ricotta (or cottage)*
  cheese
2 *eggs*
2 *egg yolks*
1 *teaspoon wheat germ*

  *A pinch each of nutmeg and
  sea salt*
2 *cups Chicken stock
  (see page 74)*

SERVES TWO

Place ricotta (or cottage) cheese in a blender container. Beat together the eggs and egg yolks. Place half of the beaten egg in the blender along with the wheat germ, nutmeg, and sea salt. Blend until fairly smooth. Place the cheese paste in an oiled glass baking dish, place the dish in a pan of hot water, and bake until firm (approximately 20 minutes) in an oven preheated to 300° F. Cool the cheese and cut into 1-inch squares. Heat the Chicken stock to boiling and beat in the remaining raw egg mixture. Place the cheese squares in a soup dish and pour the stock over them. Serve immediately.

[401]

Sweet and Sour Cabbage Soup

170 calories per serving

½ head cabbage, with hard stem
   removed

2 small onions

2 small apples

3 cups Chicken stock
   (see page 74)

1 cup tomato juice

4 teaspoons lemon juice
   Pinch of allspice

3 teaspoons honey

SERVES TWO

Shred the cabbage. Peel and chop the onion. Core the apple and cut into slices. Combine all ingredients and simmer for 30 minutes, or until the soup is fairly thick. Serve hot.

Hot Tomato and Yoghurt Soup

220 calories per serving

2 large ripe tomatoes

2 small onions, peeled

2 teaspoons butter

½ cup Chicken stock
   (see page 74)

1 teaspoon honey

1 cup milk

4 tablespoons yoghurt

½ teaspoon basil leaves
   Sea salt and pepper to taste

SERVES TWO

Chop the tomatoes and onions, and sauté in butter until the onion is transparent. (Add 3 or 4 tablespoons of stock, if necessary, to keep the vegetables from browning.) Add the Chicken stock and honey, and simmer for 5 minutes. Stir in the remaining ingredients, and continue simmering for 3 minutes more. Serve hot.

Egg Drop Soup

9 grams of carbohydrate per serving

1 cup raw veal, ground

1 teaspoon soy sauce

¼ teaspoon dulse

2 cups Beef stock (see page 67)

½ cup alfalfa sprouts

1 cup spinach

2 eggs

2 teaspoons water

SERVES TWO

Mix the ground veal and soy sauce. Crumble or cut the dulse into tiny pieces. Fry the meat, soy sauce, and dulse over medium heat for 3 minutes. Add the meat stock and simmer while you chop the alfalfa sprouts and spinach. Add these chopped vegetables to the soup and boil for 3 minutes. Beat the eggs and water together in a cup. Remove the soup from the stove and beat in the eggs. Simmer for 30 seconds, without boiling, and serve immediately.

Chilled Shrimp and Avocado Soup

9½ grams of carbohydrate per serving

Try this for a summertime lunch!

2 cups icy cold Chicken stock
(see page 74)

1 cucumber

½ avocado

4 large cooked shrimp

2 scallions with 3 inches green
top

2 teaspoons soy sauce

A pinch each of powdered
cloves and chili powder

½ teaspoon vegetable salt
seasoning

2 tablespoons yoghurt

SERVES TWO

Place the Chicken stock in bowl. Refrigerate. Peel and chop the cucumber, avocado, and shrimp. Mince the scallion. To serve, stir cucumber, avocado, shrimp, scallion, soy sauce, and spices into the chilled Chicken stock. Top with yoghurt. Serve immediately.

Oriental Sprout Soup

No carbohydrates

2 cups Chicken stock
(see page 74)

2 eggs

4 teaspoons water

4 teaspoons soy sauce

4 tablespoons winter wheat
sprouts

SERVES TWO

Heat the Chicken stock to simmering. Beat the eggs with the water. Use a spoon to dribble the egg into the simmering soup. Stir in the soy sauce. Chop the sprouts and sprinkle them over the soup. Serve hot.

Asparagus and Egg Luncheon Soup***

7½ grams of carbohydrate per serving

This nutrition-packed soup is a lunch in itself.

1½ cups Beef stock
(see page 67)

1 teaspoon nutritional yeast

Small piece of dulse

12 asparagus spears

1 tablespoon butter

2 eggs

2 teaspoons alfalfa sprouts

SERVES TWO

Heat the Beef stock, yeast, and dulse. Wash and peel the asparagus spears and simmer them in the stock for 5 minutes. Melt the butter in a skillet and fry eggs as you like them. Place the soup and asparagus spears in a bowl. Top with the fried egg and alfalfa sprouts. Serve immediately.

Cold Senegalese Soup with Yoghurt

3¼ grams of carbohydrate per serving

2 cups Chicken stock
(see page 74)

½ cup cooked chicken, finely
chopped

2 egg yolks

½ cup cream

½ teaspoon curry powder

2 teaspoons yoghurt

4 watercress leaves

SERVES TWO

Heat the Chicken stock and the chicken. Beat together the egg yolks, cream, and curry powder. Add the egg yolk mixture to the stock, and stir over low heat until the soup is just thickened. *Do not boil,* or the egg will curdle. Cool the soup and chill in the refrigerator. Serve cold, topped with yoghurt and watercress.

Lettuce Soup

10¼ grams of carbohydrate per serving

2½ cups Chicken stock
(see page 74)

1 cup iceberg lettuce, shredded

2 egg yolks

2 tablespoons sunflower seed
kernels

2 teaspoons parsley, chopped

¼ teaspoon sea salt

SERVES TWO

Bring the Chicken stock to a boil, stir in the shredded lettuce, and let boil for 3 minutes. Beat the egg yolks in a bowl and gradually beat the lettuce and stock into it. Stir in the remaining ingredients and serve immediately.

Glossary

ABALONE   A shellfish often used in Oriental cooking. When it is canned, it requires little additional cooking.

ACORN SQUASH   A nut-shaped winter squash about 6 inches in diameter; its exterior is dark green and its flesh is a distinctive bright orange.

AL DENTE   An Italian phrase describing foods, mainly pasta, that are not cooked to the very soft stage.

ALLIGATOR PEAR   Avocado.

ALLSPICE   The round, aromatic berry of a tropical American tree. It gives a sweet, fragrant flavor to desserts. Allspice is more commonly used in powdered form. It is also called *pimento* and *Jamaica pepper*.

ALMONDS   The seeds of the almond tree. *Blanched almonds* are those whose outer skins have been removed by a brief plunge into boiling water.

ANADAMA BREAD   A hearty, yellow-brown yeast bread.

ANISE   A licorice-flavored seed that is widely used in cookies, cakes, and breads. It also blends well with cabbage and cauliflower dishes.

AQUAVIT   A traditional Scandinavian liquor, also called *akvavit*, that is made by distilling potatoes or grain and flavoring it with caraway seeds.

ASPIC   Meat, fish, or chicken broth (or vegetable juice) that is jelled by the addition of gelatin to make a mold for meats, fish, or vegetables.

BARMBRACK A traditional Irish yeast fruitcake, also called *barn-brack*.

BASIL A piquant herb popular in Italian cooking. It can be added to tomatoes, seafood, fish, soups, and salads.

BATTER A flour mixture (usually of liquid consistency) that does not contain yeast.

BATTER BREAD Bread made with batter rather than dough and does not require kneading.

BAY LEAF An herb from the laurel tree that imparts a strong flavor when added to foods, alone or in combination with other herbs. Try it in soups or stews, but sparingly.

BEAN CURD A custard-like cake made with puréed soybeans. It may be used to garnish Oriental soups.

BISCUIT A small, flat, flaky bread leavened with baking powder or soda.

BISQUE A thick creamy soup, typically made with shellfish.

BLANCH To plunge for an instant into boiling water. This is the method used to loosen the skins of almonds and tomatoes.

BORSCHT A beet soup of Russian origin; it may be served hot or cold, usually with sour cream or boiled potatoes.

BOUILLABAISSE This is southern France's answer to the beloved *pot-au-feu*. Since meat is expensive and fish abundant in the Mediterranean region, this highly seasoned stew is usually made with six or seven varieties of fish and shellfish.

BOUILLON A clear broth which is made by cooking beef or chicken together with vegetables and seasonings and then straining the stock.

BOUQUET GARNI A combination of several different herbs, usually a snip of parsley, a bay leaf and fresh or dried fennel, marjoram and thyme, tied together in a cheesecloth bag. It is often added to soups or stews to impart extra flavor while cooking. (The purpose of the bag is for easy removal.)

BRAN The seed husk (or outer coating) of cereal grains such as rye, wheat, or oats. The bran is separated from the flour by sifting or bolting.

BRIOCHE A soft, knob-topped roll of French origin; it is similar in shape to a muffin.

BROTH The clear soup produced when fish, chicken, or meat is cooked together with vegetables and seasonings and then strained.

BUCKWHEAT FLOUR The dark-hued flour produced by grinding the edible triangular seeds of the buckwheat plant.

BULGHOUR A nutritious cracked wheat native to the Middle East.

CARAWAY SEEDS   Strong and aromatic seeds that are often used in breads and team up well with cabbage.

CARDAMOM   A sweet and pungent Indian spice of the ginger family that is used to flavor curries and also in Scandinavian dishes; it can be purchased whole or ground.

CAYENNE PEPPER   A sharp red pepper, from ground ripe chilies, that is one of the hottest seasonings. Don't be too liberal in its use.

CELERIAC   The root of a variety of celery, often utilized in soups or eaten raw in salads.

CELERY SEED   This seed imparts a strong celery flavor. Use it sparingly in soup recipes.

CHALLAH   The traditional Sabbath bread of the Jews is a soft, braided or round, egg and yeast loaf.

CHERVIL   An herb of the parsley family, it harmonizes beautifully with soups as well as salads, meats, and vegetables.

CHIFFONADE   Shredded strips of lettuce or other vegetables that are used to garnish clear soups.

CHILI POWDER   A blend of different chilies, ground up together with cumin, oregano, garlic, and salt.

CHILIES   Hot red peppers, popular in Mexican dishes, that have a piercing taste. Use them sparingly.

CHITTERLINGS   The intestines of a pig that have been fried in deep fat. They are of Southern origin.

CHIVES   First cousin to the onion, this herb has hollow leaves that are extremely versatile and popular. They may be chopped for use as a garnish or to flavor almost anything.

CHORBA   A seasoned broth made with a meat, fish, or vegetable base, and thickened with sour cream or sour milk. It is common in the Balkans and Turkey.

CHOWDER   A soup or stew that is thick with vegetables or seafood, or both.

CINNAMON   A sweet and pungent spice, from the bark of a tropical Asian tree, that comes in stick or powdered form.

CIOPPINO   A fish stew similar to *bouillabaisse*.

CITRON   A fruit that is larger and less acid than a lemon; it is usually available in chopped and candied form.

CLARIFY   To clear a stock or broth of cloudy particles. Egg whites and egg shells are stirred into boiling stock; the stock should then be stirred constantly while it boils for 10 minutes, and then strained.

CLOVE   A dried spice that is available in whole or powdered form; its piquant flavor is good in certain soups and desserts.

COCIDO   A Spanish soup traditionally made with chick peas. It is similar to *puchero*.

CONCH   A large shellfish from the Caribbean Sea.

CONSOMMÉ   A clear soup that is made by enriching soup stock with extra meat or chicken and then clarifying it with egg whites and shells.

CORIANDER   The chopped leaves of this plant, similar to parsley, may be used as an herb. The dried seeds, whole or ground, are an important ingredient in both Oriental and Mexican cookery.

CORNMEAL   Yellow or white meal ground from corn.

CORN PONE   A Southern style cornbread that is made without milk or eggs.

CORNSTARCH   A purified flour prepared from corn and used as a thickener in cooking.

COURT BOUILLON   A clear seasoned broth that is used for poaching fish or vegetables.

COUS-COUS   A North African dish of any crushed grain (but usually wheat), that is steamed and served with meats and vegetables; also the grain itself.

CRACKLING   The chopped, browned salt pork after it has been rendered in a skillet.

CROISSANT   A traditionally French, crescent-shaped roll with a flaky crust.

CROUTONS   Slices or cubes of bread, browned in butter or oil, and used as a garnish for soups.

CRUMPETS   Light soft cakes, typical of the British Isles, that are baked on a griddle and then toasted.

CUBE   To cut into small dice or squares.

CUMIN   A nut-flavored seed that is available in whole or powdered form; it is a seasoning for Mexican and Indian dishes.

CURDLE   A term that usually applies to eggs that have separated after they have been combined with a very hot liquid or cooked over a high heat. To avoid curdling, add hot liquids to eggs a little at a time. Keep soup from boiling *after* eggs have been added.

CURRY   A blended powder of spices from India that ranges in strength from mild to very hot; traditionally used in East Indian dishes.

CUT IN   To cut any solid shortening into dry ingredients. The best method is to use two knives held at right angles.

DIJON MUSTARD   A mild French mustard prepared with spices, vinegar, and white wine.

DILL   An herb that is related to the parsley family. Its subtly flavored stem and leaves, called *dill weed,* lend a distinctive taste to seafood, lamb, veal, and chicken. *Dill seed* can be used for pickling, in breads, or as flavoring for stews and vegetables.

DOUGH   A firm flour mixture that can be kneaded or worked with the hands.

DULSE   A reddish-brown seaweed that is sometimes eaten as a vegetable.

DUMPLING   A small ball of dough that is boiled in stew or soup.

ENGLISH MUFFIN   A thick, flat, round bread, usually baked on a griddle and then toasted.

ENGLISH MUSTARD   A dry, powdered mustard that becomes a pungent seasoning when mixed with water or vinegar.

ENRICHED FLOUR   The addition of vitamins and minerals to white flour to partially compensate for those lost through the milling and bleaching process.

FENNEL   A close relative of parsley, with a strong licorice flavor, that is also known by its Italian name *finocchio.*

FETA   A crumbly Greek cheese made of goat's milk.

FILBERT   A nut from the hazel tree that is also known as a hazelnut.

FILLET   To cut into slices or to remove a bone.

FINE HERBES   A mixture of chopped herbs used for seasoning.

FOLD   To mix a light ingredient into a heavier one by gently cutting through both with a spatula and bringing the heavy one up and over the light one. This procedure is repeated until the two are well blended.

FRENCH BREAD   A thin, elongated loaf with a crisp crust and soft interior.

GARLIC   The bulb of this plant, which is related to the onion, consists of small cloves. It is very popular, whether in fresh, powdered, or salt form, despite its strong odor and flavor.

GARNISH   To decorate one food with another.

GAZPACHO   A traditional Spanish soup made of fresh tomatoes, oil, vinegar, and seasonings; it is served cold.

GINGER   A pungent, spicy root that is available in whole or powdered form; it is an attractive staple of Indian, African, Jamaican, and Chinese cookery.

GRATE   To reduce cheese or firm vegetables to tiny shreds.

GRITS   Any grain (such as corn, oats, or barley) that has been coarsely ground.

GUACAMOLE   A spread or garnish made from mashed avocado pulp, tomato, onion, lemon, and hot seasonings.

GLOSSARY

GUMBO   A soup made from tomatoes, vegetables, seasonings, and seafood or chicken, and usually thickened with okra. It is quite common in the South.

HEARTHCAKE   A round, flat cake made of yeast, coarse flour, butter, and walnuts.

HLODNIK   A cold soup, popular in Eastern Europe, and made of beets, cucumbers, veal, and sour cream.

HUSH PUPPIES   Fried cornmeal fritters, commonly eaten in the South.

IRISH SODA BREAD   A slightly sweetened bread, made with flour, baking soda, baking powder, eggs, and buttermilk.

ITALIAN BREAD   A shorter and thicker loaf than French bread, but very similar in texture and crust.

JOHNNYCAKE   A thin, flat cornbread, much favored in the South.

JULIENNE   To cut vegetables or meats into long thin strips.

KIELBASA   A spicy Polish sausage, made of ground pork and beef and flavored with garlic.

KNEAD   To fold, press, and stretch dough with the hands into a smooth, uniform mass.

LEEK   Related to the onion, this vegetable has a bulbous stem and dark green leaves; it is popular as a soup ingredient.

MACE   An aromatic ground spice that is obtained from drying the thin scarlet covering that lies between the husk and seed of the nutmeg. It is slightly more pungent than nutmeg.

MADRILÈNE   Whether served hot, or jellied and chilled, this soup is made from consommé or broth and flavored with tomato and seasonings.

MARJORAM   This practically all-purpose seasoning is an herb that belongs to the mint family.

MEAL   Coarsely ground grain. Less coarse than grits.

MINCE   To cut or chop into very small pieces.

MINT   Properly called spearmint (since there are many herbs related to the mint family), this green-leaf herb affords a cool, pleasant flavor.

MORTAR   A container made of any hard material in which spices (usually) may be crushed or ground with a short, club-like implement called a pestle.

MUFFIN   A small, cup-shaped bread, often sweetened and usually served hot.

NAVY BEAN   A nutritious white variety of kidney bean.

NUTMEG   A sweet tropical seed; although it is available in ground form, it is even better when purchased whole and then grated by hand. It is excellent for soups.

OATS The edible seeds of oat grass. When hulled, softened, and rolled, they are popular in cooking.

OKRA Often used as a thickener for soup (especially gumbo) or as a vegetable, it is the green seed pod of a tropical plant and a favorite ingredient of Creole cookery.

OLLA PODRIDA A traditional highly seasoned Spanish soup containing vegetables and meats. It is similar to *cocido* or *puchero*.

OREGANO Similar to sweet marjoram, this herb has a strong fragrant taste and is especially favored by Mediterranean food enthusiasts. It goes well with tomatoes, eggs, cheese, and vegetables.

OYSTER PLANT This is another name for the salsify plant, whose edible taproot has a slight oyster flavor.

PANETTONE An Italian holiday bread shaped in a large round. Raisins and candied fruits are kneaded into the dough before baking.

PAPRIKA A ground red pepper that ranges in pungency from mild to hot. The Hungarian variety has the best reputation. It is good for both flavoring and decoration.

PARMESAN CHEESE Made from skim milk, this cheese is easily grated because of its hard, dry consistency; it gives a pungent flavor to many soups. Its Italian name is *Parmigiano*.

PARSLEY Probably the most popular of all herbs. Both the common dark-green variety and the pungent Italian type can be used in soups, stews, sauces, and salads; with meats, eggs, and vegetables; as a garnish; or in combination with other herbs.

PASTA A dough made from hard wheat flour (*semolina*) and water; it comes in many different shapes and sizes; including lasagna, linguine, macaroni, spaghetti, and vermicelli.

PEARL BARLEY A round, highly polished barley that is an attractive addition to many soups.

PEPPER Derived from the dried young berries of an East Indian plant, it is best when ground fresh from whole peppercorns. White pepper, which is ground from the same berries when mature, has a more subtle taste.

PETITE MARMITE A broth made with vegetables and meat and cooked in a special covered earthenware (or metal) soup casserole essential to French kitchens.

PINTO BEAN Pale pink beans mottled with brown. They are popular in the Southwest.

POACH To simmer gently in just enough liquid to cover.

POPPY SEEDS The dried black seeds of the poppy plant. They are used for baking and as a decoration for bread and rolls.

POT-AU-FEU   A soup made from stock, beef, beef bones, root vegetables and seasonings. It is a favorite among the French.

PUCHERO   A traditional Spanish soup that combines beef, bacon, sausages, seasonings, and vegetables.

PUMPERNICKEL   A dark sourish bread made from coarsely ground rye flour.

PURÉE   To force cooked or soft foods through a strainer; also foods whirled in an electric blender until smooth.

QUENELLES   Feather-light, oval shaped dumplings, made of ground chicken, fish, or veal, and blended with egg white and cream. When poached and added to soups, they provide a classic garnish.

QUICK BREADS   Any bread made with baking powder as a leavening agent instead of yeast. Biscuits, cornbreads, muffins, and popovers are all quick breads.

RASSOLNIK   A traditional Russian soup made of meat and vegetables, flavored with pickles, and garnished with sour cream.

REDUCE   To concentrate the flavor of liquids by boiling away some of the water.

RENDER   To reduce animal fat to a liquid state by sautéeing.

ROSEMARY   Whether used fresh and chopped, or dry and crushed and then soaked in water, the leaves of this herb are popular in soups, meats, and vegetables.

RYE FLOUR   A dark flour which, when mixed with wheat flour, is used in making rye bread.

SAFFRON   A pungent, yellow spice made from the dried stigmas of an autumn-flowering crocus; though expensive, it need only be used sparingly when called for in Spanish, French, or Italian recipes.

SAGE   Another herb that must be used with frugality because of the strong flavor it imparts to soups, stuffings, and gravies.

SALLY LUNN   A fairly sweet quick bread, properly served warm with lots of butter.

SALT-RISING BREAD   The fermentation of salt, milk, flour, cornmeal, and sugar provides the leavening for this type of bread.

SAUTÉ   To fry rapidly and lightly in fat in a shallow, open pan. In preparing foods to be sautéed, it is best to dry them well to ensure that they will brown nicely.

SAVORY   Whether using *summer savory* or its less commonly available twin, *winter savory* (which is similar to thyme), this herb makes a pleasant addition to bean and pea soups, stews, salads, and sauces.

SCALD   To heat a liquid almost to the boiling point.

SCALLION   A mild young onion with an edible small white bulb and green top.

SCHAV   A cold sorrel soup, of East European origin, usually garnished with sour cream.

SCONE   An enriched baking powder biscuit.

SCOTCH BROTH   A traditional soup consisting of mutton or lamb and vegetables, and thickened with barley.

SEMOLINA   A fine flour, from ground hard wheat, that is used in making pasta.

SENEGALESE SOUP   A thick curried soup with vegetables, seasonings, and a chicken stock base, puréed and blended with cream before serving.

SESAME SEEDS   The almond-like flavor of these seeds makes them popular in bread and rolls, for coating chicken and fish, and in soups and vegetable dishes. Browning brings out their nutty taste.

SHALLOT   Similar to both onion and garlic, this is a favorite ingredient in French cooking.

SHORTENING   Any fat such as butter, lard, or vegetable oil that makes bread or cake light and flaky.

SHRED   To cut or slice into long thin strips.

SIEVE   A utensil of wire mesh or closely perforated metal that is used for straining or puréeing liquids and soft foods.

SIMMER   To cook gently just below or just at the boiling point.

SLIVER   To cut or slice into long splinters.

SORREL   The green, acid-flavored leaves of the perennial herb sour grass are used in salads and soups, or they can be cooked as a vegetable.

SOURDOUGH   By combining equal portions of milk and flour and then letting it sit in a warm place, bacterial action takes place in the milk and serves as a "starter" or leaven for making bread.

SOYBEAN   The protein-rich, nutritious, and edible bean of an Asiatic herb; soybeans are often processed to become milk, meat, or cheese substitutes.

SPONGE   Dough is called sponge after the yeast has been added, but before kneading.

SPOON BREAD   A quick bread, usually made with cornmeal and soft enough to eat with a spoon; it is a favorite in the South.

STOCK   The broth that results when meat, chicken, or fish are slowly simmered with vegetables, seasonings, and water to cover. By straining and skimming off the fat, it can be used as a base for soups, gravies, or sauces.

GLOSSARY

SUIMONO   A traditional Japanese clear meat or fish stock, garnished with cooked vegetables.

TABASCO SAUCE   The trade name for a highly seasoned and spicy pepper sauce, which is occasionally used in soups. One or two drops are sufficient.

TARRAGON   A popular herb with a licorice-tinged flavor; it may be used in a wide variety of foods.

THYME   One of the most familiar and widely used herbs. It serves as a welcome addition to soups, stews, broths, and stocks in particular.

VELOUTÉ   A white sauce made by blending butter and flour and then adding fish, chicken, or veal stock. Velouté may serve as a base for other white sauces, or it may be enriched by adding cream or eggs.

VICHYSSOISE   A thick, creamy purée of potato soup flavored with leeks; it is usually served chilled.

WATERCRESS   The pungent leaves of this herb, which grows in fresh-water ponds and streams, are popular as a garnish for soups and salads.

WATERZOOI   A traditional Belgian soup made by simmering chicken or fish in a richly seasoned stock.

WHEAT GERM   The vitamin-rich embryo of the wheat kernel; it provides additional nutrition and enrichment to many baked foods.

WHOLE WHEAT FLOUR   Flour ground from the entire grain of wheat, including the bran; it is very rich in natural vitamins and minerals.

WON TONS   Popular in a clear Chinese soup called *won ton* soup, these are made from a noodle-type dough wrapped around a meat mixture.

YEAST   A leavening agent that is available commercially either in powdered or compressed form; it is composed of yeast cells and inert material, such as meal.

YEAST BREAD   Bread made with yeast as the leavening agent.

Index

[417]

INDEX

INDEX

INDEX

INDEX